FROM MASK TO ICON

S. A. Mousalimas

FROM MASK TO ICON:
Transformation in the Arctic

HOLY CROSS ORTHODOX PRESS
Brookline, Massachusetts

© Copyright 2003 Holy Cross Orthodox Press
Published by Holy Cross Orthodox Press
50 Goddard Avenue
Brookline, Massachusetts 02445

LIBRARY OF CONGRESS CATALOGING–IN–PUBLICATION DATA

Mousalimas, S. A.
  From mask to icon : transformation in the Arctic / S.A. Mousalimas.
    p. cm.
Includes bibliographical references.
  ISBN 1-885652-63-1 (pbk. : alk. paper)
  1. Aleuts—Religion. 2. Aleuts—Missions. 3. Pacific Gulf Yupik Eskimos—Religion. 4. Pacific Gulf Yupik Eskimos—Missions. 5. Russkaëiìa pravoslavnaëiìa ëtìserkov§—Missions—Alaska. 6. Shamanism—Alaska. I. Title.
  E99.A34 .M64 2003
  266'.19798'0899719—dc21
                                    2002153779

The Aleuts believed, and taught their children, that daylight is the life for all, while the night is ruination and death. For health and strength and longevity, everyone had to perform the following custom or rule: not to sleep through the dawn; but at the first light, to go naked outside and stand facing the east, or where the dawn appeared. Then, opening the mouth wide, one should swallow the light ...

Veniaminov, *Notes*, II, i, 5.

γιὰ ὑποστήριξη καὶ συντήρηση
ῥωμιοσύνης καὶ ῥωσσίας
+
ῥωμαῖος, ῥοῦμ, русь

CONTENTS

ACKNOWLEDGEMENTS

In the first instance, I should like to acknowledge the people of the Tlingits' Russian Orthodox Church of St Nicholas in the city of Juneau, Alaska. Too much time has passed. I had imagined my return, but the return has only been through vivid and constant memories. I hope that these pages may indicate that the way, while richly meaningful, has not been so easy and that my absence and silence have not been playfully remiss. I have never forgotten and shall never forget. We lived together. The people whom I met, the things that I saw, the many things that I learned, are not exposed in these chapters, because I was never among you to conduct research for a book (I never foresaw this while I was there). Yet I hope the learning will be recognized in these chapters; and therefore it is you whom I acknowledge in the first instance. The name given to me by Fr Michael Williams, who took me under his 'wing' and whose journey was so very difficult, is in me:

Sa-dao-axkh

This Tlingit name was pronounced. It was added to my ancestral and baptismal name Soterius. May their meanings shine forth through these pages.

From southeastern Alaska, I came to Oxford to compose a doctoral dissertation in a purely patristic theme, 'The concept of *theosis* in the writings of St Cyril of Alexandria', from my earlier studies in Greek Orthodox theology. The Alaskan experience was so profound, it remained ever so vividly with me, that I took a master's degree in social anthropology (my second master's degree), so that I could then apply patristic theological insights to social anthropology and produce this study, instead. I did not depart from the original vision regarding *theosis*. It is involved here, to forge the theory of *correspondence and transformation* that is contained in this book.

I am grateful to the Rt Revd Dr Kallistos Ware who allowed me the scholarly latitude to pursue this endeavour, to combine fields of research unusually, and ultimately to develop these concepts. All the while, he patiently provided his own expertise in the sources of patristic theology and in the interpretation of patristic texts, and applied valuable academic advice to the numerous versions and revisions that have come to comprise these chapters. I am also grateful to

Dr L.T. Black who generously provided supervision from her expertise in Russian-American history as well as Alaska anthropology. Dr Black was designated as co-supervisor of the doctoral research. It is rare for anyone from outside Oxford University ever to be designated as a co-supervisor. This indicates her international standing. It also indicates Dr Ware's assistance, as he arranged this, agreeing with and supporting the suggestion that was put forward. They did not create the concepts that are expressed here (the responsibility is entirely my own, and any criticism should be directed to me alone). They were superb academic supervisors who facilitated this expression by allowing a creative application across academic disciplines. I emphasize this because I am aware that the process was long and that their patience and contributions were generous. I am truly honoured to have benefitted from such expertise in their respective fields; and I hope they will consider their efforts to have been worthwhile.

The doctoral dissertation, from which this book derives, was examined by the Revd Dr George D. Dragas, then of the theology faculty in Durham University, as external examiner; and by Dr Godfrey Lienhardt, of the social anthropology institute in Oxford University, as internal examiner: both of whom comprehended this theory and then provided solid encouragement. Dr Lienhardt had been my tutor for the master's degree in social anthropology, and towards him I remain ever appreciative as he had the insight to recognize that I had come into this discipline already with field experience, an advanced degree and a definite focus.

Acknowledgment with sincere appreciation is also due to Professor Andrew F. Wall who immediately understood the value of this theory once it had been finished and who brought it into the centre that he had established: the Centre for the Study of Christianity in the Non-Western World, the University of Edinburgh. He has offered vital academic support and vision. Indeed, he has assisted innumerable people worldwide, and I am certain that his constructive legacy will be appreciated and acknowledged for generations in very many parts of the world.

Sections of my research were read and assessed by Dr Richard Dauenhauer of the Sealaska Foundation in Juneau, by Professor Richard A. Pierce of the History Department, in the University of Alaska at Fairbanks, and by Mrs Alice Petrivelli the President of the Aleut Foundation in Anchorage. I acknowledge with gratitude their constructive advice and their encouragement. An expression of gratitude is due to Fr Innocent Fryntzko and to Fr Joseph Kreta who provided accommodation for me in Juneau and Kodiak respectively; and also to Miss Barbara Mastrud, in the city of Oxford, who kindly read the proofs of the initial publication of this study.

My final words *with my deepest gratitude* belong to my parents and to our family's close friend Mr Nicholas Gavrilov-Gozzard for their unwavering support through all of these years — especially my parents: Andrew and Mary.

PREFACE

Much has happened, especially in Iakutia, since this research was completed. Iakutia (Yakutia) is the Sakha Republic in the Russian Federation, where I have had the distinct pleasure of knowing and the privilege of becoming a colleague of Dr Egor Spiridonovich Shishigin. We first met through introduction by a mutual friend and colleague Dr Semeon Nikolaevich Gorokhov, also of Iakutia, when we three happened to be in Fairbanks, Alaska, together in 1990. Egor Spiridonovich had chosen to write his dissertation about the Christianization of the peoples of Iakutia and northeast Asia. He did this during the last years of the Soviet era. I believe this was courageous. He could not have known consciously that the climate was changing; therefore, a more politically correct topic would have appeared to be in his better interest professionally at that time. Yet this is the topic he chose; and he produced a remarkable piece of work that opens out into a vision that is securely his own. In this work, he affirms the role and contribution of this religion among the Iakut people as well as the minority peoples of northeast Asia. Since then this expertise has been able to come to the fore with real, practical application in the republic; and he has pursued his commitment to this field of learning by promoting scholarship among his students in the Sakha State University, by publishing more work, and also by involving himself internationally in cooperative endeavours. During a visit of his to the United Kingdom in 1994, he proposed the international commemoration of the bicentennial of the birth of St Innokentii (Veniaminov), who will appear often through the chapters forthcoming.

The result was a remarkable series of commemorative events during 1996 and 1997. The initiative derived from this man: Egor Spiridonovich Shishigin of Iakutsk; and he served as the General Coordinator. Care was exercised to assure that each and every event included in this series was academically credible for international standing. Coordinating committees were organized in each location accordingly. Conferences, symposia or commemorative lectures took place within this series in these locations: Pembroke College of Oxford University; the CSCNWW of New College in the University of Edinburgh; the PAOI of the Graduate Theological Union in Berkeley, California; the

University of Alaska at Fairbanks; and Holy Cross Greek Orthodox Theological School in Brookline, Massachusetts. Participants at Oxford, Edinburgh and Fairbanks came from many countries, including France, Greece, Korea, Russia. Support was forthcoming from Greece. Interest was expressed from African missions. Furthermore, academic conferences took place in Moscow, Vladivostock and Irkutsk.

The culminating event of our series was the international conference convened in Iakutsk, the capital city of the Sakha Republic. It involved the republic's government, including representatives of the president's office, and involved the directors of all of the relevant major civic institutions, including the state university, the academies of sciences, the state museums and the state library. This was extraordinary. One of the outcomes is described in this study's introduction: the Sakha (Iakut) philanthropic organization known as 'Iakutskii Dom' presented and distributed their republication of a compilation and biography about Veniaminov, originally published in Moscow in 1883. A significant part of their statement can be read by quotation in my Introduction (sec.5.iii).

This type of international cooperation and achievement would not be possible without brilliant talent such as that of Dr Claudia Ivanovna Fedorova. She is a qualified academic of Sakha (Iakut) philology in her own right, while she serves in the Sakha State University professionally in a dual capacity: as director of the International Programs Office and as head of the English language department. Dedicated to the well being and advancement of the peoples of Iakutia, and to the establishment of affirmative international relations, she works tirelessly. This is a woman of high intellect with proven academic and administrative ability and with a gifted capacity for international relations, or cross-cultural relations. Yet she deigns to serve as a translator. She is recognized as the best, of course. I say that Claudia Ivanovna deigns to do this, because I am aware of her professional stature and also aware of the humility that is required of a good translator, who, if truly proficient, becomes transparent during the conversations.

Personal qualities such as these — the high talent complemented by humility — facilitate correspondence, they allow international cooperation to reach successful affirmative dimensions. Exemplary qualities such as these also indicate the depths of practical spirituality that are actively in place.

Even now as I write these final lines in this final version of the work over which I have laboured for such a long time, I am preparing to visit again the town of Mirny in the Sakha Republic where a conference will be held in the state university branch about 'education, society and technology', March 1999. This branch of the state university hosted a symposium in 1996 as part of the Veniaminov bicentennial, which was the inaugural event for a long internal series of events within the republic that culminated, as did our whole international series, in the main international conference in Iakutsk the following year. The theme of this university symposium in Mirny was 'the revitalization of spirituality among the peoples of Iakutia'. It was organized under the auspices of the rector of this university branch Dr Albina Abramovna Goldman, and with the support of the mayor of Mirny Mr Vitalii Nikolaevich Basigisov.

Particularly memorable for me was the breadth of their understanding of spirituality. It encompassed the various expressions of the spirit. It was not limited to otherworldly considerations or pursuits. Poetry, music and other arts were involved, as were ethics and education. We could compare their encompassing creative vision with the conceptions of education that will be read in the notes of Chapter 6 in this study.

Here is a vitality, a forward looking aspiration for renewal with a successful effort to regain the heritage of the past — and with hands outstretched to make friends.

The potential for cooperation and mutual development is great. Much can be done. Hands can grasp hands in true friendship, in mutual admiration.

I believe that the contents of this book will reflect this potential today. The contents may appear to be retrospective; and indeed the focus is historical. But history is with us. Ancestors surround us, they exist in the very marrow of our bones. Their legacy is our inheritance. It is contemporary. The strengths and potential reflected through these pages are strengths and potential that exist today, and perhaps even more so today.

The tensions and conflicts in these pages are modern also, particularly those in the first chapter and in the final conclusions: so much so that the same tensions tend to obscure today's potential for interpersonal correspondence (cooperation) and affirmation.

We live in a world where there are so many mistakes, so many divisions, so much hatred, so much unnecessary suffering. Even those of us who are older now, and who have had ample experience, feel ourselves to be working as if trying to patch up the tears in a fabric that keeps being pulled apart. It feels as if we are labouring away, each in isolation from others in diverse far corners of the earth: labouring until the body aches and the eyes go sore. But every once in a while, as at the Veniaminov bicentennial, our collective work unfurls surprisingly and magnificently. Our individual handiwork become visible alongside those of many generations before us as part of a long sturdy fabric, one that unifies us (like a rich tapestry) and propels us (like a sail) .

To have added my own labours has truly been a privilege for me, comparatively little though they may be. The effort will have been worthwhile if anyone reads to the very last words in the Epilogue and smiles *affirmatively*. The last words are those of an Aleut old man. My finishing hope is that a reader who reaches them may perhaps apply those words and his wish to me too.

* * *

I am very pleased to be able to publish this revised and final work through the printing house of my original *alma mater*, where I was taught a respect for patristics and where I was able to assimilate many of the theological and some of the cultural concepts that have been applied here to forge this theory of *correspondence and transformation*.

The current publication supersedes all previous ones. If the current work diverges substantially from a previous publication, then the divergence is specified in the appropriate chapter's notes. Substantial divergences are few, almost none, because the components of the theory had already been tried before any publication, and the theory has stood. By bringing my findings into academic forums, I have been able to put the concepts and vocabulary to the test prior to their consolidation here. Vocabulary has been refined and detail has been corrected through this process into this final version, while the central concepts of the theory have remained constant.

Formal research began effectively in 1983. Findings have been presented internationally in various conferences and publications since 1987. These are cited in the first note of each chapter whenever the chapter includes previously published material (therefore the list of publications under my surname in the bibliography must be longer than the lists of publications for the esteemed authors cited).

I shall not cite the initial publication of the dissertation as a book (1995, same title as the dissertation 1992), because the publication was marred by that publisher's errors. I appreciate this opportunity to present the work anew.

I have been able to make additions with this opportunity to republish. The 'substantiation of the premise' (Intro., sec. 1) is being brought forward for the first time in a properly expanded form, because its contents can not be readily found through library requests and the contents may prove to be valuable to some readers. The Epilogue is entirely new also. The final Conclusions are basically the same, as the theory has not changed.

In this, the final version I have attempted to make the whole work more easily readable. I have streamlined the text: taking aside almost all of the references and all other material that are supportive but superfluous to the main development, and placing them back into the notes, where they originally were (before initial publication) and where they belong. Also I have attempted, painstakingly, to shorten sentences, to split paragraphs and to change (the overbearing occurrences of) the passive voice to the active.

Nevertheless, the reading is challenging. Whether this is due to my own lack of popular style in writing or whether it is due to the very complexity of the theory, I can not say. I know that a good writer's task is to make the complicated readable. At least, I have tried. But the work was never meant to be a popular read. Inspirational popular literature has been written in this field. My intent has been to set perceptions on an academic basis and to provide criticism along with insights wherever constructive criticism is warranted.

So if this work is academic in tone as well as in content —well, so be it: this is an academic work. And if it is a challenge to read, then I hope the challenge will be accepted.

Abbreviations

Abbreviations for unpublished archival material cited in the notes are as follows.

HRS/RR/LCM: 'Holy Ruling Synod Documents' [HRS] filed in 'Russian Reproductions' [RR], the United States Library of Congress Manuscript Division [LCM].

VM/RR/LCM: 'Valaam Monastery Documents' [VM] filed in 'Russian Reproductions' [RR], the United States Library of Congress Manuscript Division [LCM].

RAC/Iudin/LCM: 'Russian American Company Documents' [RAC] in the Gennadii V. Iudin, or 'Yudin', collection, the Library of Congress Manuscript Division [LCM].

Abbreviations in the bibliography are listed there.

Method of Notation for Patristic Texts

Parts of a published patristic text will be signified in descending order by differing types of numerals, as follows:

Book:	Upper case Roman numeral
Chapter:	Lower case Roman numeral
Section:	Arabic numeral
Line(s):	Arabic numeral(s)

For example:

I.ii.3.4-5   = Book 1, chapter 2, part 3, lines 4-5.

Or, if a text is comprised of a single book, and the reference does not require the citing of the lines:

vi.7   = Chapter 6, part 7.

Whenever the numbering of lines differs between editions, then the line numbers will be specified after the page number; for example, *Ap.* viii.9 (1900:10, lines 11-12; 1990:13) would signify line 11-12 on page 10 of the 1900 edition of a text whose lines were not numbered in the later edition.

INTRODUCTION

Responding to a twofold question — how did the transition occur; and what were its implications for the ancient cultures? — this study places an emphasis upon the transition as *an indigenous movement involving a transformation of the ancient*. The emphasis may open areas for further discovery, or rediscovery, of Russian Orthodoxy also as a far northern phenomenon by its very nature, be it within societies of hunters or herders of the tundra and taiga; sea-hunters and gatherers of the coasts; agrarian folk from the steppes; or merchants. This emphasis may offer far northern peoples additional insights into, and a mode of interpretation for, their religious histories; and may, more widely, stimulate an awareness that relationships exist between theology and cultures here.

While the theory that is brought forward in this book does apply to diverse peoples of the Arctic (and manifestly now, as the the theory has been espoused in northeast Asia), the primary focus, or case study, is comprised of the Aleut and Alutiiq peoples of Alaska. They converted in the later eighteenth century, and then maintained this faith themselves within their village structures (the latter premise will be substantiated in the final section of this Introduction). The Aleut people derive mainly from the tip of the Alaska Peninsula and the long arc of the Aleutian Island archipelago, extending for more than 1500 miles from Asia to North America, and comprising a chain of islands, many of these islands volcanic. During the Russian period, the Pribylov Islands in the Bering Sea and the Commander Islands near the Kamchatka Peninsula were also settled by Aleuts and by other peoples assimilated to them.

Distinct from the Aleuts, the Alutiiq people derive from Kodiak Island and its archipelago, a region known collectively as the Kodiak area, situated approximately four hundred miles east of the Aleutians. They also derive from the mainland coast nearby, and from the Chugach Bay (Prince William Sound) area farther east. Theirs is a distinctly North Pacific rim culture with a Russian infusion; however, their language is classed as 'Eskimoan' because it is related more closely to the Yup'ik and Inupiaq (Inuit) languages; and these people have been categorized academically as 'Pacific Eskimos' in some mid-twentieth century literature. Another term sometimes applied to the Kodiak area Alutiiqs in anthropological literature today is 'Koniag', a term that derives from eigh-

1

teenth century Russian sources who, coming eastward, evidently assimilated an Aleutian Island word *Kanaain* for the Kodiak area people. In this study, I shall transliterate their self-designation *Alutiiq* from their own language according to a convention established (as I understand it) by J. Leer in the Alaska Native Language Center, the University of Alaska at Fairbanks. Although pronounced 'Aleut' by some of these people speaking English, 'Alutiiq' is the direct transliteration and it will be written to render them distinct and readily identifiable in this text.

(1) Substantiation of the Premise

The premise upon which the study has been based is that Russian Orthodoxy became these Arctic peoples' religion and has been their own for generations now: that is to say, the transition was actual. This premise can be substantiated for the Aleuts and for the Alutiiqs from 1867 and into the 1970s. Decade after decade during this period, linguists, social/cultural anthropologists, ethnographers, sociologists, school-teachers, a demographer, a botanist, a Red Cross officer, a USA army lieutenant and government agents including census takers — French, British, Danish, Japanese and American observers — have recognized Russian Orthodox Christianity as the Aleut and Alutiiq peoples' religion. All have written similar statements in this regard.

References could also be made to sources in Russian-America before 1867, but I shall emphasize the sources from the American era in Alaska history, post-1867, because I intend that the substantiation should be easily recognizable as objective. I have not proceeded beyond the 1970s, because some field research conducted in the later-1980s and in the 1990s may still be unpublished or may still be in-progress, and I intend that the evidence should be as exhaustive as reasonably possible for each decade. I have ceased in the 1970s furthermore because some attitudes might have changed within the generation raised after that watershed decade, due to changes in ecclesiastical structures, and I shall await the maturity and comments of this generation.

I have taken into consideration every source that I could find through normal library research. All of them but two concur decade after decade from 1867 into the 1970s. There are only two exceptions, and those two are self-contradictory. In the 1950s, the Aleuts' religion was defined as 'pure animism' without any reference to their Christianity by G. Marsh (1954, 1967). Thirty years later, it was described as a type of animistic shamanism by M. Lantis (1984:177-179), whose field research had taken place earlier. The Aleuts' Christianity was acknowledged by Lantis as she had witnessed it on site, but this was acknowledged merely in a paragraph while her article proceeded to define the 'Aleuts' religion' from pre-Christian patterns nevertheless. I shall mention Marsh's and Lantis's descriptions again in my final Conclusions (sec.3), and Marsh will re-appear in the Epilogue (nt.3).

The principal source was the same for both of those publications and is cited in both. It is a section of an ethnography published in 1840, written by Ioann (Ivan) Veniaminov in the 1820s and 1830s from information conveyed to him retrospectively by the then-elder generation. In another section of the same ethnography, Veniaminov identified the contemporary Aleuts of the 1820s and 1830s in terms consistent with the scores of sources that will be presented here. Veniaminov himself described the Aleuts as 'exemplary Christians'.[1]

Veniaminov was not alone in his assessment at that time; and earlier yet, in 1807, *hieromonk* Gideon had written:[2]

> The inhabitants of the Unalashka Island, as well as of the entire Aleutian Chain, are strongly devoted to the faith. They know and reverently observe all major Feasts, lovingly and very willingly listen to the teachings offered, and follow these in real life. They are very intelligent, gentle, industrious, and honest.

Now, let us listen to the other sources. They will speak themselves: firstly those about the Aleuts, then those about the Alutiiqs.

(i) The Aleuts

1868: Soon after the purchase, Charles Bryant, a special agent for the USA Treasury Department, with orders to examine the resources of the new territory, reported regarding the Aleuts: 'All are members of the Greco-Russian church and follow its observances in letter and spirit'; and specifically for the Pribylov Islands, Bryant stated:[3]

> All are members of the Greco-Russian church and all are presided over by a subordinate of the priest at Unalaska. They carefully observe all rites and ceremonies of the church, which goes far in relieving the monotony of their lives. The leading men are sufficiently educated in the Russian language to be able to read and write, and keep account of their labor correctly. The marriage obligation is strictly observed, the women are modest and reserved in their deportment.

The same year, H. H. McIntyre, another special agent for the same governmental department, described the people of southwestern Alaska south of fifty-seven degrees north latitude, whom he designated the 'Aleutians' or 'Aleutian family':[4]

> The Greco-Russian Church prevails among them, and nearly all are devout Christians. The precepts of the church are scrupulously observed, and therefore the marriage rite and all civilized social relations are closely adhered to.

Regarding the Pribylov Islands specifically, McIntyre likewise stated: 'The natives are an honest and industrious Christian people.'[5]

1870: The same information for the Pribylovs was conveyed by S. N. Buynitzky, clerk of the Treasury Department stationed there.[6]

1871: Alphonse Pinart, a linguist and ethnographer from Pays-de-Calais preparing to journey by kayak from Unalaska Island eastward to Kodiak Island by way of Belkovsky, a village on the Alaska Peninsula, remarked:[7]

> Le 4 septembre 1871, l'aurore, tout était en émoi dans le village d'Illiouliouk [the harbour village, Unalaska Island]: les Aléoutes qui devaient m'accompagner jusqu' a Belkoffsky allaient faire leurs dernières prières a l'église et recevoir la benediction du pope.

On the way through the harbour to the open sea, Pinart observed (ibid):

> Avant que le clocher de l'église n'êut entièrement disparu à nos regards, mes Alèoutes se decouvrirent et se signèrent piesement par trois fois.

During the journey that took him to villages in the eastern Aleutian Island and onto the Alaska Peninsula, he noticed (ibid.):

> Tout village, si petit qu'il soit, se rèjouit gènèralement de la possession d'une église ou chapelle orthodoxe russe où le service se lit regulierement chaque semaine.

1880: Ivan Petroff, collecting information about Alaska's population and resources for the USA government census, wrote:[8]

> The piety of the Aleutian people is very pronounced as far as outward signs and professions go; they greet you with a blessing and a prayer for your health; they part from you murmuring a benediction; they never sit down to the table without invoking the blessing of God upon them, and in a great many other respects, down to the trifling details too numerous to mention, they carry the precepts and phraseology of the church upon their lips incessantly.

He reported that the Aleut villages themselves were providing the church leadership and were maintaining their own churches or chapels materially and financially.[9] Henry W. Elliot on the Pribylov Islands reported likewise for the census the same year: the Aleuts 'are remarkably attached to their church, and no other form of religion could be better adapted or have a firmer hold upon the sensibilities of these people'; 'they respond, on these islands, to all outward signs of Christianity, as sincerely as our own church-going people.'[10]

1890: For the next census, Samuel Applegate, a resident of Alaska who had traveled across the Aleutian archipelago, along the Alaska Peninsula and to Pribylov Islands — he had been an observer for the 'U.S. Signal Service' and later an independent fur trader based at Unalaska — informed the USA government that 'they are devotedly attached to the Russian Orthodox Church'.[11]

The census taker, Robert Porter, adding his own conclusions to the information he had collected from Applegate, advised the federal government:[12]

> The teacher who comes as the avowed representative of some Protestant or Roman Catholic mission to one of these communities, every individual of which is a member of the Russian church, can scarcely expect to be popular, even if there was not Russian clergy to watch his doings with suspicion. His quasi official position as a government employee does not help him with the people who resent what they look upon as an assault of the government upon their established church.

1936: A botanist in transit across the Aleutian archipelago, collecting for the British Museum, Isobel W. Hutchinson observed the proficiency of the 'chief', Mikhail Hodikoff, in liturgics at Attu:[13]

> A small, intelligent native, with a group of his friends, met us with outstretched hands on the shores of his little Eden. He was a young lively man with rather bluish eyes, a wide mouth and nostrils, and dark hair and face, reminding me a good deal in type of his cousins in distant Greenland. He was accompanied by his little brown-eyed, brown-faced son. All were dressed in their Sunday best. Gone were the 'kamleika' waterproof parkas of their ancestors with seal-skin lining. ...

The quotation needs to be interrupted, because the visiting botanist presumed that the change in type of clothing had occurred long ago: 'cheap woolen and cotton clothing [from the commercial store] now replace the native waterproof "kamleika" coat of seal-gut and birch-bark "hat"' trimmed with sea lions' whiskers which graced the Aleut dandy of a century ago,' she said also at Akta (ibid., p.123). But it was not a century ago: the change had occurred recently, as a result of the commercial pressures imposed across the islands. The quotation continues:

> In the absence of a resident priest the Chief conducts (with considerable ability) the service in church in his own tongue, though, like most natives, he speaks good 'American'.

The 'tongue' in which he conducted the church services would actually have been Slavonic with some formal Aleut (nowhere does Hutchinson evince the awareness to distinguish between the two languages, or even an awareness that this 'considerable ability' among the Aleuts involved more than one language.) The 'considerable ability' that she noticed in the Attu 'chief' Mikhail Hodikoff requires competence with the Slavonic church books and in Orthodox rubrics as well as competence in leading the chanting. All this knowledge is evident in addition to this man's other skills, including his ability to converse with Hutchinson in her own language, which was his third language after Aleut and Russian, or his fourth if his ability in Slavonic is counted.

At Atka Island, Hutchinson noticed that the chapel was maintained materially and liturgically by the villagers themselves (ibid., pp.87-88); and at Unalaska she described a liturgical service (p.122):

> Though the patience was astonishing with which the natives, and especially the children would stand for two hours or even more throughout the long service, listening to a liturgy and sermon unintelligible to most of them, the stranger may be pardoned for suggesting that this service might be more profitable to all were it to be conducted in English, which is spoken or understood by practically all the natives nowadays, and is the only language taught at the Government school at Unalaska where the rising generation receives free education at the hands of a generous government.

Significant in this quotation, beyond the piety that 'astonished' the transient, is her presumption that the service and sermon were unintelligible to those 'natives'. While presuming them to be ignorant, she evinces no knowledge of either Aleut or Russian language herself. Moreover she asserts that it would be in *their* interest for *their* liturgy to be conducted in English, 'the only language taught at the Government school'. Her presumptions reflect the same bigotry that had caused education to become monolingual on the islands under USA control, 'at the hands of a generous government'. The attitude can be contrasted with the activities of an unusual school-teacher in the same location at the same time, who provides the next quotations.

1936-1937: The school-teacher Jay Ellis Ransom took the effort to learn the Aleut language, as he was living among the Aleut people; and he even incorporated bilingual education into his lessons at Unalaska and Umnak Islands himself. He was therefore described as the 'Maverick Teacher of the Aleutians'.[14] Having learned the Aleut language, he could read literature written in this language; and he reported that 'nearly every letter and diary perused by myself — and these run into the score, by several different native authors — contain references to the Russian Orthodox faith'.[15] He observed moreover that 'Russian language and churches still wield considerable influence and favor in the coastal regions of Alaska, particularly in the Aleutian area'; and that village life was centered on the church, and that religious faith was the supreme power in daily life.[16]

WW2: During the Second World War, the Aleut population along the length of the island chain were deported: the Attu Aleuts by the Japanese to Japan, the other Aleuts by the USA to southeastern Alaska, the only wholesale deportation of the Aleut population in history. Through the Attu Aleuts' three year incarceration in Japan, a leader among them, Alexei Prokoff managed to preserve the village's 'church money', according to a school-teacher at Atka after the war who collected an oral history from him.[17]

1945: A more complete account is provided by the Head of the Red Cross

Repatriation of Prisoners of War in the Pacific, Monroe M. Sweetland. The money was entrusted to him by Prokoff in 1945 at a repatriation camp in the Pacific for prisoners of war. Prokoff recognized Sweetland as trustworthy. He deposited the sum of money with him because the bills had become soaked during a typhoon and had to be exposed to the sunlight to be dried and saved, so that they became exposed to the risk of theft. Sweetland, proving himself worthy of the trust, described the event in writing later. Sweetland's description, a narrative, reflects Prokoff's use of English as a third language, after Aleut and Russian. Neither of Prokoff's primary languages requires articles. The Aleut language furthermore contains postpositions (instead of prepositions), and includes adverbs as well as aspectual elements as infixes. These grammatical elements, proper to his first and second languages, are reflected in Prokoff's use English as a third language. Reflecting the grammatical discrepancies between languages, the narrative contains a rather colourful quality, which leads to the irony at its conclusion. .I shall quote the account in its entirety as it is unpublished:[18]

> Among the recovered Allied military personnel flown to Okinawa for staging after release from the Japanese Prison Camps were the 24 survivors of the 40 men, women, and children removed by the Japanese from Attu in 1942.

> They were a brave and loyal troupe, with Russian names, Mongoloid features, Catholic [*sic*] faith, Aleut dialect, and American citizenship. Upon arrival at Okinawa two of the children came down with measles, so all 24 stayed with us for three weeks.

> The day after the second typhoon on Okinawa Alex Prokoff came into my Red Cross office, carrying something which looked like a small metal fishing tackle box. In broken English he explained that the box contained the money for the church at Attu, of which he had been treasurer.

> 'American money?' I asked incredulously, remembering that for three years and more they had been in Japanese hands, and that the Japanese diligently sought every American bill and coin.

> 'Sure, American — three hundred eighty-eight dollars, twenty cents. It got wet from the big wind. Drying it out everybody see it. Now you Red Cross gotta lock up. Maybe lose from my tent. O.K.?'

> 'Of course we'll help you, Alex,' I replied, 'but tell me, you mean you brought this all the way from Attu to Japan and now here?'

> 'Sure,' said Alex. 'Can't let the Japs get Church monies. Belong church, see.'

> 'Did the Japanese know you had this money?' I inquired in amazement.

> 'No. No. No. We hide it always when Japs there. When Japs come Attu I bury it

by house. When Japs take us on ship, I quick hand box to sick man hide under blanket. Get off ship I quick give little boy when Japs look everything. So bury box by house in Otaru until Americans come.'

We put this precious, sacred treasure in the headquarters safe until morning and then took Alex to the APO to convert it into a postal money order to assure its safekeeping.

But it seemed blasphemous somehow, to turn in those moldy, water-stained bills and corroded coins — $388.20 — in which were invested the faith and bravery of these frontier Americans.

To Alex there was nothing exceptional about the money. It belonged to their little Orthodox Church on Attu, and he was the steward. And since the Japanese had destroyed his church, they would need this "monies" more than ever when they returned.

As I write, this brave group is traveling home — from Okinawa to Manila, to San Francisco, to Seattle, to Dutch Harbor [Unalaska Island], and back again to their barren rock at the western tip of the Aleutian chain. And the little church will have $388.20 to start with — all because of the stewardship of a 20th century Christian named Alex Prokoff.

'Can't let the Japs get Church monies. Belongs Church, see?'

— And I wondered whether we really did 'see'.

1946: Following the repatriation, the USA school-teacher at Atka, Ethel Ross Oliver, observed 'these people are deeply religious and much of their lives centers around their church'.[19]

1948: Similarly on the eastern Aleutians, a scholar with the Peabody Museum Aleutian Expedition, Charles I. Shade, stated for the village of Nikolski on Umnak Island: 'The Nikolski people are religious. The church is probably the best built building in the village and is undoubtedly the best cared for'; and 'like all present day Aleuts, the people ... belong to the Russian Orthodox Church.'[20]

1952: Another scholar, Gerald D. Berreman, observed the same phenomena during fieldwork in the same location:[21]

The Russian Orthodox Church is the most significant association in contemporary Nikolski. Its unifying and coordinating value is immense. There is no factionalization, no disagreement on religious matters. It is a source of village-wide interest, common purpose, participation, and belief. There is a well-established organizational set-up surrounding the church, and everyone attends its services most of the time. Church days and holy-days are anticipated by everyone. The church has the most elaborate and immaculately kept building in the village.

'Integrated into village life' to such a degree that this faith and its practices were considered the traditional way of life, 'the church' was considered 'a part of the old culture';. moreover Berreman observed that 'Christianization had not been superficial', and he noted that no priest had ever stayed here for an extended period of time.[22] He repeated these observations and conclusions in a subsequent publication.[23]

1953: Fieldwork at Akutan by Philip T. Spaulding, funded by the Arctic Institute and the U.S. office of Naval Research, , conducted mostly during 1953, resulted in the same conclusion:[24]

> The church is the most unifying institution in the village today. Membership is villagewide and most of the Aleuts attend the services most of the time. For the people of Akutan, village membership is coincident with church membership.

The Akutan Aleuts maintained and supported their own church financially and materially, from essential details such as the *iconostasis* carved by the men, to the altar cloth and icon cloths made by the women (ibid.).

1960s: A comparative study between two villages in eastern Aleutians by Dorothy Jones, a sociologist, found that in the one village the Aleuts had retained social and economic control, but in the other village an influx of 'white settlers' with their own economic interests was being suffered. American 'fundamentalists' had established missions in both locations. In the one village the parents were 'devoutedly Russian Orthodox and consider the church as a dominant symbol of their old culture'. And in the other village, 'the majority consider the Russian Orthodox church a distinctly Aleut institution'.[25] In both these villages, despite the differing circumstances, the Aleuts' own religion had remained a stable, traditional and integrative factor.

1976: Dorothy Jones wrote regarding the Pribylov Island Aleuts:[26]

> After years of suppression of their language, they now seek to reinvigorate it through bilingual programs in the schools and parents' efforts in the home. And they remain devotedly committed to the Russian Orthodox Church, which they view as a powerful cultural symbol.

All of these descriptions derive from American, French and British observers; and all of these sources were compiled through a normal process of library research (except Sweetland's manuscript). I have merely juxtaposed them all, so that they may speak together themselves to substantiate the premise for the Aleuts. Ethnographers, anthropologists, linguists, a sociologist, even a botanist, school-teachers, USA government agents including census-takers, consistently decade after decade, have recognized Russian Orthodox Christianity as the religion of the Aleut people.

I could have confined myself to statements by Aleuts whose life-spans extend beyond the 1970s. For instance, the Aleut state senator of Alaska Moses Dirks could be quoted from September 1987 at Atka:[27]

> The church is still a very important part of the community. Traditional Russian Orthodox holidays are still observed. There is still no priest residing at Atka; lay readers conduct services regularly, and a priest periodically travels to Atka from Unalaska to conduct divine liturgy and perform weddings in church, baptisms, etc.

Or Ilarion Merculieff from St Paul, Pribylovs, in 1984, then the Commissioner of the Alaska State Department of Commerce and Economic Development, could be quoted as he likened the village community to a family and stated 'the center of our family is the church.'[28] Or Alice Petrivelli, originally from Atka, who stated in 1990 as President of the Aleut Foundation: this religion 'has sustained our people'.[29] Moreover, the million dollars could be mentioned that the Aleuts corporately designated in 1989 for the restoration of their churches from the partial monetary compensation that they won from the USA federal government for some of the wanton destruction of their property by USA military forces during the Second World War.[30]

(ii) The Alutiiqs

1868-1870: A USA army first lieutenant, Eli Lundy Huggins, having learned Russian and having learned to distinguish between 'Creoles' and 'natives' (Russian-Alutiiqs and Alutiiqs), noticed the religion of both groups. 'The Creoles of Alaska are the most devout people at church I have ever seen,' he wrote.[31] The 'natives' were perhaps even more pious in his eyes: 'the bishop as well as the priest' seemed to be held in higher esteem 'by the natives than by the Russians or Creoles'. In each of the Alutiiq-Russian homes, icons were kept with a votive lamp lighted; and among Alutiiqs, icons 'were numerous', some of them much worn by veneration.[32]

Huggins was impressed by the attention of people worshipping in church in Kodiak town. On nearby Afognak Island, he observed the 'natives' and 'Creoles' constructing a new and larger church building for themselves together:[33]

> The site was about midway between the creole and native villages, so as to serve them both; for although the Russians and creoles in other respects assume a haughty tone with the natives, they would think it unchristian to make them worship in a separate church, or even in a separate part of the church.

Their Christianity was reflected in their civic deportment: 'unless the church be so considered, there is no law or authority whatever upon the island [Afognak, where the army had not been stationed], yet serious disputes seldom occur' (ibid., p.27).

Each spring, 'a fleet of several hundred bydarkas' (kayaks) assembled at Kodiak to be blessed by the priest before the annual sea hunt: 'nothing could induce the expedition to start before receiving' a blessing (p.14):

> Every year in the month of May a fleet of several hundred bydarkas is assembled at Kadiak [*sic*] for the purpose of hunting the sea otter. The hunters remain with the bydarkas at Kadiak for several days, procuring supplies and making other preparations. Nothing could induce the expedition to start before receiving the formal sanction and blessing of the pope, or priest, a ceremony which lasts two or three hours. Each native, if not already supplied, also receives from the priest a fetish or amulet, consisting of a picture of the Virgin and Child. These pictures are painted on little pieces of thin board of some hard, highly polished wood.

In January 1870, a procession took place from Kodiak to the ice fields on the nearby small island of Woody Island, to bless the ice for a very practical reason (p.21):

> The natives on Woody Island are anxious to have cold weather so they can have employment at cutting ice [for the San Francisco Ice Company]. Day before yesterday they sent a deputation to the priest, requesting him to go and bless the lake so it would freeze over. He went and got the people together, and the procession was formed which marched to the lake chanting, some carrying lighted wax candles, and censers.

This procession warrants some more attention because, with visualization, it will reflect the wider cultural context in which all of this was taking place. The Alutiiqs in the procession would have been wearing the clothing typical of them at that time as noted by Huggins in a general observation as follows (p.5):

> The natives for the most part continue to wear their ancient dress, which is alike for both sexes. The principal article, called a *parka*, consists of a gown or dress of fur, fur-lined, with the flesh side of the furs laid together, so that the garment can be worn either side out. ... Sometimes the *parka* has a hood which falls to the back or is drawn over the head at pleasure. Under the parka is worn a jacket of fur or cloth, sometimes with and sometimes without sleeves; also leggings of the same material wrapped and bound about the limb below the knee. Sealskin boots, waterproof and water tight, complete the costume. In wet weather or at sea, a waterproof shirt of *kamlayka* is worn over it. The kamlayka worn upon land extends to the ankles. The kamlayka also has a hood, or rather a cap, which, when worn is drawn about the face with a string so as to cover the cheeks and forehead, leaving exposed the eyes, nose and mouth. Sealskin caps are sometimes worn. Both men and women are fond of beads and other ornaments.

Their priest was 'creole' himself, a married man, distinctly Russian Orthodox in appearance, 'his hair and beard, which was never trimmed, flowed in profusion over his shoulder and breast, and on occasions of ceremony his appearance was dignified and impressive' (p.12) This is the way these people and their priest appeared while making their procession up the mountain. The description concludes by stating that 'it turned clear and cold that night, and has been freezing steadily ever since' (p.21).

In Huggins' descriptions, we may see that a far northern custom such as the *banya* ('steam bath', sauna), a frequent Alaskan and generally far northern practice, had become incorporated even into the religious calendar: 'The creoles rarely pass a week without a steam bath, in fact there are many occasions upon which it is enjoined by the rules of the Greek church' (p.10). Reciprocally, we may see that church customs such as the nameday had become deeply ingrafted into native life (p.13):

> They seldom celebrate their own birthdays, but a sacred day to each individual is his 'name's day' or the day of the saint for whom he is named. These 'name days' are a serious tax on the time of a large family. Ivan [John] is the most common name for boys, Ivan the Evangelist being more popular than Ivan the Baptist. As elsewhere in Christendom, Mary is the most common name for girls, most of the Marys being named for the mother of Jesus. New Testament names are the most common and next to them, names of the Byzantine or Eastern Empire, as Porphyry, Procopius, Sophia, and Irene.

1873: Alphonse Pinart, the linguist and ethnographer who travelled from Unalaska to Kodiak by kayak, observed at his destination: 'Ils sont tous a present membres de l'Eglise orthodoxe russe.'[34]

1880: In a report for the USA census, Ivan Petroff mentioned the religion of Nuchek, a village in the Chugach Bay area (Prince William Sound region), approximately four hundred miles east of Kodiak. This village was comprised of sixty 'Eskimos' (Alutiiqs), eleven 'Creoles', and three 'whites'; and he stated that the people were conducting church services there themselves.[35]

Similarly at Chenega, another village in this area, the people were 'very religious', 'went to church nearly every day', and conducted the church services (ibid.):

> There is a Russian chapel, but it is eight or nine years since a priest made an appearance here. A creole reads prayers every Sunday in chapel, which is kept in excellent repair with the aid of donations from the surrounding villages. It is touching to observe the constancy and faith of these people, who have gathered at this central point from a circuit of one hundred miles every spring for the last nine years in the expectation of seeing a priest come at last to give them a blessing and to solemnize the marriages that have been contracted during his long absence. Baptism can be performed by the church reader under the rules of the Russian church.

He provided the same kind of advice to the federal government that was being provided concurrently by another collector in the Aleutian Islands that year:[36]

The natives and creoles all along the coast, from Mt. St. Elias westward are too strongly wedded to the faith of the Greek Orthodox Church (adopted by their forefathers nearly a century ago) to take kindly to sectarian schools of another denomination.

1933: In the same location two generations subsequently, virtually the same observations were recorded by the Danish ethnographer Kaj Birket-Smith:[37]

> There is no Russian priest in the Sound now, but at intervals a priest from Kodiak will visit Chenega, where the ordinary service is taken care of by a 'second priest', i.e. a lay reader or catechist.
>
> In a way the Chugach [Alutiiq] are very religious. A holy picture is probably found in all the houses of Chenega. When a man leaves the village he will look back toward the place, uncover, and bow and cross himself, and when he comes back from a hunting or fishing trip, he will walk right up from the beach and enter the church. They go to church almost every day, and all cross themselves after eating. Both Russian and American holidays are observed, but the former are by far the most important. The inhabitants of Chenega always return to the village for church holidays.

1946: A liturgy was observed in the village of Karluk on Kodiak Island by a USA school-teacher in transit to her assignment at Atka in the central Aleutians. When the steamer stopped at Karluk, Ethel Ross Oliver went to see the church:[38]

> As we entered the main part of the church we smelled a strong odor of burning incense. There are no pews in these Russian churches. Everyone was standing, the women to the left of the center aisle, the men to the right. The singing was all in Russian; the women's high pitched voices sang in unison with the lay priest, while the men's voices sang tenor, baritone and bass parts. It was thrilling to hear. Wild flowers in great abundance decked the altar and we caught some of their fragrance through the odor of the burning incense. Simeon [the writer's husband] recalled that this was the holiday which the Russian churches in Alaska celebrate with the season's first flowers. We left quietly a few minutes later.

The 'lay priest' would have been the village's own псаломщнк (ἀναγνώστης: church reader) who is proficient in rubrics and in Slavonic. Karluk did not have a resident priest. The teaching of this proficiency by village elders to village youth was observed in the 1950s, as follows.

1950 and 1953: A knowledge of 'church texts' (liturgical books and scripture written in Slavonic) was being imparted in leading village families on Kodiak Island and the Alaska Peninsula, according to field research by Louis L. Hammerich.[39]

1960: Conducting ethnographic fieldwork in Old Harbor on Kodiak Island, Harumi Befu found that the villagers had recently reconstructed their church building themselves; and that the village's 'lay priests or acting psalm-ists took care of the religious activity.'[40] Furthermore the village had maintained their religion despite the activity of Baptist missionaries who had placed them-selves there in the 1950s: no one had been converted from Russian Orthodoxy.

1964-1965: After the great earthquake of spring 1964, five villages, all of them Alutiiq, that had been affected most severely were studied by Nancy Yaw Davis who observed the centrality of Russian Orthodoxy in them:[41]

> The frequent and spontaneous references to the Russian Orthodox church, espe-cially during the disaster, emphasized its importance in the lives of the people.

> No other institution touches so many of the people as deeply, consistently, and thoroughly.

> ... modern Orthodoxy is an integral part of the distinctive way of life proudly maintained by the Pacific Eskimo villagers.

'The most traditional' and least 'enculturated', or 'modernized', of these five villages was Chenega, with a population of seventy; and this village was placed foremost by Davis in a continuum of 'church pervasiveness in village life': When asked about social activities a villager stated, 'Church is mostly what we do.'[42]

The village of Kaguyak, the smallest of these five, received special attention by Davis. A 'kinship based, conservative' village with a population of thirty-six at the time of the earthquake, maintained their own church liturgically and materially themselves; and the liturgical calendar was dominant in the social life here, also.[43]

The findings were similar in each of these five Alutiiq villages in the Chugach Bay area; and Davis observed among them collectively that 'the church is the only institution sustained entirely by local funds.'[44] (Other institutions, such as the state schools and foreign missionary churches in these villages were maintained by outside funds.)

1966: In Karluk on Kodiak Island, the village's maintenance of liturgics was observed by Kenneth L. Taylor:[45]

> Once a year, generally in the autumn after the fishing season is over, the priest is called to Karluk by the villagers. On the occasion of this visit confessions are heard and holy communion is celebrated ... Throughout the remainder of the year regu-lar weekly church services are held; there is a preparatory service on Saturday evening [the Vigil] and the service proper on Sunday morning. These services are conducted by a lay reader who is one of the villagers.

He noticed the relationship between Alutiiq identity and Russian Ortho-doxy here (ibid., p.212):

Two major features of present-day Konyag [Alutiiq] culture ... largely determine the particular character of contemporary village life in Karluk. These are the membership of all villagers in the Russian Orthodox Church and the modern commercial salmon fishery. It would be hard to overestimate the importance of the Church in the life of the villagers. Its influence is felt at all levels of socio-political life.

1977: The same conclusions were reached by Robert R. Rathburn who observed that the villages in the Kodiak area had 'remained Orthodox', and were maintaining their own churches themselves. He was impressed by their tenacity 'despite the Church's inability to provide them with little more than a yearly visit by a Russian Orthodox priest', and he concluded:[46]

> The Russian Orthodox Church can not be understood simply as a transplanted foreign institution. ... Traditional Koniag [Alutiiq] behavior today includes membership in the Orthodox Church. Assimilation to white society includes surrendering inter- and intra-village ties, both of which are part of church membership.

Again, all of the references, now for the Alutiiqs, derive from international academic sources and from USA government-affiliated sources from 1868 into the 1970s, collected through normal library research: an army lieutenant, a census taker, a school-teacher, a linguist, a demographer, a sociologist, an anthropologist, each American; a French linguist and anthropologist; a Japanese anthropologist; and a Danish ethnographer. I have merely compiled them to have them speak. I have omitted none that I could find. All these voices agree: they concur, decade after decade.

I could have included other statements; for example at the village of Karluk on Kodiak Island in 1988, the Holy Week services were celebrated by Peter Kreta, a priest from Kodiak town. No priest had conducted these very complex services at Karluk for a decade, as he told me; yet they were conducted by the village with proficiency (rituals require the cooperation of laity with clergy), because the village had been observing these rites annually during Pascha (Easter). They knew the intricate services of their church.[47]

It is not on my own knowledge that the substantiation rests, but on all of these sources dating from the 1860s to the 1970s, so that the premise from which our study commences may be recognized manifestly as objective. This religion became the Alutiiq and Aleut peoples' own and remained theirs. The transition to Russian Orthodoxy occurred.

(2) Summary Chronology

A summary chronology is provided for an orientation to the relevant history. The summary may furthermore provide an initial indication that Native Alaskan peoples have themselves comprised the mainstay of their churches while ecclesiastical suprastructures have been in flux with political suprastructures.

Data until 1867 derive from primary sources and scholarly analytical sources, as I shall explain below (Intro., sec.5). Details from these sources and references to them will be provided in my chapters, while the following chronology is meant just to be an expedient summary. Data after 1867, which are outside the main focus of my research, have been drawn mainly from a short history attributed to a bishop who was resident in Alaska from 1972 until recently, *circa* 1995 (Afonsky 1977, 1990): only the data after 1867 have been drawn from this source. The emphases are my own.

1741: Bering's Expedition proceeds from Kamchatka eastward to the Gulf of Alaska.

1745: The first commercial fur hunting enterprise from Kamchatka arrives at the Aleutian Islands, specifically the Near Islands.

1747: A young Aleutian Islander travels to Kamchatka on that enterprise's return, and is baptized as Pavel.

1762: Initial contacts have taken place across the length of the Aleutian chain; and a number of young men have been baptized, some through alliances of their elder kinsmen with, particularly, Kamchadals who came to the Aleutians for the sea hunt.

post-'66: New commercial enterprises begin on the eastern Aleutian Islands.

1784: A company of entrepreneurs pacify and colonize Kodiak Island.

1794: A religious mission arrives at the commercial colony, but is reduced within four years from ten members to only four, all in the Kodiak area.

1796: The leader of the religious mission returns to Irkutsk to be elevated to the 'bishop of Kodiak'.

1799: The newly elevated bishop drowns in a shipwreck on his return voyage to Kodiak. The same year, the Russian-American Company is formed by imperial decree with a renewable charter for monopoly rights.

1804-7: The surviving mission is reinforced by cathedral *hieromonk* Gideon.

1820s: A renewed charter period begins for the Russian-American Company in 1821. Subsequently, four vast parishes, each with a parish priest, are designated for the Russian-American Pacific coast territories and Kurile Islands. These parishes are: the Kodiak parish (where the religious mission had been sent), the Unalaska parish, the Atka parish, and the *Novo Arkhangel'sk* (Sitka) parish. The latter in this list had its priest assigned earlier, in 1816.

1840: Ioann (Ivan) Veniaminov is elevated in the priesthood to become the bishop of a newly created diocese of Kamchatka, the Kurile Islands, and the Aleutians Islands: for his elevation, he is tonsured a monastic and given the name Innokentii.

1841: Bishop Innokentii (Veniaminov) arrives at his see at *Novo Arkhangel'sk* (Sitka), company headquarters: a site on the American northwest coast more than a thousand miles farther east than the closest location designated in the diocesan title.

1840s: Innokentii conducts an indefatigable series of pastoral journeys through this immense diocese; establishes missions in Russian-America — at Ikogmiut on the western Alaska mainland; at Kenai on the Pacific coast; and around *Novo Arkhangel'sk* (Sitka) in the southeastern archipelago; and he creates a new parish at Nushagak on the southwest mainland. He himself spends most of this decade not in Russian-America however, but in Kamchatka.

c.1852: The diocese is incorporated into an archdiocese. Innokentii is elevated to archbishop with his see in Asia, initially at Aian, ultimately at Iakutsk, from where he administers the auxiliary parishes (those not specified in the diocesan title) and the missions in Russian-America. An auxiliary, or vicar, bishop, named Peter is placed at *Novo Arkhangel'sk* (Sitka).

1867: Russian-America, including the Aleutian Islands, is sold by Petersburg to Washington, DC. The vicar bishop Peter vacates for Iakutsk.

The ecclesiastical suprastructure wanes in Alaska.

1872: A bishop assumes the designation 'of the Aleutians and Alaska', but he is not resident in these locations: he maintains himself mainly in the USA proper instead. (Alaska is not yet in the USA, but is a federal possession.)

1876-9: The see is vacant.

1882-8: The see is vacant again.

1889: It becomes the 'Archdiocese of the Aleutians and North America'.

1903-7: Three 'vicar bishops of Alaska' are appointed in succession, but they reside mainly in the USA proper. (Alaska is now a federal territory.)

1917: Due to the revolution in Russia, the 'vicar bishop of Alaska' returns to Russia from the USA. The Patriarchate of Moscow is newly reconstituted under the government of the USSR. Within the Russian *diaspora*, ecclesiastical divisions result. A faction in North America that recognizes authority of the Moscow Patriarchate becomes known as 'the Metropolia'. Episcopal jurisdiction over the Alaskan churches remains confused due to factional claims and counterclaims, and the diocese is intermittently vacant, until 1970.

1959: The territory of Alaska becomes the forty-nineth state of the USA.

An ecclesiastical suprastructure waxes new.

1970: Leaders of the 'Metropolia' gain for themselves the status of an autocephalous church from the Moscow Patriarchate, and designate themselves the 'Orthodox Church of America' ('OCA'). The decision is unilateral, without reference to the other Orthodox patriarchates established in America.[48]

1972: An 'OCA' bishop becomes resident at Sitka, and a seminary is opened in Alaska.

Ecclesiastical suprastructures have been in flux with political suprastructures in Alaska: waxing initially in the 1790s with the Russian-American Company, then waning with the selling of the possession in 1867, and waxing anew after Alaskan statehood, and particularly more recently from 1972.

Throughout this flux, the Russian Orthodox communities consisting mainly of Native Alaskan peoples have been the mainstay, as the following additional data should indicate. In 1858, nine priests, mainly Native Alaskans, served forty-four Orthodox churches and chapels in Russian-America.[49] In 1972, the number of priests, still mainly Native Alaskans, remained the same, while the number of churches and chapels had increased to as many as eighty-four.[50] Even if the later figure is a high estimate, there was an increase in the number of churches and chapels. As this occurred during the period when the ecclesiastial suprastructures had waned in Alaska — no formal ecclesiastical seminary existed in Alaska between 1858 and 1972 — much of the credit for the stability and increase must be assigned to the indigenous mainstay.

The causes for this stability and increase should be sought within indigenous processes. A preliminary insight into these processes can be gained from W. Oswalt,[51] who conducted field research in 1957 at the Yup'ik village of Napaskiak where conversions had taken place in 1905 and 1906. The villagers had constructed a church building, yet had never had a resident priest. Priests would visit occasionally. The priests who would visit to serve in Napaskiak derived from this region themselves. They had an ability in the Russian vernacular language and the Slavonic liturgical language.[52] Monolingual men who spoke only the Yup'ik language had indispensable leading roles in the village church as well, however not as priests. These visiting priests had been schooled in the major parishes, particularly Unalaska and also Sitka.[53] Distances from the Yup'ik regions to those major parishes are equivalent to the distances from England to Thessalonica or from England to Moscow. A particularly motivating force behind the village church in 1957 was an Aleut resident.

A further insight that we may gain from the Napaskiak example is that these dynamics, which sustained and augmented the church life during these years when the ecclesiastical suprastructure had waned, were certainly indigenous dynamics but they were not insular. These dynamics bridged and united the relevant peoples and regions. Similar dynamics are evident far earlier than this source. For example, more than a century earlier, I.E. Netsvetov had travelled an even greater distance, from his family's home on the Pribylovs to seminary in Irkutsk (for Netsvetov, see Ch.1, sec.1.ii), to study before returning to the Aleutian Islands as a priest. He was proficient in the Russian and Aleut languages alike. He was himself 'Creole' by social status; and his ordination reflected a general characteristic at that time in Russian-America where 'Creoles' were the only Alaskans ordained to the priesthood. Evidently, a type of ideal was reflected for spiritual leadership that could span the relevant cultures. The evident ideal was also realized in the exemplary clergyman I. Veniaminov, although not in most of the foreign clergy who came to Alaska after him.

These examples may suffice preliminarily to indicate that insularity is not implied when I refer to the processes as indigenous.

(3) *Initial Definitions*

The terms (i) 'Aleut'/'Alutiiq', (ii) 'Russian Orthodoxy', and (iii) 'shamanism' are explained initially. Other definitions will be provided in the chapters.

(i) *'Aleut'/'Alutiiq'*

Assimilated throughout much of southern Alaska, these terms derive from Алеут, designating a civil status during the Russian era. In nineteenth century Russian sources, general distinctions between Алеут groups were rendered by predicating the term with regional designations, for example 'Atka Aleut', 'Fox [Island] Aleut', 'Kodiak Aleut'; and I shall do the same in this study but with other regional designations and also by distinguishing 'Aleut' from 'Alutiiq' as follows: 'western Aleut', 'central Aleut', and 'eastern Aleut'; 'Kodiak Alutiiq' and 'Chugach Alutiiq'.

Another civil status from the Russian era in Alaska was Креол ('Creole'). This term is maintained today as a social distinction mainly by members of the eldest living generation in my experience. Otherwise it has been absorbed more-or-less into the words 'Aleut' or 'Alutiiq'; therefore, I shall not use the term 'Creole' in this study. Instead I shall write 'Russian-Aleut' or 'Russian-Alutiiq'.

Other southern Alaskan peoples likewise assimilated these terms for themselves, most notably Yupiit of the Nushagak and Bristol Bay areas, and some Athapaskans of the Iliamna Lake and Kenai Bay (Cook Inlet) areas. They are not included in the primary focus of this study; yet their assimilation of the term Алеут as a self-designation merits particular attention, as it indicates that similar historical processes and influences had affected all these groups who refer to themselves alike as Алеут. Yet each group remained distinct in their respective culture, distinct in language and in other cultural aspects, such as traditional clothing and dance. These Алеут identities, thus, involve the complementary qualities of interrelatedness and distinctiveness.

A precedent for an interpretation of Алеут identities along these lines, involving such complementary qualities, might be found in the identities signified by the Greek word Ῥωμαῖος, and its cognate Ροῦμ. Originally signifying citizenship in the Roman Empire this word became a designation for Greek

Orthodox Christians of various ethnic groups in the eastern Mediterranean, progressively from the later first and through the second millennia AD: each group with its own language or dialect, each with distinct traditions, yet all interrelated through their mutual religious beliefs and practices embodied within the respective cultures. A similar precedent might perhaps also be found in the identities signified by the Russian word Русь, or Русский, that once indicated Russian Orthodox Christian identities across Eurasia. The identities of Ρωμαῖος, Ροῦμ and Русь could be a likely precedent for an interpretation of Алеут identities. And the interpretation could well be predicated upon a patristic theological model: an appropriate one being the Trinitarian proto-type: the Trinitarian hypostases who coinhere would be analogous with the distinct cultures or ethnic groups while the divine nature inherent in each hypostasis would be analogous with the mutual religious beliefs and practices infused into each group (also see Conclusions, nt.22).

(ii) 'Russian Orthodoxy'

This term is the English language designation used most frequently by Native Alaskans today for their religion in my experience, substantiated by written sources.[54] Often pronounced as if a single word, it derives from Православне ('Orthodox') with 'Russian' prefixed. The prefix reflects their traditional liturgical language, Slavonic, that was maintained within their chapels and churches with the Native language incorporated more-or-less depending on the location. The maintenance of Slavonic was mostly by these people themselves, from the introduction of this faith and its practices here beginning in the late eighteenth century and continuing until relatively recently, as will be indicated in the summary chronology in this Introduction. In the 1970s, newer clerical institutions were established, which began displacing the Slavonic through English-only practices.[55]

The term 'Russian Orthodoxy' also reflects religious history, as this faith and its practices were communicated initially from Russia. People are aware of this history; for example in the Tlingits' church in Juneau in 1981, four people were chanting *troparia* as others present were venerating the icons at the conclusion of vespers. These four happened ethnically to be a Tlingit (the choir master), an Aleut, a Russian, and a Greek; and some of the more senior people there said afterwards, 'We have just seen history.' They were referring to the communication of this faith and its practices from Greeks to Russians to Aleuts then farther eastward to the Tlingits. The symbol reflected spontaneously, by chance, through the four singers was recognised because the history was known.

The phrase 'Greek Orthodox *ecumene*' has been created for this study to highlight, through the word 'Greek', a continuity from biblical and patristic times and writings; and furthermore to highlight, through the word '*ecumene*', the expanse of this religion. My incorporation of this phrase into this study has a certain precedent in the nineteenth and early twentieth century sources, where the terms 'Greco-Russian Church' and 'Greco-Russian religion', as well as 'Russo-Greek religion', occur. Some instances have appeared in this text (Intro., sec.1, above). Historically earlier instances can be found in the writings of *hiermonk* Gideon, the documents compiled by P.A. Tikhmenev, and other then-contemporary sources.

The terms 'Orthodox Christianity' and 'Orthodoxy' will be used seldom here, only when doctrinal formulations and/or liturgical rituals are signified alone. These terms will be used infrequently, because they tend not convey a sense of the comprehensive cultural context, or embodiment. The focus in this study is clearly on the embodiment.

The use of these terms sometimes tends to imply that an orthodox essence can be extracted away from its context, even where this faith and its practices have for many generations been embodied in home life, in rites of passage, in festivals, in the preparing of foods, in folk dance, songs and tales. The simile to a body may allow me to express this perception. Just as it would be impossible for one to gain a person's processes of affection by extracting and transplanting a heart; so, it seems to me to be improbable for one to obtain the affective processes of liturgy by extracting and transplanting rubrics. Just as it would be impossible for one to grasp the processes of intellection by extracting and studying a brain; so, it seems to me to be improbable for one to comprehend the noetic processes of theology by extracting and memorizing a set of doctrines. A living body is more than the body's parts.

This problem may be expressed with reference to christology. The propensity for such an extraction away from the cultural embodiment is similar to Nestorius' inclination to abstract the divine nature away from the fully human incarnation. This may be observed more clearly by seeing Nestorianism in the larger complex into which it fits (that complex is described in Ch.3, sec.3). When the divine is posited categorically apart from the physical, be this by Nestorius or Arius, the Iconoclasts or the Platonists: then, the separation of divinity from any embodiment would appear possible and even desirable to attain a purer contact with the divine, away from physical attachments. I am not implying a confusion between the distinct realities: the reality of the divine essence is distinct from the reality of the physical embodiment. I am emphasizing the christological formulation by which we are taught that these realities, while unconfused, remain indivisible. Through the incarnation, the qualities of the body are assumed by the divine and they are transformed through participation within the divine energies, thus they are themselves imbued with divinity. The qualities of the body are therefore more than mere attachments, which can be shed or stripped.

The reader will find the dynamics about divine participation and embodiment indicated in Chapter 3 especially, where other sorts of activities are contrasted with them; and the reader may notice a nascent theme about this problem throughout these chapters, as I shall criticize the propensity towards a division of the divine away from the physical embodiment and shall indicate that such a propensity has influenced some theories of asceticism and of ecstasy in particular (Ch.4, sec.1).

(iii) 'Shamanism'

Entering the Russian language from Tungusic terms designating a comparably specific type of functionary,[56] the term 'shaman' and its derivative verb, 'to shamanize' were extended in Russian sources to like phenomena in Asian Russia and Russian-America. The original Russian-language references to 'shaman' and 'shamanizing' were more specific than the modern abstract noun 'shamanism', which has since been coined and is now being applied in literature to phenomena as different as 'magic' and even 'Hasidism'.[57] Because the term 'shamanism' has become so diffuse, and therefore too indefinite, it will be excluded from the text of this study.

Another reason for excluding the term is that 'shamanism' exaggerates a single pattern constellating around the shaman. The exaggeration is particularly inappropriate within southern Alaskan contexts where shamans' practices remained circumscribed, certainly vital but limited in social scope (see Ch.5, sec.2). The exaggeration is rather like that which would result if the term 'clericalism' or 'mysticism' were assigned to Christian cultures because 'clergy' or 'mystics' had captured the imagination of some observers.

Only the abstract noun, 'shamanism', will be omitted from the text of this study. The verb, 'to shamanize', will be incorporated with reference to the geographically specific, original sources where this verb is found. And the term 'shaman' will be used, as defined in Chapter 5 with reference specifically to the Alaskan words that it is meant to represent. I shall use the phrase 'far northern culture(s)' to signify the wider relevant cosmological and social relationships.

(4) Transliteration, Including Personal and Place Names

Aleut, Alutiiq, Tlingit and Yup'ik words have been spelled in Roman script according to the current usage at the Alaska Native Language Center, University of Alaska at Fairbanks, and (for Tlingit) at the Sealaska Heritage Foundation.

Russian words have been transliterated from the Cyrillic alphabet according to the Library of Congress system, slightly modified as I have omitted the 'soft-sign' and 'hard-sign' when they occur at the ends of words. For proper names, I have deferred to popular usage when a name is well known, such as: 'Dostoyevsky'. I shall write 'Peter', instead of the direct transliteration Petr, for Peter I (the Great); 'Catherine' for Catherine II (the Great); 'Gideon', instead of Gedeon; 'Herman', instead of German — as the direct transliteration in instances such as these might cause confusion and can be unsightly.

For Russian place names, I have transliterated and italicized the historical designations, for example: *Pavlovskaia gavan* for today's Kodiak town, *Novo Arkhangel'sk* for today's Sitka. When the historic Russian and modern American designations are very similar — for instance, *Unalashka* and Unalaska, *Atkha* and Atka, *Kad'iak* and Kodiak — I have opted for the modern as it allows fluency while yet conveying the historical sense. But I have broken these rules at the Pribylof Islands, where the final consonant has been transliterated as a 'v' to accord with the ultimate consonant in the other transliterated Russian surnames. Pribilov is a surname. The 'f' appeared to me to be rather incongruous among so many resonant v's.

An engaging problem was posed by the imperial capital. Санктпетербургъ is itself a euphonic composite evidently from the Latin *sanctus* and the Germanic *Petersburg*. The normal English term 'St Petersburg' is a rendition, not the transliteration. If the English term were translated directly into Russian it would become Св. Петроградъ, a term that is not found in these sources. The difference is significant in this study. The euphonic composite, Санктпербургъ, may convey a sense of splendour, however not necessarily a sense of saintliness that the name Св. Петроградъ may carry. It is rather like the city name San Francisco, evoking to an English speaker some sentimental images without the religious connotation of the name St Francis. Where a meaning of holiness does not necessarily exist in the original sources, care should (I believe) be taken not to impute such a meaning into studies of those sources, especially in a study that involves theology. Therefore, I shall use the normal English term 'St Petersburg' in my bibliography, while using 'Petersburg' in my text and notes. An alternative would be 'S.-Peterburg', the transliteration of the then-contemporary abbreviation С.- Петербургъ. This is not an idiosyncrasy on my part: in the eighteenth century primary sources for this study, Петербургъ and С.- Петербургъ were written, not Санктпетербургъ.[59] I am conforming my terminology to these primary sources.

For Greek patristic names, I have opted for the normal English usage as written in the *Oxford Dictionary of the Christian Church*, the *Encyclopaedia Britannica*, and the post-1920 Bodleian Library catalogues; because this normal usage in English approximates the immediacy of the personal names in Greek. For example, the full form of the name 'Cyril of Jerusalem' is 'Cyrillus Hierosolymitanus' in academic Latin, which is in use in some studies today.

But doesn't 'Cyrillus Hierosolymitanus' appear more like a palaeontological specimen, a fossil, than an influential human being? Even the first name alone, 'Cyrillus', might appear too remote. As for the direct transliteration from the Greek, 'Kyrillos' would be nearly incomprehensible to many, and pendantic to others.

Whenever the normal English usage maintains the Latin form, so shall I. I will not transliterate these Greek names into English in preference over the Latin forms as some authors do; because, while a transliteration such as 'Athanasios' would be easily recognizable, other names might not be. Further-more, it seems to me that the direct transliteration passes-by the original Greek and Latin affinities, or Graeco-Roman as I shall refer to them. A divergence of medieval Latin systems from the Greek patristic sources did occur, and preci-sion about this divergence is vital for this study, indeed for any study of Christian missions; but equally vital are the affinities between the earlier Latin churches and the Greek patristic sources. Therefore, I shall incorporate Latin forms for Greek names whenever these coincide with the normal English usage.

(5) Method of Study

Three fields of study have been involved in this research: (i) theology, espe-cially patristics; (ii) social/cultural anthropology; and (iii) history.

(i) Patristic Theology

My references to patristic texts are to the critical editions whenever possible, and otherwise to the most recent publications, as specified in the *Clavis Patrum Graecorum* corrected and kept updated by the Bodleian Library catalogues, and also as specified in the third edition of the *Thesaurus Linguae Graecae*. Due to the number of texts being published in theology, it is very possible that a critical edition or recent publication has not come to my attention. Yet even with this possibility, the bibliography should be fairly current in most in-stances into the 1990s if not through the duration of this decade. This concern is bibliographic. It does not affect my argument.

A patristic writer's authority as a saint in Orthodox Church will be specified in the initial references to an author in each chapter. The dates for patristic and other religious writers will be given according to the dates in the *Oxford Dictionary of the Christian Church*.

My selection of patristic texts is straightforward. They begin in Chapter 2 with St Justin the Martyr (c.100-c.165), because he is specified in Chapter 1 by a key historical source inside the focus of this study precisely. Published in 1894, the key source quoted and cited in the history in Chapter 1 thus pro-vides the starting point for the patristics in Chapter 2. But this historical reference is not the only reason for my study to begin with Justin the Martyr.

He was among the first known Christian academic writers; and he was involved with concerns that parallel the theme of this study: the relationships between Christianity and aspects of non-Christian culture (or now, retrospectively, the pre-Christian) culture in which he lived. From Justin, the study proceeds to patristic writers who followed him in the second and early third centuries, and who also were involved with the same theme. Whenever they do not develop other themes that become relevant to this study, I shall proceed chronologically to the first known patristic writers who do. For example in Chapter 4 when 'ecstasy' becomes a theme that Justin and his immediate predecessors did not address in their writings further than an occasional reference to it, I shall proceed to St Epiphanius of Constantia and to Didymus of Alexandria, both of whom wrote on this theme in the fourth century. When the meaning of icons is considered in Chapter 3, the references will be to Sts John of Damascus, Nicephorus of Constantinople, and Theodore the Studite who articulated the theology about icons.

There is an apparent exception to this method: St Athanasius of Alexandria has been selected to provide examples from patristics in Chapter 3, Βίος Ὁσίου Ἀντωνίου has been selected in Chapter 4, and Ἡ κατ᾽ Αἴγυπτον τῶν μοναχῶν Ἱστορία in my last chapter, when other patristic writers and lives were possible. By choosing these sources, I have striven to strengthen a thematic link between the patristic world and the North: specifically between the Egyptian Thebaid and the 'Russian Thebaid', as the latter was known by analogy in the mid-nineteenth century (see Ch.6, sec.4).

I have striven to bring the thematic patristic focus into the regional focus throughout my writing, as with Justin initially and with the Thebaid ultimately. When the meaning of the Divine Liturgy is considered in Chapter 2, I refer to the ninth century commentary by St Germanus of Constantinople, because his text in translation was incorporated into Slavonic church books that would most probably have been read at Russian seminaries (see Ch.2, sec.4), whence the initial priests who served in Alaska had derived. Also, the Divine Liturgy as he wrote about it would have been virtually the same as that celebrated in Alaska. The thematic patristic focus has been brought into the regional focus, and *vice versa*.

(ii) Social/Cultural Anthropology

Research in this field has combined library study with field experience. The library study was conducted into ethnographies and other descriptions contemporary or nearly contemporary with the conversions of Alaskan peoples to Russian Orthodoxy; and the material in these sources were then compared. Certain problems with the comparative method have been explained particularly definitively by E.E. Evans-Pritchard (1963). Insights gained from him have been applied by me elsewhere (Mousalimas 1990a). I have attempted to avoid the weakness in this method myself while building upon its strengths. The method is strong when the sources can be ascertained as credible, and when the material they contain is incorporated with integrity into analyses.

Works that have been excluded are, for example, the ethnographic descriptions by G.I. Davydov and G.H. von Langsdorff, due to immaturity in the first instance and gross bias in the second. Born in 1784, Gavriil Ivanovich Davydov became a cadet at the imperial naval academy, then entered into service with the Russian-American Company with whom he was employed from November 1802 until June 1803, and again from June 1805 until July 1806, but with two-and-a-half months in California during the later phase.[59] Keeping himself occupied by writing, he produced material that has value as a primary historical source, certainly; however not as a credible ethnography, particularly not with regard to the aboriginal religious attitudes that he described briefly for the native people whom he had observed in a cursory manner. Following his untimely death by drowning in the Neva in 1809, the material was published as a book by the patronage of an influential friend of Davydov's family who composed a preface to the volume himself. Thus endorsed and beautifully bound, the volume might belie the author's age and own qualifications. He was a teenager during the initial phase and only three years older during the second phase of his stay in Alaska.

Georg Heinrich von Langsdorff, born in 1774 of a baronial family in Rheinhessen, had never been far into Russia. It was the circumnavigational voyage of the *Nadezhda*, Petersburg's first round-the-world voyage, that brought him to Russian-America from Europe by way of Cape Horn and Kamchatka. Remaining here from June 1805 until June 1806, he journeyed during that time also to California in the company of Davydov and others including N.P. Rezanov.[60] (Rezanov will be introduced in Ch.1, sec.2.i.) Langsdorff, aghast by his surrounding, did not conceal his reaction which was worse towards the Russian seamen and hunters with whom he had, of necessity, to come into proximity, than towards the Alaskans whom he could observe at his leisure from a distance.

Regarding the Unalaska Aleuts, he wrote: 'Their religion consists like that of most uncivilized nations, in superstitions and a belief in charms.'[61] At Kodiak, he wrote statements such as the following as if a matter of fact: 'An Aleutian whom I questioned upon the subject, answered me with perfect indifference that his nation, in this regard [sexual behaviour], followed the example of sea-dogs and sea-otters.'[62] Langsdorff's writings appeared as a book in no less than two languages, very soon after his return: nicely bound for posterity, accessible, and interesting as an historical source; but not quite a credible source with regard to these peoples' behaviour and beliefs.

How have I ascertained the credibility of sources for anthropology? My primary criterion has been the author's familiarity with the people(s) about whom he is writing. This involves a proficiency in communication with them, of course; yet it need not require his own fluency in their language(s) for the purpose of ethnography: therefore, I have allowed for an ethnographer's cooperation with a competent translator. I should concentrate on this dynamic before proceeding. In other parts of the world, I have experienced this process of communication through an interpreter myself, and have thus gained some primary knowledge of the possibilities. Communication occurs through more than an exchange of words. It occurs within an active social context that can be called *participatory*, as the ability and willingness of one party to learn is combined with the ability and willingness of another party to impart. When a good translator is present who has rapport with all involved, then the possibilities for real communication become greatly potential. I could well argue that this combination of factors is most important for the purpose of ethnography, while the author's own proficiency in the language can be a desirable further addition. Would proficiency in the language alone, without these social and personal factors, enhance communication or inhibit it? Let someone be an accomplished linguist, his fieldwork would be hardly accomplished if he were unable himself to participate in the social context; and his liability would increase where a people valued warmth of heart as much as, or more so than, a meeting of minds; where they valued social propriety and rapport as much as, or more so than, an exchange of ideas. For the credibility of an ethnography, much of the criteria can indeed be met through a competent translator; and I have allowed this insight into my consideration of the sources. However, when the field research is meant to be anthropological and analytical, requiring that precise terms be ascertained, then proficiency in the language has become a necessary condition for me to ascertain the credibility of a source.

Having compiled information from a source ascertained as credible, I have compared information from it with that from other credible sources. Thus have I established *corroborated facts*. For the comparison, I assigned each source to one of two arcs, a smaller one encompassed within a larger one, according roughly to the actual geography. Material from the outer arc was employed to substantiate further the material from the inner arc. The inner arc was comprised of the specific focus of my study: the Aleutian Islands, Kodiak Area, and Chugach Bay Area including the Aleut and Alutiiq peoples. The outer arc included the neighbouring people: the Yupiit, the Ingalik Athapaskans, the Kolchan Athapaskans, the Dena'ina Athapaskans, the Eyaks, and the Tlingits. (The outer arc is directly north and east of the inner arc. To the south and west of the inner are oceans, gulfs, and formidable straits.) The peoples of the Kamchatka Peninsula were not brought into this comparative study, because pre-historic contact between northeast Asia and Alaska took place mostly farther north, across the Bering Strait, and earlier yet across the Bering Land Bridge. Kamchatka becomes central in my study during the early historic period with the coming of Christianity, as I shall explain in Chapter 1.

Corroborated facts — established thus through regionally specific comparisons between credible sources — were employed inductively to give rise to regionally specific concepts; and these concepts were then compared with analyses of international repute, as cited in these chapters.

Experience in Alaska comprised a vital aspect for the formation of my perceptions. The personal relationships that came through this experience created the motivation as well as much of the theoretical foundation for my writing. However, these personal relationships were never entered into for the sake of research, they remain personal and they will not be cited. There were a few exceptions: I conducted interviews in Anchorage in March 1988, followed by Kodiak and Spruce Islands in April 1988 (before and after the First Kodiak Area Heritage Conference); I identified my intent, which was to conduct research in those instances; and I have cited those sources (for example, in Ch.1, sec.2.ii). Exprience in Alaska began with my first visit to Kodiak Island in 1978. Subsequently, from winter 1981 until autumn 1982, I lived in Barrow on the North Slope and Juneau in the southeast; and I returned to various locations in the state of Alaska until 1994.

Since 1991, I have had the honour of becoming increasingly involved in the Sakha Republic (Iakutia) in the Russian Federation. I became involved initially by invitation from the Ministry of Culture in July 1991 and again in June 1993 through the auspices of Egor Spiridonovich Shishigin, who is now an academic of the Sakha State University at Mirny and who has himself forged ground admirably into the study of Christianity in northeast Asia. I have returned to Iakutia almost yearly since.

My relevant field experience has not been confined to the Arctic, nor could it be for a study such as this. Indepth experiences in Greece, from 1966 intermittently until the present, have been essential for the formation of my concepts by providing immediate insights into cultural dynamics within traditional village and monastic settings. My references to Arcadia are actual, not figurative. The very kind, indeed forebearing, hospitality that I received from *hegoumenos* Dositheus of the Monastery of Παναγία Τατάρνης near Carpenision in Eurytania, Greece, where I was able to stay for a season and participate with the monastics in their way of life, in autumn into winter 1976-1977, provided me with a vital experience in my youth that has been integral to the theory that I have attempted to express here. My references to Egypt are existentially specific also: I have visited the Copts' Patristic Centre at Cairo and monasteries in the desert.

Cultural contrasts have also proven vital for this type of thought and writing; because without them, some of the cultural dynamics described in this book might have appeared to me to be universals and might have remained conceptually dormant. These contrasts derive particularly from more than a decade-and-a-half of everyday life in the south of England, and from professional involvements in London, Edinburgh and Geneva. I mention all of this for a purpose: to emphasis the fact that international experience has thus combined with academic research to create the concepts for the social anthropological aspect of this work.

(iii) History

The primary sources for this history are late eighteenth and early nineteenth century manuscripts contained in various archives in Russia, America, and Finland. A number of these regarding the political history of Russian-America (as the possessions in North America were known) are published in editions, to which I have had recourse, by P.A. Tikhmenev in 1863, by A.I. Andreev in 1948, and by N.N. Bashkina in 1980.

I have had access to transcripts in the 'Holy Ruling Synod Documents' filed among the 'Russian Reproductions' in the United States Library of Congress Manuscript Division (HRS/RR/LCM, as I shall abbreviate this collection). The manuscripts themselves are located in Petersburg: the Central State Historical Archive, 'Archive of the Holy Governing Synod', catalogue numbers 643 and 564, as cited in the HRS/RR/LCM catalogue list (p.6) and also cited by F. Golder (1917:9). The transcriptions were made by Golder. He also copied four drawings from the Valaam Monastery archives that are relevant to this study. They are catalogued as 'Valaam Monastery Documents', also filed among the 'Russian Reproductions' in the Library of Congress (VM\RR\LCM, according to my abbreviation for this study). The four have been published as plates in the Limestone Press Alaska History Series translation of a book published by Valaam Monastery (Valaam 1978). The original book (Valaam 1894a) contains reproductions of three of these four drawings.

Golder conducted archival research in Russia in 1914 by invitation from the Russian imperial government.[63] In the same year, a book he had written on the history of Russian expansion to the Pacific was published in his home country, the United States. In 1917, he went to Russia again to conduct further research, and he visited the Monastery of Valaam. Returning to the United States, he produced a readable booklet, meant for distribution to his own friends, about one of the original missionaries from Valaam to Kodiak, the monastic Herman. In 1921, Golder became a professor of history at Stanford University, where he died in 1929. I have established my own archival research upon his transcriptions.

I have also had access to the documents collected by G. V. Iudin ('Yudin'), stored on microfilm in the Library of Congress Manuscript Division. Among them, a single document is most relevant to this study: the letter from Kodiak by Archimandrite Ioasaph to Grigorii Shelikov, dated 18 May 1795. It is the second item, first reel, first container, in the 'Yudin Collection' at shelf number 18, 292-2N-2P.

Translations into English of Russian primary sources have been provided with substantial introductions, appendices, notes, and reproductions, in the Limestone Press Alaska History Series (LPAH), edited by R. A. Pierce, a professor emeritus in history from Queens College in Ontario, presently continuing as a professor of history at the University of Alaska at Fairbanks. Some of these materials are published for the first time in any language. In addition to translations of Russian primary sources, this series also includes American primary sources. The series furthermore includes Russian analytical studies in English translation as well as American analytical studies in first editions.

Recognizing its accuracy, I have used LPAH throughout my work. I am aware, of course, that some editors are selective about the materials they chose to bring forth; but a characteristic of this edited series is an on-going effort for ever greater accuracy in the publications For example, a translation of primary source materials containing letters by a missionary *hieromonk* (priest-monk),[64] written between 1805 and 1807 (in Valaam 1978), has been reissued in this continuing series in a revised translation from a critical study accomplished by L.T. Black (cited here as Gideon 1990); and both these LPHA compilations include a reissuing of ethnographical material by Gideon published in English translation earlier (Black 1977b). This primary source material has been made available through consistently cooperative effort for ever more refined and inclusive editions to promote accuracy for studies in Alaska history.

Supplementary material from an unrelated translation project known as 'Documents Relative to the History of Alaska' (DRHA) has been appended to some publications in LPAH. A voluminous early translation project, DRHA is different from LPAH: the standard of accuracy is not the same. Copies of DRHA are available on microfilm in the University of Alaska Library system, and also in the Alaska State Historical Library at Juneau. Another copy exists on microfilm in the Library of Congress Manuscript Division, filed under 'Alaska University: Alaska History Research Project', at shelf number 10,612, serviced through the library's Microfilm Reading Room. The value of this pioneering project can be found in the effort to make Russian language primary sources available in English. While I refer to the LPAH appendices from DRHA, no detail in my study has been based on them. Nor have quotations been incorporated from them into my text. My few references to them are, in each case, to the entire appendix in LPAH, and refer to the general content, not to details.

Whenever I cite an appendix in LPAH, be it from DRHA or from another source, I provide LPAH appendix's own reference to its own source: in quotation marks within brackets in my note. I provide also my own reference directly to the published Russian primary source except in one instance where the original has not been published, and then I specify this circumstance. My intent is to provide direction to scholars, whether they have proficiency in Russian or not; and for those who do not, I have differentiated the better translations.

Analysed data from North American and Russian scholars have been incorporated into my study, principally for the details of dates and for the analyses of population figures. These sources are: L.T. Black and R.A. Pierce of North America; S.G. Fedorova, R.G. Liapunova and R.V. Makarova of Russia. Substantial contributions to the religious history in Russian-America from the 1820s have been provided by L.T. Black in her introductions, notes and appendices to Russian primary source materials published in English translations: this is important analytical work. Further archival research that she conducted in Petersburg, May-June 1993, has been incorporated into her forthcoming book, provisionally titled *Russians in Alaska, 1741-1867*. Details from this research are included in my Chapter 6.

I have had to place aside the volumes of primary source material compiled and edited by I. Barsukov and the additional volume of biography by him, all published in the 1880s, because I am unable to assess the accuracy of the various contents myself. They relate to the highly gifted churchman I. Veniaminov, who arrived in Russian-America in 1823 and who later influenced the history of northeast Asia. Barsukov's work is certainly important, as reflected through its republication in 1997 by the Iakutskii Dom, a philanthropic organization in Moscow comprised of leaders of the Sakha Republic (Iakutia) who produced this volume to commemorate the bicentennial of Veniaminov's birth. They have written the following message in English in the front pages of this beautifully created republication:

> The Moscow charitable commune 'Yakutsky Dom' has made the reprint of this rare book with the intent of confirming the grateful memory of the Sakha [Iakut] people for the great deeds of the famous Russian Orthodox missionary and educator of the peoples of America, Yakutia and the Far East: a great scientist and Apostle of the Faith ... a man who loved the citizens of the North so much.

This clearly expresses the vitality of Veniaminov's contributions and legacy. It also signifies the value of Barsukov's edition and biography about him. Assessments of Barsukov's work will probably be forthcoming from academics qualified in that field, as interest in Veniaminov has revived in Russia during the 1990s. An international conference of remarkable dimensions took place in Iakutsk in 1997 to commemorate the bicentennial of Veniaminov's birth, convened as the culmination of a series of commemorative conferences that spanned the globe during 1996 and 1997 (and the republication of Barsukov's work was presented by representatives of Iakutskii Dom in the city of Iakutsk at that time). Earlier conferences devoted to Veniaminov's life and accomplishments were held at Vladivostock in 1990 and at Petropavlovsk soon afterwards in 1993. All of these gatherings involved specialists in various disciplines. Without demeaning the importance of Barsukov's work, I have set it aside for the purpose of this study, until its various contents are assessed by specialists.

I have had direct access, instead, to first editions of Veniaminov's published works. I have also had recourse to archival research by qualified colleagues regarding Veniaminov's life and his written works. L.T. Black has been particularly helpful in this regard, assisting me while I laboured through these sources whose authenticity has already been established credibly.

Excluded from this study is any primary source about which there is a question of authenticity, and any analytical source about which there is a question of credibility — except when the credibility is itself the matter of my concern, and then that work is cited and the concern about it is expressed in my text.

Entirely excluded from my text is the three volume series of Russian documents loosely rendered into English by B. Dmytryshyn, E.A.P. Crownhart-Vaughan, and T. Vaughan, published by the Oregon Historical Society between 1985 and 1989. I have listed this series in my bibliography to signify my knowledge of it. Impressive by bulk and arty format, it was funded by USA national endowments and other grants; but its scholarship, as I have found, can hardly be considered commensurate with such funding. For example, *baidara* is repeatedly mistranslated (Dmytryshyn, Crownhart-Vaughan and Vaughan, vol.2, 1988:380-381). Where the original document refers to an open skin boat that could carry as many as twenty men (a *baidara*), the 'translation' has rendered the boat repeatedly as a kayak. A kayak is a *baidarka*, different from the *baidara*.

In another document (ibid., vol.2, pp.215-216), an error is made in geography. The locations of men with entrepreneur S.G. Glotov and cossack S.T. Ponomarev from 1759 to 1762, have repeatedly been rendered as Unalaska and Unimak Islands. But Glotov and Ponomarev camped on Umnak Island (not Unimak), before dispatching hunters northeast along the Bering Sea coast of neighbouring Unalaska Island. Unimak is separated from both Umnak and Unalaska by three other major islands. The location bears directly upon studies such as mine; because this document contains a report regarding an Umnak leader named Shushak entrusting a young kinsman to Glotov who baptized the youth. The erroneous rendition has placed this event in an altogether different location.

The problems with yet another document rendered in that series are indicated by the title attached spuriously to this other document (ibid., p.497): 'A Report from Ieromonk Makarii, head of the Russian Orthodox mission in Alaska ... detailing the treatment of natives by Russians.' But Makarii was not the 'head of the mission'. Archimandrite Ioasaph was the head: this is an uncontested fact, readily available in any publication: primary, secondary and tertiary sources, and analytical studies alike. Furthermore, the term 'native' never occurs in Makarii's own report.[65] This term rarely occurs in eighteenth century Russian reports from the Aleutians and Kodiak, as far as I know. But the connotative term is used in the spurious title attached to this document and used throughout the rendition of the text. It is used in place of Makarii's original terms, such as the 'Aleuts' and the 'voiceless people' (the latter emphasizes Makarii's appeal on their behalf).

Finally in the spurious title and occasionally through the loosely rendered text, these 'natives' are set against 'the Russians', although Makarii's protest was more specific. He was protesting against a ruthless capitalistic enterprise that he very clearly named and emphasized in his report: the Shelihov-Golikov enterprises; and he was protesting *to* imperial Russian authorities! Just as the Aleuts become undifferentiated 'natives', and Makarii's own standing is changed, so that the culprits are obscured in that series.

Were a point of merit to be found in the series, it would be that the 'translators' and editors recognized in their introduction that no history has yet interpreted the initial contact periods, before the mid-1760s, across the Aleutian Island archipelago (p.xl). Overlooking this period however, they embark on a treatment of events after the 1770s as if that were the totality nonetheless. Their brief statement remains significant: no work had concentrated on the early contact periods.

Perhaps my study may provide some insights into the initial contact periods, as the first baptisms took place across the length of the Aleutian Island chain then. I have attempted to analyse the relevant interactions from those early periods, and to compare them with interactions from later periods, the 1770s into the 1820s.

The dates from the Russian-American history sources are given here according to the Julian Calendar, as found in these sources.

NOTES

[1] Veniaminov (1840b:144; 1984:229). Also see id. (1840a:44; 1840b:144-148; 1972:51; 1984:230-231). The following is an example of the descriptions he wrote during his parish ministry, a note to a journal entry dated 4 May 1825 during his first pastoral visit to the village of '*Recheshnoi*', known today as Nikolski, on Umnak Island (id. 1993:36, nt.13):

> It is impossible to remain silent about the zeal, devotion, and affectionate manner of all the local Aleuts. They have only to catch sight of the baidara, and all — from the small to the great, and even those on crutches — come to receive us, to greet us, and to receive the blessing with great joy.

For others contemporary with Veniaminov, see, e.g., F.P. Litke (Friedrich Luetke), an imperial Russian naval captain of a sloop-of-war on a voyage round-the-world, reporting from Unalaska in 1826 (Litke 1987:101): 'They are all Christians ... very zealous in carrying out the services of worship. They attend church very diligently.' Also consider the descriptions by Ivan Kriukov, a Russian or Russian-Siberian settler in the Unalaska region who had intermarried here and had more than forty years of experience on the Aleutian Islands by the early 1820s when he visited Irkutsk to tell of 'the zeal of the Aleuts for prayer and [the zeal of the Aleuts] to hear the word of God and to be blessed in the name of God'. For the citation, and for Kriukov and his descendants, see Epilogue, nt.10

[2] Gideon (1989:122). A well educated cathedral *hieromonk* (priest-monk) of the *Aleksandr-Nevskaia lavra* (monastery of St Alexander Nevskii) in Petersburg, Gideon spent nearly three years in Russian-America, mainly in the Kodiak area, to bolster the spiritual mission. Although he stayed on Unalaska Island for about seven days only, from 29/30 June until 7 July 1807, while returning to the Russian mainland from Kodiak, his statement is indicative because he ministered here to numerous people from various locations who had come to the Unalaska harbour village to meet him, 1-6 July 1807 (see ibid., pp.131-143). His statement is indicative furthermore in light of Veniaminov's extensive experience and consistent statements a generation later. But cf. the statements by N.P. Rezanov and G.H. Langsdorff who were in Russian-America concurrently with Gideon, and who will be quoted in my final Conclusions, sec.1, at nts 13-15.

[3] Bryant (1870:8, 22).

[4] McIntyre (1870:8).

[5] Ibid., p. 12.

[6] Buynitzky (1871:6).

[7] Pinart (1874b:6, 9).

[8] Petroff (1881:14). But for Petroff, see Sherwood (1963; 1964) and Pierce (1964).

[9] Petroff (1884:18, 21).

[10] Elliot (1881: 21, 22).

[11] Applegate in Porter (1893:82).

[12] Porter, ibid., p. 187.

[13] Hutchinson (1942:150-151).

[14] See Miyaoka (1978:177-178).

[15] Ransom (1945a:337).

[16] Ibid., p.333, ftnt.3; pp. 337, 340.

[17] Alex Prossoff's Story, personal account dictated on 16 March 1947, Appendix 2 in Oliver (1988:242). Prossoff in Appendix 2, and also in the list of Attuan war prisoners in Appendix 3, in ibid., is the same as Prokoff in Sweetland (ms.), cited next; and I shall maintain Sweetland's spelling.

[18] Sweetland (ms.). The manuscript is held by his daughter, Barbara Sweetland Smith in Anchorage, and I am grateful to her for allowing me access to it.

[19] Oliver (1988:56).

[20] Shade (1949:96).

[21] Berreman (1953:148).

[22] Ibid., pp.151-152. The statement about clergy is correct.

[23] Id. (1955:51).

[24] Spaulding (1955:134-135).

[25] Jones (1976:80-82). The researcher maintained anonymity about the villages to honour confidences. She referred to one as 'New Harbor' and the other as 'Iliaka', which are fictitious names. American religious missions had been established in both villages. (Yes, USA authorities sent missionaries into the Christian Aleut villages to convert them.) But the Aleuts 'tend to view the fundamentalist mission as a white man's church'. If 'Iliaka' is Dutch Harbor on Unalaska Island, which is probable, then the American mission would have been operative since the later years of the nineteenth century, sometimes aggressively with 'hostile acts' reported,[30] but in fact with nearly no conversions through three generations. For reports of the missionaries' hostile aggression at Unalaska, see, e.g., Report of Rev. Priest Alexander Kedrovsky of Unalaska, including correspondence with Mrs. Agnes Newhall [missionary and matron of the Methodist Home], 11-24 November 1900, in Oleksa, ed. (1987, 328-339).

[26] Jones (1980:168).

[27] Dirks (1988:xiv).

[28] Merculieff (1984). Also see St. Paul, Pribilov Islands, schoolchildren's self-description in Jones (1980:168): 'We have traditions ... We go to church, church school, and learn about the church. We have our own community, and our family life is pretty good too. And we are hunters...'

[29] Petrivelli (1993).

[30] See WW2, above. When the Aleut population was deported, abruptly with merely a few hours warning, and the military occupied their villages as part of the war campaign in the north Pacific, many of the churches were looted and damaged or destroyed through the occupation. Compensation in part was won three-and-a-half decades later through prolonged legal action by the Aleuts, and this large portion of the money was designated by them for the reconstruction of their churches. This information can be substantiated with reference to the documents from the legal proceedings that can be located through USA federal government sources, the Alaska state archives, and the Aleut Foundation. Among the sources cited here, above, see: Oliver (1988:16, 56), the schoolteacher assigned by the USA government to Atka immediately after the

repatriation, who mentions the villagers' own reconstruction of their church, with their own resources, because the church building had been burnt by the military and a valuable icon along with a nineteenth century cast iron bell had been lost.

[31] Huggins (1981:13).

[32] Ibid., pp.13, 27.

[33] Ibid., pp.13, 28.

[34] Pinart (1873b:673).

[35] Petroff (1884:28).

[36] Ibid., p. 42. Cf. Porter (1893:187), quoted above.

[37] Birket-Smith (1953:132).

[38] Oliver (1988:9). See id., cited above for Atka.

[39] Hammerich (1954:424).

[40] Befu (1970:31).

[41] Davis (1970:125, 129, 145).

[42] Ibid., p.128-129. The same village was described by Birket-Smith in 1933 and by the USA census taker in 1880, both of whom have been quoted above.

[43] Id. (1971:78, 189-190).

[44] Id. (1970:129).

[45] Taylor (1966:121).

[46] Rathburn (1981:12, 20).

[47] Personal communication, Peter Kreta, priest of the Resurrection Russian Orthodox Church, Kodiak, April 1988.

[48] Therefore, I shall enclose the self-designation 'OCA' in inverted commas; and in the bibliography, I shall append the adverb *sic* to this designation.

[49] Veniaminov (1975:28-29). Each altar is counted as a church in this source; therefore, the specified number has been reduced in my text to forty-four chapels and church buildings, as two buildings contained two altars each.

This source requires further clarification, because he assigned credit for this number to the patronage by the Russian-American Company whose shareholders he was addressing in Petersburg on 17 December 1857. The address was published in the Company's annual report for 1858 (Lada-Mocarski 1969:413; trans. Veniaminov 1975, as cited above). While specifying that the Russian-American Company had been responsible for the construction of churches at only the company's main locations, he yet commended them for the promotion of Christianity throughout this vast region in general. Was he being tactful?

The Russian-American Company had at times actually impeded the missionaries' work and had at times opposed the functioning of churches. Here are a few examples. A local chapel had been appropriated by the company's chief manager, P.E. Chistiakov, who rendered it a warehouse in 1826, then had it destroyed when the stores were depleted (see Black 1984a:98, nt.30). The dwelling of the last surviving missionary had been axed by order of the company district manager in the Kodiak area at about the same time (P.F. Kashevarov, 'Information about Fr Herman', 7 Sept. 1866, in Valaam, ed., 1894:185-186, 1978:111; also see S.I. Ianovskii, Letter to Damascene, 22 Nov. 1865, in ibid. 1894:142, 1978:87). Earlier, another district manager for the company, I.I. Banner, attempted to impede a gifted young man from being prepared for church service (cathedral *hieromonk* Gideon to the Kodiak Office, 11 March 1805, in Gideon 1989:85; also see Gideon to Metropolitan Amvrosii [no date], in ibid., p.82). For yet earlier instances of antipathy and impediment, see Ch.1 at nts 96-99, below. And for further information regarding Veniaminov in this context, see Ch.1 at nt.103.

[50] Kodiak, anon. (1985:6).

[51] Oswalt (1963a:131-146).

[52] See, e.g., ibid., p.132. Also see e.g., Intro., sec.1, at nts 13, 38, 39, 47, above.

[53] See Appendix in Oleksa, ed. (1987:377-386). Fr Nikifor Amkan in ibid., is 'Fr Nichafor' in Oswalt (1963:132); Bereskin is the 'songleader Matthew Berezkin'.

[54] For published substantiation see, e.g., McClanahan (1986): 'Russian Orthodox' is found in the transcribed interviews spoken in English by elder Native Alaskans from various regions, who were residing at the time of these interviews in the Cook Inlet region. Also see the use of this term reflected in the descriptions by numerous observers in Intro., sec.1, above.

[55] For substantiation see Davis (1984:201). Also see Kodiak (anon. 1985:6) acknowledging that 'in many areas, English was not the language of the people' in 1972. For those few regions where English had become the dominant language, see Ch.2, nt.44, below.

[56] Shirokogoroff (1935:268); Eliade (1964:4, 1987:202). Also see Tugolukov (1978:426). The term occurs in the Manchu language also.

[57] See, e.g., Nicholson, comp. (1987).

[58] See, e.g., Valaam (1894a:45), and Valaam, ed. (1894:131, 141); but translated as 'St Petersburg' in Valaam (1978:28), and Valaam, ed. (1978:80, 87).

[59] See Pierce (1990:113-114).

[60] See ibid., p.288.

[61] Langsdorff (1814:47; 1812:42).

[62] Ibid. (1814:64, 1812:58).

[63] For biographical data about Golder, see the 'Introductory Note' by J. Franklin Jameson in Pt1 in Golder (1917); also see the Preface in Pt2 in ibid. The latter part was issued in 1937, but is bound with the first part as vol.37, dated 1917.

[64] A *hieromonk* is a monastic ordained to the priesthood. Not all monastics are thus ordained in the Orthodox Church.

[65] *Hieromonk* Makarii, Report to the Holy Synod, 5 Oct. 1797, HRS/RR/LCM 643:13-23.

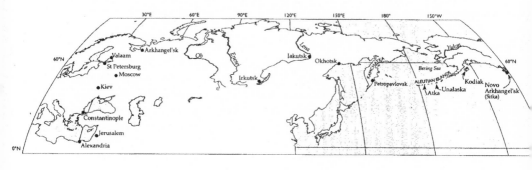

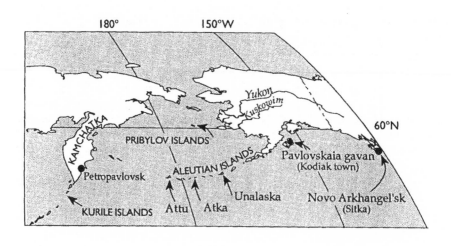

Maps of Alaskan Territories

Chapter 1

Initial Contacts, First Baptisms

The purpose of the first chapter is to indicate that the transition was indigenous and corporate: it involved indigenous spiritual and social processes; and it involved the whole bodies of peoples' societies, or kinship-based polities. The opening sections of this chapter will concentrate on the Aleutian Islands, the concluding sections on the Kodiak area. In the latter location, the historical circumstances differed about the initial contacts and first baptisms; yet the characteristics of the transition were very much the same: indigenous and corporate.

(1) The Aleutian Islands

When the first parish priest assigned to the eastern Aleutian Islands arrived in 1824, the Aleut laity of his parish were already conducting Orthodox services that did not require clergy. Throughout his ministry from 1824 to 1834, whenever Fr Ioann Veniaminov made pastoral visits to the villages that comprised this parish, he conducted those sacraments that require an ordained minister: chrismation, confession, and communion. This is evident in his journals where he recorded the sacraments he had ministered. To marry, he 'sacramentally blessed' the couple (a phrase from his journals): in other words, he performed the marriage ceremony for a couple who had already been bonded through local customs. Rarely did he baptize: he would chrismate those who had been newly baptized. Very rarely did he bury: he would sometimes lead a memorial service. Only at the harbour village on Unalaska Island where he himself remained most of the year, did he conduct baptisms and funerals regularly. Elsewhere the village laity were ministering these sacraments themselves, throughout the vast parish.[1]

The parish was vast indeed. Known as the Unalaska parish, it extended from Unalaska Island eastward along the Aleutian archipelago to Unga Island and to the tip of the Alaska Peninsula, westward to Umnak Island, and northward across the Bering Sea to encompass the Pribylov Islands. Veniaminov made pastoral visits to various locations through this parish during the summer and spring months of each year of this decade. During autumns and winters, he remained mostly in Unalaska's harbour village (near today's Dutch Harbor).

The same type of ministry is evident in the journals of the priest of the neighbouring Atka parish, Fr Iakov Netsvetov, who arrived in 1828, soon after Veniaminov, and ministered for almost sixteen years. The Atka parish encompassed the central and western Aleutians and extended farther westward to the Kurile Islands; so that this parish together with the Unalaska parish encompassed the Aleutian archipelago and locations beyond.

How had these parishes come into being? Their formation was a development by the laity, beginning three generations prior to the arrival of the first parish priest.

(i) Chronology of clergy prior to Veniaminov

No clergyman had been assigned as a missionary to the Aleutian Islands before Fr Ioann Veniaminov arrived as the parish priest in 1824, except one missionary who had served for approximately a year, from summer 1795 to summer 1796: *hieromonk* Makarii whose ministry was located mainly in the vicinity of the harbour settlement on Unalaska Island.[2]

Other clergy in transit had made brief landfalls at Unalaska Island, the port-of-call for east-west voyages between Okhotsk/Kamchatka and Kodiak/Sitka, and for north-south voyages between the north Pacific and the Bering Sea. Their combined total of time amounted to less than a year. A chronology is provided below:

(a) Briefly in 1790: Fr Vasilii Sivtsov, chaplain to the *Slava Rossii*, Billings/Sarychev expedition, performed baptisms and marriages (Sarychev 1802:26, 1807:13).[3]

(b) Two days in September 1794: missionaries in transit from Okhotsk to Kodiak Island stopped at Unalaska. They also harboured through inclement weather at a remote bay on the same island. They performed baptisms.[4]

(c) A week in July 1807: *hieromonk* Gideon in transit from Kodiak to Okhotsk performed baptisms, chrismations, and marriages at Unalaska.[5]

(d) Briefly during a period in June 1820, at the end of August 1820, and mid-June 1821: Fr Mikhail Ivanov chaplain to the Vasil'ev/Shishmarev circumnavigational expedition, on the *Blagonamerennii*, might have landed while that vessel was anchored in the Unalaska harbour (Ivashintsov 1980:141).

In August 1824, Veniaminov arrived as the parish priest and recorded nearly the same list of clergy in the region before him, but without the chronological details.[6] He overlooked only point (b) in the chronology: the missionaries in transit to Kodiak.

In summary, prior to Veniaminov's arrival a single missionary had been assigned who had served for approximately a year. Otherwise, chaplains and missionaries in transit had made landfalls at Unalaska Island, for a combined total of less than a year. Thus the combined time of all clergymen was less than two years prior to Veniaminov's arrival; and their presence was located mainly on a single island, Unalaska, and more specifically at the harbour settlement.

Yet when Veniaminov arrived, sacraments were already being performed by laity on the islands throughout the region; and he was assigned as the parish priest who ministered within an existing parish comprised of Aleut villages, or kinship-based polities.

The history in the neighbouring Atka parish is even more impressive in this respect. Encompassing the central and western Aleutian Islands, this parish had known its first baptism by 1747. Four generations later in 1828 Iakov Netsvetov was assigned as the parish priest. Yet never had a clergyman been in these regions prior to him; and he had roots here himself, as his mother, Maria, was an Atkan Aleut.

(ii) Social dynamics that brought forth Russian Orthodox leadership

How had such leadership developed prior to the arrival of parish priests? Intermarriage was one social dynamic that brought it forth. An example is provided by the parents of Fr Iakov Netsvetov. His mother Maria Alekseevna from Atka married his father Egor Vasil'evich from Tobolsk, a man of particular piety.[7]

Egor Vasil'evich had arrived in 1794 within the second generation following the first baptisms in this region that later came to comprise the Atka parish. The couple were married according to local customs; and their first child Iakov was born in 1804. In July 1807, they had their marriage blessed sacramentally by *hieromonk* Gideon; the only priest in this region since 1796, he had landed at Unalaska for a week while journeying from Kodiak to Okhotsk. It is significant that the couple sought him. They received an anointing with blessed oil from him, as well. At that date, Egor was 34 years old and Maria was in her 20s, according to Gideon's records.[8] They raised a family on St George, Pribylov Islands, a location that eventually became part of the Unalaska parish. Their children distinguished themselves: one son as a master shipwright; another as a navigator; one daughter as the wife of a company manager at Sitka; another as the wife of a Russian-Aleut educated at Petersburg; and the eldest son Iakov as a graduate of the Irkutsk seminary, then as the first priest of the Atka parish (1828-1844). Later, Iakov became the first clergy missionary to the Yukon and Kuskokwim River regions (1845-1863).

The leadership this marriage brought forth was bilingual. Netsvetov translated into Atkan Aleut and cooperated with Veniaminov in creating an alphabet based on the Cyrillic for the Aleut languages. Netsvetov instructed the next generation of parish priests for both the Atka and Unalaska parishes: Fr L.S. Salamatov and Fr I. Shaiashnikov. These men who also derived from inter-marriages were fluently bilingual: they translated scriptures and authored original work in Atkan and Unalaskan Aleut respectively.

A fact has been indicated that deserves attention. From the beginning the priests had kinship ties within the parishes. Netsvetov, Salamatov, and Shaiashnikov were raised and were kindred on islands where they served. A foreigner intervened in the Unalaska parish between Shaiashnikov and Veniaminov: Fr Golovin, who may have been a Kamchadal. As for Veniaminov who had come from Irkutsk, he became competently bilingual and he devel-oped kinship ties through the marriage of a brother to an Aleut woman and the marriage of a daughter to a Russian-Aleut man. The combination of dual kinship and dual language (Russian-Aleut) must have been instrumental in the communication and indigenization of this faith, instrumental for its im-planting from Asia and engrafting in the Aleutians.

The combination of dual kinship and language should be emphasized to avoid any misinterpretation of this dynamic of intermarriage. While inter-marriages in other historic and modern contexts result in monolingualism and monoculturalism, the dynamic here resulted in multilingualism and a blending of cultures for an ingrafting of Russian elements into Aleut culture (and similar dynamics occurred throughout Russian-America and in Asiatic Russia).[9]

Intermarriage was thus a vital social dynamic for the development of Rus-sian Orthodox leadership. An even earlier social dynamic began with the initial contacts, within alliances formed between hunters across the Aleutian Islands.

Shushak, a leading man of Umnak Island, entered into alliance with Stepan Gavrilovich Glotov, a hunter who had come from northeastern Asia and who remained in the Umnak region from 1759 to 1762. Shashuk entrusted a nephew to him, and the ally baptized the youth. This was the first baptism, or among the first, in the Unalaska region. Names were given and shared: the godson received the baptismal name Ivan (Ioann) and he assumed his godfather's names as his own patronymic and surname; thus the youth Mushkal (Mushkalyax) became the Aleut Ivan Stepanovich Glotov.[10] He remained alongside his god-father for the next three years. Together in 1762 they departed Umnak aboard the *Sv. Iulian* and travelled to Kamchatka where they stayed from August until October 1762. They then journeyed aboard the *Sv. Andreian i Natal'ia* to Kodiak Island where they spent the winter of 1762/63, before returning along the eastern Aleutian Islands to Umnak, Ivan's home island, in spring of 1764.

Eventually succeeding his uncle Shushak and becoming the primary *toion* of Umnak, the Aleut Ivan Stepanovich Glotov exercised mature political and spiritual leadership into the next century, including the conducting of Orthodox services in the chapel on Umnak, as recorded in 1807.[11] (*Toion* is the word, probably of Iakut origin, assumed by leading Aleut men during the Russian era.)

Another example of this social dynamic is evident concurrently at the other side of the island chain, on the western Aleutians. On Attu in 1761 a leading man named Makuzhan had his young kinsman baptized by men who had come there from northeast Asia for the hunt. The young kinsman received the baptismal name Leontii and also assumed his godfather's names as his own patronymic and surname, becoming the Aleut Leontii Vasil'evich Popov.[12]

Entrusted thus to his godfather, he journeyed alongside him, departing that same year on the *Sv. Ioann Ustiuzhskii*, sailing east to the islands of Buldir, Kiska, Segula, Awadax, Little Stikin, and Amchitka; then turning westward to hunt on Shemya (a Near Island) in summer 1763, before continuing to Kamchatka. In September of the following year, the merchant Popov funded the same vessel for a voyage that spent nearly a year on Bering Island before returning to the Near Islands in summer 1765.[13] The latter voyage would have been the one that brought Leontii home. By then, he would have had four years in his godfather's company, hunting, exploring, and learning the ways of these men who had come from northeastern Asia.

(iii) An indigenous social process

A process occurred in these parallel, concurrent examples that corresponded to an indigenous social process guiding the successions of leaders. Three key elements were involved. Firstly, succession occurred among 'customary lineage chiefs' on the eastern Aleutians, and within a 'hereditary kin group' on the central and western Aleutians.[14] Hence among the examples, on the eastern Islands the Aleut Ivan Stepanovich Glotov succeeded his own uncle Shashuk as *toion* of Umnak. A further example derives before 1786 when the Aleut Sergei Dmitrievich Pan'kov succeeded his own brother as *toion*. The successor's names clearly indicate baptism, for Sergei is a baptismal name. The successor's names may also indicate an alliance with the Russian Dmitrii Pan'kov who had made a number of voyages into this region and had evidently entered into a number of lasting alliances.[15]

The second component in the social process was the fostering of children. Parents permitted their children to be raised by kinsmen or even by non-consanguine affines.[16] Non-consanguine affines would be friends and allies. Hence the young men were entrusted to their godfathers by elder kinsmen. The Aleut Ivan Stepanovich Glotov's godfather and the Aleut Leontii Vasil'evich Popov's godfather clearly honoured the trust by returning the youngsters to their elders after years of traveling, exploring, and hunting.

Succession depended also on skill and on valour. A successor was expected to have distinguished himself by mastering techniques of seafaring and of hunting. He was expected also to have completed expeditions to foreign lands and thus to have gained experience of wider geography and of other peoples.[17] This was the third component. Hence the successor journeyed alongside his godfather for a series of years in each example: exploring, hunting, and learning the ways of these men who had come from northeast Asia.

In each example the godson went to Kamchatka. What would he have seen? By the early 1740s, the Kamchadals were Russian Orthodox; churches (with priests) or chapels (without priests) existed in the major settlements where Kamchadal men exercised leadership.[18] The first clergy had been assigned in 1705, from Tobolsk.[19] A priest was described at Petropavlovsk in 1779, an embarkation site for the Aleutians since 1741: the 'benevolent and hospitable pastor' was 'native on his mother's side'.[20]

The Kamchadals themselves comprised up to fifty per cent of the men who came to the Aleutians for the sea hunts during the initial contact period, between 1745 and the 1760s. Later during the 1770s when the purpose of enterprises and the nature of contacts changed, the percentage of Kamchadals involved decreased.[21]

(iv) The merging of faith and polity

This merging is evident through: (a) the successful exercise of leadership by Russian Orthodox Aleuts on behalf of their people in the 1780s and 1790s; (b) a continuity in this leadership from the 1760s; and (c) specific examples of this leadership from the 1760s into the time of Veniaminov's ministry.

The merging is evident in the exercise of leadership by Russian Orthodox Aleuts in the 1780s and the 1790s in protests against an influx of enterprises and imperial interests into the Unalaska region during the later 1700s. The following is a chronological summary of these protests. Before June 1787, a *toion*'s kinsman named Izosim Polutov dispatched a written protest from the central Aleutian Islands to the Okhotsk district commander.[22] At the same time, Tukulan Aiugnin dispatched a report also to the Okhotsk office from the 'third Fox Island' — an eastern Island: Akutan, possibly Akun, or even Unalaska. Before 1791, a *toion* Algamalinag named in baptism Mikhail and bilingual Saguakh named Ivan Chuloshnikov spoke out in person to the naval captain G.A. Sarychev who had anchored at Unalaska, whose expedition for the government had been charged in part to collect such testimony.[23] In 1796, *toion* Ivan Stepanovich Glotov of Umnak led twenty-two other men, each a leader in this region, in a protest directed to the imperial capital Petersburg.[24] In 1797, a *toion* Ielisei Popachev travelled with the Aleuts Nikolai Lukanin and Nikifor Svin'in and with the missionary *hieromonk* Makarii toward Petersburg.[25] The key to the chronology exists in the men's names. Only one lacked a baptismal name. Russian Orthodox Aleut leaders were in place, stood firmly, and acted on behalf of their people through the influx.

An extended example is found in the *toion* Sergei Dmitrievich Pan'kov. By 1791, he had visited Kamchatka and had made at least two journeys to Okhotsk from where, in response to protests received, official communications had been dispatched that clearly articulated the Aleutian Island peoples' civil rights as Russian subjects.[26] This *toion* had travelled to Unimak Island (in the Unalaska region) where he consulted with kinsmen in that year, 1791. He then journeyed to Unalaska to meet with naval captain Sarychev whose governmental expedition was charged, in part, to investigate. Pan'kov came with twenty-five Aleut men: fourteen with him in a *baidara*, an open skin boat; another eleven alongside in single-hatch *baidarkas*, kayaks.[27] At the meeting, other leading Aleut men were present as well, among whom Pan'kov presided. Addressing Sarychev in Russian, this primary *toion* wore a head-covering and a over-garment of light red cloth and of velvet with gold or golden trim, presented to him by a government office in northeastern Asia. Outstanding in colour, unusual in texture, they distinguished him from the other men in the council and from Sarychev: for the clothing was unlike a European uniform. Dressed as an Aleut of high status, the primary *toion* stood and spoke.

Through leadership such as this, the Aleuts maintained remarkable autonomy on the Aleutian Islands and achieved an unusual degree of independence. As observed by Veniaminov in the 1830s, they were more independent than the Kamchadals and were freer than some Asians: 'in their own locale, the Aleuty [*sic*] are more independent and free than the people of Kamchatka and even baptized Asians.'[28] Autonomy was reflected in the moral qualities described for them consistently by Veniaminov;[29] it was reflected as well in their intellectual pursuits in their own language, evident in these journals and also in the work of subsequent generations on the Islands. With autonomy and with the language, the culture prevailed.[30] The leadership was successful.

The Aleut leadership on behalf of polity in 1780s and 1790s can be seen in continuity from leadership in the preceding generation, but with new tactics now. In the 1760s, to counter the escalating influx, Aleut men had created a militant alliance led from the islands of Tigalda and Akun and including the islands of Unimak, Unalaska, and Umnak.[31] These were the major islands in the Unalaska region, later to become the Unalaska parish.

In the same region by the 1790s, Aleut leaders had been empowered legally and morally: legally through information received from northeast Asia where an articulated prerequisite for trade on the islands was humane conduct; and morally through the ethics intrinsic in Christianity that had been communicated to them by this time. The leaders, who had succeeded their kinsmen as *toion* through the native social processes of upbringing and succession, especially would have known themselves to be empowered in these ways; because they had travelled to Kamchatka and moreover had Christianity imparted to them through alliances with men like themselves.

The Aleut leaders in this generation articulated complaints, and they sent petitions, directly to the Petersburg government for the enforcement of the legal and moral requirements. These leaders were Russian Orthodox; and they were already in place on the eastern Aleutian Islands when they were joined by the missionary *hieromonk* Makarii.

Who was Makarii? A *hieromonk* from the Konevskii Monastery in Karelia, he was a member of the spiritual mission to Kodiak Island. Arriving at Kodiak in September 1794, he was dispatched with an interpreter to the Unalaska region in summer 1795, where he travelled to a very few islands, including Unga and Akun, on the route to the harbour settlement at Unalaska Island. Remaining in the latter vicinity, he joined Aleut leaders against the escalating commercial enterprises of the Shelikhov-Golikov company; and the following June, with six Aleut men he journeyed towards Petersburg, carrying a petition of protest from regional leaders.

The dimensions of the task become clear when one considers the purpose and circumstances of the journey: they were traveling to protest against a commercial power which had representatives in the towns of Okhotsk and Irkutsk and which was gaining influence over the northeast Asian coast, the North Pacific archipelagos, and the southern Alaskan coast. The men had to arrange transportation through those regions and had to travel through those towns. Makarii himself was a monastic without title, and would have had few if any sources of financial support. Furthermore he lacked authority to travel: he had departed without authorization. He journeyed resourcefully and (one may well imagine) cleverly.

Of the original group of seven men, three survived to arrive at Petersburg in spring 1798: *hieromonk* Makarii, Nikolai Lukanin and Nikifor Svin'in were granted an audience with the emperor. Makarii was reprimanded for unauthorized activity. Intercessions by the Aleut men spared him from punishment.[32] On their return journey eastward, all three died: Lukanin and Svin'in on the overland route across Siberia; Makarii on the sea crossing, off the Aleutians, towards Kodiak. This was the only Russian missionary to the Aleutians: the conscientious and resourceful Makarii who gave his life with these Aleut leaders.

Russian Orthodoxy thus merged with the people's own leadership, with their own struggle, with their destiny. This merging of faith and polity is reflected particularly in a person who recurs in Veniaminov's journals: Ivan Pan'kov the *toion* of the islands of Tigalda and Akun. The same islands had provided the leadership for the Aleut wars in Pan'kov's grandparents' generation during the mid-1760s; and in his parents' generation in 1791, the *toion* Sergei Dmitrievich who presided at the council at Unalaska had had the same surname.[33] Yet, prior to Veniaminov's arrival, Ivan Pan'kov was providing instruction in the faith within his polity himself.[34] And when Veniaminov arrived, Ivan Pan'kov donated money for the reception and settlement of the priest and family: indeed he donated more than the average sum.[35] Elder in age to the priest, Pan'kov accompanied him on pastoral visits to Tigalda and Akun where the priest was warmly received.[36] This *toion* co-translated the catechism and the Gospel. After Veniaminov's transfer, Pan'kov had chapels constructed in 1842 and 1843 on both those islands for his own people.[37]

An earlier example of the merging of faith and polity is provided by Ivan Stepanovich Glotov the Aleut *toion* of Umnak. It was he who had led twenty-two men of the Unalaska region in a protest written directly to the imperial capital in 1796. Yet when *hieromonk* Gideon landed briefly at Unalaska in 1807, the *toion* came to receive an anointing from him. This *toion* was conducting daily services for his own polity in the chapel at Umnak himself. Indeed, 'he may have substantially assisted in spreading Christianity among the Aleuts'.[38]

Subsection (iv) summary. How had the Aleutian Island parishes come into being? They were a development by the people beginning three generations prior to the arrival of the first parish priest on the eastern Aleutian Islands, and four generations prior on the central and western Aleutian Islands. When the priests Veniaminov and Netsvetov arrived in 1824 and 1828 respectively, the Aleuts were Russian Orthodox; and these clergymen were assigned as parish priests, who ministered within existing parishes. Indeed Veniaminov described his parishioners as 'exemplary Christians'.[39]

The transition on the Aleutian Islands was thus an indigenous movement, involving indigenous social and spiritual processes, such as intermarriages, and earlier the process of alliances in which baptisms occurred and through which Russian Orthodox Aleut leadership was generated.

(v) Insights into these processes within the alliances

Before proceeding to the next major section of this chapter that will concentrate upon the Kodiak area, the study should provide descriptions of the process of diffusion of the religion as this process was taking place on the Aleutian Islands within alliances that had formed among hunters. Descriptions derive from two hunters' camps: one on the western Aleutian Islands between 1759 and 1762; another on the eastern Aleutian Islands in 1778.

The report from the western Islands, specifically the Near Islands, was written by Stepan Cherepanov, a leader among Russian hunters with the small vessel *Sv. Zakharii i Elizaveta*. He had earlier spent two winters on Agattu Island, a Near Island; and he would make at least one other voyage, between 1768 and 1773, farther east to the Andreanov Islands, central Aleutians.[40] Observing propriety, distributing gifts, sharing meals, cooperating, Cherepanov and his men found themselves in a 'special position of friendship' with the Near Islanders, and also found themselves to be 'kinsmen by affinity' with the Andreanov Islanders, according to contemporary accounts.[41] The reported relationships are substantiated by the tone and content of Cherepanov's own report, as he referred to the Aleuts virtually as his equals. Nowhere does he refer to them as 'savages' or 'heathens', appellations that are found in abundance in later reports by other men (for example, by G.I. Shelikhov in his account of his own *Voyage to America*). Instead, Cherepanov referred to the Near Islanders as 'these foreigners'; indeed at one point, Cherepanov stated that they are 'like ourselves'.[42]

Among other information, Cherepanov's report includes an account of the baptism of Leontii Vasil'evich Popov who was one of the primary examples in section 1.ii, above. Cherepanov provides the circumstances about this baptism and describes a healing that took place.[43] An Aleut *toion* named Makuzhan had brought the youngster, his own kinsman, into the Russian hunters' camp for baptism. (Baptisms were already known on the Near Islands, the first having occurred in the later 1740s.)[44] The youngster had requested to be brought himself because, badly injured with a compound fracture (mauled by a sea lion), he was suffering nearly to the point of death, and he believed, according to Cherepanov, that when he was baptized he would be cured. The baptism was performed by the Russian Orthodox hunters, a practice among laity when clergy are at a distance. He recovered. This healing was a 'special incident', as Cherepanov explained it, 'an evident blessing by God' that made these foreigners 'very understanding of the Orthodox Christian faith':[45]

> They are very understanding of the Orthodox Christian faith and do not think that there is untruth (in our faith), because there was a special incident which was an evident blessing by God. To whit: the foreigner Leontii Vasil'evich Popov who travelled hither in the year '761, suffered at home cruelly in his arm which was wounded; the bone could be seen, and all despaired that he would survive. He could not even raise from his place of repose unless others lifted him. The father, whose name is Makuzhan came to our ship and said that his son wanted to be baptized to see if he might get better. We responded that he should have hope, as our God is great and merciful and is quick to be compassionate to those who call upon him with faith. Makuzhan answered: If your God is good, my son will recover. The son in that year 1761 was baptized with holy baptism by the company of another vessel that was at the island, that of Vasilii Popov, merchant of

Lal'sk. As soon as he was baptized, he showed immediately better and eventually recovered. Then Leontii's father Makuzhan in his joy was saying: your God is very good, that means great.

Very significant in this description is that the Russians and the Aleuts perceived that a miracle had occurred among the them. Evidently, these men lived alike within a cosmos that embraced the divine and the miraculous.

A further indication is forthcoming in Cherepanov's report when he stated: 'We did not observe among them any special faith, except what is proper to any kind of faith. They live and act in everything very simply.' What might he have meant by the phrase 'no special faith, except what is proper to any'? Today, it would probably indicate a quasi-agnostic theism; but what did the statement mean there, then, as written by Stepan Cherepanov, a leader among men of the traditional far north? An answer derives from Iakov Netsvetov, the first priest of this greater region (the central and western Aleutians), himself the son of an Aleutian and Russian marriage:[46]

> while acknowledging the Creator of the universe, they also believed in spirits who ruled the world. ... The supreme being they called the Creator of Heaven, and the Creator of the nether regions or the base of the world. ... The lore on spirits ... was extensive. They believed in birds, fish and other living things; and in the sun, the sky, and other inanimate beings, thinking that spirits dwelt in them.

This was the 'faith' that seemed to Cherepanov not particularly 'special': this cosmos imbued with the spiritual seemed to him 'proper to any kind of faith'. Indeed was it not universal in Cherepanov's own Eurasia then? Moreover, numerous prescriptions and just as many prohibitions applied within Aleut traditions, including: prayers; fasts; seclusions; community and public rites; offerings at sacred places or at sacred times.[47] All seemed to be not 'special' but 'proper' to Cherepanov, as these men lived alike within *a sacred cosmos.*[48] Thus, together they perceived the miracle at baptism.

The Aleut hunters furthermore had spiritual traditions similar to the Russian hunters, as described by Cherepanov who compared their spiritual preparations for the hunt. Beginning with a generality about his own men, he wrote that before any endeavour 'we Russians invoke the name of the Lord God to aid us and to bless'. He then became specific, referring to the preparations before the sea hunts from these islands. Before setting out in the *baidaras*, 'we Russians' would observe a moment of silence and would pray, 'God come to our aid'.[49] Turning to the Aleuts he noted a similar practice: 'In the same way these foreign peoples, leaving for the hunt say the prayer: *Lord bless.*' The Aleut hunters, moreover, would join the Russian hunters in prayer as they set out together in the same *baidaras*: 'like us they say *God come to our aid.*' Cherepanov's comparison follows:[50]

As we Russians when we set out on any endeavour and invoke the name of the Lord God to aid us and to bless, or when we proceed on any sea hunt in the *baidaras* observe a moment of silence by all, calling on God to aid us and expecting his mercies, say 'God come to our aid', in the same way these foreign peoples, leaving for the hunt say the prayer: 'Lord bless'. Also, when traveling in the *baidaras*, like us they say 'God come to our aid'.

The Aleuts had corresponding traditions and corresponding perceptions. As the hunters themselves had thus merged in the camp and in the *baidaras* for the sea hunt, so their faithful practices had meshed; and in this way, Russian Orthodoxy was being communicated from far northerners to far northerners within personal alliances. This theme will be developed to greater depth in subsequent chapters of this study, while it should be indicated at this point: the communication of the religion was taking place within interpersonal alliances that had formed among men on the Aleutian Islands.

This merging of men and their traditions and this communicating of religion is evident in another report, this one from the other side of the Aleutian archipelago, from Unalaska Island (among the eastern Aleutians) in 1778. In this instance, the observer was John Ledyard, a corporal of marines on James Cook's third voyage. Dispatched by the captain to accompany an 'Indian' who had made contact with them, Ledyard became most probably the first of his own kind ever to enter a hunters' camp in the eastern regions of Russia, and certainly the first of Cook's voyage.[51]

Through the night in the month of October, he accompanied some 'Indians' (as he referred to them) to the Russian hunters' camp. They literally carried him there. He was transported over water in a two-man kayak, as he himself lay inside the thin hull between the two kayakers. Remaining inside, he felt the kayak strike the beach, then felt it being lifted and being carried. Finally, he was pulled up and out by his arms, and he found himself in the hunters' camp. Immediately he was taken, still by the arms, into a yurt aglow with oil lamps within. (A yurt is a semi-subterranean dwelling then-typical of the Aleutians and also of regions of northern Asia.)

Many men were therein. Having enjoyed these men's hospitality despite the language barrier (he did not speak Russian or any of the local languages),[52] he was then made comfortable so that he might sleep; and from his bed he observed the hunters at evening prayer. The 'Indians' (as he continued to refer to them) particularly impressed him, as they prayed together 'after the manner of the Greek church':[53]

> I could not but observe with what particular satisfaction the Indians performed their devoirs to God through the medium of their little crucifixes, and with what pleasure they went through the multitude of ceremonies attendant on that sort of worship.

These 'multitude of ceremonies' that he observed would have been the ritual acts that these men would have repeated as they were oriented eastward together while the prayers were being chanted or recited 'after the manner of the Greek church', including their making of the sign the cross, bowing, and sometimes making obeisance by kneeling to bring the forehead humbly to the ground.

Who were these 'Indians'? They remained undifferentiated in the corporal's account of the men in the yurt except in contradistinction to the 'Russians', or those men who appeared to him to be 'European, fair', until the following morning when he collected a few vocabulary items from only some of the 'Indians'. He then discovered two languages: one was 'Kamchadal', the other 'American' (It was Aleut.) In his subsequent account, these 'Indians' therefore became either 'Kamchadal Indians' or 'American Indians'; and he applied this categorization when he presumed to estimate the number of 'Indians' in contrast to the number 'Russians' in the larger camp, consisting of thirty yurts:[54]

> The number of Russians were about 30, and they had with them about 70 Kamchadales [*sic*], or Indians from Kamchatka[;] these with some American Indians whom they had entered into friendship with occupied the village, enjoyed every benefit in common with the Russians, and were converts to their Religion.

This was a snowy day in October: he would have been observing men who were clothed for this weather. And his collection of vocabulary was cursory and sparse: only a few numerals from some of the men. He made no further collections during his brief stay of merely the previous night and part of this day. Therefore, his estimate cannot be considered accurate. Other 'Indians' may have been there also; for by this time, 1778, the Russian hunters included — in addition to the Kamchadals — Iakuts, Evenks and other men from northeast Asians as well as men from northwestern Russia.[55] The latter derived from approximately the latitude of Vologda northwards to the White and Pechora Seas, and included the Komi, a people who had been likened in physical appearance to the Kamchadals at the initial contact on the Kamchatka Peninsula.[56] Any of these men who were Asian or Eurasian in appearance would have been subsumed under Ledyard's categories as the 'Indians'.

Many of the nations from which these men derived were already, or were well in the process of becoming, Russian Orthodox. The Kamchadals had already been identified as such by this time.[57] The Christianization of the Iakuts had begun in the mid-seventeenth century.[58] The Komi had been Christianized as a nation by the fourteenth century.[59] Therefore when Ledyard presumed that these 'Indians' (categorically) were 'converts', and was impressed with them performing their devotions to God 'after the manner of the Greek church', he was actually observing men who had derived from the Greek Orthodox *ecumene* themselves. In other words, Russian Orthodox men were virtually indistinguishable from the Aleuts in the corporal's unaccustomed sight, especially as these hunters prayed together.

As the far northern hunters lived and prayed together, themselves merging in the yurt, their faithful practices meshed. In this way, Russian Orthodoxy was initially communicated on the Aleutian Islands from men of the Arctic to men of the Arctic: from like to like.

(2) The Kodiak Area

The history was different in the Kodiak area. The kinds of alliances that had comprised significant dynamics during the initial contact periods on the Aleutian Islands (1745-1760s) are evident here as well. However unlike the Aleutians, a planned invasion and colonization took place at the initial major contact in the Kodiak area, in 1784; and a religious mission was dispatched into this setting a decade later.

Yet, merely nine months after the missionaries' arrival, their leader reported that they had baptized more than six thousand people: 'we baptized more than 6,000 people through the winter on Kodiak, who were so willingly baptized that they destroyed and burnt all their shamanistic array.'[60]

If attention is focused squarely on the more definite aspect in his statement — that is the number of baptized, that the source himself would have been able to ascertain from the records he was keeping — the reader encounters an extraordinary number representative of whole lineages or of an entire population.[61] Such a number could not have been achieved by the missionaries themselves within the nine months between their arrival at Kodiak in September 1794 and the date of this report in May 1795. Therefore, causes for the baptisms must be sought within dynamics preceding, or immediately contemporaneous with, the missionaries' arrival. What were these dynamics? Credit for the baptisms was claimed by the colonizers; and those claims have been repeated from their own generation to the present day. But are the colonizers' claims credible?

(i) Grigorii Ivanovich Shelikhov: In his own Words, the First Missionary

The colonization was spearheaded by an invasion in 1784, effected by Grigorii Ivanovich Shelikhov. Born in 1748 at Ryl'sk, Kursk *gubernia*, southwest Russia, he had moved to Irkutsk, near Lake Baikal, where he entered into the employ of a compatriot from Kursk, Ioann Larionovich Golikov. In 1775, Grigorii married Natal'ia Alekseevna, 'probably the daughter or widow of some rich merchant, and thus an initial source of Shelikhov's capital'.[62] The following year, he financed the first of his ventures in the north Pacific maritime fur trade; then during the years 1777-1797, mostly in partnership with Ioann

Larionovich, he funded ships in rapid succession for overlapping enterprises that extended progressively across the Aleutian Islands, into the Kodiak area, and eventually to the American northwest coast.[63] The final expeditions were dispatched from a permanent base that the partnership had, in 1784, established on Kodiak Island. The establishment was daring, absorbing the personal interest not only of Grigorii Ivanovich Shelikhov, Ioann Larionovich Golikov, and Golikov's nephew, but also of Natal'ia Alekseevna Shelikhova who ventured to Kodiak alongside her husband, and was thus at the helm from the start. Their daring was profitable; for with this advantage, and with subsequent astute political management, their enterprises prevailed. The major shareholders formed the Russian-American Company with monopoly rights over much of the north Pacific archipelagos and coasts by imperial charter in 1799.

It was not Grigorii Ivanovich who achieved this consolidation, however. Four years earlier (1795), the active forty-seven year old had died very suddenly at home. Nor did the partner Ioann Larionovich enjoy the consolidation; because soon after Grigorii's untimely death at home, the widow Natal'ia Alekseevna through her connections in the capital city took over Golikov's interests in the company; so that those connections, and her family, were the major shareholders when the monopoly was formed.

(a) From the Aleutians, as in a single voice. The fur trade along the Aleutian Islands had been inaugurated earlier, between the mid-1740s and the mid-1760s. The next phase began in the 1770s, when a proliferation of companies began coming increasingly more frequently along routes that were known now, and were therefore less risky. Passing the western Aleutian Islands, a very few stopped at the central islands, while almost all concentrated on the eastern Aleutians. Competition and violence increased. It was during this phase, into these predatory waters, that Shelikhov's enterprises entered in 1777; and reports from the Aleutian Islands to the imperial government during subsequent decades implicate or explicitly identify his enterprises, including those of the Shelikhov-Golikov partnership, in the deeds of violence and gross exploitation. These reports have been mentioned in the context of Aleutian Island history (sec.1.iv, above). They will be repeated briefly with reference now to Shelikhov's involvement.

Before June 1787, the Aleut *toion*'s kinsman named Izosim Polutov, dispatched the protest from the central Aleutian Islands.[64] It did not identify Shelikhov by name; but in that region during the decade prior to that date, there had been two ships: both belonged to the Shelikhov enterprises: one had remained for a period of four years.[65] A decade after the Polutov protest from the central Aleutians, the report from the eastern Aleutian Islands was carried

across that immense distance of the breadth of northern Eurasia to Petersburg
by Aleut leaders and the *hieromonk*. They identified the Shelikhov-Golikov
partnership explicitly.[66] Shelikhov-Golikov company hirelings were accused
of deeds of extreme brutality; for instance:[67]

> The Shelikhov-Golikov company men act like barbarians toward the people. They
> exhibit no humanity whatsoever. They forcibly take women and children as con-
> cubines. They beat people to death. Beginning in early spring they send both the
> healthy and sick to hunt sea otter against their will. The sick often die on the way.
> They force them to continue hunting until autumn so that they have no time to
> attend to their own subsistence activities, to store food for themselves, or to take
> animals to make winter parkas.

A plea was voiced succinctly in a sentence in this report: 'The newly-enlightened
people cry not tears but blood.' The newly-enlightened were the recently baptized.

Despite such reports, the controlling interests in the Shelikhov-Golikov company were awarded the monopoly by imperial decree in 1799. Part of the
articulated rationale was that a monopoly would control the harsh treatment
of the natives by the traders.[68] But those traders were the hirelings of the
monopoly's progenitors, and the harsh treatment was itself the condition
through which the progenitors had prevailed, and in which the monopoly had
been spawned.

The widow Shelikhova, family and associates would later laud Grigorii
Ivanovich for even implanting the Orthodox faith in Russian-America, as we
shall see. The reality was more clearly the inverse, however. As we have seen,
Russian Orthodox Aleut leaders were already in place on the Aleutian Islands,
and had been speaking out as in a single voice against them.

Nearly twenty years subsequent to the granting of the monopoly, another
plea was voiced, now from the Kodiak area. Written by a monastic missionary
Herman, it was addressed to the monopoly's new on-site chief manager; and it
sounded strikingly like the one earlier carried from the Aleutians:[69]

> I the most humble servant of the local people and their nursemaid, stand before
> you with bloody tears and write my request: be a father and protector to us. We, of
> course, know no eloquence, but we say, with the halting tongue of children, wipe
> away the tears of our defenseless orphans, soothe the sorrows of aching hearts, let
> us know what joy is like.

This plea came directly from the Kodiak area where the Shelikhov-Golikov
partnership, with Natal'ia Alekseevna also at the helm, had established their
company's permanent base. Later, after a relocation, it had become the
monopoly's initial on-site headquarters.

(b) The establishment of the Kodiak base: Three independent, corroborative reports. How had the permanent base been established? Aware that the people of the Kodiak area had earlier repelled other companies' attempts to locate even temporary camps, the Shelikhov-Golikov partnership went prepared to establish a permanent base, not in one but in three ships, equipped not only with arms but with two-pound cannons.[70] Their little fleet was a small armada. Regarding the events subsequent to the landing, three independent eyewitness accounts corroborate each other: one by a Kodiak elder; another by an assistant surgeon with the company; and yet another by a navigator, also with the company. Shelikhov's own report reflects basically the same events, that is, once his euphemisms are decoded.

In the early 1850s, seventy years subsequent to the events, Arsenii Aminak, a Kodiak elder who had been a boy at the time, related his eyewitness account to an ethnographer from Finland. An ultimatum had been sent from the ships to Sitkalidak ('Sakhliadak'), a populous stronghold, to warn of the danger if the people did not capitulate by relinquishing children as hostages. Twice it was sent, twice these people refused; then they were attacked:[71]

> This happened in April. When our people revisited the place in summer the stench of the corpses lying on the shore polluted the air so badly that none could stay there, and since then the island has been uninhabited. After this every chief had to surrender his children as hostages; I was saved only by my father's begging and — many sea otter pelts.

Aminak's account is corroborated by a testimony submitted four years after the event, in retrospect, by assistant surgeon M.S. Britiukov to the Billings/Sarychev expedition, an imperial government expedition. Britiukov had been aboard with Shelikhov.[72] Britiukov presented the same sequence of events: the armed assault; many casualties — 300 fatalities according to Aminak; over 500 according to Britiukov — the subsequent capitulation with the relinquishing of children as forced hostages.

This was only the initial attack, described alike by unrelated eyewitnesses. The one witnessed it from among the Kodiak Islanders, the other from among Shelikhov's men. The one account was collected by an ethnographer on Kodiak Island in the 1850s, the other account was collected by a naval officer in northeastern Asia in 1788. The two independent accounts are fundamentally the same.

Subsequent attacks elsewhere on the island were described by Britiukov,[73] who also reported that a number of adult captives were executed as public examples, and on one occasion when kinsmen came to ransom child hostages, these kinsmen were tortured for information, then executed on Shelikhov's order by an employee, namely the navigator Izmailov.

When Izmailov himself was questioned by the Billings-Sarychev expedition,

he admitted that he had shot two individual men on Shelikhov's orders, although in a context different from that described by Britiukov (according to
Izmailov, Shelikhov had eventually freed all surviving captives without further
harassment of their relatives who had come for them).[74] Moreover, the navigator reported instances of executions of small groups of men (not by Izmailov
himself), each execution by Shelikhov's orders; and he emphasized that he had
reported this to the government office at Okhotsk in 1787. The executions
had included the spearing of six to ten old men selected specially for this
purpose from among the initial captives, who themselves numbered from two
to three hundred people. Regarding the initial attack, Izmailov described the
same pattern of violence which had been described by Britiukov and Aminak,
so that the three independent eyewitness accounts corroborate each other.[75]

Shelikhov's own account reflects the same information when he himself
mentions the establishment of forts and the subjugation of the populace during the pacification of Kodiak.[76] Once decoded, these euphemisms are deadly
accurate: for why are forts established; and how would such numbers be so
quickly pacified, indeed pacified to 'obedience'? Reaching either a height of
triumphant pretence, or a crescendo of subtle humour, in a petition to the
empress, he himself proclaimed 50,000 savages obedient to a single Shelikhov.[77]

(c) The distinguished citizen. The euphemisms were linked to an articulated
motive, which together created a self-justifying circle enclosing and submerg-
ing those deeds. Shelikhov wrote to Empress Catherine II: 'Through
innumerable labors and dangers, we have had no object in view except love for
our country and zeal for the public good; these have been the main motives in
our enterprises'.[78] Such ostensibly noble motives ringed such brutal deeds.

The motive was reflected in Shelikhov's own portrait.[79] Looking squarely
ahead, he holds a telescope in his hand, while behind him a masted ship sails
out of harbor: signs of his vision and his ventures. He wears a large medallion
given to him by imperial decree in 1788 for noble activities on behalf of civilized society. This medallion and some other rewards he received were minor
in comparison to the recognition and patronage he had requested from the
Crown.[80] Yet they were honours nonetheless. Whether he had been shunned
by Petersburg society, as the limit of the patronage would suggest, is inconsequential here. Regardless of how he might have been perceived, he was
advancing certain interests in this way, and he was rewarded. A distinguished
citizen of the empire, he has his sight set on the expanding horizon: he is an
empire builder (similar to Cecil Rhodes, for example) expanding the sphere of
'civilization'. Having donned a short wig worn by men of that class and of that
era in the United States and in Western Europe, and having shaved his face
according to the same fashion, Shelikhov wears a contemporary waistcoat and

tailcoat, replete with a slight belly visibly extending the waistcoat: signs of his modernity and of his affluence in the new society. These are also vivid signs of this merchant's break with Russia's own past. Gone are the Eurasian merchants' caftan and beard.

The new society he was intent on extending was that inaugurated by Peter I, the first emperor.[81] Just as this emperor had shed the Moscow tsars' symbolic oriental robes for a military uniform, so this merchant shed the caftan for a suit. Shelikhov was a minor image of Peter I, his object for the colony a minor image of Peter's for the empire.

The intent was two directional: while reaching out for new territories and resources, Grigorii's enterprises would bring in new subjects, and would bring them to 'innumerable advantages', particularly to the benefits of 'security and prosperity' ('безчисленные выгоды, безопсность и благоденствие').[82] While the benefit of security is ironic, that of prosperity is rather interesting. A type of prosperity was envisioned: warehouses bustling with productive workers on busy docks; fields and pastures in the countryside; offices, houses, a school along proper streets in the town. Kodiak town (*Pavlovskaia gavan*) was to be a proper colony.[83]

We should see, however, that Kodiak remained mostly Alaskan in reality nevertheless. Alutiiq maritime technology prevailed, so did the Alutiiq language. The richly artistic culture was not supplanted.[84] Indeed the Alutiiq people were never entirely 'subjected' during the occupation which itself was localized, geographically limited:[85] on the contrary, while personally allied with some Russians,[86] they remained opposed to and defiant of others, and according to Aminak,[87] 'did them harm in many ways'.

The colony envisioned by Shelikhov was to have its church. Shelikhov himself had boasted of baptizing a number of Kodiak people:[88] the same writer who had also boasted of subjugating the fifty thousand and of bringing them to 'obedience' to himself. He requested from the Crown the assignment of 'two priests and a deacon' for the church. This request was specifically distinct from a petition for missionary priest-monks. Priests would be married men, who could be imagined as cooperative colonial clergy indeed, isolated as they would be across the 'Eastern Sea' (the Pacific), dependent as they would be on the company for necessities as basic as transportation and communication, not for themselves alone but for their families. 'Two priests and a deacon' were specifically requested to propagate 'the Greek-Catholic faith'.[89]

A score of missionaries were sent instead (see Ch.6, nt.2). Most of them were from the monastery of Valaam, at vast Ladoga in Karelia: far northern men of the taiga themselves, strangers neither to the far northern climate nor to far northern subsistence. They were received with remarkable alacrity by

Shelikhov at Irkutsk, who arranged their transportation to Kodiak; but when they arrived in September 1794, they found no provisions there for themselves.[90] Among them was *hieromonk* Makarii, assigned to the eastern Aleutian Islands the following year.

(d) Laudation in stone, echoed to the present. The year after the mission arrived at Kodiak, Grigorii died very suddenly at home in Irkutsk. He and Natal'ia had just married their daughter, or the widow Shelikhova herself would soon arrange the marriage (the date of the wedding is unclear), to N.P. Rezanov, a thirty-one year old ascendent courtier, then in Irkutsk. The daughter, Anna, half his age, was wed with a dowry of company shares.[91] Her sister had been married, or was soon to be married, to a merchant with eastern involvements, M.M. Buldakov.

Within five years, a series of events took place through which the social and financial standing of Shelikhova and family was consolidated. In 1797, the widow and associates merged with Grigorii's partner Golikov and with most remaining rivals to coordinate the far eastern and north Pacific enterprises.[92] The next year, Shelikhova and progeny, including Buldakova and Rezanova, were 'ennobled' by imperial decree through patronage at Court.[93] In 1799, the merger was reorganized to form the Russian-American Company with monopoly rights by imperial decree and with controlling interests secured for the Buldakov, Rezanov, and Shelikhov family members and their financial and social connections.

The extended family erected monuments immediately prior to the granting of the monopoly. They had an obelisk constructed in 1800 at Grigorii's gravesite on cathedral grounds in Irkutsk, the imperial administrative center for the Far East including the north Pacific. It was constructed against the will of the local bishop who complained: 'it is higher than the altar'.[94] An imperial decree silenced him. Erected tall on cathedral grounds, the stone would itself express laudations such as these:[95]

He Proclaimed
Among the Uncivilized People
...
The Name of God Unknown to Them,
And in the Name of the Life-Giving Trinity,
Implanted the Orthodox Christian Faith
in the year 1794.

That was the year Grigorii Shelikhov had, with alacrity, transported the monastics whom he had not requested, and for whom he had not made provisions. As for the monastics, their mission had included protests against the company management on Kodiak[96] and also against the company activities on the Aleutians;[97] and would continue to involve protests,[98] indeed no less than a plea,[99] against the monopoly's management.

The commendation, now written in stone, would apply by extension to the Shelikhov family name and enterprises. The extension had already been articulated in the ennobling of the widow and descendants when the *ukaz* of 1798, bearing the signature of the emperor, proclaimed:[100]

> Our attention has been drawn to the services of the late citizen Shelikhov, who gave his life and property in annexing to our Sceptre the peoples inhabiting North America. He laid the foundation there for the Greek-Catholic [*sic*] Christian Faith and for various trades useful to the State. Most graciously we bestow upon his widow ... and to their children, the merit of nobility ... [*etc.*].

The laudation was then repeated, indeed it has been echoed from those times to the present day. Praise for Grigorii's 'Christian mission' was voiced, for example, in 1817 by an imperial naval officer (V.N. Berkh) in a history of the company's circumnavigational frigate the *Neva*:[101]

> The well-known Grigorii Ivanovich Shelikhov was the first of all the Russian Argonauts, who, upon conquering the island of Kad'iak [*sic*], founded upon it a regular colony, and after settling more than two hundred Russians there, took to America the Religious Mission, built a church and started to convert the savages to the Christian faith.

(Very significant in this source is the explicit coupling of Christianity with conquest, and explicit confusion of nobility with barbarity: which had been implicit in the *ukaz*.) A footnote was added (ibid.):

> The reader should know that for these exploits Mr. Shelekhov [*sic*] was raised to the dignity of a nobleman and wore the insignia of the favors of the Most Wise Empress Catherine of Blessed Memory.

(The empress, however, had not bestowed the rank of nobleman upon Grigorii, but had recognized him as a distinguished citizen; her successor Paul had decreed the nobility upon the widow and descendants.)

The laudation for Grigorii's 'Christian mission' was repeated predictably in a history commissioned by the company directors in preparation for a renewal of the monopoly charter:[102]

> everything Shelikhov did was done much more from zeal for the good of the country than for his own personal advantage. The way he made savage and hostile peoples see the advantage of dealing peacefully with visitors to their shores was truly amazing. After they had shown clear hostility toward Shelikhov and his men, he not only pacified them to the point where they entrusted themselves to his leadership and defended his interests against other natives, but he persuaded them to give him their children as voluntary hostages. When Shelikhov taught these children reading, writing, and Christian doctrine, their fathers were favourably impressed ...

Less predictably, it was echoed by Ioann Veniaminov. Mentioned in the preceding sections regarding Aleutian Island history, he was the first parish priest
to the eastern Aleutians (1824-1834) who became fluent in Aleut; he then
became the first bishop, named Innokentii, of Russia's newly created eastern-
most diocese of Kamchatka, the Kurile Islands, and the Aleutian Islands, was
finally elevated to the Metropolitan of Moscow, and recently in 1977, was
canonized a saint by the Moscow Patriarchate. Veniaminov said:[103]

> Mr. Shelikhov, the founder of the present company, in his plans and designs for
> the benefit of this land, had the main aim the wider and wider spread of Chris-
> tianity and the establishment of churches. For this reason, on his return from Kadiak
> [sic] in 1787, before everything else, he presented the idea to the Government and
> asked for the appointment of a spiritual mission.

The mistake is understandable. Veniaminov had been born in a village in
the Irkutsk region in 1797, during the consolidation by the Shelikhov enterprises. He had been schooled during the monopoly's initial charter period:
schooled at seminary in Irkutsk, under a shadow cast by the obelisk, cast by
persons distinguished and ennobled by an anointed monarch. His statement
was a repetition of verses he would have heard from his youth, a paraphrase of
the claims the distinguished citizen had made for himself, a recitation of the
claims the family and company continued to make for themselves.
   Another bishop associated with Alaska repeated the commendation, in this
instance in 1896, after the centennial celebration of the arrival of the mission
to Kodiak. He wrote imperatively in a 'proclamation':[104]

> I on my part hold it my duty to remind the Orthodox Christians of Alaska of their
> moral obligation to show their gratitude to G. I. Shelekhof [sic] for the good he
> did them while he lived.

Evidently, Shelikhov had been ignored by the Alaskans at the centennial, so
that this 'duty' was felt by that bishop to remind them of their 'moral obliga-
tion'. The bishop further instructed them to collect funds for a monument to
express 'their gratitude' to this 'distinguished citizen' for 'the good' he had
done them. But no such monument was ever built here.
   In 1943, Shelikhov was again commended as 'pious', now in a history of
religious missions written by an ecclesiastic (S. Bolshakoff), as follows:[105]

> Shelekhov [sic], accompanied by his companions, the brothers Golikov, landed on
> Kadyak [sic] Island, on July 22nd, 1784, and founded the first Russian settlement in
> America. Within three years Shelekhov subjected to his rule the neighbouring natives
> and returned to Russia. The Empress Catherine II recognized Shelekhov's conquests
> and decorated him, granting him also a reward of 20,000. Shelekhov continued his
> fur trade very successfully, but being a pious man, he grew uneasy at the harsh treat-

ment of the natives by Russian traders. He decided to do everything possible to protect them. In 1793 he requested the Holy Synod to send a mission to Alaska.

Surely the author could not have intended to couple Christianity with such
'conquests', as he did.

In 1970, the commendation was repeated by yet another bishop (G. Afonsky)
who described Shelikhov as 'a staunch member of the Church'. The actual
deeds — encircled as they were by euphemisms, covered as they were by deco-
rations for 'nobility', indeed by the decoration of a cross — remained hidden
from this source. And yet again:[106]

> Shelikhov also became the first missionary to the native people. In his own words:
> 'I exhorted them to keep the Orthodox faith which they had accepted according
> to law.'

Thus 'in his own words' was Shelikhov the first missionary. And in the words
of his widow, family, their companions, he was the patron of the mission from
Valaam to Kodiak.

(e) A Sounder Voice. Gavriil the Metropolitan of Novgorod (or Novgorod
and St Petersburg), who had himself been instrumental in dispatching the
score of monastic missionaries in 1794, did *not* assign any credit for this mission to Grigorii Shelikhov however. The metropolitan assigned the credit to
Shelikhov's partner, Ioann Larionovich Golikov: 'Golikov ... sought to send
the missionaries [and] ... the Archimandrite and monastics are maintained at
Golikov's expense.'[107] Metropolitan Gavriil mentioned Shelikhov very briefly
only as having 'organized the commercial enterprise in America'; and the metropolitan subordinated him (ibid): 'Golikov had initially recruited Shelikhov
from the lower ranks and then elevated him to a full partner.'

Metropolitan Gavriil provided this information in a letter to Prince Platon
Zubov, dated three months after a letter by Natal'ia Alekseevna Shelikhova to
the same influential person.[108] She was appealing for support in the struggle
for company control that had ensued from Grigorii Ivanovich Shelikhov's
untimely death, a few months earlier. Metropolitan Gavriil, on the other hand,
was championing Golikov.

Metropolitan Gavriil's sounder voice from that very time, before the preva-
lence of company propaganda, should itself clearly indicate that the initial
laudations of Shelikhov were pretentious and that the repetition has been naïve.

(ii) The Account from Old Harbor regarding the Baptism of the Kodiak Alutiiq, 1794/95

To reach an understanding of the Christianization of the Kodiak Alutiiq, the
study must therefore delve more deeply into the history than the company's
claims. How can this be accomplished? I shall attempt it by complementing

the more credible written historical sources with an oral historical source about the baptism of the Kodiak Alutiiq, and showing that they corroborate each other point by point.

The oral historical source derives from the village of Old Harbor on Kodiak Island, recounted to me by a *toyuk* of longstanding, Semeon Haakanson.[109] (*Toyuk* is the Alutiiq rendering of the word *toion*.) He is a tradition bearer of stature and particular abilities. His account relates to Kodiak Island and also to the Alutiiq regions of the Alaska Peninsula where the sequence of events was fundamentally the same. Three leaders, all originally from the village of Belkovsky on the Alaska Peninsula, were cited by him by name as having received the same account and having communicated it also. They, too, were tradition bearers of stature and of particular abilities.[110] Old Harbor is today's village nearest the historical site of *Tri Sviatitelia gavan*, the initial settlement founded by Shelikhov in 1784. The settlement was subsequently relocated to *Pavlovskaia gavan* (today's Kodiak town) in 1792; and it was to the latter location that the missionaries arrived in September 1794.

According to the account from Old Harbor, the Alutiiq people continued to resist the invaders, and were selective in their contacts. Yet when the missionaries arrived, the Alutiiq people welcomed *them*, and willingly received baptism, because the Alutiiqs' own leading 'shamans' had had visions and had given advice. Whole villages accepted baptism with these receptive leaders, while a few dissenting shamans went to live apart; and thus did village membership coalesce around baptism and Russian Orthodoxy. Each element in the account — (a) the Alutiiqs' continued resistance; (b) their reception of the missionaries; (c) the exile of the few dissenting shamans; and (d) the receptivity by leading visionaries — is consistent with historical sources and substantiated by parallel events elsewhere in Alaska.

(a) Continued resistance. The oral history today is corroborated by a statement from the Kodiak eyewitness to the initial events of 1784, Arsenii Aminak (see sec.2.i.b, above). It is corroborated furthermore by information in letters written from the 1790s into the 1800s by the on-site manager of the company's enterprises. In letters to company associates outside Russian-America, the on-site company manager A.A. Baranov reported the danger from Kodiak Alutiiqs and other Native Alaskans[111] — a danger that reached the proportion of a possible large scale revolt.[112] While the invaders of Kodiak were pretending otherwise in public statements,[113] the Alutiiq had never actually been 'pacified'. On the contrary, they remained actively defiant and continued to resist: indeed, they counted fatalities among the invaders. Aminak stated that yet long afterwards 'we did them harm'; and he provided the description of a specific instance as follows:[114]

The lake contained sea hedgehogs (sea urchins), which are poisonous. We knew of this but smartly kept it to ourselves. We never ate them; not even gulls touched them. Many Russians died upon eating them. But in other ways, too, we did them harm.

Continued resistance is evident later yet, through the 1830s, in another way. The Kodiak Alutiiqs reportedly refused to be submissive to Church 'duties' ('обязанности'), according to Veniaminov:[115]

All who have been to Kad'iak [*sic*] unanimously agree that the Aleuts there [the Alutiiqs] almost never go to church. ... and very few fulfill their duties with regard to the Church, usually only those living in the main settlement.

In other words, those who were visibly fulfilling such 'duties' were the Kodiak Alutiiqs who were living in the company's main settlement, who had probably conformed themselves to the foreign occupation and to the imperial designs. Otherwise, non-conformity was observed by 'all who had been to Kodiak'. It was noticeable enough to elicit the 'unanimous' opinion, and disconcerting enough to be reported. Instead of conformity to the occupying authority, there was resistance.

'All who have been to Kodiak unanimously agree': the source Ioann Veniaminov was conveying an opinion which had been expressed by others. He had not yet been in the Kodiak area himself. No record of a visit is contained in his journals from the date of his arrival in Russian-America in October 1823 until the eve of his initial departure in November 1838 when he sailed from *Novo Arkhangel'sk* (Sitka) to visit Petersburg and Moscow. He sailed from *Novo Arkhangel'sk* southward to round Cape Horn. He returned to Russian-America in 1840, the same year as the publication of the statement quoted here, above.[116] Only subsequently did he visit the Kodiak area, in the year 1842 for eighteen days.[117] Thus without immediate experience in the Kodiak area before the publication, Veniaminov had relied on information from 'all who had been to Kodiak', as he himself admitted forthrightly. They were 'unanimous' in their opinion. He was conveying their opinion.

Their opinion is invalidated, however, by evidence in other sources contemporary with or preceding the period of this report. These sources describe 'Aleuts' gathering on Sundays and feastdays to worship with the last surviving missionary on *Elovoi* island (today's Spruce Island), a considerable distance away from the company settlement, *Pavlovskaia gavan*, on Kodiak Island.[118] As the term 'Aleut' is unqualified by a geographical designation in these sources, it signified or included Kodiak Alutiiqs. The last surviving missionary was 'Монах Германъ' (the monastic Herman) who had acted alongside Alutiiq leaders against the on-site company management at the turn of the century.[119] He had since removed himself from *Pavlovskaia gavan* to isolated forested *Elovoi* (sometime after 1807 and before 1819) where he resumed the anchoretic life that he had known in the forests of Karelia at the Monastery of Valaam;[120] and from this forest hermitage at *Elovoi*, he extended his mission to the colonial administration:[121] a direction inverse to the more usual thrust of missionary work. Some 'Aleuts' and 'Creoles' had settled at *Elovoi* to live in proximity to him;[122] and they would then be joined by others on Sundays and feastdays. The evidence from these other sources regarding the activity at *Elovoi* into the 1830s mitigates the generality published in 1840.

The generality is contradicted furthermore by evidence deriving twenty-eight years subsequent to Veniaminov's conveyance of the 'unanimous opinion'. On Afognak Island, away from the (now former) company settlement, Alutiiq and Russian-Alutiiq villagers were constructing a new church-building for themselves through their own labour and with their own resources to replace their previous building that had become too small for their needs.[123]

The generality asserted in the 'unanimous opinion' is thus discredited. Instead of remiss in 'their duties to the Church', the Kodiak Alutiiq were evidently selective. Yet the unanimity among 'all those who had been to Kodiak' remains significant; because it implies that the 'duties' that they would themselves impose were not being fulfilled by a people who remained resistant.

(b) The reception of a missionary. An otherwise resistant people welcomed the missionaries and received baptism, according to the account from Old Harbor; and this point is also corroborated by historical sources.

Two missionaries had travelled to Kodiak area villages within the initial nine months of the religious mission's arrival, from September 1794 until May 1795.[124] Each evidently travelled singly with an interpreter. Both returned alive, although either missionary could easily have disappeared as if by an accident (we may recall the 'accident' in the Kodiak area which had killed an entire group of Russian hunters as reported by Aminak). The villages were coastal, joined not by land routes over the island's glaciated mountainous interior, but by sea routes along which fatal accidents by drowning did occur. Yet both missionaries returned, indeed well enough to be enthusiastic about their next journeys to locations farther afield.[125] Soon afterwards in 1795, each commenced on his subsequent journey alone with an interpreter: the one missionary, Makarii, to the eastern Aleutian Islands; the other, Iuvenalii, to the southwest mainland where Iuvenalii did disappear but among a people other than the Alutiiq.[126]

This element in the account from Old Harbor about the reception of a missionary is not idiosyncratic. Missionaries were similarly received in other locations in Alaska. On their way to Kodiak in 1794, the original group of missionaries were compelled by inclement weather to harbour in the eastern Aleutian Islands, and were received spontaneously there as recalled by the monastic Herman:[127]

during our journey through the Aleutian Islands, we were driven against our will into one bay by unfavorable winds, and the Aleuts there caused us great amazement by their kindness to us in distress and their willingness to be baptized.

Similar receptivity and readiness among the Yupiit and Athapaskans of the Kuskokwim and lower Yukon Rivers region were reported by Russian-Aleut priest Iakov Netsvetov in the 1840s and 1850s, when whole lineages, or kinship based polities, sought him and invited him for baptism.[128]

(c) Exile of dissenters. A few shamans dissented however. Refusing to accept baptism, they went to live apart, away from the villages, according to the account from Old Harbor. Whether the dissenters chose to go or whether they were banished, the effect would have been the same: they went into exile. Exile is known to have been a traditional method for the maintenance of social cohesion and identity among the ancestral Alutiiqs in the Kodiak area.[129]

While the dissenting shamans went into exile, the villages followed the receptive leaders into baptism. Just as the dissenters were referred to as 'shamans' in the account from Old Harbor, so were the receptive visionaries; although it should be possible to refer to the latter instead as 'leaders with exceptional prophetic gifts', in order to render a difference in terminology that would reflect the difference in response. As the villages followed them into baptism, village membership and mutual identity would have coalesced around baptism and Russian Orthodoxy.

(d) The receptivity by leading visionaries. Those leaders who were receptive among the Alutiiq had had visions, according to the account from Old Harbor. Visions heralded the conversions of other Alaskan peoples, also. Among the Tlingit in the Juneau area in the 1890s the following reportedly took place, precipitating Orthodox baptisms:[130]

> A young Indian man had a vision. A venerable old man came to him and advised him to go to Sitka and to be baptized. The young man followed the advice. A few years later he became sick, and on his death bed he called for the elders of his tribe and told them that the same venerable old man came to see him again and told him to advise the other Indians to be baptized. The young man died, but his message did not die with him. Other Indians started having the same vision and the urge to be baptized spread like wildfire.

Although this account from the Juneau area refrained from referring to the prophetic Tlingit young man as a 'shaman', another account regarding the baptism of Unalaska Aleuts makes the reference explicitly, and the reference clearly corroborates the Old Harbor account: 'It seems proper to remember the predictions of the Shamans. It is probable that they much facilitated the work of the missionaries.' This source is Ioann Veniaminov.[131] With regard to the Unalaska region (unlike the Kodiak area), he remains a most credible source:

as he had lived with the Unalaska Aleuts for a decade previous to the publication of this statement; he spoke their language; and he was informed about
many aspects of the workings of Unalaska region shamans from that earlier
era. Neither did he off-handedly dismiss the information that he had received
about shamans-of-old in the Unalaska region, nor did he embrace them naïvely
in his historical considerations.[132] And in his pastoral practice he demonstrated
an ability, deriving from regional knowledge and from patristic guidelines alike,
to differentiate between types of 'shamans' (see Ch.5, sec.3.i, below). Furthermore, he himself derived from the Lake Baikal area in proximity to the 'Tungus'
from whose language the very word 'shaman' originated.

Having considered whether the predictions were 'truly the words of the shamans', or whether they had derived from 'the fictions of old men' (in other
words, from the elder Aleuts who had related this account from their parental
and grandparental generations), he arrived at the following conclusion:[133]

> I leave it to anyone to judge for himself, but I, for the most part, am on the side of
> the former because the Aleuts all suddenly and without the slightest compulsion
> accepted the Christian faith.

In the Kodiak area, the final proof likewise may be found in the acceptance
of this faith by the Alutiiq people, and moreover in the ingrafting of this
religion into their own community life and identity.

Subsection (ii) summary and conclusion. The account from Old Harbor is
thus corroborated throughout; and Semeon Haakanson is himself a leader of
longstanding, of stature and of particular abilities within a community in a
significant location. According to this account (I shall repeat this for emphasis
and clarity), these people continued to resist the invaders, and were selective
in their contacts. Yet when the missionaries arrived, the Alutiiq people welcomed *them*, and willingly received baptism, because the Alutiiqs' own leading
'shamans' had had visions and had given advice. Whole villages accepted baptism with these receptive visionary leaders, while a few dissenting shamans
went to live apart; and thus did village membership coalesce around baptism
and Russian Orthodoxy.

This corroborated account takes us much further into the history of the first
baptisms than the colonizers' pretentious reports and 'unanimous' opinions.
And through this account and the corroborative material, we may see that
dynamics similar to those precipitating the baptisms in the Aleutian archipelago during the initial contact periods there, were operative in the Kodiak
area. Here too, the transition was indigenous and corporate: involving indigenous spiritual and social processes, and involving the whole bodies of people's
societies, or kinship-based polities.

Also, the transition occurred here within the Alutiiqs' far northern hunting culture, as these people continued to exercise many of their own traditions confidently. Their confidence remains evident well throughout the nineteenth century in the many intricate hand-crafts held today in museum collections, as noted earlier in this chapter (see nt.84, above): Huggins reflected the complement of traditional culture, language, dwellings, artifacts, dress from 1868 to 1870; Pinart collected oral traditions, tales, ornamentation, masks, and carvings from 1871 to 1872; Fisher collected numerous artifacts including embroidered clothing, intricately carved sea hunting equipment, symbolic ornamentations of many kinds in the 1880s. The latter's rich and varied collection derived from various locations in the Kodiak area, including Woody Island, Three Saints Bay, Karluk, and the Alaska Peninsula.[134] These locations are both near to and far from Kodiak town, the former *Pavlovskaia gavan*.

Self-confidence in their traditions is evident furthermore in the indicative although hasty reference by Veniaminov to the 'unanimous opinion of all who had been to Kodiak',[135] when he wrote the following statement between the two sentences already quoted. Omitted as irrelevant in the quotation above, it becomes relevant now from Veniaminov, and will be emphasized by my italics:[136]

> All who have been to Kad'iak unanimously agree that the Aleuts there [the Alutiiqs] almost never go to church. *Secretly and openly, they adhere to their own shamanism* ['своихъ шаманствъ']; and very few fulfill their duties with regard to the Church, usually only those living in the main settlement.

Types of traditional functionaries were practicing among a decisively baptized yet resilient people who were visibly attached to them. And some practiced openly.

What was 'their own shamanism' ['своихъ шаманствъ'] that had been seen? Earlier, Archimandrite Ioasaph (the leader of the missionaries who arrived in 1794) had reported: they 'were so willingly baptized that they destroyed and burnt all their shamanistic array [шамаскіе наряди]'.[137] The term 'array [наряди]' is indefinite, and it remains indefinite even if it is allowed the more definite gloss that is sometimes assigned to it, 'garments'. Evidently not everything had been destroyed, or not all practices had been abandoned: some phenomena had been maintained that elicited the 'unanimous opinion' in 'all who had been to Kodiak' (foreigners, non-Alutiiq). When Ioasaph's and Veniaminov's statements are combined, a two-fold reality is yielded: the discarding of shamanistic array; but also the continuity of some kind of 'shamanizing', or rather a continuity of phenomena within Kodiak culture that appeared to outsiders to constitute shamanizing. The challenge for us is to discern between the two aspects of this reality, thus to achieve a perspective into the nature of the 'shamanizing' maintained, and the nature of the 'array' discarded, among a resilient people decisively baptized. This challenge will be accepted in Chapter 5 of my study, while currently my focus remains upon the dynamics about the baptism of the Kodiak Alutiiqs during 1794 and 1795.

Once the dynamics expressed in the corroborated Old Harbor account are highlighted, then we may begin to perceive far deeper than the colonizers' pretences. We may see that significant meetings occurred, and synergy existed, between spiritually gifted indigenous people and spiritually gifted allogenous people. Most notable among the latter in the Kodiak area was the forest-dweller from Valaam Монахъ Германъ, the monastic Herman, who merits a chapter of this study himself (Ch.6). Other folk were also here, who merged with the Alutiiq people and who will be considered next.

(iii) Affinities and Attachments

Indications of the interpersonal attachments that existed between some indigenous and some allogenous peoples in the Kodiak area at this time, as well as indications of certain affinities that engendered these attachments, can be gleaned from George Vancouver in the general region in 1794, and from Gonzalo Lopez de Haro in the company's Kodiak settlement four years earlier. Both were explorers without interests invested here.

Vancouver's observations were predicated upon greater experience than those by other explorers. Vancouver had had prior experience in the Kodiak area in 1778, as a midshipman on Cook's third voyage (that voyage then proceeded to Unalaska; and the reader may recall the adventure of John Ledyard there, as described above). Vancouver moreover had had extensive global experience, as he had taken part not only in Cook's third circumnavigational voyage but in the second also; and most recently, prior to the circumnavigational voyage that he was himself now commanding (1791-1794), he had had nine years in Dutch service in the East Indies. He thus benefitted from considerable experience in various parts of the world, both in Dutch and British service; and his observations of the 'Russians and Indians' in 1794 would have been predicated on that experience. Finally as a consideration regarding the credibility of his observations, I should mention that his perceptions regarding social life in these regions was described by him in considerable detail. He described them in a combined total of twenty published pages, from which the quotations below have been taken.

Vancouver explored the regions relevant to this study during May and June 1794. Coincidentally, this was immediately prior to the missionaries' arrival in September of that same year. The regions he explored more extensively were in the Kenai Bay (Cook Inlet) and the Chugach Bay (Prince William Sound) areas. And, again coincidentally, these were the very regions whence people would come to Kodiak to be baptized the following winter. He also explored along the eastern and northern coasts of the Kodiak archipelago, from Sitkalidak to Shugak Islands, before voyaging eastward to the mainland and those bay areas. Although his explorations of the Kodiak archipelago were less intensive that those of the Kenai Bay and Chugach Bay areas, yet his generalizations may be extended to the Kodiak archipelago, inasmuch as he observed Kodiak people in those bay areas, and included Kodiak people in his statements (quoted and cited below).

Were a qualification to be placed on Vancouver's observations, it would be that most probably he had not had contact with the Shelikhov-Golikov enterprises. Vancouver did not enter the settlement at *Pavlovskaia gavan* on Kodiak Island (where the missionaries would arrive); nor did he visit that company's outpost at the tip of the Kenai Peninsula, but instead he proceeded farther into Kenai Bay where the last competitors were located: the Lebedev-Lastochkin company, belonging to a merchant of Iakutsk.

Vancouver was impressed that Russians 'appeared to be perfectly content to live after the manner of native Indians':[138]

> They appear to be perfectly content to live after the manner of native Indians of the country; partaking with equal relish and appetite their ... food adopting the same fashion, and using the same materials for their apparel, and differing from them in their exterior appearance only by the want of paint on their faces, and by not wearing any of the Indian ornaments.

Wearing the same clothing, sharing the same food, they differed only slightly from each other in this explorer's eyes. He recorded the affinity yet again, while remarking on a mutual assimilation that he observed:[139]

> Without deviating much from the habits and practices of their earliest infancy, the Russians can readily adopt many of the Indian customs, by which means the manners of the two people become much assimilated. This is greatly furthered by their partaking of the same sort of food, and wearing the same sort of clothing. Their external appearance differs little from the natives.

These perceptions by Vancouver in 1794 are consistent with the actual origins of the men at this time. By 1799, the majority of the Russian hunters derived from the towns of Siberia and eastern Russia.[140] During the earlier phase, from the 1770s into the 1780s, the majority had derived from Russia's far east and northwest (as mentioned in context earlier in this chapter: see nt.55, above).

Culture(s) indigenous to all these regions were more-or-less that of far northern hunters. Such culture(s) might not be expected in Russia's northwest, which extends from approximately the latitude of Vologda northward to the White and Pechora Seas and includes Karelia as well as Komi-land: but these too were regions of the traditional far northern hunters. Karelia for example was

the cradle of runes that came to comprise that great saga of the Arctic, the
Finnish *Kalevala*. These runes were collected between 1824 and 1845, contemporaneous with Russian-America.[141]

The regions of the Russian northwest, moreover, had fostered Arctic maritime hunting and exploration recorded since the sixteenth century.[142] Hence
these men would have the ability for the sea hunt in the north Pacific, and also
the ability to construct seaworthy vessels from local materials for the open sea
crossings from Kamchatka.

The indigenous far northern culture(s) might not be expected in Siberian
and eastern Russian towns either; however, in the town of Iakutsk where the
merchant Lebedev-Lastochkin was registered — a town that had been founded
in the early 1600s — the settlers had become Iakutized, as they had assimilated the Iakut language to the demise of the Russian language among
themselves as late as the 1890s, a century later than Vancouver's observations.[143]
Vancouver's perceptions regarding affinities and mutual assimilation can thus
be supported by analytical studies and other historical data.

Affinities can engender personal attachments; and certain attachments were
also perceived by Vancouver. 'Principles of attachments', as Vancouver expressed
it, had formed as 'the Russians seemed to live upon the most intimate terms of
friendship with the Indians of all descriptions'; and as 'the Indians' had an
interest in these Russians' 'success and welfare':[144]

> The interest the Indians seem to take in the success and welfare of the Russians,
> originates in principles of attachment which do not appear likely to be easily re-
> moved by the influence of strangers to the prejudice of the Russian commercial
> interest, and which from the practice of the present day may probably be strength-
> ened in the succeeding generations.

As these men lived closely and comfortably together, these Russians had
found a way to the heart and secured 'an affectionate regard' among the 'Indians':[145]

> Although we could not gratify our curiosity to the extent I could have wished re-
> specting the situation of the Russians, yet I could not avoid feeling a degree of
> satisfaction in observing the comfortable manner in which they seem to live amongst
> these untutored children of nature; having gained them over to be obedient to their
> wishes, they appear to maintain their influence not by fear, as their conquerors, but
> by having found the way to their hearts, and by securing an affectionate regard.

These 'Indians' were particularly Alutiiqs ('people of the Kodiak') and
Dena'ina Athapaskans ('people of the Cook Inlet'). They spoke of their 'attachment' with 'praise':[146]

> This was manifested in all their [these Russians'] transactions, though more espe-

cially in their intercourse with the people of Cook's inlet and the Kodiak; many of whom, the women as well as the men, are retained in the service of the Russians, who speak of their attachment and fidelity in the highest terms of praise and approbation, and indiscriminately employ them with their own parties on business of the most confidential importance.

These observations by Vancouver describe people living intimately with each other in relationships of affection, confidence and trust.

Some affinities between 'Indians' and Russians described by George Vancouver at locations other than the Shelkhov company's camp in 1794, are evident also to a considerable extent even at that company's initial camp on Kodiak Island in 1788. In this case the observations by Gonzalo Lopez de Haro were based on merely a sojourn of a single morning and without previous experience in the region. Yet they are indicative as a complement to Vancouver's perceptions; and moreover it is interesting to glimpse these dynamics through the eyes of an explorer from Mexico also. The practice of religion becomes evident as well.[147]

The 'officers' whom Lopez de Haro met at *Tri Sviatitelia gavan* were from 'Siberia'. An 'officer' had a lovely wife fair-of-skin. She was dressed in oriental fashion: 'very modestly in the manner of Chinese women with very good clothes of this kind'. Two other women, whose beauty he also admired, were dressed in similar fashion and were themselves 'daughters of Siberia'. The 'captain' here was 'del Aro'. There were many 'Indians' in the establishment, who remained undifferentiated from each other in Lopez de Haro's account as some were preparing whale oil, others a catch of fish; yet others were 'attending school' to learn the Russian language — and yet others were attending to pelts highly valued for sale in China and in Europe. Religion becomes evident when Lopez de Haro mentions 'many well painted pictures of saints in the captain's and officers' rooms'. A beached galliot served as a 'chapel'; and Lopez de Haro mentions the presence of a 'chaplain'.

The descriptions, except perhaps one, are consistent with historical data. Men from Siberia and eastern Russia were among the prominent figures here. Let us consider Gerasim Grigor'evich Izmailov, for example. A decade earlier, in 1778, at Unalaska, Izmailov had made contact with Cook's third voyage. Journals from that voyage described him as a 'native of Iakutsk' and a 'leader among the Russians'.[148] He had studied navigation at the imperial navy's institute and was accomplished as a navigator and explorer in the north Pacific. Accomplished indeed, he had corrected the maps carried on the *Enterprise* and the *Discovery*, as reported by Cook himself (as cited earlier in this study). Later, in 1795, this 'native of Iakutsk' would take his own Alaskan godson away from the company's relocated camp.[149] When Lopez de Haro was visiting on

Kodiak Island in 1788, Izmailov was away exploring the Chugach Bay area.[150] The unnamed 'officers' whom Lopez de Haro met here at this time would have been yet other men from 'Siberia'.

Captain 'del Aro' was the company's chief manager Evstratii Ivanovich Delarov, whose Slavicized surname became Hispanicized through Lopez de Haro's ear and pen. He had been hired by Shelikhov in 1787, a year prior to Lopez de Haro's visit, and had not been here at the founding of the Kodiak settlement in 1784. Shelikhov had returned from Kodiak to Okhotsk where he convinced Delarov to assume this position on Kodiak. By then, Delarov had had more than twenty years of prior experience with other companies on the Aleutian Islands. He would remain in this position until 1791. Captain 'del Aro' was originally from the Peloponese.[151]

Regarding the evidence for religion, the placing of icons in dwellings is normal, as the capitan and 'Siberian' officers had placed them in their rooms. Early voyagers eastward across the north Pacific would carry icons with themselves.[152] For the 'chapel', the galliot would have been propped on its side, thus providing a ceiling and interior. As for the 'chaplain', this might have been the error if Lopez de Haro meant a priest: there was no such clergyman here or anywhere in proximity at this time. That man may have been a псаломщик, ἀναγνώστης (a 'reader' as these words are usually rendered into English usage today). Proficient in chant and ritual for the formal cycles of prayers and for the formal life-crisis rites, a псаломщик conducts the laity's role in ceremonies with a priest and may conduct services performed by the laity without a priest.

(3) Conclusions

The communication of the Russian Orthodox faith and its practices took place along lines of personal attachments, engendered by certain affinities, from like to like: that is to say, from northeast Asians and far northern Eurasians to Aleuts and Alutiiqs within the far northerners' own culture(s); and it took place throughout the whole bodies of peoples' kinship based polities.

So that these qualities could come forward, periods in the early contact history have been demarcated in this study. The initial periods between 1745 and the 1760s along the length of the Aleutian archipelago have been differentiated from the subsequent period involving the escalation of commercial enterprises on the eastern Aleutian Islands beginning in the 1770s. The escalation has been shown to have extended eastward into the Kodiak area through Shelikhov's invasion of 1784. Later periods were coincidental in the Kodiak area and on the Aleutian Islands, from the beginning of the monopoly in 1799 and then from the change in company administration in 1818.

Successful cultural resistance and resilience of Aleut and Alutiiq peoples continued through these periods (and throughout the nineteenth century into the twentieth indeed). Cultural affinities and amicable interpersonal relationships with some of the new-comers were clearly observed.

Insights along these lines of close interpersonal attachments were particularly forthcoming in the Aleutian archipelago where leading men entrusted their young kinsmen to Russian Orthodox godfathers, and these godsons later assumed the leadership in their home polities. The relationship between the godfather Stepan G. Glotov and his godson Ivan Stepanovich Glotov was indicative in this respect: Ivan eventually became the bilingual and literate *toion* of Umnak and was conducting the lay services in the first chapel on the eastern Aleutians.

This dynamic — the entrusting of young Ivan by his elder kinsmen to Stepan, predicated on the general Aleutian Island custom of kin exchange — should be differentiated categorically from the actual hostage-taking which occurred by force in other instances. The distinction is incisive. In the latter instances, some captured youth were baptized: examples can be found in Shelikhov's invasion of Kodiak, according to his own reports. If the distinction between these categories is lost, then the constructive interpersonal dynamics will remain obscured.

Such an obscuring began deliberately with H.H. Bancroft, but then persists without his (if I might say, redeeming) motive. Bancroft's motive was expressed by him in the preface to his volume on Alaska (1886), which he wrote as one in his series about the American West. Intent on refuting a comfortable misconception that his American contemporaries were entertaining about themselves, he emphasized the barbarism through which the West had been won. Authors who have followed him, however, appear to be motivated less by a concern such as his, as they co-join brutal deed after brutal deed with their pens while describing Russian Alaska alone. I wonder whether they would depict their own society in those macabre tones. Bancroft did, correctly.

I have concentrated on violent characters and their deeds whenever they were directly relevant to the religious history. Shelikhov and his ilk were directly relevant. (Also relevant is the culpability of generations who have so readily believed his and his associates' pretensions.) Arguably, they were the most violent. Certainly, they managed to present themselves as the most 'civilized' and 'enlightened'. I have explained this above. The paradox will be brought forth again, in the final sections of this study. But I have not allowed their brutality to eclipse the greater humanity in this history.

Even in the Kodiak area where the historical circumstances at the initial contacts differed from those on the Aleutian Islands, the main characteristics of the transition were fundamentally the same: *indigenous and corporate, predicated on cultural affinities and close interpersonal relationships*. In the Kodiak area, these characteristics became clear in the account from Old Harbor. They were also especially evident in the observations by Vancouver in the Kodiak area, Kenai Bay area and Chugach Bay area. The affinities described repeatedly by Vancouver in 1794 were similar to those observed by Ledyard in the eastern Aleutian Islands in 1778. Neither could Ledyard distinguish 'Indians' from Russians. Unlike Vancouver however, Ledyard was unaware of the affinities, and therefore of his own confusion. The personal attachments described by Vancouver are reminiscent of those reflected by Cherepanov in his report from the western Aleutian Islands between 1759 and 1763, as Cherepanov described the cooperation, the similar customs, and the coinciding perceptions among the men who were living and hunting together.

These qualities explain much about the communication of the new faith and its practices. This was an indigenous movement, involving indigenous Arctic social and spiritual processes; and it was corporate movement, involving the whole body of the Aleut and Alutiiq peoples' societies, or kinship-based polities.

NOTES

[1] For Veniaminov's and Netsvetov's journals in English translations, see Veniaminov (1993) and Netsvetov (1980). Both publications contain scholarly notes and appendices providing carefully researched data by L.T. Black. For material in this chapter previously published, see Mousalimas (in print (a), 1993a, 1991, 1990e, 1990f): the current work supersedes these.

[2] For Makarii see sec.1.iv, below. Not every monastic is ordained: hence the qualification in his designation, *hieromonk*; for example in contrast, the monastic Herman who was also a member of this mission remained unordained (for him, see Ch.6).

[3] Research in Russian archives would consult the following document as described by Golder (1917:2): 'Archive of the Holy Ruling Synod ... 1768, May 12 [the opening date of this catalogue]. No. 297. The priest Vasili [*sic*] Sivtsov reports, June 4, 1792, that when he was in America with Billings many natives desired to be baptized and married by the church; list. 20 ff.' It should be noted that the surname 'Sivtsev' occurs among the Iakut.

[4] Archimandrite Ioasaph [head of the mission] to '*Vladika*' [bishop], 19 May 1795, HRS/RR/LCM 643:47. Monastic Herman to *hegumen* Nazarii of Valaam Monastery,19 May 1795, HRS/RR/LCM 643:54; for the latter, also see trans. in Oleksa, ed. (1987:40).

The term *hegumen* is transliterated from игумен, a word deriving from ἡγούμενος, itself deriving from the verb ἡγέομαι, to lead the way, to guide: an *hegumen* is the leader of monastics, someone who leads the way, one who guides. I have chosen to transliterate the Russian but with the initial vowel adapted to the conform to aspirated Greek, so that the relationship between the words can be readily recognized: ἡγούμενος, игумен, *hegumen*. And I have chosen to incorporate this adapted Russian transliteration into my text for congruity with the men's Slavicized Christian names: *hegumen* being congruous with Damascene, as *hegoumenos* would be with Damaskenos, and (perhaps) *hegoumenus* with Damascenus.

[5] Gideon (1989:131-143); also see Pierce (1990:161).

[6] Veniaminov (1840b:160-161; 1984:238).

[7] See Appendix 3, Inscription on the Gravestone of E.V. Netsvetov, in Netsvetov (1980:271).

[8] Gideon (1989:137-138, 141). Gideon administered chrismation instead of Holy Communion, because he was travelling without an *antimins*. For Maria's age, cf., Gideon (1989:138) where she is listed as twenty, with ibid., p.132 where she is listed as twenty-five. Notice in the latter that Maria is recorded among the 'children born to Russian *promyshelennye*'. Was she a Russian-Aleut herself? An intermarriage in her parents' generation would have been very early indeed.

[9] For Iakutia, see Iakutsk Church Brotherhood (1897:3). In Iakutia, initial contacts with Russians took place in the early 1600s; intermarriages were frequent from the start. As late as the 1890s, the settlers were being assimilated to the Iakut language. In 1897, a primary concern of the Orthodox Brotherhood in the town of Iakutsk was to teach the Russian language for bilingualism among the Russians and Iakuts alike. The town of Iakutsk was a eastern centre in the Russian empire, probably next in importance to the city of Irkutsk, located far to the southwest of Iakutsk; and the town of Iakutsk and people of Iakutia were influential in Russian-American history, as the references in this study may indicate. For intermarriages in Siberia, also see Czaplicka cited in context in Ch.5, nt.33, below.

For a further example in the Aleutian Islands, consider Ivan Vasil'evich Kruikov mentioned in context in Epilogue, nt.10, below; and see Pierce (1990:268-270). For an example in the Kodiak area, consider the Kashaverov family mentioned in Ch.6, nt.43, below; and see Pierce (pp. 213-220). For an example on mainland southwest Alaska, consider the Lukin family mentioned in Ch.2, nt.51, below; and see Pierce (pp.318-321) and esp. Black (1984c:469-479). For an example on the Kenai Peninsula, consider Ivan Moonin, according to his grandson of the same name, John Moonin, interviewed and transcribed by Kathy Kvasnikoff in *Alexandrovsk* (1980-1981), p.33:

... my grandfather John Moonin arrived from San Francisco. He was part Russian and some kind of Indian. Cherokee, I believe. He was the only one who baptized the people here and converted them to Russian Orthodox. That was in early 1800s, and yes, of course he taught the people how to sing in church.

Also see Appendix, 'Aleut and Creole Churchmen in Alaska: nineteenth and early twentieth centuries', comp. M.J. Oleska, in Oleksa, ed. (1987:377-386).

[10] See Pierce (1990:169).

[11] Gideon (1989:122), at Unalaska while in transit westward from Kodiak, 23 October 1807:

On the Island of Umnak, through the efforts of the literate toion Ivan Glotov, a chapel has been built which is dedicated to the Church Teacher Nikolai [St Nicholas]. He himself conducts there morning and evening prayers services and the Hours on Sundays and Feastdays.

Also see Veniaminov (1840b:151; 1984:233). For the origin of the chapel on Umnak Island, see Epilogue, nt.10, below.

[12] S. Cherepanov, 3 August 1762, in Andreev, ed. (1948:117-118). For an indication of types of Aleut-Russian contacts, see Sardy (1985/86:43-58). For a summary historical analysis, see Black (1981b:117-121). And for a summary description of social interactions, see Black (1989a:46-57).

[13] For these voyages, see Black (1984a:67, 83); also see Makarova (1975:60-61, 63).

[14] Netsvetov (1840:12-13; 1984b:370); Veniaminov (1840b:171; 1984:244). For the *toions*' patriarchal, or conciliar, manner of leadership, see: Veniaminov (1840b:165; 1984:240-241) and Netsvetov (1840:12-13; 1984b:370). Aleutian Island societies comprised several regional groups: see *Unangam Ungiikangin*, map (1990:xviii); compare Black, map (1980a:83); reprinted in id. (1984a:x). For relevant geographical/demographic analyses see: Black (1984a:41-71; 1980a:82-84); Bergsland (1990:2-5).

[15] Black (1984a:83-84, 94, 187-188; 1977a:99).

[16] Netsvetov (1840:10-11; 1984b:369); Veniaminov 1840b:72; 1984:191).

[17] See Veniaminov (1840b:58, 72, 99-100, 143; 1984:184, 191, 206, 229).

[18] Krasheninnikov (1764:180, 205, 263-267), referring to the early 1740s. From his own field observations on the peninsula for successive years, affiliated with Bering's expedition, this educated Russian describes the Kamchadals as 'Orthodox', counts four churches/chapels, one in each of the major towns and villages, and refers to Kamchadal leadership in the villages. A generation later, in 1779, the Kamchadals were again described as 'Orthodox', this time by King (1784:303-304, 367, 368), an educated Englishman who was a lieutenant with Cook's third voyage (for the Kamchadals at this later date, see nt.57, below). Between the dates of these reports, the initial crews of sea hunters had embarked for the Aleutians and had returned to Kamchatka. Cf., Krasheninnikov with Gideon (1989:124-126), a secondary source from a brief stay in 1807, reporting two churches/chapels for the 1740s, and others from the 1760s to 1790s.

The reference here is to the original population: see, e.g., Krasheninnikov (1764:170), who differentiates lexically between Kamchadals and Cossacks. The latter were settlers very similar to the Kamchadals in their lifestyles as Krasheninnikov describes them both. King differentiates likewise between these two groups. This vocabulary found in Krasheninnikov (1764) and King (1784) differs from modern terminology. In modern popular usage according to Levin and Potapov (1964:876), the term 'Kamchadal' encompasses: (a) aboriginals, (b) progeny of aboriginal-settler intermarriages, and (c) descendants of the early Cossack settlers. In modern academic usage in Arutiunov (1988:34), the term 'Kamchadal' is applied to the progeny of such intermarriages, referred to as an 'ethnographic group of Russians'; while the aboriginals are differentiated as 'Itel'men'.

[19] See Glazik (1954:92); Smirnoff (1903:12).

[20] King (1784:368); see ibid. in Beaglehole, ed., (1967:1253); also see nt.57, below.

[21] Black (1984a:77, 1980:92); also see nts 55 and 140, below.

[22] Kozlov-Ugrenin, 15 June 1787, Okhotsk, in Tikhmenev, ed. (1863:20; 1979:16). Also see Liapunova (1987:116).

[23] Testimony from the Aleuts I. Chuloshnikov and Mikhail Algamalinag from Unalaska Island, 7 June 1789, in Appendix 6 ['LCM, Yudin collection, Box 2, folder 23; trans. DRHA, vol.2, pp.237-240'] in Shelikhov (1981:128). As explained in the Introduction: sources for appendices in LPAH will be cited from LPAH *verbatim* and placed within quotation marks and brackets. The first instance has occurred in this note.

[24] Liapunova (1987:124).

[25] *Hieromonk* Makarii, Report to Holy Synod, 5 Oct. 1797, received 20 Dec. 1797 (no. 3056), HRS/RR/LCM 643:13-23. Also see ibid., trans. Black in Oleksa, ed. (1987:288-290).

[26] Black (1984a:94); Kozlov-Ugrenin in Tikhmenev, ed., (1863:19-20; 1979:15-16); Liapunova (1987:116).

[27] Black (1984a:95).

[28] Veniaminov (1840a:30; 1972:47). Veniaminov's primary knowledge was of the Unalaska district. For autonomy in the Atka district, see Netsvetov (1980:12). For specifically Atka Island and Amchitka Island (central Aleutians) see ibid., pp.18-19, 30. For specifically the Near Islands (western Aleutians) with adaptation to a commercial economy, see Appendix 1, 'Notes on the Western Aleutians and the Commander Islands by Navigator Vasil'ev (1811-1812), in Black (1984a:151-170, esp. pp.160-161).

[29] Veniaminov (1840a:42-48; 1840b:19-66, 319-321, 326-327; 1972:50-52; 1984:166-188, 319-320, 323); but not for company dependents at Sitka: id. (1840a:30; 1972:47).

[30] See *Unangam Ungiikangin* (1990) photographs as well as various texts. Also see the artifact collections from the Aleutians, e.g.: under Etholen and Wrangell 1820s-1830s; by Voznesenskii, 1840s; by Pinart, 1870-1872.

[31] Black (1977a:97), Pierce (1990:391).

[32] See Pierce (1990:325).

[33] For a possible kinship between these leading men, see Black (1978:32-33).

[34] Veniaminov (1993:78-79), journal entry dated 24 April 1828.

[35] Black (1977a:97).

[36] Veniaminov (1993:76, 78, 113), journal entries dated 13 April and 24 April 1828, 16 September 1829. Pan'kov was forty-six years old in 1824 (Black 1977a:96); and Veniaminov, born in 1797, was twenty-seven years old that year.

[37] Black (1978:29-32; 1977a:98); Pierce (1990:392).

[38] Veniaminov (1840b:151; 1984:233). See Gideon (1989:122, 142), quoted in nt.11, above. See text at nt 11, above: He had been baptized during or before the year 1762, through his uncle's alliance; he journeyed to northeast Asia; he was literate and bilingual; and he became proficient in Orthodox rubrics.

[39] Veniaminov (1840b:144; 1984:229). See Intro., nts 1-2, above.

[40] Black (1984a:76); Makarova (1975:213).

[41] Respectively in Liapunova (1987:110) and in Black (1977a:99). For the Near Island stay, see Liapunova (as cited); also see the original statement by Cherepanov in

Andreev, ed. (1948:117). For the Andreanov Island stay, see Black (as cited).

[42] In Andreev, ed. (1948:117).

[43] In S. Cherepanov of Tot'ma, An Account of his Stay on the Aleutian Islands (1759/60-1762), 3 August 1762, in Andreev, ed. (1948:117-118), trans. Black (personal communication, 1985).

[44] The first known to have been baptized was the youth Temnak (his name) who visited Kamchatka with M. Nevodchikov from the latter's voyage to the Near Islands (Liapunova 1987:111). A subsequent reported baptism was that of a boy from the Near Islands, taken to Kamchatka on the 1756-1758 voyage of the *Petr i Pavel*, and baptized there, who later became Cossack Ivan Cherepanov (ibid.): the coincidence of his surname with Stepan Cherepanov's surname may be significant, as the latter had spent two winters on the Near Islands before 1759. Was Stepan Ivan's godfather?

[45] In Andreev, ed. (1948:117-118), trans. Black.

[46] Netsvetov (1840:2; 1984b:365).

[47] Ibid. (1840:1-14; 1984b:365-371). Also see Veniaminov (1840b:130; 1984:222) for the Unalaska Aleuts: 'Every activity or undertaking and almost every step required its own elaborate signs and talismans.'

[48] Cf., Eliade (1959:17): 'sacralized cosmos'.

[49] Cherepanov in Andreev, ed. (1948:117). Cf., the following accessible source: Pascal (1976:19-20), describing laity's own practices properly without clergy. (But Pascal stresses the dichotomy somewhat unrealistically in my opinion. Laity can be as independent as he describes; however, close inter-relationships and a mutual dependence may also exist between the laity and their clergy. In either case, the point remains: laity perform ritual appropriately on their own, as in Cherepanov's report.)

[50] Ibid.

[51] Ledyard (1963:92-100).

[52] Nor did any of the officers of this voyage speak any of these languages. See Capts Cook and Clerke, and Lt King, in Beaglehole (1967:449, 1335, 1445).

[53] Ledyard (1963:95).

[54] Ibid., pp.97-98. The 'American' numerals were actually the Unalaskan Aleut cardinal numbers for 'two' through 'nine' with the Atkan Aleut 'one' and 'ten'. Ledyard's transcription was nonsequential: cf., Veniaminov (1944:30, sec.58).

[55] Black (1984a:77; 1980a:92); Fedorova (1971:155; 1973:168-169). In summary, from these analytical sources combined: Into the 1760s, the majority were Kamchadals. From the 1770s, the proportion of Kamchadals decreased. Into the 1780s, the majority derived from various regions in Russia's east and northwest. For the 1790s, see nt.140, below.

[56] Lantzeff and Pierce (1973:197), citing Report by Vladimir Atlasov at Moscow, 10 Feb. 1701, in Al'kor and Drezen, eds. (1935:29-33). Atlasov was himself from Komi-land. For the term 'Kamchadal', see nt.18, above.

[57] See nt.18, above. For descriptions of the Kamchadals' religion in 1779, see King (1784:303-304, 367, 368). For descriptions of Russian and 'Kamchadal' (Itel'men) language, leadership, and customs, including dances and foods, combined here: see ibid., pp.189, 214, 218, 367. Refer directly to him as cited, not to Beaglehole, ed. (1967) who includes King's journals incomplete and piecemeal, often omitting his

references to religion and other cultural aspects.

In 1779 at Petropavlovsk, the primary port on this peninsula for embarkation to the Aleutians and Alaska, the priest was himself 'native on his mother side' (King 1784:368): mentioned already in my text. Members of Cook's voyage met him. From Unalaska, the voyage went to Hawaii for the winter, 1778/79; then, the next season, now under the command of Capt. Clerke, they proceeded to Petropavlovsk. There, Clerke succumbed to illness, and received pastoral care from this Orthodox priest. During a subsequent exploration of the Bering Sea and Strait, aware of his imminent death, Clerke requested that his body should be returned for burial, not deposited at sea. This priest interred him. Notice that the voyage had arrived here subsequent to Unalaska, their initial landfall in the north Pacific.

[58] Shishigin (1991:32-35, 80-81). See nt.9, above.

[59] Generally accepted: see 'Komi', *Encyclopedia Britannica*, 15th ed. A major figure in Komi history was St Stefan of Perm (c.1340-1396). My reference to the Komi and Russian Orthodoxy should be understood as including the Old Believers, those groups that resisted the reforms imposed by the imperial government in the seventeenth century. Northwestern Russia, from Komi-land to Karelia, were and remain Old Believer strongholds.

[60] Archimandrite Ioasaph to *hegumen* Nazarii of Valaam, 19 May 1795, HRS/RR/ LCM 643:50. See this letter in Valaam, ed. (1894:68). Compare trans. id., ed. (1978:42), reprinted in Oleksa, ed. (1987:38). See this number (in Ioasaph, HRS/ RR/LCM, as cited) reported also in: Archimandrite Ioasaph to '*Vladika*', 19 May 1795 HRS/RR/LCM 643:41; and conveyed in: Veniamin bishop of Irkutsk [and Nerchinsk] to 'Archbishop', 22 Nov. 1795, HRS/RR/LCM 643:33; and conveyed also in: Gavriil Metropolitan of Novgorod [and St Petersburg] to Zubov, 18 Feb. 1796, HRS/RR/LCM 643:30. Compare the rounded number of 'slightly less than 7,000' in: Monastic Herman to *hegumen* Nazarii of Valaam, 19 May 1795, HRS/RR/ LCM 643:54.

This number included virtually the entire population of Kodiak Island, according to Ioasaph to Nazarii (as cited in this note). It also included some people from the Alaska Peninsula, the Kenai Bay area, and the Chugach Bay at Kodiak, according to Archimandrite Ioasaph to Shelikhov, 18 May 1795, RAC/Iudin/LCM, p.1; in Tikhmenev, ed. (1863:101), trans. in Tikhmenev, ed. (1979:77); also see trans. in Oleksa, ed. (1987:58).

[61] For the population of Kodiak Island as 'more than 6,200' in winter 1795/96, see Tikhmenev (1978:47), published originally in 1861. For the entire extended Alutiiq population including the Chugach Bay area at first contact, see: Clark (1984:187) estimating at least 9,000; and Crowell (1988:134) estimating at least 10,000. Compare the number baptized according to Ioasaph in nt.60, above. This comparison allows the statement that whole lineages certainly, and quite likely virtually the entire population, of Kodiak were baptized during winter 1794/95. Later in 1795, a missionary named Iuvenalii traveled from Kodiak to the Chugach Bay area, and baptized numbers of people there (see nts 124-125, below). From that later date, it should be possible to speak of the baptism of the Alutiiq nation, or people (ἔθνος, народ).

[62] Pierce (1990:454). For detail, see (Sitnikov 1990).

[63] For the dates of these enterprises, see Makarova (1975:213-216). For finer detail with regard to the chronology of Russian voyages from northeast Asia to the Aleutians and eastward, from 1745 to 1799, see Dominique Desson, research in progress, University of Alaska, Fairbanks. Also see Pierce (1990:454): 'In eight years [from 1776], he participated in at least ten voyages.'

[64] See Colonel G. Kozlov-Ugrenin, Commandant of the Okhotsk *oblast*, 'Document, to the Toions and Peoples inhabiting the Northeastern Ocean and Aleutian Islands who are subjects of the Russian state', 15 June 1787, in Tikhmenev, ed. (1863:20; 1979:16). Also see Liapunova (1987:116).

[65] See the chronological tables in Makarova (1968:185-186; 1975:214).

[66] *Hieromonk* Makarii, Report to Holy Synod, 5 October 1797, HRS/RR/LCM 643:13-23l. See sec.1.iv, above.

[67] Ibid., trans. L.T. Black in Oleksa, ed. (1987:288-289).

[68] See, e.g., the history commissioned by the company asserting that 'this event [the granting of the monopoly] was significant not only in consolidating the company's position, but also because it enabled the company to introduce proper government' (Tikhmenev 1978:53).

[69] Monastic Herman to S.I. Ianvoskii, 28 Dec. 1818 (transcript, Valaam Monastery) in Valaam, ed. (1978:92); reprinted in Oleksa, ed. (1987:310). See ibid. (1894:151). For the transliteration 'Herman', see Ch.6, nt.1, below.

[70] Pierce (1981a:12). Two ships landed at Kodiak in summer 1784; the third, separated from the others and then repeatedly delayed, arrived much later, in spring 1786 (ibid, pp.10, 16). Nonetheless, the three were constructed near Okhotsk for the purpose of this voyage; they were equipped and departed together for Kodiak.

[71] Aminak in Holmberg (1985:59). For the full account, see Aminak in Holmberg (1855:13; 1856:416-417; 1985:59): original publication 1855, abstract reprint 1856, translation 1985. Written 'Arsentii' by Holmberg, Aminak's name should be Arsenii through the Russian from Ἀρσένιος.

[72] Testimony by *podlekar* [подлекарь, assistant surgeon] M.S. Britiukov to navy captain J. Billings, 2 Nov. 1788, Appendix 5.2 ['LCM, Golder collection, Box 3, from Russian State Archives, Petersburg, 1789, vol.7, no. 2742; also in *Pamiatniki novoi russkoi istorii, Sbornik istoricheskikh statei i materialov*, vol.3 (Petersburg, 1873), pp.373-383, trans. in DRHA, vol.2, pp.332-336'], in Shelikhov (1981:123-126). For my references to such appendices, see nt.23, above.

[73] Ibid. Also, Britiukov submitted a report of assaults to the governor-general of Siberia during the previous year, 1787, according to Pierce (1990:70).

[74] Testimony of navigator G.G. Izmailov to naval captain J. Billings, 1 July 1790, Appendix 6.3 ['LCM, Yudin collection, Box 2, folder 23; trans. DRHA, vol.2, pp.237-240'], in Shelikhov (1981:130-131).

[75] A correlation has been noticed also by Pierce (1981a:12-13) and by Black (n.d.).

[76] Shelikhov and Golikov, Petition to Catherine II, [13] Feb. 1788, in Andreev, ed. (1948:266); also in Bashkina et al., eds. (1980:166): the words укрепление and крепость are used; they are fortifications. Also see Shelikhov, Report to Irkutsk governor-general I.V. Iakobii, after 18 Nov. 1786, published as G.I. Shelikhov, *Российскаго Купца Григорья Шелехова Странствовніе в 1873 году* (St

Petersburg, 1791; 2nd ed. 1792; 3rd. ed. rev. 1793), trans. in Shelikhov (1981:36-48). For the contents of and circumstances about the publications of the Russian editions of 1791 to 1793, see Pierce (1981a:32-35).

[77] Shelikhov and Golikov, Petition to Catherine II, [13] Feb. 1788, in Andreev, ed. (1948:266); also in Bashkina et al., eds. (1980:166). 'пятидесяти тысяч человек' in the edition by Andreev; '50 тыс. человек' in the edition by Bashkina et al. See Appendix 4 ['LCM, Golder collection [box ?], photostat of ms. copy, Soviet archives, Vorontsov collection, File 476, no. 416- 419; DRHA, vol.2, pp.330-331'], in Shelikhov (1981:121): 'up to 50,000 in all'. Also see Grigorii's statement immediately subsequent: 'до пятисот [*sic* (пятьсот)] детей в аманаты принял' (Andreev, ed. 1948:266); '500 детей в аманаты' (Bashkina et al. 1980:166). An аманаты was a hostage: 'about 500 children were taken as hostages'.

After Grigorii Ivanovich's death, Natal'ia Aleeksevna (his widow) asserted a number higher than Grigorii's own, '120,000 people' subjugated by 'my husband, the late Shelikhov', in her Notes concerning 'The duties and the success of the American company', written not before 3 Aug. 1798, in Bashkina et al., eds. (1980:208).

[78] Shelikhov and Golikov, Petition to Catherine II, [13] Feb. 1788, trans. in Appendix 4, Shelikhov (1981:121). See ibid., in Andreev, ed. (1948:266-267); and in Bashkina et al., eds (1980:166).

[79] See the portraits reproduced in Shelikhov (1981). Also see the portrait reproductions of numerous colonial figures in Bashkina et al., eds. (1980) and in Pierce (1990). Differences in bodily features in various portraits of Shelikhov are noted by Sitnikov (1990:378, nt.2) who considers the portrait reproduced in Tikhmenev (1861) frontispiece, to have been 'most probably the official representation': see it replicated in Tikhmenev (1978). The bodily differences are slight however, and all the portraits contain the same symbols in his clothing and in the background. These symbols are the key. The theme implicit in them was expressed in then-contemporary written sources, and could be developed at length with reference to those written sources: see, e.g., the *ukaz* granting nobility to the Shelikhov family for Grigorii's extending of empire (cited below). For a relevant study, see Riasanovsky (1985).

Shelikhov's portrait can be contrasted to another merchant's portrait painted in 1840. The latter was exhibited at *Costumes Historique Russes du Musée de l'Hermitage de Leningrad*, Musée Jacquemart-André, Paris, 1-31 May 1989. A merchant of the town of Rzhev on the upper Volga, Petr Vassilievich [*sic*] Filatov was affluent enough to commission a portrait of himself and another of his wife. Yet he posed for his own in the traditional appearance of a Russian Eurasian merchant, in a caftan and with a beard. His wife posed in regional costume with flowered embroidery and flowered headdress. They remained attached to these traditions, nearly two generations after Shelikhov and Shelikhova.

[80] For these requests, see Pierce (1981a:20-21).

[81] Peter I was the first Russian ruler to adopt the term 'emperor'. 'Tsar' remained the popular term, maintained from the earlier era, that of the Moscow rulers. See Riasanovsky (1985).

[82] Shelikhov and Golikov, Petition to Catherine II, [13] Feb. 1788, in Andreev, ed. (1948:266); also in Bashkina et al., eds. (1980:165-166). See trans. in Appendix 4

['DRHA'], in Shelikhov (1981:121).

[83] For indications of the colony envisioned, see Shelikhov to A.E. Polevoi, 9 Aug. 1794, in Tikhmenev, ed. (1863:71-73, 1979:54-56); Governor-General I.A. Pil' to G.I. Shelikhov, no. 991, Irkutsk, 12 May 1794, points 2-7, in Appendix 7 ['LCM, Yudin collection, Box 1, folder 4; trans. DRHA, vol.2, pp.161-163'], in Shelikhov (1981:132-134).

[84] See, e.g.: the Pinart collections from 1871-72 in the Bancroft Library, University of California, Berkeley, and in the Château-Musée, Bologne-sur-mer; the Fisher collections from the 1880s in the Smithsonian, Washington, DC. For an accessible published source see Huggins (1981:3-7, 14, 23-24, 29-30, 33). Also see nt.134, below.

[85] The approximate average of Russians through the expanse of Russian-America was 500 per year, according to Fedorova (1971:117, 136-147; 1973:124, 147-159).

[86] See Vancouver (1984:1241, 1308-1309), according to observations in 1794 in areas of Kodiak other than the company settlement and also in the Kenai Bay (Cook Inlet) area. See sec.2.iii.a, below.

[87] Aminak in Holmberg (1856:415; 1985:59).

[88] Shelikhov (1981:43-44).

[89] Shelikhov, regarding privileges for his company, May-Nov. 1787, in Andreev, ed. (1948:224): Да сверх сих чинов [military personnel and artisans] нужны к просвещению пришедших народов в греко-кафолическое исповедание и впредь пожелавших в чем ни малейшего нет затруднения, 2 священника и диакон.

Also see Governor-general at Irkutsk, I. Iakobii, Report regarding the activities of Golikov and Shelikhov's company on the Pacific Ocean islands, 30 November 1787, in Andreev, ed. (1948:264): 'послатв туда для проповедывания христианской веры хотя двух из ученых священников [two from among the educated priests to propagate the Christian faith].

[90] Archimandrite Ioasaph [Bolotov, head of the monastic mission] to G.I. Shelikhov, from Kodiak, 18 May 1795, microfilm reel no. 1 [pages unnumbered], Iudin [Yudin] collection of Russian-American Co. papers, LCM [henceforth: RAC/Iudin/LCM]. See ibid., trans. Black in Oleksa, ed. (1987:58-59, 61). Also see this source in Tikhmenev, ed. (1863:101-104; 1979:77-79, 80).

The publications of this source pose a problem that requires explanation. Tikhmenev, ed. (1863) is an edition of collected sources supplementing a history commissioned by the Russian-American Company, which was meant to influence opinion favourably for the renewal of the company's monopoly charter (see the translators' and editors' Preface in Tikhmenev 1978:vi). Many segments of Ioasaph's letter that were particularly damaging to the on-site company manager were omitted: the omissions were indicated with ellipsis points. The segments included in the 1863 edition were translated for LPAH (Tikhmenev, ed. 1979:77-85); but the omissions were inserted from DRHA, indicated by underscoring as the two translations were thus merged. For the differences between LPAH and DRHA, see my Introduction, sec.3.iii. A congruent translation was subsequently accomplished by Black from a copy of the original document, and was published in Oleksa, ed. (1987:58-63); however only the initial two-thirds of Ioasaph's letter was included there: the last part was not.

⁹¹ Having moved to Petersburg, young Anna died in 1802, after her second child-birth. Within the next year, Rezanov (now a major shareholder in the Russian-American Company) became Court Chamberlain, was assigned as Petersburg's first ambassador to Japan, and commenced on a tour of the north Pacific that combined the brief embassy with a subsequent inspection of the company's on-site operations.

⁹² For the merger, see Partners of the United Company to A.A. Baranov, 19 July 1797, in Tikhmenev, ed. (1863:114-115, 1979:90-91).

⁹³ *Ukaz*, granting Madam Shelikhova and her descendants nobility, 15 Feb. 1798, in Tikhmenev, ed. (1863:116, 1979:91).

⁹⁴ Veniamin bishop of Irkutsk to Amvrosii metropolitan of Petersburg, quoted in Radchenko (1979:349), citing: 'f. 859, k. 33, no. 12, Shil'der collection, *Otdel rukopisei Gos. publichnoi biblioteki SSSR*'. See Radchenko, trans. in Appendix 9 in Shelikhov (1981:143).

⁹⁵ Drafts for the inscriptions, Appendix 8 ['LCM, Yudin collection, Box 1, folder 5; trans. DRHA, vol.2, pp.164-166'], in Shelikhov (1981:136).

⁹⁶ Archimandrite Ioasaph to Shelikhov, 18 May 1795, in RAC/Iudin/LCM. See nt.90, above. Ibid. partly trans. Black in Oleksa, ed. (1987:58-63). Also see this source partly in Tikhmenev, ed. (1863:101-107, 1979:77-85). Also see the following source, seven years later: Complaint by the monastic missionaries Athanasii, Nektarii, Herman, and Ioasaph from Kodiak to the Holy Synod against Aleksandr Baranov, 31 July 1802 [filed 1 August 1804], HRS/RR/LCM 564:1-5. 'Ioasaph' in the latter instance is not the archimandrite but another man.

   While critical of the on-site management at Kodiak, what was Archimandrite Ioasaph's attitude towards Shelikhov who was then in Irkutsk and towards the Shelikhov-Golikov wider view and enterprises? The answer may not be as important as the question itself. An insight by Florovsky (1979:121) regarding Russia in general may be significant here in specific: 'The upper realm of clergy maintained an ambiguous silence'.

⁹⁷ Makarii to Holy Synod, 5 Oct. 1797, HRS/RR/LCM 643:13-23.

⁹⁸ *Hieromonk* Gideon, Secret report from Kodiak, to Metropolitan Amvrosii, 2 June 1805, critical ed. and trans. Black in Gideon (1989:75-79); Gideon to Holy Synod, 1-2 June 1805, trans. Black in Oleksa, ed. (1987:290-292).

⁹⁹ Monastic Herman to Ianovksii, 28 Dec. 1818, in Valaam, ed. (1894:150-152; 1978:92-93); trans. reprinted in Oleksa, ed. (1987:309-310).

¹⁰⁰ *Ukaz*, 15 Feb. 1798, in Tikhmenev, ed. (1863:116; 1979:91). Also see Natal'ia Alekseevna Shelikhova, 3 Aug. 1798, in Bashkina et al., eds (1980:208): she claims that her deceased husband, Grigorii Ivanovich, had himself requested these Orthodox missionaries who, upon their arrival, baptized 'more than 8,000 souls'. The number exceeds that in Archimandrite Ioasaph's report of May 1795 by 2,000 (Ioasaph's report is cited in nt.60, above). For her penchant for exaggeration, see also nt.77, above.

¹⁰¹ Berkh (1979:42). In contrast, research would probably bring to light a critical view on Shelikhov from the reports by naval officer V.M. Golovnin who examined the Russian-American Company officially on site in 1818: Golovnin became 'major general', and eventually 'head of the Naval Ministry', according to (Pierce 1990:177).

¹⁰² Tikhmenev (1861:19-20; 1978:21).

[103] Veniaminov (1840b:153; 1984:234). Or perhaps did Veniaminov not write this himself? Записки[Notes] was published by the Russian-American Company. Did they edit it and insert the claim? Compare Veniaminov (1840b:313-327; 1984:317-323), where he questions the wisdom and practicality of aspects of the colonial aim.

[104] Nicholas, bishop of the Aleutians and Alaska in *The Russian Orthodox American Messenger*, no. 9 (13 Jan. 1897), p.157.

[105] Bolshakoff (1943:84-85). Bolshakov places the 'brothers Golikov' on the scene as Shelikhov's 'companions'. But I.L. Golikov and nephew (not brother) did *not* travel to Kodiak Island with Shelikhov.

[106] Afonsky (197712, :32). Although it is still too early to know for certain, it appears that the bicentennial in 1994 for the arrival of the religious mission did not include a repetition of such panegyrics to Shelikhov and his enterprises from anyone in authority today. If it did not, this would have been due to the historical research that was made available well in advance.

[107] Gavriil Metropolitan of Novgorod [and St Petersburg], Letter to Prince Platon Zubov, 18 Feb. 1796, HRS/RR/LCM 643:30-32.

[108] N.A. Shelikhova, Letter to Count [*sic*] Platon Zubov, Adjutant-General and Representative of the Empress in the Crimea, 22 Nov. 1795, in Tikhmenev, ed. (1863:108-113; 1979:85-89).

[109] Personal communication, Semeon Haakanson ('Sven Sr.'), Old Harbor, Kodiak, 26 April 1988, written with his permission. Among other official and local governmental titles, he had been the 'Council President' for ten years (or eleven?) until spring 1987, and had become the vice president by April 1988 to elevate the development of younger leadership.

[110] Their names, contained in my fieldnotes, will be withheld because I have not maintained communication with these men to request permission to make their names public. The specification of their derivation, and the indication of their social status, should be sufficient here, and will be particularly significant for anyone familiar with the Kodiak area.

[111] Baranov to Shelikhov and Polevoi, 20 May 1795; Baranov to Malakhov, 11 June 1800; Baranov to Larionov, 22 March 1801: in Tikhmenev, ed. (1979:68, 105, 126-127). Also see the uprisings in the Kenai and Chugach Bay areas in Baranov to Shelikhov and Polevoi, 20 May 1795; Baranov to Polomoshnoi, 28 April 1798; Baranov to Radionov, 14 May 1800; Baranov to Larionov, 24 July 1800: in Tikhmenev, ed. (1979:76, 92, 107, 115).

[112] Baranov to Larionov, 24 July 1800, and 22 March 1801, in Tikhmenev, ed. (1979:115, 126-127).

[113] E.g., Shelikhov (1981:42-45).

[114] Aminak in Holmberg (1856:415; 1985:58-59).

[115] Veniaminov (1840a:39; 1972:49).

[116] Also in 1840, his comprehensive notes were published, and they too contain the assertion about the Kodiak Alutiiq (Veniaminov 1840b:14; 1984:231): 'Of the Kad'iak [*sic*] people only about a hundredth part fulfill the obligations of Religion [обязанности Религіи] to any extent and very few of them may be acknowledged as diligent in it.'

[117] For an incident during his visit to Kodiak in 1842, see his retrospective account: Archbishop Innokentii (the bishop had subsequently become an archbishop), letter to *hegumen* Damascene of Valaam, in Valaam, ed. (1894:169-170; 1978:101). Also see an Alutiiq retrospective account from Afognak Island, Kodiak area, recorded by Huggins (1981:29). For a summary chronology of Veniaminov's movements, see Pierce (1990:524). I am assuming that the vessel *Okhotsk*, transporting Veniaminov from the town of Okhotsk to *Novo Arkhangel'sk* between 19 August and 26 September 1841, did not stop at Kodiak on the way; but if it happened to harbour there, the fact would remain that he had not been to Kodiak prior to 1840. (He came in that year as the newly elevated bishop Innokentii of the newly formed diocese of Kamchatka, the Kurile Islands and the Aleutian Islands.

[118] S.I. Ianovskii to *hegumen* Damascene of Valaam, 22 Nov. 1865, in Valaam, ed. (1894:134; 1978:82). Also see Ianovskii to Damascene, 3 Sept. 1866, in ibid. (1894:153; 1978:93). For Ianovksii, see Ch.6, sec.2.i.

[119] Baranov to Larionov, 24 July 1800, in Tikhmenev, ed. (1979:121); Gideon to Amvrosii, 2 June 1805, in Gideon (1989:77); Ianovksii to *hegumen* Damascene, 22 Nov. 1865, in Valaam, ed. (1894:134, 1978:82). For Herman, see Ch.5 (sec.3.ii) and Ch.6, below. The Cyrillic is quoted from M.F. Chumovitskii in Birket-Smith (1953:130).

[120] He had been well steeped in this tradition, and was recognized by the Monastery of Valaam as being securely within this tradition: qualities that differentiate him from merely anyone who might don monastic garb, live in a forest, and claim affinity with the same. See Ch.6, sec. 1, esp. nt.44, below.

[121] Ianovskii to *hegumen* Damascene, 22 Nov. 1865, in Valaam, ed. (1894:138-139; 1978:84-85). Also see, K. Larionov, 'Information about Father Herman', [dated in postscript, 7 Sept. 1866], in ibid. (1894:174-175; 1978:104). For Larionov, see Ch.6, sec.2.i. Herman converted naval officer Ianovskii, according to the latter's own account to *hegumen* Damascene, 22 Nov. 1865, in Valaam, ed. (1894:135-136; 1978:83). According to the same source (pp.138, 85), he also converted a certain naval captain 'G.', whom the editor of the translation (Pierce 1978:177) has assumed to be L.A. Gagemeister, also spelled L. von Hagemeister. A Baltic German of landed gentry who had been sent to England as a youth to be trained with the British fleet, Gagemeister assumed the position of chief manager of the Russian-American Company, briefly from January 1818 at Baranov's retirement. In his communications in this position, Gagemeister referred to Herman as старец (in Pierce, trans. and ed. 1984:20): meaning 'elder', this is a term of respect that is applied to monastic spiritual fathers (see Ch.6, sec.2.ii). A decade earlier, Gagemeister had spent the winter of 1807/08 at Kodiak, and returned during summer 1809 and spring 1810 (Pierce 1990:185). He relinguished his duties to Ianovskii, who became acting chief manager in mid-1818.

[122] Monastic Herman to *hegumen* Ionafan of Valaam, 13 Dec. 1819; Herman to Ianovskii, 20 June 1820; Larionov, Information [postscript at *Novo Arkhangel'sk* dated 21 May 1867], and Narrative of the Pilgrim Lazarev [inscription at Valaam dated Oct. 1864]: in Valaam, ed. (1894:193, 147-148, 122-123, 178-179; 1978:115, 91, 76, 107), respectively. For these sources, see Ch.6, sec.2.i, below.

[123] Huggins (1981:28-29).

[124] Archimandrite Ioasaph to 'Archbishop', 19 May 1795, HRS/RR/LCM 643:39-40; Monastic Herman to *hegumen* Nazarii, 19 May 1795, HRS/RR/LCM 643:55. According to Ioasaph to 'Archbishop', the two missionaries who travelled around the island had sent a report to Veniamin, bishop of Irkutsk and Nerchinsk. Research into Russian archives is needed to locate that report.

[125] See Monastic Herman to *hegumen* Nazarii, 19 May 1795, HRS/RR/LCM 643:56-57.

[126] For Makarii, see sec.1.iv, above. For Iuvenalii, see Oleksa (1990:340-341, cf. pp.336-337); also see Black (1981a:33-58).

[127] Herman to *hegumen* Nazarii, 19 May 1795, trans. in Oleksa, ed. (1987:40); see ibid. HRS/RR/LCM 643:54. Also see Archimandrite Ioasaph to *hegumen* Nazarii, 19 May 1795, HRS/RR/LCM 643:50: 'We spent two days at Unalaska and baptized more than 100 people'.

[128] Netsvetov (1984a:47-50, 250-253, 349-350), esp. the journal entries dated 25 and 30 May 1851. Subsequent to his ministry in the Atka parish, he was assigned as a missionary in the Kuskokwim and lower Yukon River regions where he served from 1845 until 1863.

[129] KANA (1987:56-66). Also see Veniaminov (1993:82, nt.9), note to the journal entry dated 29 Dec. 1827:

All Aleuts are unanimous in affirming that on the Alaska Peninsula there live Aleuts who have fled from this island arc [Aleutian archipelago] or from Kodiak Island, and that they travel along the entire arc in secret.

While roaming, they did 'nothing greatly offensive', and 'rarely took young men off with their group' (ibid.). I have noted this information because, while it is secondary, it is significant. Veniaminov was relaying, and responding to, a concern that he had received from the eastern Aleuts: a concern that may relate to the Old Harbor account regarding exiles.

Also, he mentioned that the Russian-American Company office denied their existence (ibid.). And on 19 August 1828, during a pastoral visit to the village of *Recheshnoi* on Umnak Island, eastern Aleutians, he told the villagers: anyone who sees 'nomadic Aleuts' should 'greet them and tell them that I feel sorry for them and desire that they should settle some place permanently and that they are pardoned' (ibid., p.87).

[130] H.A. Shenitz, 'The Legend that Built a Church', *Capital City Weekly*, 9 June 1967, pp.1-2, Juneau, AK; quoted in and cited by Stamey (1979:74). Shenitz and Stamey were associated with this parish.

[131] Veniaminov (1840b:148 nt.; 1984:231 nt.).

[132] Ibid. (1840b:123-126; 1984:219-220).

[133] Ibid. (1840b:124; 1984:219).

[134] Alan Crowell, Smithsonian Institution, 1st Kodiak Area Culture Conference, Kodiak, AK, 28-30 March 1988.

[135] The statement was hasty, because (as explained above) it was hearsay. Veniaminov is a primary source with regard to the Unalaska region (eastern Aleutian Islands) where he had extensive experience and gained personal insights. For example on Akun Is-

land in the Unalaska region, he exerted the initiative to meet an elderly man who was referred to as a 'shaman' by the local populace; then discovering that this baptized man differed from normal shamans, he advised the people there to cease referring to him as a 'shaman' (see Ch.4, sec.3.i, and Ch.5, sec.3.i, below). In the Kodiak area however, Veniaminov had no such experience, and exercised no such personal insight.

[136] Veniaminov (1840a:39; 1972:49).

[137] Archimandrite Ioasaph to *hegumen* Nazarii, 19 May 1795, HRS/RR/LCM 643:50.

[138] Cited with reference to the edition, Vancouver (1984:1241).

[139] Ibid., p.1309.

[140] Fedorova (1971:158-159; 1973:172-173). I shall employ the expression 'culture(s)', because these men derived from different nations, or peoples (ἔθνη, народы) that in contrast to each other would be considered different cultures; but together the affinities between them might be described as a general type. Also see Fedorova (1971:156; 1973:169): 'It is a characteristic that among the northern gubernias of Russia most of the departing peasants and tradesmen came ... specifically from those uezds where agriculture and cattle breeding were weakly developed ... and the chief regional occupations were crafts (hunting, forestry, salt-boiling and others).'

[141] See Pentikäinen (1989:229). It is noteworthy that all the major sources but one for these runes were Orthodox and Old Believer Karelians: ibid, pp.99-115, 124-130.

[142] Lantzeff and Pierce (1978:20, 127).

[143] Iakutsk Church Brotherhood (1897:3). One of the primary aims of this organization in 1895-96 was to teach the Russian language to Iakuts and Russians alike, because Iakut was the predominant language among the latter as well. This has been emphasized also in nt.9, above.

[144] Vancouver (1984:1241, 1309).

[145] Ibid., p.1308.

[146] Ibid.

[147] Lopez de Haro (ms.:104-107), trans. and ed. Moore (1979:67-69). For his biography, see: 'Lopez de Haro (Gonzalo)', *Enciclopedia Universal Ilustrada*, vol.31, pp.146-147 (n.d.): photocopy and citation provided by the Manuscripts Division, Huntington Library, San Marino, CA.

[148] Cook, Clerke and King in Beaglehole (1967:450, 1335, 1446, 1450).

[149] Baranov to Shelikhov and Polevoi, 20 May 1795, in Tikhmenev, ed. (1863:91; 1979:69).

[150] For his explorations, see 'Izmailov' in Pierce (1990).

[151] See Pierce (1990:115-117). But Lopez de Haro (ms.:104) writes: 'navida [*sic*] en Constantinopola'.

[152] See Ch. 3, nt. 43, below.

CHAPTER 2

Correspondence

For the transition to have been indigenous and corporate — involving these peoples' social and spiritual processes, and occurring through the whole body of their societies, or kinship polities — there must have been vital characteristics within their own ancestral cultures that corresponded to and could engage the Russian Orthodox Christian faith and practices. Correspondence means similarity, or analogy in significant ways, not necessarily equivalence. Can we establish a theory for such correspondence in the Arctic?[1]

Firstly, precedents within patristic theology will be identified that would support a theory of correspondence, from patristic and other Christian writings that together span many centuries, beginning from the early second century AD.[2] Then, the possibility for such a theory will be tested briefly, before it is applied with greater depth to pre-Christian Aleut and Alutiiq cultures in subsequent chapters. The test case will involve the Aleutian born priest Iakov Egorovich Netsvetov as he ministered among the Yupiit (Yup'ik Eskimos) and neighbouring Athapascans beginning in 1845, a generation after the transition had taken place in the primary focus of this study.[3]

(1) Precedents Within Patristics for a Theory of Correspondence: the Affirmative Outlook and Dual Complement

Are there precedents within patristic theology that would support a theory of correspondence? An appropriate starting-point is St Justin the Martyr (c.100-c.165), because he considered ancient Greek culture within the Graeco-Roman world, and may thus provide a theological prototype for the consideration of a pre-Christian culture. Furthermore, Justin was cited and quoted in Russian translation by Valaam Monastery in a commentary published specifically for the 1894 centennial anniversary of the 1794 mission to Kodiak, as most of the members of this religious mission were monastics of Valaam.

Let us consider the bicentennial commentary firstly, to see the context in which Justin was cited and quoted. The commentary's author, who remained anonymous as he wrote for the monastery, described many of the moral traits of the Aleutian Islanders and Kodiak Islanders including patience, loyalty, hospitality, truthfulness, charity, humility, sensitivity toward others, respect for parents, and care for children: He described these qualities in considerable detail, having compiled the information retrospectively from an ethnography of the Kodiak Islanders and an ethnography of the Aleutian Islanders.[4] He found their charity especially impressive, 'their complete readiness to share their last crust with anyone in need.'

Perceiving that the hand of God had touched their heart, he spoke for Valaam: 'To us, at least, this seems the appearance of an inner moral law, inscribed in the hearts of men by the Creator of the universe.' Regarding their pre-Christian 'religious concepts', he concluded that these were 'not bereft of God's Grace'; they involved 'elevated moral ideas ... in accordance with God's Holy Revelations'. The 'spark of God's truth' was 'visible'.[5] It was this perception that he referred to Justin the Martyr, whom he cited and quoted.

The quotation from Justin (*2 Ap.* vi.3) is presented here in the Russian translation by Valaam, with the Greek original and an English translation:[6]

Богъ не есть имя, но мысль, всажденная въ природу человъческую, о чемъ-то неизъяснимомъ.

οὐκ ὄνομά ἐστιν, ἀλλὰ πράγματος δυσεξηγήτου ἔμφυτος τῇ φύσει τῶν ἀνθρώπων δόξα.

[God] is not a name, but glory inexplicable implanted in the nature of humanity.

In Valaam's Russian translation, the subject 'God' derives accurately from verses 1-2, immediately preceding the quotation from Justin. The translation is otherwise literal; and it contains a certain kernel that would generate the affirmative outlook expressed in the Valaam commentary. The phrase 'God is not a name' signifies that the divine is not merely a concept to be taught and learned, professed by one group to be understood by another. Instead, the divine glory is present within the very nature of humanity and extends beyond explication. It is 'implanted' (ἔμφυτος, всажденная), intrinsic within our creation.[7]

Justin, in his own text, had referred to Genesis 1:26, that humanity has been created in the divine image and likeness; and described this image as the 'seed of the Logos' (σπέρμα τοῦ λόγου), a 'share of the divine Logos disseminated' (μέρος τοῦ σπερματικοῦ θείου λόγου).[8] Even through the Fall (the distancing of humanity from divinity), this 'seed', or 'share', had not altogether been destroyed, because it had been implanted within our very nature. Our contact with the divine persisted, indeed within the very nature of humanity universally. Thus despite the Fall, extraordinary people could live according to the seed of the Logos within them, and a divine likeness could become evident in them, according to Justin. Yet their illumination and righteousness would remain partial in comparison with the fullness that was to come. Through the Incarnation of the Logos in Jesus Christ, the image of God would be completely regained and the likeness would become completely visible:[9] then, the fullness could be known and received.

Aware that the phrase σπέρμα τοῦ λόγου had been employed by the Stoics,[10] Justin appropriated this phrase but not necessarily their interpretations of it, as he emphasized the possibilities that have (as he believed) been given uniquely through Jesus Christ.

Justin thus affirmed two complementary realities: (i) the universal dissemination, or presence, of the divine Logos from whom no one was entirely separated, and in whom everyone participated to greater or lesser degrees; and (ii) the fullest possibility for union with God (hence, salvation), given uniquely through the Incarnation. These complementary realities comprise a *dual complement* (as I shall term it).

This can be seen especially in Justin's most vivid example, Socrates, who, conforming to the divine within, and living a life of truth and virtue, became highly illumined and righteous. Socrates was following the Logos, as Socrates heeded the divine disseminated in his own nature; so that Justin boldly described him as a Christian before Christ.[11]

This bold statement about Socrates has caused Justin to be imagined as equating Christianity with 'the best elements' in philosophy, as if Justin had considered them to be 'almost identical ways of apprehending the same truth' (H. Chadwick 1966:10-11). But was Justin such a relativist? However, the dual complement in his thought should itself preclude the possibility.

It could be more accurate to state that Justin had recognized the godliness evident in Socrates, and therefore affirmed the potential within those elements of philosophy that Socrates embodied. After all, it was not to 'elements of philosophy' that Justin was referring. He was referring to a teacher who had elevated his own disciples' minds towards an apprehension of virtue, a person who had taken the heroic stand for this virtue himself. It was this person whom Justin affirmed in the boldest terms as conformed to, and thus guided by, the Logos before the Incarnation of the Logos: conformed to, and thus guided by, Christianity before Christ. Justin affirmed this potential in a manner superlative to any other patristic writer except perhaps St Clement of Alexandria.

Yet even Socrates' extraordinary stature remained incomplete in comparison with the fullness that was to be given in Christ, according to Justin. When he wrote about the 'fullness' in Christ, he was (or it appears to me that he was) referring to the very heights and depths. At the hands of a writer of lesser stature than Justin, this perception could be perverted; as if Christians know the 'fullness' and are 'saved' over even someone of Socrates' stature, simply by virtue of their profession of faith (that notion is influenced by a negative outlook, to be explained soon). Justin's perception about Socrates was about someone who had reached heights of development, never reached by most of us. When Justin spoke about the fullness-to-come in relation to Socrates, this would be the manifestation known to the greatly illumined. We may glimpse this through the Gospels (Mt. 17:1-8, Mk 9:1-8) when even the Disciples Peter, James and John could not yet behold the more complete manifestion of divine presence and divine glory.

As Justin perceived a presence of the Logos in Socrates, so should a theory of correspondence recognize this presence within other pre- or non-Christians. And as the dual complement precludes relativism from Justin's affirmative outlook, so would it exclude the same from a theory of correspondence predicated upon Justin's thought and upon the patristic tradition to which he belongs.

He wrote two generations after Christ's Apostles: Justin's πρὸς Ἀντωνίνον (1 Ap.) and πρὸς Ῥωμαίων Σύγκλητον (2 Ap.) were written around the year AD 155. Earlier, the affirmative outlook, so beautifully developed by him, had been expressed also in the Gospel according to John. Rather than stressing the distancing of humanity from divinity, which it clearly recognizes (John 1:10-11), the Gospel emphasizes the affirmative aspect that everyone exists in, and is illumined by, the divine Logos (John 1:3, 9). The Gospel then brings forth the full life and illumination now possible in Christ.

This affirmative outlook with its dual complement were expressed by mainstream theologians who immediately followed Justin in the late second century: Sts Theophilus of Antioch, Irenaeus of Lyons, and Clement of Alexandria. It becomes especially vivid when the latter describes philosophy as 'a kind of schooling ... coming beforehand, preparing the way' (προπαίδειά τις ... προπαρασκευάζει τοίνυν ἡ φιλοσοφία προοδοποιοῦσα).[12]

The context of Clement's description within the Στρωματεῖς is important. He likened the efforts of Greek philosophers to the efforts of Hebrew prophets to elevate their respective people towards virtue. Clement did not set philosophy as a prerequisite for Christian illumination; just as his predecessor, Justin the Martyr, had not equated philosophy with theology. They both recognized, and did affirmatively emphasize, the facility of some teachings of philosophy or some philosophers to elevate the human spirit towards godliness.[13]

Similarly in the early fourth century, St Athanasius of Alexandria expressed this affirmative outlook with its dual complement. He stated that the Fall had not entirely annihilated the divine image in humanity; instead, the Fall had

precipitated a process towards entire corruption,[14] until the Incarnation intervened with the fullness made possible in Christ. Just as the destruction of the
divine image was not total, neither was the separation of humanity from divinity; on the contrary according to Athanasius, the divine Logos continued
within the cosmos, 'giving light and movement by His providence to all things
in it'.[15]

The perception regarding the divine presence in the cosmos is an integral
aspect of this outlook, and was expressed later in the same century especially
by St Basil of Caesarea (Basil the Great, c. 329-379). Just as the bishop of
Alexandria had confronted the Arian heterodoxy that would diminish the divinity of the vivifying Logos, so this bishop of Caesarea confronted a heterodoxy
that would diminish the divinity of the Holy Spirit.[16] Thus both these bishops
in their generations affirmed, indeed defended, the operation of undiminished divinity within the cosmos. And just as Athanasius had stated that
undiminished, uncreated divinity was itself illuminating and animating 'all
things',[17] so Basil stated that divinity is itself immediately present in creation
through the divine energies, or operations (ἐνέργειαι).[18] While terms varied,
the same fundamental perception of the divine presence in the cosmos remained consistent among these sainted early patristic writers.

In the next generation, St John Chrysostom (c.347-407) articulated this
perception in terms of God's οἰκονομίαι.[19] Chrysostom's term οἰκονομίαι
etymologically indicates the management of the cosmos as if of a household.
It is not exactly synonymous with Basil's term ἐνέργειαι. Yet the concepts
involve each other, for how else is the cosmos managed except by the vivifying
divine operations?

The perception was articulated further in patristic writings by St Maximus
the Confessor (c.580-662) who preferred the term λόγοι, reminiscent of Justin's
own expression, to signify the divine presence that sustains all creation. The
articulation was advanced yet further by St Gregory Palamas (1296-1359)
with the term ἐνέργειαι, that had been used by Basil in particular.

Thus, Justin's perception of the divine presence in the cosmos — that vital
aspect within the dual complement that engenders an affirmative outlook —
is found within this patristic tradition; and when Valaam cited and quoted
Justin in the 1894 centennial publication regarding the 1794 mission to Kodiak,
the monastery was in effect referring to this tradition.

The reference in Valaam's centennial publication may increase in significance when the quotation from Justin is related to certain writings by Basil
and Chrysostom that were meant to correct the Eunomians. The latter had
interpreted the phrase σπερματικοὶ λόγοι as if the λόγοι were actually words,
or names, which had been disseminated by divine providence to indicate the

essences of phenomena. The Eunomians supposed that no less than the essence of divinity could be grasped and professed in this way, through reflective and dialectic exercises of their intellect upon the names revealed for God.

Against such misinterpretations of the σπερματικοὶ λόγοι, Basil and Chrysostom wielded a two-edged sword. It was etched on one fine edge with the 'incomprehensibility of the divine essence', to sever the presumption that the intellect could encompass the essence of the divine. It was emblazoned on the other fine edge with the 'energies', or 'economies', to defend the presence of undiminished divinity that actually, not nominally, sustains and illumines all things.

This presence of divinity had itself been 'implanted' in the nature of humanity, as Justin would state (*2 Ap.* vi.3), and as Valaam (1894a:35) would cite:

> It is not a name, but glory [*the energy*] implanted within the nature of mankind, about something [*the incomprehensible essence*] that can not be explained.

> Богъ не есть имя, но мысль, всажденная въ природу человѣческую, о чемъ-то неизъяснимомъ.

> οὐκ ὄνομά ἐστιν, ἀλλὰ πράγματος δυσεξηγήτου ἔμφυτος τῇ φύσει τῶν ἀνθρώπων δόξα.

(2) A Negative Outlook, in Contrast

There was another attitude in a very few early Christian writers. It derived from a conviction that the Fall resulted in a radical separation of humanity from divinity, and that evil had prevailed over humanity's primal goodness, so that the very nature of mankind had become utterly corrupt. Major proponents were Tertullian (c.160-c.225) and St Augustine of Hippo (354-430). This is generally recognized; for instance, the *Oxford Dictionary of the Christian Church* states: Tertullian 'prepared the way for that pessimistic doctrine of the Fall and Original Sin which came through Augustine to dominate Latin theology.'[20]

Accordingly, fallen humanity was wholly ruined, 'marked' with 'a sentence of transgression': totum hominem elogio transgressionis inscripsit (Tertullian, *de Resurrectione carnis* 34).[21] Sinful at its root, 'that mass of perdition' was a 'stock condemned': massa illius perditionis, perditionis massa (Augustine, *Enchiridion* xxiii.92).[22] The mark was progenitive, the condemnation inherited (id., *De peccato originali* xxxviii.43):[23]

> Where God did nothing else than by a just sentence to condemn the man who willfully sins [Adam], together with his stock; there also, as a matter of course, whatsoever was even not yet born is justly condemned in its sinful root.

Ubi nihil deus fecit, nisi quod hominem voluntate peccantem iusto iudicio cum
stirpe damnauit, et ideo ibi quicquid etiam nondum erat natum merito est in praevari-
catrice radice damnatum, in qua stirpe damnata tenet hominem generatio carnalis.

No one was exempt, not even children according to Augustine. Belonging
by nature to this 'massa damnata', thus corrupted essentially, they too were
eternally damned unless saved through baptism.[24]

It is as if salvation were a type of census in which only some individuals,
having passed through the baptismal font as through an actual laver, were
enrolled. So, Tertullian asserted that a soul remained unclean (immunda) unless recounted (recenseatur) in Christ.[25]

The severity of his assertion is mitigated in some English-language versions
of this work when the verb he did write (recenseatur) is rendered as 'reborn' or
'born again'. The renditions occur evidently by transposition from the Biblical
verse to which he was alluding. In that verse known today as 1 Peter 1:23, the
original word ἀναγεγεννημένοι is properly translated in the Revised Standard Version of the Bible as the phrase 'born anew' and in the King James
Version of the Bible as the phrase 'born again'.[26] But Tertullian did not write
ἀναγεγεννημένοι. Nor did he write its proper Latin translation (renati), as
found in the Vulgate for this verse 1 Peter 1:23. Tertullian's term is different,
deriving not from this verb (renasci, renascor: renati), but from another
(recensere, recenseo: 'recenseatur') that is found instead in Old Testament
Pentateuch verses such as Exodus 30:12, where the saved are described as numbered against impending doom:

> When thou takest the sum of the children of Israel after their number, then shall
> they give every man a ransom for his soul unto the Lord, when thou numberest
> them; that there be no plague among them, when thou numberest them.

Numbers 1:18, 22, 24, 29, 30 also contain that verb (recensere, recenseo:
'recenseatur') when the chosen people are described as counted by Moses and
Aaron before their entrance into the promised land.[27] That is the term Tertullian wrote into his own allusion to the epistle; and when a word proper to the
epistle is rendered instead into translations of his work, the rendition glosses
over his own meaning. For Tertullian, as if in a census, some individuals only
had been counted for salvation from the damned.

Among the unredeemed, little if any possibility could exist for illumination
and righteousness. This depravity was imputed even to the ancient philosophers whose partial morality and revelation had, according to Tertullian, come
from outside themselves: from the Biblical prophets, communicated to the
Greeks indirectly through the Egyptians. The notion is not entirely unreason-
able; for eastern Mediterranean cultures were in proximity and had long been

in contact. In Tertullian's mind however, it assumed a particular importance. For him, the prophets became the philosophers' main source of truth and virtue, and had to be as the pagan soul was essentially depraved, altogether severed from the divine: any goodness reflected there being a 'stray beam', whether it be in Socrates at Athens, or among the common people at Rome when, for instance, the latter would by 'accidental outlet' bid each other 'Deo commendo'.[28] Thus a wide wedge was thrust, sundering non-Christians from Christians — a sundering which Tertullian recapitulated in his succinct rhetorical question: 'What has Athens to do with Jerusalem?' The gulf between them was ontological in his view: the difference existed in the very nature of the 'non-elect' whose redemption would entail an entire change of nature, should they ever be numbered among the saved.

Similarly according to Augustine of Hippo, the rest of humanity remained depraved, therefore justly damned and eternally alienated from the divine, while a predestined elect had been chosen by God to be saved.[29]

I am aware that this is a literal interpretation of sections from Augustine's voluminous writings, let them be major sections in major writings in his *corpus*; and that another interpretation is possible with regard to his entire work. His later 'Retractions' can be emphasized, thus admitting his earlier writings as speculative, not definitive. His value would then be posited, not in any of those writings specifically, but far more generally in his religious devotion through the very act of his writing itself, and through his own personal struggles. But such an approach to him rather skirts around the thrust of his pen, does it not? Speculations they may have been, but he expressed them with vigour nonetheless; and they have hardly been neutral in their effects.

His negativity in these matters was criticized in his own generation especially by St John Cassian (c.360-435) who established two monasteries near Marseilles. In contrast to Augustine of Hippo in the province of Africa, statements such as these within the affirmative patristic tradition were expressed by Cassian in Gaul (*Conlatio* XIII):

> For we should never hold that God made man such that he can never will or be capable of what is good. [Nec enim talem deus hominem fecisse credendus est.][30]

> The Divine protection then is inseparably present with us, and so great is the kindness of the Creator towards His creatures, that His providence not only accompanies it, but actually constantly precedes it. [Adest igitur inseparabiliter nobis semper diuina [sic] protectio tantaque est erga creaturam suam pietas creatoris, ut non solum comitetur eam, sed etiam praecedat iugiter prouidentia.][31]

> We must not think that the philosophers attained such chastity as is required of us... But they had a sort of μεϱικἠ, i.e. some particle of chastity. [primum

philosophos nequaquam credendum est talem animi castitatem qualis a nobis exigitur ... habuerunt autem illi quandam μερικὴ, hoc est portiunculam castitatis.][32]

Even the Council of Carthage, AD 418, a local council held in Augustine's own province during his own lifetime, did not entirely endorse the bishop of Hippo's pessimism in these matters.[33] Rather more of it was expressed in Gaul a century later, after the barbarian invasions and barbarians' consolidations in that region; yet the Council of Orange, AD 529, remained less severe than he, and that was the only important early conciliar pronouncement of that sort.[34]

As for Tertullian, he came into conflict with the greater affirmative attitudes, and separated himself from mainstream Christianity, becoming a leading member of a rigorist sect, the Montanists, in the Roman province of Africa (present-day Tunisia and north-easternmost Algeria) where he lived as would Augustine. Their negativity was a provincial current surpassed by the greater affirmative patristic outlook in the early Church.

It was later that the negative outlook somewhat eclipsed the affirmative, an occurrence which the Council of Orange, AD 529, can be seen as having heralded in that part of the world. By the sixteenth century, a thousand years later, it was being propounded in political and historical theories by churchmen related to the Vatican: theories correlated directly with elements in the writings by Augustine of Hippo.[35] Augustine's speculations, so confidently expressed by him, and then read as if Christian doctrines, would provide a justification for the denigration of the heathen in colonized America and elsewhere, would they not? Or perhaps the inverse is truer: that the propensity for such denigration in that pattern of barbarity, yet repeating itself unmitigated through those further invasions and subjugations, had been the engaging factor, the cause for Augustine of Hippo's peculiar doctrines to have become so engaged and exalted. In either case if long a primary focus, then his Predestinarianism should be expected as an ingrained concept with various manifestations; that is to say, with manifold correlations.

Also during the sixteenth century, it received vigorous expression in specifically religious terms in two important works: the *Institutes of the Christian Religion* and the 'Formula of Concord'. The latter was written by a number of Lutheran theologians in 1577, however not by Luther himself from whose view it deviated, according to Gustaf Aulén (1931) who argues convincingly that Luther's own view, in contrast, was patristic.[36] The 'Formula' had limited acceptance: the book in which it was published, *The Book of Concord*, was rejected by the Danes and by others.[37]

As for the *Institutes of the Christian Religion*, its author, John Calvin (1509-1564), referred his opinions directly to Augustine of Hippo, as if the latter represented the mainstream in early Christian thought.[38] John Chrysostom also was cited conspicuously in that treatise; but precedence was taken even over Chrysostom by Augustine in Calvin's thought. His view of the bishop of Hippo as an authority in the early Church, and of himself in relation to Augustine, was expressed in the following summary passage in another work (*De aeterna Dei praedestinatione*), appropriately an essay on predestination:[39]

> But since the authority of the ancient Church is offensively brought against me, it is perhaps worthwhile to say at the outset how unjustly the truth of Christ is smothered by this enmity, partly in error and partly in frivolity. But I would rather disperse this accusation, such as it is, with the words of Augustine than with my own.

> Sed quia odiose nobis ingeritur veteris ecclesiae autoritas, breviter etiam praefari operae pretium est, quam iniuste hac partim falsa, partim frivola invidia, prematur Christi veritas. Augustini tamen verbis potius quam meis, hoc quidquid est criminationis diluere malo.

Following Augustine, Calvin extended this indictment even to infants; and interpreted the Gospel along those lines, for instance in his *Institutes of the Christian Religion*:[40]

> For a heavenly Judge, even our Saviour declares that all are by birth vicious and depraved, when he says that 'that which is born of the flesh is flesh' (John 3:6), and that therefore the gate of life is closed against all until they have been regenerated.

They brought 'condemnation with them from their mother's womb'; their nature was 'a seed-bed of sin': 'odious and abominable to God'.[41]

What, then, might the heathens be? By 'natural instinct', they had 'some sense of deity'; however, rather than a highly potential point of participation in, and sanctification by, the divine, it had been given to them as a judgement:[42]

> God himself, to prevent any man from pretending ignorance, has imbued all men with some idea of his Godhead, the memory of which he constantly renews and occasionally enlarges, that all to a man, being aware that there is a God, and that he is their Maker, may be condemned by their own conscience when they neither worship him nor consecrate their lives to his service.

By such admonitions Calvin, Augustine of Hippo, and Tertullian might have incited their own people to pursuits of virtue, and the last quotation from Calvin could be reviewed in this manner. In their own cultures, such preachers might comfort their own people with the emphasis on election, a surety of redemption. But that severity could have destructive effects if applied to other peoples in other cultures from whom, thus denigrated, a radical change in personal and cultural nature would be demanded if ever the 'damned heathens' were to be counted among the saved. The wedge had been driven.

The anvil need not be overtly doctrinal: Sharp wedges can be forged on harsh social principles, as indicated already with reference to sixteenth century Vatican-related political theories. A wedge of that sort was wielded intellectually also in the nineteenth century by the naval officer V. N. Berkh who coupled the Cross with the battleaxe in his account of Russian-American history, as mentioned in the preceding chapter; and in the mid-twentieth century by S. Bolshakoff, the Orthodox Church history writer also mentioned in the preceding chapter, who likewise coupled them in his hasty account of the history of the Kodiak mission.[43]

The same sort was wielded by a chaplain to Petersburg's embassy in London at the turn of the twentieth century. Writing a short general history of Russian missions, E. Smirnoff (1903:4) described the wholesale assimilation of some Finnic tribes as a commendable result of the conversions. The key phrase in my criticism is *wholesale assimilation*. A degree of assimilation is to be expected in any conversion process that may involve an integration, or ingrafting, of an *ethnos* (ἔθνος), but not its annihilation. He commended the cultural annihilation of those Finnic ethnic groups.

While the Orthodox chaplain Smirnoff was writing in Europe, a Presbyterian minister was coincidentally effecting a parallel ideal in Alaska for the wholesale assimilation of the heathen, or those he perceived as heathens, to Anglo-American structures now. Having become the territorial Agent of Education during the last decades of the nineteenth century, Sheldon Jackson instituted a policy which separated Native Alaskan school-children from their parental environments, their families and villages; and demanded wholesale unilateral conformity from them. The same wedge continued to be wielded through the first half of the twentieth century when, for example, Native Alaskan schoolchildren who spoke any language other than English had their mouths washed with soap by territorial schoolteachers across the breadth of southern Alaska.[44]

Farther north in Alaska, at Tununak, during the first half of the twentieth century, general cultural aspects were being destroyed wantonly to effect conversions, thus salvation, by Catholic Vatican-related missionaries who suppressed, for instance, even the demure Yup'ik dancing.[45]

Should we discover in Alaska that even today native languages and other cultural aspects are being demeaned and tacitly suppressed by churchmen in favour of the currently dominant colonial culture, then the insidious permeation of the negative outlook would have manifested itself through time as well as across doctrinal boundaries. The wielding in the current circumstances would be in rather another direction however, not bluntly against those perceived as heathen, but sharply against people identified as Christian whose ethnicity is being denigrated. And we will then have uncovered a paradox if any such smiths are speaking ostensibly purely in patristic terms while working their hands in such grimy counter principles. Therefore while the Augustinian-Calvinist doctrines form a readily recognizable anvil; similar wedges can be, have been, and may yet be forged and driven by other legions. Against them all, on all sides, the patristic outlook can guide along an actually affirmative way.

(3) Summary Contrast, and an Extension of the Affirmative Outlook

Different outlooks on, or broad currents regarding, the same pre- or non-Christian cultures can be identified through the course of Christian history. The negative outlook concentrates on the separation between divinity and unredeemed humanity, and posits a gulf so wide that any good evident on the other side is seen as but an epiphenomenon overlaying the reality of an essentially depraved nature.

The affirmative outlook perceives an enduring, highly potential quality implanted in the very nature of mankind where humanity meets divinity. Relative righteousness and illumination are seen, because the presence of the divine Logos is affirmed universally: Righteousness and illumination are expected more-or-less depending upon the relative degrees of people's participation in the divine; and this participation may reach extraordinary degrees indeed, as in Socrates. This affirmative outlook has the greater historical depth, and in the early Church a wider distribution.

Within the patristic theology that engenders the affirmative outlook, we have found precedents for a theory of correspondence between the pre-Christian Aleut and Alutiiq cultures and Russian Orthodox Christianity; and we saw that these precedents were cited retrospectively by Valaam with regard to these pre-Christian cultures specifically.

Just as aspects of ancient Greek culture (philosophy) were interpreted through the affirmative outlook as a kind of preparation for, or prefiguration of, Christianity; so by a reasoned extension, we may expect that certain dynamics in the ancestral Arctic culture(s) may be interpreted likewise. And just as a naïve equivalence was avoided through the dual complement inherent in this affirmative outlook with regard to Graeco-Roman culture; so we should expect that naïvety and excessive sentimentality would be avoided with regard to the Arctic, while wanton negativity is also spurned on the other hand.

Justin's outlook in particular was not naïve or overly sentimental. Ultimately he chose to be martyred instead of compromising inappropriately; and thus was he dissimilar from adherents of Gnostic sects contemporary with himself. The Gnostics promoted an inappropriate syncretism between philosophies, mythologies and rites.

It is into a consideration of rites and ritual symbols that we shall proceed next. But can we proceed so easily into this field from the patristic precedents? Justin as well as Athenagoras, Clement and Irenaeus were generally disparaging about the pagan rites in the Graeco-Roman world that were contemporary with themselves. There were sound reasons for their criticism. We shall glimpse these reasons in Chapter 4. Contrary elements existed also within philosophy; yet Greek philosophy became a challenge for Justin, Athenagoras, Clement of Alexandria. It occasioned their creative thought, Justin's bold affirmation. Therefore let us ask whether we may reasonably expect that some dynamics in the ancient rites might also be interpreted as a kind of preparation for, or prefiguration of, Christianity? After all, the very word 'mysteries' from the ancient Greek religions was retained transformed, becoming the word for the Christian sacraments: τὰ μυστήρια. Do we have an extension of the affirmative outlook that would speed us along this line of reasoning?

The Graeco-Roman Mystery Religions have been embraced within a 'vast *preparatio evangelia*' as 'foreshadowings' of the 'ideal and supreme', as follows for example:[46]

> [the objective observer] would see no reason why the 'Creed of creeds' should not include, side by side with an ethic loftier than that of Socrates, and a theology richer and grander than that of Aristotle, 'Mysteries' more pure and ennobling than those of which Sophocles wrote ...

Should it be surprising that the same author developed the contrast between the affirmative patristic tradition and the Augustinian-Calvinist divergence as the theme for his ever timely Bampton Lectures? It is hardly coincidental; and therefore I have chosen to quote N.P. Williams.

An affirmation along this line of reasoning has been expressed directly from the field of missions within the Greek Orthodox *ecumene* by bishop Anastasius (Yannoulatos). Regarding the ancient religions of Kenya, he has written:[47]

> The ancient religions should not be considered on the one sided basis of demonic domination in the sense of Romans 1:21: '... [they] became vain in their imaginations, and their foolish heart was darkened'; ... but also in light of Acts 14:17: 'he left not himself without witness'.

His conclusions are of particular significance: he recognizes the ancient religions of Kenya as already 'on a high level'.[48] His perception is not sentimental or diffuse. He is writing specifically and insightfully about particular groups of people, some Bantu tribes, especially the Kikuyu, with whom he lived and whom he knows. His affirmation is like that found in Veniaminov's ethnography regarding the moral qualities of the ancient Aleut people and in the Valaam commentary regarding the moral qualities of the ancient Aleut and Alutiiq peoples: specific qualities were delineated among particular groups of people. It is not my intention to equate the experience in Alaska and the experience in Kenya: they remain distinct. Yet affirmations have been expressed in both instances, each specifically, then and now, with regard to pre-Christian religion and rites.

Let us see whether dynamics in ancient Arctic rites might have corresponded with elements in Russian Orthodox Christianity: a correspondence (not an equivalence) that would allow the engaging of the one with the other, and that may even allow some essential qualities to be retained transformed, imbued with new meanings and new orientations.

(4) A Test Case for the Theory of Correspondence

This test case will involve a succinct comparison between ritual symbols that reflect the cosmos, proper to the pre-Christian Yupiit of that time and proper to the Russian Orthodox religious mission among them then.[49] Major rituals have been chosen from each: for the ancient Yup'ik, the ritual festivals known as *Nakaciuq* and *Kelek*; and for the Russian Orthodox, the Divine Liturgy.

The commentary to be quoted for the Divine Liturgy is Ἱστορία ἐκκλησιαστικὴ καὶ μυστικὴ θεωρία by St Germanus of Constantinople. Written in the eighth century, this commentary was incorporated into Slavonic service books in Russia beginning in the thirteenth century.[50] The form of the Liturgy described in this commentary remains virtually the same throughout the Greek Orthodox *ecumene* today, including the characteristics that will be described here. The complete Liturgy is celebrated by clergy and laity chanting in cooperation, each properly within their respective roles according to long established rubrics. (An abbreviated version is conducted in Alaska today by laity, whenever a priest is not at hand.)

The missionary priest who will appear and who was the main celebrant of the Divine Liturgy in this region of the comparison at that time is Iakov Egorovich Netsvetov (introduced in Ch.1, sec.1.ii).[51] Born of Russian and Aleut parents on the islands, he went to Irkutsk to study for the priesthood. In 1828, he was assigned to become the first priest of the Atka parish, encompassing the central and western Aleutian Islands, his mother's homeland. From 1845 until 1863, he served as the first clergy missionary of the expansive *Mikhailovskii-Kvikhpak* (Yukon) Mission among Yupi'k Eskimo and neigbouring Athapascans of the Yukon and Kuskokowim River regions on the mainland. Ikogmiut was the centre of this *Mikhailovskii-Kvikhpak* (Yukon) Mission. Ikogmiut was the site where Netsvetov lived for most of each year from 1845 until 1863, and whence he travelled to other locations throughout the vast mission region. Peoples as distant as the Athapaskans from the upper

Kuskokwim River region would travel here to visit him.

Ikogmiut was also the location of Yup'ik ceremonial festivities, such as *Nakaciuq* and *Kelek*, as well as Yup'ik major memorials for ancestors. Participants included Athapaskans from the middle Yukon River region, Inupiat from the Norton Sound area, and central Yupiit from the Kuskokwim River region, as well as the Yupiit of the lower Yukon region.[52] These festivities were occasions not only for rituals, but also for gift-giving, feasting, the trading of goods, the exchanging of ideas, myth- and story-telling, pantomime, and dancing.

(i) The Divine Liturgy

A view into the Orthodox Christian cosmos can be gained through the symbolism of the Divine Liturgy, as Netsvetov would have celebrated it.

Let us begin with the structure of the space where the Liturgy is celebrated. The sanctuary is divided from the nave by an *iconostasis*, a screen of icons. This symbolic arrangement – sanctuary, *iconostasis*, nave – is reproduced for the celebration of the Liturgy whether in a church building, a chapel or a church tent (the latter was used by Netsvetov wherever a church building or chapel had yet to be constructed). In the church tent, icons may be placed on stands that are set in a row with a primary opening in the middle between them. In the middle of the *iconostasis* are doors, the 'Royal Gates', opening into the sanctuary. (I have been told that Netsvetov carved an *iconostasis* and other church items from ivory at Ikogmiut.)

The division of the nave from the sanctuary symbolizes our separation from the divine due to the Fall. The gates into the sanctuary symbolize the opening of our way to union with the divine.

The actual union with the divine is represented in the icons: especially the icon of Christ always present on one side of the gates in the *iconostasis*; and on the other side, always the icon of Mary the Mother of God in whom the Incarnation occurred uniquely. While these two are always present thus, each on either side of the gates, icons of various saints and angels may be included with local variations in the extension of the *iconostasis* (and also on stands in the nave, and on the sides, even on the ceiling, of the structure).

The laity stand in the nave facing the *iconostasis* during the Divine Liturgy. The ordained clergy stand mostly in the sanctuary. So do their acolytes. The clergy are robed in liturgical garments according to rank, be they bishop, presbyter, or deacon. They make symbolic processions at times around the altar, and from the sanctuary into the nave, and again into sanctuary.

At a relatively early point in the Liturgy, the presbyter carries the Gospel in procession with his acolytes from the sanctuary, and then he re-enters the sanctuary through the Royal Gates, still carrying the Gospel: thus symbolizing the High Priest, Christ, attended by angelic and human hosts, coming into the midst of the people, and opening the way.

Later in the Divine Liturgy, a similar procession is made, now to offer the bread and wine for the Eucharist. The presbyter is again in the midst. He carries the offering through the Royal Gates to the Holy Table. The offering of the bread and wine is censed by another of the processionists, while yet another leads the procession by carrying a tall cross with images of the Resurrection and, on the inverse, the Crucifixion. Other processionists carry fans, actually solid fan-like circles on poles, slightly taller than the height of a man.

Known as τὰ ἐξαπτέρυγα (the six-winged), these fan-like circles are embossed or carved with figures of the 'the six-winged seraphim' and 'the many-eyed cherubim' who are present iconically in the procession, proceeding 'invisibly before the great king Christ who is coming to the mystical sacrifice'. During this procession, the Cherubic Hymn is chanted, beginning with these words: 'Let us who mystically represent the Cherubim'. Thus, through this verbal and visual imagery, 'the earthly imitates the heavenly, other-worldly, noetic order', and the Liturgy in heaven conjoins with that on earth.[53]

While the visual and verbal representations in the Divine Liturgy are richly more encompassing than these, the representations of the seraphim and cherubim may provide us with an expedient focus for our succinct comparison.

Images of these heavenly hosts are found also in Isaiah 6:1-3, where the Lord, 'enthroned, high and lifted up, his train filling the temple', is surrounded by and hymned by them. The imagery from Isaiah is extended in the commentary by Germanus to Revelation 4:7-8, where ζῷα hymn antiphonally:[54]

And the four-formed animals [ζῷα] antiphonally giving to, receiving from each other: the first, a likeness of a lion exclaims, HOLY: the second, a likeness of a calf exclaims, HOLY: and the third, a likeness of a man exclaims, HOLY; and the fourth, a likeness of an eagle exclaims, LORD OF SABBAOTH.

Written in the verse in Revelation and in the Greek commentary, rendered as 'animals' in the quotation (as cited), ζῷα is translated in the King James Version of Revelation as 'creatures', because one is a man. These figures indicate the heavenly choirs. They are also often interpreted as symbols of the four Evangelists, each exclaiming the Lord.

Either these zoomorphic and anthropomorphic images from Revelation or the seraphic and cherubic images from Isaiah are normally depicted in the pendentives of the central dome in church buildings (or the central upper ceiling where a dome is lacking). They may also be depicted on the Royal Gates, opening inward. Christ is depicted inside the dome, thus lifted up, surrounded and exalted by these other represenations.

Iconography and architecture, hymnography and processional movement, are symbolic in the celebration of the Divine Liturgy. The earthly opens to the heavenly. The heavenly co-celebrates at one with the earthly.

After the Divine Liturgy, co-joined with it, memorials for the deceased may follow. These occur on the fortieth day after the funeral, and then periodically at anniversaries of the funeral. Prayers are recited and chanted for the person's repose, 'where there is no sickness or sorrow or sighing but life everlasting'. The person is mentioned by name in the prayers offered to God through Christ. And in honour of the person for whom the memorial is specific, boiled rice (in Alaskan tradition today, but boiled wheat in Mediterranean tradition), always sweetened and usually decorated, is brought forward, blessed, then distributed to all present.

(ii) The ancient Yup'ik Mid-winter ritual festivities

A view into the ancient Yup'ik cosmos can be gained likewise through symbols in major rituals. These rituals took place in the *qasgiq*, or according to Russian vocabulary the *kazhim*: a communal house that was itself a representation of the cosmos, with the smokehole in the structure's roof being an image of the passage to the spirit world.[55]

The latter image (of the passage to the spirit world) was evident particularly during *Nakaciuq*, an annual mid-winter ritual festival honouring primarily the spirits of sea mammals, especially seals, that had been caught through the hunt and that were so vital to Yup'ik subsistence. Known as *yua* in the Yup'ik language, they were represented by certain internal organs preserved from the caught animals throughout the year in anticipation of this ritual. Escorted ceremoniously on their way from the hunters' world to their own, they would be raised by the celebrants through the smokehole in the *qasgiq* at a ritual climax; then, outside, they would be returned into moving water through a hole in the winter ice. All this was done with invitations that they may come again to the hunters' world in due time, and with assurances or promises that they would be honoured at that time again.[56]

The animals' *yua* were represented also by ritual masks, as were various other spirits, especially during *Kelek*, following *Nakaciuq*.[57] In many sizes (as large as a man; as small as a finger), and in many forms (human, animal, surreal), some worn by celebrants (over faces, on fingers), others placed on the *qasgiq* sidings, yet others in some instances suspended from the ceiling, these masks represented various powers active in the cosmos and active in the ritual.[58]

A ritual procession that took place during an ancestor memorial at Ikogmiut in 1847 was described as follows.[59] 'Dressed in their best garments which had been prepared beforehand especially for this occasion', the processionists emerged from the *qasgiq*, made a round of the cemetery, then returned into the *qasgiq*. A drummer led. The men who were offering the memorial ceremony followed slowly. Next came their wives, carrying rods decorated with feathers, and swaying from side to side to the solemn drum beat and the chant.

Ancestor memorials primarily honoured and nourished the deceased, and also supplicated more generally. The ritual actions could be personal, for particular kin who were addressed, for instance:[60]

> Return, our father;
> We wait for you;
> Come back to us;
> And we, who are lonely,
> Will give you food.

To provide the ancestor, or the departed, with nourishment, food and water would be consumed by a namesake, or bits and drops would ritually be either cast into the fire or deposited through cracks in the floor, for example:[61]

> The [deceased's] namesake would take [a bowl of water provided by the host], dip his fingers, and shaking drops of water three times to the side into a crevice in the floor, would say quietly: 'Drink, our dead.' Then when he was given another bowl of food, he would take small bits of each food, and likewise throw them into the fire pit, with the words: 'Accept, dead ones, from our supplies, and help us secretly next summer.'

Thus the ancestor memorials, as well as the ceremonial festivities of *Kelek* and *Nakaciuq*, took place where the eternal and temporal intersected symbolically. Visual and verbal representations would effect this meeting or would make this meeting manifest.

(iii) Similarities and Dissimilarities, in brief

Dissimilarity exists not only about some of the types of spirits that were involved in the respective rituals (we shall proceed into this difference in Chapter 5), but more significantly in the ways the spirits were involved. At times in *Nakaciuq* and *Kelek*, the central ritual acts were directed *to* the represented spirits, which were meant to be appeased. The angelic hosts symbolized within the Divine Liturgy are not propitiated: they co-celebrate with humans to worship something greater, encompassing themselves and all.

Differences notwithstanding, some of the words written by Germanus of Constantinople to describe the Divine Liturgy would apply to the *Nakaciuq* and *Kelek* at Ikogmiut, would they not? He said: 'the earthly imitates the ... other-worldly.' Symbolic representations manifested a meeting of the eternal with the temporal in each instance throughout our comparison. Dynamics corresponded. The representations were visual as well as verbal, including the movements of processions. They even included the structure of the space through which the 'other-worldly' opened symbolically into this one, and reciprocally this world opened into the other. Space and movement, words and visual imagery, manifested a participation of this world vividly with the 'other-worldly', and reciprocally a participation of the 'other-worldly' vividly within this one.

(5) Conclusions

We may draw conclusions in this chapter by focusing on Netsvetov's response to the ancient Yup'ik ceremonial festivities. How did this Native Alaskan (Russian-Aleut) priest respond? He clearly advised his flock, those people who had been baptized, that they should refrain from involving themselves in the main rites during ritual festivals such as *Nakaciuq* and *Kelek*, because he considered those rites to be superstitious.[62] Otherwise, evidently, he was not adverse regarding the activities of the mid-winter festivities: nowhere in his journals did he pointedly advise anyone against these other activities, from gift-giving to traditional dancing.

His response towards the wider activities in the ancient Yup'ik mid-winter festivities reflects an *affirmative outlook*. This outlook is available in a line of tradition through patristic theology from the first and second centuries that recognizes the presence of the divine Logos disseminated universally. This was expressed with patristic references in the Valaam commentary in 1894, regarding the ancient Aleut and Alutiiq cultures. Recognizing the divine presence, the patristic theologians acknowledged some elements or patterns in the ancient world as prefigurations of and a preparation for Christianity. We may say that these patterns *correspond*. Therefore the patristic theologians were prepared to 'retain some cultural elements'.[63] And we may expect that this kind of attitude would allow an appropriate synthesis, would it not?

This affirmative attitude differs from a negative outlook, which in contrast would demand a radical separation of things considered to be Christian on the one hand from everything considered to be non-Christian on the other hand, causing a severe disjunction: a severance even of ancestral languages and demure dancing along with folklore, folk-healing, gift-giving, etc. The negative outlook has been traced through the history of doctrine in this study. We have seen that the affirmative outlook obtains the greater depth in mainstream Christian history, although it has been eclipsed by the negative outlook in some locations at times.

The affirmative outlook does not project a naïve equivalence between differing things. Correspondence does not imply equivalence. Distinctions were marked in the biblical and patristic literature during the first and second centuries. Distinctions were marked in Netsvetov's ministry in the nineteenth century. The patristic theologians were discerning. He was discerning when he advised his flock to avoid the main rites during *Nakaciuq* and *Kelek*, while he was not disparaging against the wider context in which the ancient mid-winter festivities took place.

He furthermore marked distinctions by celebrating the Divine Liturgy in a special structure apart, instead of celebrating it in a yurt or a house. Especially sacred space was thus defined and maintained for the Divine Liturgy at each site where he celebrated this divine service in the vast *Mikhailovskii-Kvikhpak* (Yukon) Mission: be this in a church building or in a chapel or in a church tent, depending on the location.[64] Respective rituals would have remained clearly distinct and unconfused during his spiritual mission (cf. Matt. 9:17).

This marking of distinctions by him reflects the *dual complement* that we found within the patristic outlook. Accordingly, while the Logos is recognized to be disseminated universally, a fullness is believed to become available uniquely through the Incarnation in Jesus Christ. This fullness could be explicated from a theological viewpoint, and that type of explication is very important with regard to the spiritual ascent to heaven, the spiritual descent into the heart: in other words, with regard to the potential of the human person for participation in the divine presence and for union with the divine (this will be indicated in subsequent chapters).

It can also be seen from an aesthetic or artistic viewpoint, which is more accessible. It becomes evident even through the structure of the Divine Liturgy of St John Chrysostom itself in comparison to the ancient rites, be they the Yup'ik *Nakaciuq* and *Kelek* or the Graeco-Roman mysteries. The Divine Liturgy is more sublime and majestic even as art, surely. Let us pause to consider this aspect as it will yield a coincidence that may be meaningful.

Simultaneously while the Divine Liturgy was being engaged in Yup'ik villages, the same Divine Liturgy was engaging the genius of European composers of fine music. Tchaikovsky composed his opus 'The Liturgy of St John Chrysostom' in 1878. Rachmaninoff composed his opus 31, 'The Liturgy of St John Chrysostom', in 1910. Coincidentally at the same time, Yup'ik Eskimo villages were converting in Alaska: for example, the conversion of the village of Napaskiak took place during 1905 and 1906, as we saw briefly in my Introduction (sec.2); and we have seen from that example that the Yup'ik villagers with an Aleut resident came soon to maintain the liturgical services themselves (they were visited only occasionally by one of the ordained priests, who were also Yupiit). In Alaska, the music that accompanies the Divine Liturgy of St John Chrysostom developed according to Native tones while the structure of the divine service has remained integral, including the wording of the hymns. In Europe, these masterpieces of music were written to accompany the celebration of the same divine service and they follow precisely the same structure (the same that is found in the commentary by Germanus of Constantinople in the eighth century and earlier). This is an amazing quality in my eyes: that something as refined as the Divine Liturgy of St John Chrysostom could be engaged by Yup'ik people, while simultaneously the refinement would engage the genius of European fine artists. This coincidence reveals much about the sensitivities and the potential of these Alaskan people, in accord with their own unsevered spiritual and social processes. It reveals much about the spiritual qualities, including aesthetic endowment, of the ancestral Arctic culture(s) that could engage these dynamics and would retain them.

This kind of engagement may allow a real possibility for elements to combine creatively. A creative synthesis did occur. Ancient Yup'ik Eskimo elements and Russian Orthodox elements have combined. Now during the Twelve Days of Christmas (from the Nativity to the Theophany), the Yup'ik villages visit each other. They feast and give gifts in a distinctly Yup'ik manner. This takes place in harmony with the celebrations of the Orthodox liturgical services: indeed the customs flow to and from the church buildings or chapels. For instance, at Christmas a representation of the star of Bethlehem is blessed during a liturgical service in the village chapel. The star is then carried through the village by processionists intoning seasonal hymns and carols. The processionists thus 'follow the star' from the chapel to homes, where they are received into each home and are hosted generously in each. At the end of the day's round of visits, the star is returned in procession to the chapel. The procession occurs day after day during Christmastide. This ritual festivity is known as *Selaviq* in the Yup'ik language today. It is known as 'Starring' in Alaskan English.[65]

As the Yup'ik *Selaviq* flows to and from the liturgical services, we may see that these liturgical services have been ingrafted within the Yup'ik mid-winter ceremonial festivities and that the mid-winter ceremonial festivities have been imbued with Christian meanings and orientation now. Similar 'Starring' is known among other Alaskans, and quite similar customs are known also among Carpatho-Russians, Ukrainians, and Romanians (it may have been known furthermore in regions across Russia from where men who assumed vital roles in the initial Christianization in Alaska had derived: further research could bring this to light). Yet among the Yupiit, characteristics that corresponded are held in continuity from the Yupiit's own antiquity, so that we may say: Their antiquity is *retained transformed* — drawn up in their own way from their own roots unsevered.

It is deeper into the corresponding dynamics that we shall proceed next, with solid footing on the foundations provided by patristic theology: further into the dynamics of divine participation, to discover a point of comprehension where these ancestral Arctic culture(s) could engage and retain the new faith and its practices.

NOTES

[1] To achieve historical specificity as well as thematic economy, I shall exclude the missiological discussions, or debates, about 'contextualization'. My reason is twofold. Firstly, this transition took place before those discussions about 'contextualization' began. They are relatively current, occurring for merely a century now. We may recognize that the outlook described in this chapter gives rise to perceptions and methods known as 'contextualization'. We should recognize that such perceptions and methods had already been realized in Russian-American in the early nineteenth century and in other locations earlier yet. Furthermore, the theory of correspondence that will be developed here from a patristic viewpoint is predicated upon 'panentheism', a concept that has not yet entered squarely into the missiological discussions about 'contextualization' (this concept will be described in Ch.3, while some aspects essential to it are introduced in the present chapter).

For material in this chapter previously published, see Mousalimas (1989b, 1988c): the current work supersedes the previous. Also see id. (in print b).

[2] This transition among the Aleut and Alutiiq peoples took place within the expansive Greek Orthodox *ecumene* (for this phrase, see Intro., sec.3.ii) where patristic theology remains authoritative. Therefore the sound basis, or precedents, for a theory of correspondence here must be found with reference directly to the patristic sources. My references to St Irenaeus of Lyons and St John Cassian of Marseilles should suffice to indicate that the patristic 'affirmative outlook' was widespread geographically. Another example would be St Gregory of Rome who could provide a complete example of the 'affirmative outlook' if a chapter were to concentrate on the history of missions. The purpose in this chapter is to contrast two outlooks as succinctly as possible.

[3] Why include a contiguous group of people? While focused on the Aleut and Alutiiq peoples, the theory generated by this study extends to other peoples in the Arctic, and this extension should be demonstrated clearly and securely in the body of this text. Netsvetov serves as a link: he was Aleut by maternal descent; and therefore through this example we may appreciate one of the effects of the transition among the Aleuts: their giving rise to spiritual missionaries who evangelized neighbouring Alaskan peoples in subsequent generations.

[4] Valaam (1894a:20-37; 1978:13-23). Cf., Gideon (1989:33-680), also in Black (1977b); Veniaminov 1840b, 1984. Cathedral *hieromonk* Gideon, compiler of the Kodiak ethnography had been sent by the Holy Synod of the [Russian] Orthodox Church to bolster and examine the mission between 1804 and 1807. The priest Ioann Veniaminov ministered in the Unalaska and the *Novo Arkhangel'sk* parishes between 1824 and 1838, having arrived in Russian-America for this assignment in late autumn 1823. Veniaminov has already been introduced and will appear often in this study.

[5] Valaam (1894a:23-24, 36; 1978:15, 22-23).

[6] Ibid. (1894a:35). Cf., Valaam (1978:22); but an error occurs as that translation continues (p. 23): 'originally God's Revelation was limited in all its purity to the

European peoples alone.' But Valaam (1894a) wrote, 'the Hebrew people': 'народа еврейскаго'. Justin, πρὸς Ρωμαίων σύγκλητον [henceforth: 2 Ap.] vi.3, will be cited with reference to the editions as Justin (1915:83, 1987:204).

[7] For the word δόξα, translated as 'glory', see Liddell and Scott (1940:444): (i) expectation; (ii) notion, opinion; (iii) opinion others have of one, mostly of good repute; (iv) glory, splendor, generally magnificence. For this word for the glory of God, see: Gen. 31:16, Ex. 16:10, 24:17, 40:34, John 1:14, Acts 7:55, 22:11, 2 Cor. 3:18.

[8] Justin, 2 Ap. viii.1, xiii.3 (1915:84, 88; 1987:208, 216).

[9] Ibid., viii.1 (1915:84, 1987:208).

[10] Ibid., x.1-8, xiii.6 (1915: 85-86, 89; 1987:210, 216).

[11] Id., πρός Ἀντωνίνον [henceforth: 1 Ap.] xlvi.2-4 (1915:58-59, 1987:160); also see 2 Ap. xiii.4-6 (1915:88-89, 1987:216).

[12] Clement, Στρωματεῖς I.v.28.1-3 (1985: 17-18). See Theophilus, πρός Ἀυτόλυκον ii.24-25 (1970:64-67, 1948:156-162). For Irenaeus, see Williams (1927:189-199).

[13] If such a description were to be extracted from context however, then a misconception might occur. It might appear to imply a contemporary typology instead of a retrospective one: as if Clement of Alexandria had been advocating the teaching of philosophical systems to students as a prerequisite for their comprehension of Christian theology. This would be a misleading appearance, particularly if applied to systems of logic such as the Aristotelian categories and the 'Porphyrian Tree'; because elements in those systems can work away from, not towards, certain principles operative within patristic theology (as I shall indicate in Chapter 3). The contrary direction should be expected particularly with regard to Porphyry who was the author of a treatise against Christianity.

[14] Athanasius, περὶ τῆς Ἐνανθρωπήσεως [henceforth: Ἐναν.] iv.16, vi.2-4 (1971:142, 146); also see ibid., lines 19 and 4-5 (1973:276, 282). Notice the verb tenses in the original: διεφθείροντο, ἠφανίζετο, παραπώλλυτο.

[15] Ibid., xlvi.24-25 (1971:236); also see ibid., line 27 (1973:414).

[16] See esp. Basil, πέρι τοῦ Ἁγίου Πνεύματος xvi-xxiv (1892:77-113).

[17] As cited above: Athanasius, Enan. xlvi.24-25 (1971:236); also see ibid., line 27 (1973:414).

[18] Basil, Ep. 234 [to Amphilochius] (1966:41-42); also see ibid. (1857a:869C-870B).

[19] Chrysostom, πέρι Ἀκαταλύπτου i.280-281 (1970:124). Also see ibid., ii.359-361, ii.370-371, iv.113-115 (1970:170, 172, 238). For the theological relationship between Chrysostom and the Cappadocians in this respect, see Christou (1973). We must be aware that the mutuality of these terms and concepts would be lost however, should οἰκονομία/οἰκονομίαι be translated as: 'le gouvernement de l'universe' and 'les desseins de Dieu'; and be interpreted apart from ἐνέργειαι. A conceptual separation of the cosmos from the divine might then result instead, except in terms of governance. See these translations in Chrysostom (1970:125, 171, 173, 239).

[20] Cross and Livingstone (1983:1352).

[21] Cited as Tertullian (1960:92, lines 5-6). See ibid. (1870:272): 'it has marked the

whole man'; but cf. ibid. (1960:93): '[it] has involved the whole man.'

[22] Cited as Augustine (1969:98, 1953:80). Also see id., *ad Laurentium*, Ep. ccxiv.3 (1911:382 [repr. 1930:408]; 1930:409); but cf. (1956:59): 'clay of perdition'.

[23] Cited as Augustine (1902:200-201); ibid. [43 (xxxviii)] (1887:252).

[24] Ibid., xxxix.44 (1902:201-202, 1887:253); id. *'De peccatorum meritis et remissione, et de Baptismo'* I.xii.15, I.xv.20 - I.xx.28, II.xxvii.43, III.iv.7 (1913:15-16, 20-27, 114-115, 133-134); see ibid. (1887:20, 22-25, 62, 71). Also see H. Chadwick (1986: 111). Also see Cross and Livingstone (1983:109): 'At times Augustine shows himself to be frankly Predestinarian. The whole human race is one mass of sin (*massa peccati*), out of which God has elected some souls to receive His unmerited mercy. There is no other explanation of the elect and non-elect than the inscrutable wisdom of God, and babies who die unbaptized go into everlasting perdition.'

Compare Tertullian, *de Anima* xxxix (1947:55-56, 1950:270-271), who assigned this condemnation to children of pagan parents and attributed the corruption to these parents' invocations of pagan gods during gestations and births.

[25] Tertullian, *de Anima* lx (1947:56).

[26] The RSV phrase is equivalent to 'reborn' in a rendition of Tertullian's verb in a comparatively modern English translation, and the KJV phrase is identical with a rendition in an older translation: See Tertullian, *de Anima* lx (1950:271, 1870:504). The Latin versions of the Bible to which I shall be referring for 1 Peter 1:23 are: the critical edition of the *Vulgate* (Wordsworth and White 1949), and the Stephanus editions of the Latin Bible. The latter are a series of successive editions printed by Robert Estienne at Paris and Lausanne during the first half of the sixteenth century.

[27] For other Old Testament verses, see 'recenseo' in Fischer (1977:4361).

[28] Tertullian, *de Anima* xli.3 (1947:57, 1950:273).

[29] See: Brown 1967:350, 398-407; H. Chadwick 1986:115-117).

[30] Cited as Cassian, *Conlatio* XIII.xii.1 (1894:428, 1886:378). For Cassian, see O. Chadwick (1968)

[31] Ibid., XIII.viii.3 (1894:426, 1886:371).

[32] Ibid., *Conlatio* XIII.v.2 (1894:424, 1886:365-366).

[33] Concilium Carthaginense, AD 418, in Munier (1974:69- 77). Also see the main phrases in Latin in the 'Canons of the Carthaginian Council of AD 418, dealing with the Fall and Original Sin', in Williams (1927:391).

[34] Concilium Arausicanum, AD 529 [Second Council of Arausio (Orange, France)] in Clerq (1963:53-76); also in Bright (1880:384-392). For this council, see Cross and Livingstone (1983:1001). For translations of the main clauses, see Bettenson (1963:86-87). Also see Bettenson (1963:84-85): 'The decisions of Carthage were not popular throughout the Church, and the full Augustinian doctrine did not win wide acceptance.' Also see Williams (1927:389): '[Augustine's doctrine] can not be said to have ever attained to acceptance in a literal sense *ubique et ab omnibus*. Not even in a modified and secondary sense of the term, therefore can it claim to be the ecclesiastical doctrine *par excellence*.'

It may be useful to note that in the Greek Orthodox *ecumene* where (as I understand it), Augustine's 'Retractions' are taken more literally than his earlier speculations, there is no special commemoration for him: he is mentioned among other saints on a single day, June 15, while the hymns of that day attend to the Prophet Amos instead. In the short *Μηναῖον* printed in Rome in 1900, and in the new edition printed by Φῶς in Athens (not dated), his name is not found at all.

[35] See Padgen (1982:19, 71, 115, 133, 178, 193).

[36] This translation (Aulén 1931) is an abridged version of his Olaus Petri Lectures for 1930, delivered while he was bishop of Lund. In 1913, he had become a professor of systematic theology at the university in that city.

[37] Cross and Livingstone (1983:327).

[38] E.g., Calvin, *Institutionis* [henceforth: *Inst.*] 2.2.4 (1962: 245, lines 18-25). See ibid. (1845:304 [1949:226]).

[39] Cited as Calvin (1961:62, 1552:886, also in 1870:265).

[40] Cited as Calvin, *Inst.* 2.1.6 (1845:290 [1949:216]). See ibid. (1962:235, lines 30-34).

[41] Ibid., 2.1.8 (1962:237, lines 24-26). See ibid. (1845:293 [1949: 217-218]).

[42] Ibid., 1.3.1 (1962:37-38). See ibid. (1845:55 [1949:43-44]).

[43] See Ch.1, sec.2.i.d. Berkh cited with reference to the translation as Berkh (1979:42). Bolshakoff (1943:84-85).

[44] For the educational policy and its affects on Alaskan languages, see: M. Krause (1980:13-25, 92-99; 1988:149); R. Dauenhauer (1980). Personal communications by people who are now over sixty and seventy years old in Juneau and in Kodiak about incidents at those locations, and in Anchorage about incidents at Unalaska. Also see: Worl (1988:320), Pullar (1991:14-19). For further published substantiation see the transcribed autobiographies in McClanahan (1986), where the multilingualism that had been maintained into the mid-twentieth century throughout southern Alaska is contrasted in almost every account with the monolingualism prevalent by the 1980s. Also see my Intro., nt.55, above. For a further correlation, see Toynbee (1935:221-227), esp. pp.221-215.

[45] Sarah Elders and Leonard Kamerling, 'Tununeremiut: the People of Tununak', Alaska Native Film Project, University of Alaska Fairbanks (c. 1977). Towards the conclusion of this century, the Christian Yupiit have themselves revitalized many of their traditional dances (ibid.). This film was shown at the 7th International Inuit Studies Conference, University of Alaska, Fairbanks, 19-24 August 1990.

[46] Williams (1950:397). Williams was the Lady Margaret Professor of Divinity at the University of Oxford, and Canon of Christ Church Cathedral, when he wrote this article, published in its first edition in 1926.

[47] Yannoulatos (1983:222-223). For considerations of the ancient rites and religion of these peoples, see ibid., pp.71-73, 108-119, 194-216; cf., English summary, ibid., p.267. Serving in Kenya, Yannoulatos was the bishop of Androussa in Nairobi, and a professor of theology at the University of Athens. Since then, he has concentrated his efforts in Albania.

[48] Ibid., p.221.

[49] A comparison of a similar kind was indicated earlier in this study from the report by Cherepanov on the western Aleutian Islands, 1759-1763, when Russian and Aleut hunters performed customary rituals similar to each others' (Ch.1, sec.1.v). A comparison can be developed with detail now, predicated on the theory of correspondence as supported by patristics.

[50] Meyendorff (1984:9), citing Taft (1980/81:46 [nt.10]). The commentary remains standard among, or typical of, the instruction provided to Orthodox seminarians in general to the present day; so, the same commentary, or another text containing the same standard concepts, would have been read at the theological school in Irkustk where Netsvetov (as well as Veniaminov) studied in the early nineteenth century. For the Liturgy in religious missionary work in general, see Bria (1986:17-23); Clapsis (1989); Stamoolis (1986:86-102).

[51] It is significant that this Russian-Aleut priest, a Native Alaskan himself, was the main celebrant of the Divine Liturgy (as well as the head of mission) in this region at this time; therefore in this note, I shall substantiate the fact that he would have been the main celebrant.

Netsvetov was assigned as the sole priest of the newly established *Mikhailovskii-Kvikhpak* (Yukon) Mission in 1844, arriving in this capacity in 1845. He was assisted in this mission by a deacon and a sacristan, each of whom was of Russian and Alaskan parentage himself also. The Russian-Aleut deacon was Innokentii Shaiashnikov. In 1848, Shaiashnikov was ordained to the priesthood by bishop Innokentii (Veniaminov) who had come to Ikogmiut on a pastoral tour; and Shaiashnikov was sent from Ikogmiut to Unalaska to serve as the Unalaska parish priest. The Russian-Aleut sacristan Konstantin Semenovich Lukin became the mission's deacon, or a rank of deacon, at bishop Innokentii's hands then. Another young man became a rank of deacon for the mission at the same time: this was Netsvetov's own nephew Vasilii, who unfortunately died sometime in the mid- or later 1850s. Lukin remained in the mission as Netsvetov's mainstay. He had derived from a family prominent at *Kalmakovskii*, the redoubt on the Kuskokwim River (for the Lukin family, see Black 1984c:469-479); and he was renowned as a hunter of special magnitude in the region encompassed by the *Mikhailovskii-Kvikhpak* (Yukon) Mission. These are very significant qualities in this context, therefore they merit emphasis: Netsvetov's mainstay, Lukin, the deacon of the mission under Netsvetov's authority, derived from a prominent Native Alaskan family of this region and was known as a hunter of special ability.

Four assistant priests were assigned in succession to this mission (Black 1984c:482-484). Netsvetov would have had seniority among them until 1861 at the earliest. *Hieromonk* Filaret arrived in the summer of 1848, but returned to *Novo Arkhangel'sk* the following summer. *Hieromonk* Gavriil arrived in 1853, but he was suspended in 1856 (evidently he was unbalanced). *Hieromonk* Theoktist was assigned here in 1858, where he remained for three years, having been transferred across the breadth of Russia for a decade previously, being sent farther eastward and northward in each instance. In 1861, *hieromonk* Ilarion arrived, a responsible man who eventually received the leadership when Netsvetov was summoned in 1863 to *Novo Arkhangel'sk* by the auxiliary bishop Petr (who had replaced Innokentii). Netsvetov soon died there, in *Novo Arkhangel'sk*. Ilarion continued here, in the mission, until 1869.

[52] Netsvetov (1984a:67).

[53] Ἱστορία ἐκκλησιαστικὴ καὶ μυστικὴ θεωρία, xxxvii, xli, cited with reference to the edition as Germanus (1984:86, 94).

[54] Ibid., xli, p.94.

[55] Fienup-Riordan (1988:266, 264, 268); Oleksa (1985:117).

[56] Fienup-Riordan (1988:264, 267-268); Morrow (1984:123- 127). For *yua*, see (see Ch.5, sec.1.ii, below).

[57] According to Morrow (1984:126), masks were not a predominate feature of *Nakaciuq* in the village of Old Kashunak.

[58] Fienup-Riordan 1988:269, 1986:52; Morrow 1984:137-138; Nelson 1899:358-359, 395; Ray 1981:27. For further descriptions of ritual masks, see Ch.3, below.

[59] Netsvetov (1984a:56-57). The drum would normally have been the wide tambourine-shaped drum, held in one hand and beaten with a drumstick; and the beat could have been solemn, as Yup'ik song and dance is often reserved and subdued.

[60] Nelson (1899:369).

[61] Zagoskin (1967:123).

[62] Netsvetov (1984a:57, remarks to journal entry dated 22 September 1847; also see p.227, remark to journal entry dated 7 January 1851). It is interesting in these entries in his journals that he was very strict about this distinction and was most intent that it should be communicated to his flock, but he was not vociferous in his writings in this regard: also see ibid., p.68, jounal entry dated 16 December 1847.

[63] Cf. Daniélou (1973:20).

[64] Previous to Netsvetov's arrival in this immense mission region, a chapel had been constructed only at the *Kalmakovskii* redoubt on the Kuskokwim River, within which people were 'continually holding prayers' themselves (Netsvetov 1984a:6-7). In 1851, during Netsvetov's ministry, a church building was constructed at Ikogmiut, the mission centre on the Yukon River towards the Bering Sea. Until that date at Ikogmiut, Netsvetov used a church tent (also known as the church's field tent). Once pitched, the church tent remained in place here. It was different from a lodging. The church tent was used for the celebration of the Divine Liturgy.

During his pastoral visits throughout the vast region, wherever a church building or chapel had yet to be constructed, he would pitch a portable church-tent for the duration of the visit. Where a church tent had been placed for the Divine Liturgy, there the tent would be set again by Netsvetov during subsequent visits: at the very same site. This practice is reported consistently throughout his journals.

Netsvetov used the church tent, wherever necessary, during all seasons. For instance at Ikogmiut in October 1845 (before the church building had been constructed there), he conducted the services of Matins and the Hours inside a yurt due to the cold, then he proceeded outside and into the church tent to celebrate the Liturgy. Due only to the more intense cold would he refrain from using the church tent. On 12 March 1849, the temperatures had fallen to '35 degrees in the morning, 26 degrees at noon, and by evening 30 degrees' below zero. (The bread and wine would have frozen in the chalice in the tent.) Furthermore, he was not feeling too well. So, he celebrated the Liturgy in a house that morning. By the end of the same month, 31 March 1849, the weather had become more seasonable and tolerable (a mere seven degrees below zero), and so he resumed his normal practice, as he wrote:

As the weather was fine, though cold, and the cold was tolerable, we were able to hold the services in the tent without hinderance, while the temperature was 7 degrees below zero.

For specifically these entries in his journal, see: Netsvetov (1984a:.5, 133, 135).

Other formal services. such as Matins and the Hours, were conducted by this priest in a yurt or a house; and we may recall that laity were observing formal prayers in their yurt at Unalaska in 1779 (see Ch.1, sec.1.v., above).

The practice of using a church tent for the celebration of the Divine Liturgy was normal in the Atka and Unalaska parishes also: there likewise church tents would be used wherever church buildings or chapels had yet to be constructed, and the church tents would be pitched anew at the very same sites — in space made especially sacred by the divine celebration. For this practice in the Atka parish, see, e.g., Netsvetov (1980:37), pastoral visit to Bering Island in May 1830; cf., p.78, pastoral visit to the same location two years later by which time a 'prayer house' had been built. For the Unalaska parish, see, e.g., Veniaminov (1993:57, 98-99, 110, 130-131, 157), pastoral visits 8-10 July 1827, 3 May 1829, 26 July 1829, 17 April 1830, 10 and 14 August 1830, 20 April 1832.

[65] For *Selaviq*, see: Fienup-Riordan (1990a:94-122); also see Inouye (199), and Oleksa (1992:190-192, 200).

CHAPTER 3

Point of Comprehension

The dynamics of divine participation correspondended, and they comprised
a vital *point of comprehension* where these ancestral far northern culture(s) could
engage and retain the new faith and practices — to comprehend not merely in
a theoretical manner, but in a profoundly existential way: for it may well be
said that the divine is ultimately communicated existentially, through direct
participation.[1]

To indicate the correspondence, and to locate this point of comprehension,
I shall describe 'panentheistic participation in the cosmos' as expressed tradi-
tionally in the Greek Orthodox *ecumene:* firstly with regard to the *dynamics*
reflected within manifold culture aspects; secondly with regard to the *concept*
evident consistently in theological articulations by the Ecumenical Councils.
Whether the dynamics in the ancestral far northern culture(s) were also
panentheistic is unknown: the evidence is insufficient to allow a credible conclusion of that sort,[2] and I shall address the question further in this chapter.
The correspondence should become evident nonetheless; and the vital point
of comprehension may then be seen through a comparison between icons and
ritual masks.

(1) Panentheism, Defined

The significance of the term 'panentheism' can be found in its Greek etymology: πᾶν meaning 'all', ἐν 'in', θεός 'God'. Inherent in this term is the
existence of '*all in God*', and equally inherent is, reciprocally, the presence of
God in all, while the transcendence of God from all phenomena is maintained
by the very word God. The term panentheism is thus able to convey divine
immanence and divine transcendence as complementary realities; indeed the
term can allow no less than boundless immanence and the most radical transcendence.

Transcendence in its most radical sense attributes to the divine the freedom
beyond every constraint:[3] a freedom that must be an attribute of the omnipo-
tent God. It allows the divine an unlimited activity free from every

116

categorization and every restriction that govern other phenomena. The divine thus transcends by being essentially different from all, instead of by being away from all. Rather than placing God in a dimension apart, this transcendence allows the divine to permeate all more-or-less, depending upon the degree of participation. Rather than placing God outside, this transcendence allows the divine a boundless activity within: a potentially unlimited, and possibly surprising, participation of God in all, and reciprocally of all in God.

This radical sense of transcendence may clarify the phrases introduced in the preceding chapter: *transcendent divine essence* and *immanent divine energy*, or *operation*. While they might seem to imply a primitive paradox, as if God were outside and inside simultaneously, up there and down here at the same time, they actually express a sublime consistent logic. As the divine is essentially different from all, and thus beyond all categorizations, the divine can be kinetic, operative, energetic fully within any category, without restriction and without diminution. This sublime logic allows the cornerstone of the Christian faith: the Incarnation of God in man in real terms.

The complementary qualities of transcendence and immanence in panentheism (*all-in-God*) can be seen in contrast against the simple immanence in pantheism (*all-[is]-God*), and in contrast at the other extreme against the simple transcendence of deism and theism. The meaning of 'deism' may be found in its own etymology. While the term might appear to derive from the word *deus*, it derives more probably from the Latin preposition *de* that more clearly represents the deists' view that the cosmos is *away-from-[God]*, or *apart-from-[God]*. Deism posits a separation of the divine from nature. This allows a natural theology but without special revelation and without divine intervention. When the eighteenth century English deists were translated into French by Diderot as 'théistes', the term deism became confused with theism; but the distinction can be useful, so that deism is reserved to signify a cosmology that allows a concept of God while precluding any divine participation.

'Theism', on the other hand, may allow instances of special revelation and intervention by God in history. In religious studies, this term has been used against polytheism to indicate One God or One Source, and also against pantheism to indicate this One existing apart from nature. But the latter usage can lead to a false dilemma, as if the alternative to pantheism were the theistic (and deistic) separation from the divine. The false dilemma is intensified by the predominance of theistic and deistic worldviews in the contemporary world.[4] For this reason, a term other than theism is needed that will serve to indicate a difference from pantheism, and at the same time allow divine immanence. This term is panentheism.

(2) Panentheistic Participation:
Cultural Dynamics in the Greek Orthodox Ecumene

The dynamics of panentheistic participation are articulated through manifold culture aspects in this *ecumene*, as evident in the following examples from: (i) patristic literature; (ii) iconography; (iii) popular literature; (iv) folk traditions; and (v) liturgical traditions.

(i) Patristic Literature

For a single example, St Athanasius of Alexandria (developing ideas expressed in the theology of St Justin the Martyr and of other early patristic writers) describes a threefold reality to explain the Incarnation of God in Jesus Christ: the divine transcendence; the divine immanence; and this immanence made specific in the Incarnation:[5]

> Being in a human body, and vivifying it himself, he [the divine Logos] is also vivifying all, and existing in everything: yet is he outside all. And known through the works in his body, he is not imperceptible also through activities in all.

Athanasius's phrase 'yet outside all' expresses the transcendence. His phrase 'vivifying all, and existing in everything' expresses the immanence. And 'being in a human body, and vivifying it himself' is the immanence made specific in the Incarnation in Jesus Christ. Clearly expressing this threefold dynamic again, Athanasius continues:[6]

> He was not bound by the body, but rather he held it, so that he was in it and in every thing, and yet outside, resting with the Father alone. And this is the wonder: that as man he was living the human life; and as Logos, engendering the life of all; and as Son, existing with the Father.

The same threefold dynamic is expressed in the Gospel according to John 1:1-14. Firstly, the transcendence is articulated:

> In the beginning was the Word [the Logos], and the Word was with God, and the Word was God. The same was in the beginning with God.

This Gospel then expresses the immanence:

> And all things were made by him; and without him was not anything that was made. In him was life; and the life was the light of men. And the light shineth in the darkness; and the darkness comprehended it not. ... That was the true Light, which lighteth every man that cometh into the world. He was in the world, and the world was made by him, and the world knew him not.

Finally, the immanence is made specific in the Incarnation:

> And the Word was made flesh, and dwelt among us (and we beheld his glory as of the only begotten of the Father, full of grace and truth).

(ii) Iconography

The same dynamics are expressed through icons of Christ. In the φωτοστέφανον — the *crown of light*: the oriental halo that encircles the whole face — there are normally three Greek letters around Jesus Christ uniquely, not found within the φωτοστέφανα of saints who have been sanctified through Christ: *omicron*, O, at one side; *omega*, Ω, at the zenith; and *nu*, N, at the other side. Together they spell the participle with its masculine article: O ΩN, 'the Being', or 'the Existing'. This is the name that God pronounces for Himself to Moses in Exodus 3:14 in the *Septuagint*, translated between the third and first centuries BC. God speaks from the 'burning bush', itself a literary symbolic prefiguration (according to an understanding within patristics) of the human nature in the Incarnation, aflame with the divine without being consumed. At the same time, the participle, O ΩN, is a designation for the existent principle permeating and vivifying the cosmos that was known in pre-Christian Greek philosophy. The icon communicates that this immanent principle has become Incarnate uniquely in Jesus Christ.

Both Athanasius and the Gospel according to John communicated the same in writing with reference to the Logos, as we have just read; and both then described this immanent principle as personal (not an impersonal force as conceived by the philosophers). Iconography through painting communicates the same dynamics that theology communicates through writing. The divine incarnate in Jesus Christ is the divine immanent in the cosmos.

(iii) Popular Literature

'God and nature are one and the same thing,' says Dostoyevsky through the voice of a humble character named Maria in the novel titled *The Possessed*. An innocent crushed by her sufferings, she articulates this suddenly, emphatically, in the presence of an important abbess who, tending toward theism and moral legalism, balks. The wise woman flounders foolishly when the simple fool states the full breadth and implication of the divine immanence.[7]

Without the slightest qualification from the mouth of this humble woman, the unmitigated articulation that is meant to contrast boldly against the abbess's narrowly rigid worldview, might seem pantheistic; but the articulation derives from the fluid pen of Dostoyevsky who describes the dynamics of panentheism with detail through another character, the saintly *starets* Zossima, whom the author insightfully develops at length in *The Brothers Karamazov*. Expressing the difference of God in relation to 'God's work' that 'strives towards the Lord', Zossima articulates the divine transcendence while the *starets* is in conversation with a young peasant:[8]

> 'But,' asked the lad, 'can Christ really be with them?' 'How could it be otherwise,'
> I said to him, 'since the Word is for all; all creation, all creatures, every leaf are

striving towards the Lord, glorify the Lord, weep to Christ, and unknown to them accomplish this.'... And I told him how a bear once came to a great saint, who was seeking salvation in a little hut in a forest. And the great saint was filled with tenderness for it, went up to it fearlessly and gave it a piece of bread: 'Get along with you,' he said to the bear, 'Christ be with you.' And the ferocious beast went away obediently and meekly, without doing him any harm. And the lad was deeply moved that the bear had gone away and that Christ was with him [the bear], too. 'Oh, how good that is,' he said, 'how all God's work is good and beautiful.'

The transcendence thus expressed, the immanence is also described by Zossima in conversation with the same peasant, whom he tells that 'Christ has been with them [the birds of air, the beasts of the field, the leaves, and the blades of grass] even before us'.

An implication of this immanence is drawn out by the *starets* as he describes even the minute creatures partaking 'in the mystery of God' (ibid.):

Every blade of grass, every small insect, ant, golden bee, all of them knew so marvelously their path, and without possessing the faculty of reason, bore witness to the mystery of God, constantly partaking in it themselves.

Further implications of the immanence are drawn out by Zossima later when he describes his 'young brother' who 'asked forgiveness of the birds'. The *starets'* condescension to his young brother's act remains unconfused with any notion of crass animism, as the personality of the *starets* has already been developed within many chapters and many discourses:[9]

My young brother asked forgiveness of the birds: it may seem absurd, but it is right nonetheless, for everything, like the ocean, flows and comes into contact with everything else: touch it in one place and it reverberates at the other end of the world.

Zossima likens 'everything' to 'an ocean' to describe the inter-relatedness of all creation. According to the perception in patristics everything is indeed sustained by and permeated with, held together by and recapitulated within, the divine Logos; or as St Athanasius would express the perception: the divine Logos is 'the source of Life to all the universe, present in every part of it.'[10]

Zossima continues with a repetition for emphasis, and then with advice:

Everything is like an ocean, I tell you. Then you would pray to the birds too, consumed by a universal love, as though in a sort of ecstasy, and pray that they too, should forgive your sin. Set great store by this ecstasy, however absurd people may think it.

He repeats for emphasis yet again: 'Love all men, love everything, seek that rapture and ecstasy.'[11]

Finally Zossima advises: 'Love to fall upon the earth ceaselessly ...' He is advising frequent prayer with the prostrations that are customarily made; yet an allusion is also involved, one that rests upon the fullest implications of panentheistic participation: the author allowed Maria to express it most boldly, and it is implied now as Zossima finishes the sentence and then continues: 'Love to fall upon the earth and kiss it. Kiss the earth ceaselessly and love it insatiably.'

The earth with its fecund beauty reveals the sacred to another insightful, however less saintly, character in the novel with Maria. In Dostoyevsky's novel, Shatov likewise admonishes: 'Kiss the earth, drench it with your tears, ask forgiveness.'[12]

(iv) Folk Tradition

Shatov's exhortation corresponds to a folk tradition recorded in Russia. A peasant woman makes obeisance to the earth to atone. A moment earlier she made peace with the members of her family, and then with 'the fair sun, the clear moon, the numberless stars, the dark nights, the soft showers, the raging wind'. Now, she atones to the earth: Why? — because she must cut the earth with a plow to bring forth food to sustain her life. So, she brings her forehead to the earth; and sighing, she prays:[13]

One further blow, my foster-mother,
I wish to touch you with my head,
To beg your blessing,
Your blessing and your pardon.
I have torn up your breast
Cutting with the iron ploughshare.
Never have I smoothed your face,
Never have I combed your locks;
I have bruised you under the harrow
With its teeth of rusty iron.
Foster-mother, pardon me,
In the name of Christ our Saviour,
Of the Holy Mother of God,
Of Blaise our intercessor,
Elias the wise, the prophet,
And the knightly George.

Her act seems lucid. She does not confuse the divine energy immanent in the earth with the specific Incarnation in Christ; nor yet does she confuse Christ with any of the saints, all of whom she invokes integrally. We may say that she is in lucid communion with the divine.

Yet while perceiving the divine in the very earth, this Russian Orthodox peasant in the north is also aware of a tragic disharmony, for her subsistence derives from her cutting that divine beauty when she plows. So, she atones. Similarly, the Orthodox Yup'ik hunter in Alaska — (this example is from modern Yup'ik Christian customs; the extended example in Chapter 2 was from Yup'ik pre-Christian ritual) — perceives the divine in the animals on whom his subsistence depends. And he atones. He restores harmony with the animals by honouring them: respectfully keeping the bones of a land animal, respectfully keeping some inner part of a sea mammal, then returning these in due season to the land or to the sea with thanksgiving, and with supplication that these animals may come again to his home.

The Greek Orthodox shepherd in Arcadia takes a lamb away from the sheepfold to slaughter to feed his family. The mother ewe, distressed by the separation, perhaps also by an intuition, is frantic, she butts, she bleats. And the shepherd sighs deeply: for in these harsh mountains, his small flock is part of his household; and in these harsh mountains, he too has known the death of offspring. The shepherd and his flock suffer alike. But on this day, the lamb has been cut in preparation for the feast of Pascha (Easter) when it will become an image of Christ the Lamb. In the middle of that coming night, the shepherd (like the hunter, like the peasant) will hold a candle in the darkness, and will sing: 'Christ is risen from the dead, trampling down death by death.' Then during the day of feast, the shepherd will dance in celebration of the Resurrected Saviour who suffers with us, who sustains us, who promises to restore life to all.

Among Romanian Orthodox folk early this century, Mircea Eliade similarly observes that 'central motif' of Pascha: 'All Nature sighs, awaiting the Resurrection'. The motif was expressed also by Dostoyevsky, as quoted earlier: 'all creation, all creatures … weep to Christ' as they 'are striving towards the Lord'. This motif is recognized by M. Eliade as being central in 'the religious folklore of Eastern Christianity'.[14]

(v) Liturgical Tradition

Cosmic participation in the suffering, death and resurrection of the Logos is articulated also in liturgical traditions: indeed there is a time on Good Friday before Easter when the unity of this liturgical articulation along with folk, iconographic and patristic articulations becomes vividly manifest.[15] During that evening in anticipation of the Resurrection, the people will cluster in the nave of their church around the *epitaphion*, the representation of the tomb of Christ that they have beflowered (but decorated otherwise colourfully in colder climates). This representation of the tomb of Christ is placed in the nave where their own members' coffins have been and will be placed. Gathered here, around the *epitaphion*, the people sing hymns of lament that become hymns of faithful joy in expectation of Christ's ultimate triumph for us over death. These hymns are so very popular in some locations, throughout Greece for instance, that they are known by virtually all; and they are sung with emotion by the people.

As the Logos is praised within the initial set (*stasis*) of these hymns, the participation of the cosmos in the Passion is articulated:[16]

> The whole creation was altered by thy Passion: for all things suffered with Thee, knowing, O Word [Logos], that Thou holdest all things in unity.

The cosmic lament is voiced for a few verses through Mary the Mother of God, who recapitulates the cosmos within her grief, before the hymns again praise the Logos with complementary images of hope:[17]

> 'Who will give me water and springs of tears,' cried the Virgin Bride of God, 'that I may weep for my sweet Jesus?'
> 'O hills and valleys, the multitude of men, and all creation weep and lament with me, the Mother of our God.'
> 'When shall I see Thee, Saviour, Light eternal, the joy and gladness of my heart?' cried the Virgin in her bitter grief.
> Thy side was pierced, O Saviour, like the rock of flint in the wilderness; but Thou has poured forth a stream of living water, for Thou art the Fount of Life.

Each set of these hymns culminates with verses such as the one above that turn sorrow into joy with the anticipation of the Resurrection. Analogously, the tomb has been turned to beauty beflowered. The tomb is expected to burst with Life, just as the winter is expected to burst into spring, just as the darkness of this night itself is turning into daylight.

In that morning, Holy Saturday morning, all creation will join in the celebration during the Divine Liturgy when flowers (or evergreens) are brought forth from the altar and are strewn throughout the nave while the 'Hymn of the Three Children' from the Book of Daniel — 'O all ye works of the Lord, bless ye the Lord. Praise and exalt Him forever.' — is sung.

But now it is the night. The time itself becomes a simile: 'Thou art hidden like the setting sun beneath the earth and covered by the night of death: but, O Saviour, rise in brighter dawn'. In the next set of these hymns, the sun stands alongside the moon in mourning, through an allusion to the solar eclipse at the Crucifixion: 'The sun and the moon grew dark together, O Saviour, like faithful servants clothed in black robes of mourning.' In the third and final set, the cosmos is joined by the people in its lament: 'Come, with the whole creation let us sing a funeral hymn to the creator.'[18]

How can the cosmos be understood thus, as suffering and sighing, and, at the same time, be perceived as imbued with the divine? We may find the answer where we began in this section of this chapter, within the theology expressed by St Athanasius who explained that the divine Logos immanent in the cosmos is the divine Logos incarnated in Jesus Christ. Once we see the divine Logos suffering for us in Jesus Christ, we may also see the divine Logos suffering for us in nature, sighing with us even there, vulnerable to us even there, indeed communicating the divine to us even there in nature.

The Difference from Naïve Pantheism

So vital and vivid is this expression in liturgical traditions, in folk traditions, in popular literature, in iconography, and in theology alike, that a question might arise, and indeed it should arise, about the principles inherent that would keep such culture(s) from tending, instead, toward a naïve pantheism. Two such principles are readily available.

To begin with, cosmic disharmony is not necessarily conceived as deriving from God. Rain may turn to hail, rivers may flood, waters shimmering with beauty may suddenly swell: yet the Logos is always represented as life-giving; always rational, never irrational, not even whimsical. Neither is the disharmonious conceived as resulting from the act of creation, but instead from a marring of the nature by the subsequent Fall.

The divine is described as benevolent through Orthodox theology, and the concept about divine participation is reserved for these benevolent aspects. However, the attribution of some malevolent aspects to the divine does remain a somewhat popular notion. This type of attribution is indicated slightly in one of the quotations from Dostoyevsky (above) when the humble innocent character Maria, crushed by her sufferings, exclaims emphatically: 'God and nature are one and the same.' This tension creates the brilliance in the biblical story of Job, who waivers between asking 'Why has God allowed this to befall me?' and 'Why has God done this to me?' The lucid difference can be obscured in the depths of one's pain. (And it need not even be something as profoundly disorienting as pain that causes the confusion: in America today, storms, fires and floods, and sometimes even epidemics, are regularly referred to as 'acts of God'.) Therefore the attitude cannot be easily dismissed. Yet it does differ from the theological articulations that are meant to guide. The difference needs to be emphasized. This difference is manifest even in folk traditions, such as that transcribed by Pascal from the Russian peasant woman (as explained above).

For this purpose, I render the distinction through the use of two extended phrases: the phrase 'divine participation in nature' permits the inclusion of non-benevolent aspects, as pests and pestilence are part of 'nature'; while the phrase 'divine participation in the cosmos' excludes malevolent aspects, and reserves panentheistic participation for the benevolent, as a meaning of harmony and benevolence is intrinsic within the word 'cosmos'.

Secondly, there is the demonic that is not imputed to the divine. Instead, the Logos Incarnate in Christ expels the demonic. This is as manifestly true in folklore as it is true in theology. We can see this represented theologically in icons of the Epiphany where Christ stands in the waters of the River Jordan. Ashore, John the Baptist attends to him. On the opposite shore, a company of angels are ready to receive him: the human and the angelic together around Christ. On both sides of the Jordan, the earth rises stylistically as if reaching upwards in an ecstasy of prayer; and inside the river, towards the banks, a very few figures of fish, or sometimes of tiny human beings, are almost imperceptible as they represent the nature of waters, innocent and neutral, who behold in amazement as Christ, looking out from the waters and from the icon, peacefully blesses us while beneath his feet is a humanoid or sauroid demon, rendered small, relatively insignificant, crushed underfoot.

We can hear the same theme in Alaskan folklore. The major tale among the Orthodox Dena'ina tells of holy water, the Bible, and church incense expelling a deadly evil spirit-person which intruded into the village.[19] A folktale among the Orthodox Alutiiq tells of an icon and church incense warding off evil spirits in the mountains.[20] This recurrent theme in Alaskan folklore is recurrent also in the Gospels and in patristic writings, and constitutes one of the principles in the culture(s) of the Greek Orthodox *ecumene* that differentiates the dynamics of their panentheism from naïve pantheism.

(3) Panentheistic Participation:
A Concept Consistent Throughout the Ecumenical Councils

It is thus mostly the dynamics of panentheistic participation within the cosmos that are reflected in such culture(s) of the Greek Orthodox *ecumene*; and it is this kind of divine participation that is articulated, and indeed defended, by the Ecumenical Councils. Although the term panentheism was not coined through these councils, the concept can be recognized as of central importance to them, when they are viewed thematically through three phases that follow sequentially, one to the next: from participation (a) in the Godhead, (b) through Jesus Christ, (c) into the physical cosmos.

(i) Three sequential phases

The contribution of the following section is the organization of the Ecumenical Councils into these phases to highlight this concept intrinsic in them. The data for the councils' dates and issues are standard. What is presupposed here is that a reader will have some knowledge of these councils and of the relevant vocabulary, so that their primary issues can be arranged succinctly and expediently in this thematic summary. Should a reader find the summary

too compact and daunting in its economy, the reader may proceed directly to
the comparison in the next section of this chapter.

Only the primary issues from the Ecumenical Councils will be presented
here; and no pretence is assumed that such expedient dimensions would encompass the breadth of the history of doctrine. Within a wider thematic
development, more detail would be given to the subtleties of the polemics,
and the historical depth would be extended: for example, greater reference
would be made to the Gnostics' dualistic view of creation which was countered by mainstream Christianity prior to the First Ecumenical Council; and
in this regard, St Irenaeus of Lyons would figure predominantly, particularly
as he affirmed Genesis 1:31 against that dualism.[21]

(a) In the Godhead. The First and Second Ecumenical Councils concentrate
on coexistence and participation in the Godhead itself, as they recognize the
Persons of the Holy Trinity as integral realities, each fully divine in essence,
who indwell perfectly to comprise the One God.

The First Ecumenical Council (Nicaea, AD 325) expresses the Son's undi-
minished divine essence, one essence with the Father, against the heterodoxy
of Arius. The latter posited an ontological divide between the Persons of the
Trinity by rendering the Son a creation, albeit a pre-eternal creation, of the
Father. The Second Ecumenical Council (Constantinople, AD 381) expresses
the undiminished divine essence of the Holy Spirit against the heterodoxy of
Macedonius who shifted the ontological divide by positing it instead with the
Father and the Son on the one side, while the Holy Spirit was diminished on
the other side, as a creation.

Thus in these two councils are the Persons recognized each as perfectly divine and coexistent. Each participates with the Others to comprise the single,
indivisible Godhead.

(b) Through Jesus Christ. The next four councils concentrate on the union of
the divine with the human in the Incarnate Second Person of the Trinity, Jesus
Christ. The Third Ecumenical Council (Ephesus, AD 431) emphasizes the
union as hypostatic, in other words as thoroughly pervasive, against the heterodoxy of Nestorius who kept divinity and humanity conceptually apart. He
posited a contiguous union in which qualities were exchanged only in name:
for example, the divinity could be only said to have been born of Mary; the
humanity could be only said to be life-giving, according to Nestorius. The
Fourth (Chalcedon, AD 451) attempts to clarify the hypostatic union further
by describing the undiminished divinity and the undiminished humanity as
integral realities alike, unconfused while yet inseparable, in Jesus Christ.

The Fifth (Constantinople, AD 553) counters a resurgence of Nestorianism
by censuring the works of Theodore of Mopsuestia that were being circulated

in place of Nestorius's own; and by stressing that God the Logos (the second Person of the Holy Trinity) became passible through the Incarnation and actually suffered, died and was resurrected in his humanity. The Sixth Ecumenical Council (Constantinople, AD 680-681) counters the opposite extreme as manifested in the Monothelite heterodoxy, which confused the integral realities, instead of separating them as did the Nestorians. The Monothelites diminished the reality of Christ's human volition in favour of an emphasis on the divine will alone. In response, this council emphasizes that the second Person of the Holy Trinity incarnated was tempted in everything as we are, and resisted those temptations through human volition in synergy with, never usurped by, the divine will. Undiminished divinity had assumed the human experience entirely.

Thus in the Third to Fifth Ecumenical Councils are humanity and divinity acknowledged as completely, pervasively coinherent in an unconfused while indivisible unity in Jesus Christ, so that undiminished divinity is totally participant with completely integral humanity.

(c) Into the physical cosmos. The Seventh Ecumenical Council as well as the subsequent Constantinopolitan councils concentrate on the participation of the divine in the created cosmos. The Seventh Ecumenical Council (Nicaea, AD 787) defends the material representations proper to the divine, particularly icons and also the relics of saints, against iconoclasts who denied that divinity could be active within created physical nature except uniquely in the elements of the Eucharist.[22] The defence is reiterated in Constantinople (AD 843) after another surge of iconoclasm.

The defence is articulated further in Constantinople (AD 1341 and 1351) to express the immanence of undiminished divine energy, and to express the potential for our own immediate participation in this divine presence, or energy: an articulation necessary against the heterodoxy of Barlaam who was, one may say, a theist of a sort. The perceptions affirmed at these later councils in Constantinople (AD 1341 and 1351) were articulated particularly by St Gregory Palamas who is commemorated annually on the second Sunday of Great Lent. The first Sunday is the liturgical celebration of the restoration of icons (their restoration after the iconoclastic assaults); and through the proximity of these annual liturgical celebrations, the theology regarding the divine particularly in material icons is joined manifestly to the theology regarding the divine immanent in creation as articulated by Palamas. Indeed just as the one Sunday follows from the other, so the theology of divine immanence articulated at Constantinople in 1351 and 1351 follows from the theology of icons articulated at Constantinople in 843 and Nicaea in 787. Together they comprise the third phase; and the later councils have a doctrinal authority 'scarcely inferior to the Seven General Councils themselves'.[23]

Thus, in the Seventh Ecumenical Council and the later Constantinopolitan councils is the immanence affirmed of undiminished divinity within integral physical phenomena, without confusion or diminution of either reality: the Creator continues to participate immediately within creation. Thus do the three phases follow one from the other thematically: from participation (a) in the Godhead, among the divine Persons of the Trinity, to (b) participation of divinity with humanity in the Incarnated Second Person of the Trinity, Jesus Christ, to (c) participation of the divine undiminished in the created cosmos. And they follow in particular direction: the participation is thematically from the divine into creation.

(ii) The reciprocal direction

Creation participating in the divine is expressed explicitly particularly during the third phase, yet it is inherent throughout from the beginning. It may have been the very reason for controversies, the Councils maintaining this dynamic against heterodox constructs which would separate the divine from the cosmos, and which would thus diminish the possibility of creation's participation in the divine.

In the first phase, the indwelling of the Divine Persons has an effect upon the reciprocal movement of creation within the divine. When the First and Second Ecumenical Councils emphasize that each of the Persons of the Trinity is fully divine by essence, these councils are affirming that divinity is fully present without diminution in the act of creation by the Father through the Son in the Holy Spirit. Creation implies no lessening, neither through emanation nor through a demiurge. In contrast Arius and Macedonius both posited a demiurge, by rendering the Logos in the one instance, the Holy Spirit in the other instance, as a lesser divinity than God the Father. Constructions such as those by Arius and Macedonius might meet the demand in some philosophical systems that uncreated divinity be categorized exclusively apart from creation: the demiurge acting as the intermediary; but those constructs would preclude the participation by creation in the fullness of divine presence. An intermediate separates. The demiurge stands between. Against this separation do the First and Second Councils affirm that creation derives from, and that creation is sustained by, no less than complete divinity. Therefore it is with undiminished divinity that we are immediately in contact.

In the second phase, the same relationship is at risk. Any division posited between the divinity and the humanity in the Person of Jesus Christ would (again) separate the fullness of uncreated divinity from the creation. Consequences would ensue affecting our reconciliation to God in Christ, because the processes of salvation would then have to be interpreted in terms other than dynamic participation. Concepts of election or merit would become dominant, while the dynamics of participation and *theosis* would be either confined to ethical development alone or altogether lost.[24]

At the other extreme during this second phase were the heterodox confusions that diminished the humanity in Christ. By compromising the integrity of creation, they would circumscribe or preclude the participation of our integral selves within the divine: they would circumscribe or preclude the possibility of the sanctification of our whole being. So vital are these dynamics of the participation of integral humanity with complete divinity that the controversy continued against the two extremes to the end of the seventh century.

The third phase follows, as the Incarnation imbues creation further with divinity. This phase begins with the relationships in iconography. Here, participation is predicated upon the relationship between image and archetype. And, here, any confusion of substance is rejected, so that realities remain integral, unconfused: all the more so because here participation is not the same as the *hypostatic* union in Christ. The icon is not the same as its archetype, instead representing it by participating in the archetype's existence.

The reciprocal movement involves the sanctification of created nature through this iconic participation, so that St John of Damascus could declare: 'Divine grace is conferred on material icons, by virtue of the persons whom they depict.'[25] While icons are the primary focus of attention, the implications for the veneration of saints' relics would be of concern at the same time: and thus the implications for our direct interaction with the saints themselves.

The later Constantinopolitan councils clearly articulate the potential of humanity to participate within divinity, indeed to participate in the divinity undiminished and immanent in the cosmos. The defence is pastoral. Simple monastics came under attack intellectually, because they claimed to have had an immediate experience of the divine, one they would not explain as being of anything other than of God. Their perception was as of pervasive, divine light, the same as that perceived by the Apostles on Mount Tabor at the Transfiguration of Christ. But their experience was rejected by Barlaam who felt that these men were coarsely imputing a material, sensible quality to the immaterial divine. Like Nestorius, Macedonius, and Arius before him, Barlaam insisted on a division of the divine from the created cosmos, and the consequences were the same: the separation of creation from immediate participation within the divine.

In defence, St Gregory Palamas, bishop of Thessalonica, differentiates between the divine essence and the divine energies, or operations.[26] He explains that creation is sustained and pervaded by divine energy while the divine essence remains radically transcendent from, and utterly unknowable by, created nature. Neither is there confusion, as the Creator is other than creation; yet nor is there division, as the divine energy is fully present, so that undiminished divinity creates and sustains creation, and therefore can be experienced in creation.

A simile may be useful for the distinction. The divine essence and energy in relation to creation is like the sun and sunlight in relation to the earth. While the sunlight vivifies us, and is perceived by us, we are utterly incapable of perceiving the source, the sun itself, not only because of its intensity, which is normally beyond our capacity, but furthermore because we are constantly in a position relative to the sun that will never allow us a perception of the source itself: by the time the sunlight infuses our world, the source is already in a different location relative to us. We always perceive the sunlight, never the source, even when we are focused directly on the orb itself. The simile however is insufficient: unlike the sun, the divine essence remains immutable; unlike sunlight, the divine energy is undiminished in intensity from the fullness of the source. Yet the simile is useful, for it is the sun that vivifies us, nothing other than the sun, in its energy, or its operation. And it is the sun that we perceive, although never the self-same source, never the essence.

Some of the implications inherent at the councils in AD 325 and 381 are thus re-articulated a millennium later, in AD 1341 and 1351; for at the earlier councils, creation is affirmed as occurring through the operation of undiminished divinity; and a millennium later the same is affirmed, that creation occurs through the operation of undiminished divinity. The implications for the human experience of undiminished divinity are then articulated at the later councils, because this experience had to be defended explicitly at the time. The way had be maintained unobstructed for this experience.

Perceived thematically through these sequential phases, the Ecumenical Councils can be understood as having been convened to defend against limiting definitions, instead of presumed to have been convened for the sake of defining. Rather than define, these councils set boundaries to guard against diminution. They set boundaries on one hand against any division between the divine and creation, and on the other hand against any confusion of integral realities. Boundaries are set and reset against that chasm on the right and against those confusions on the left, particularly against the chasm — while the way ahead is maintained open, unobstructed, for the boundlessness of divine manifestation and for the limitlessness of divine-human participation. Can there be a more rational approach to the divine than this? — an approach that defines against limitations of the divine.

A simile for this approach is that of a thimble in the sea.[27] A thimble is like the created cosmos, and more specifically the created consciousness of humanity.

The sea is like uncreated divinity. A thimble in the sea is filled and keeps being filled. Supremely rational is a stance that would allow the thimble to be so filled, and to continue to be so filled, through the operations of the uncontained sea, according to the sea's own qualities. Irrationality would occur as soon as the thimble supposed itself capable of containing the expanse, or supposed itself capable of categorizing all the possibilities of the sea's movements.

(4) Participation through Icons and Ritual Masks: a Comparison

The previous sections of this chapter have concentrated upon the concept of panentheistic participation articulated by the Ecumenical Councils, and the dynamics also reflected in other cultural aspects in the Greek Orthodox *ecumene*. The concentration has been meant to emphasize that this concept and these dynamics are centrally important in Russian Orthodox Christianity. The centrality allows the following statement: To comprehend this faith and its practices, one must be able to grasp the dynamics of divine participation, if not specifically panentheistic participation.

In the present section, evidence will be provided to indicate that this ability existed within the ancestral Aleut and Alutiiq cultures. This point of comprehension existed because divine participation, although articulated differently in some ways, was operative centrally within the ancestral far northern culture(s) also.

This point of comprehension will be indicated through a comparison between icons and ritual masks, a single example that is meant to recapitulate the correspondence. Other examples could be developed: for instance, the dynamics of naming could be compared, as a name may be an audible image analogous to the visual images of the icon and of the ritual mask;[28] and by extension from the iconic quality of names and the participatory dynamics of naming, a further example could be developed about hymns and prayers, as glimpsed in the first chapter of this study regarding the sacred cosmos of the Aleut and Russian hunters, and evinced in the second chapter regarding rituals. Yet other comparisons will be provided in subsequent chapters.

Masks were used in rituals throughout southern and western Alaska. They were used in the seasonal public ritual festivals by the ancient Aleuts of the central and eastern Islands, by the ancient Alutiiqs (Koniag and Chugach), and by the northern and central Yupiit. Masks were used in shamans' rites by the Dena'inas and the Tlingits.[29]

Likewise, icons are essential to major ritual. This is clearly explained in the following quotations from two intellectuals of the twentieth century. The first is from P. Sherrard, a Britisher knowledgeable in the history of Orthodoxy, and a translator of Greek monastic texts:[30]

The first thing that has to be said about the icon is that it is not simply a work of art similar in kind to other works of art. ... For an icon exists within the particular framework of belief and worship to which it belongs. ... An icon divorced from a place of worship is a contradiction in terms.

The framework of belief and worship to which the icon belongs is the Christian liturgy. The art of the icon is liturgical art.

The next quotation is from L. Uspenskii, an iconographer who was a member of the Russian emigrant community in Paris:[31]

It is absolutely impossible to imagine any liturgical rite in the Orthodox Church without the icon. The liturgical and sacramental life of the Church is inseparable from the image. ... As an object used in worship, the icon is not merely occasioned or inspired by the liturgy, but it forms with the liturgy a single and indivisible whole.

Il est absolument impossible d'imaginer dans l'Église orthodoxe le moindre rite liturgique sans icone. La vie liturgique et sacramentelle de l'Église est inséparable de l'image. ... Objet de culte, l'icone n'est pas seulement provoquée ou inspirée par la liturgie, elle forme avec elle un tout homogéne.

Icons are, and masks were, highly visible, essential components in the respective rituals.

Ritual masks were made with special care as sacred objects. On the central Aleutian Islands, for instance, masks were constructed by mask-makers in a special place which was safe from all impurity. Before beginning, the mask-makers performed ablutions; and while constructing, they washed the masks to keep them unpolluted. Throughout southern Alaska, masks were often burned or deposited in caves after rituals.[32] Likewise are icons made while the iconographer engages himself in asceticism for self-purification. The iconographer prays and fasts for the attainment of spiritual perception; so that he may acquire 'spiritual eyes' and 'spiritual ears', according to Ph. Kontoglou, a Greek iconographer, who explains:[33]

No one enters uninitiated into the sea of mysteries. It is necessary that his spiritual senses be attuned, that they may grasp the spiritual tones and spiritual forms and colours.

The iconographer's task is to depict spiritual dimensions, or more precisely to depict those physical dimensions transfigured within the spiritual. The depictions themselves conform to traditional types, as the iconographer exercises his own inspiration and own ability within the inherited tradition, so that the icons assume a timeless, other worldly quality.

Thus icons are, and masks were, sacred objects: integral to ritual and integral to the sacred cosmos. More to the point, icons are, and masks were, involved in the realities represented.

Ritual masks were identified with the archetypes represented; and the mutual identification could extend into a tripartite fusion that included the person wearing the mask. This has been noted by observers and commentators throughout southern Alaska:

> The mask is an object made by men that, when used ritually, transforms the wearer so that he becomes, for as long as he wears the mask, a living representation or incarnation of beings outside the human sphere but with power to affect events therein. (Black 1982a:29)

> The painting of the wooden masks [allowed] the dancer to become visible to the spirit world and in fact to embody the spirit at the same time that his human identity was hidden from the world of men. (Fienup-Riordan 1986:52)

> [Le chaman] fixera d'eux [des esprits] des images, leur permettra de s'incarner, qu'ils l'accompagneront, troupe fidèle, dans ses pérégrinations extra-terrestres auprès des grands maîtres. (Lot-Falck 1957:15)

> ... masks were not worn as concealment or disguise, but for visual and psychological transformation into the animal or supernatural being represented by the mask. During the wearing of the mask, the dancer or performer was suffused with its spirit. (Ray 1981:27)

> When worn in any ceremonial ..., the wearer [of the mask] is believed to become mysteriously and unconsciously imbued with the spirit of the being which his mask represents ... (Nelson 1899:395)

> ... when an actor puts on the mask he is supposed to become imbued with the spirit of the being represented. (Hawkes 1941:17)

> The masks of the shaman represented his spirits and, when he put one on, he not only was supposed to resemble the spirit in outward appearance, but he actually became inspired by that yek [spirit], and spoke and danced as the yek. (Laguna 1972:690)

> When the shaman puts it [the mask] on, he impersonates this particular spirit and loses his own identity. (Emmons in Laguna 1972:692)

> The Koloshi [Tlingits] believe that during the shamanistic seance it is not the Shaman himself who acts but one of the Yeik [spirits] who has entered into him. (Veniaminov 1840c:72; 1984:406)

In a similar manner, icons are associated with the realities whom they represent and whom they make perceptible, although perhaps not to the same degree. These realities are usually known as archetypes, or prototypes, in the theological literature about icons. The icons' association with their archetypes is relational, not substantial. In the words of St John of Damascus in the early eighth century:[34]

> An icon is a likeness, a similitude, a representation of someone. While showing in itself the person who is being represented, the icon is not altogether like the prototype (that is to say, the person being represented) in every way, for the icon is one thing and the person being represented is another.

The same distinction is found just as clearly in writings by, for example, St Nicephorus of Constantinople (758-828) who explains that icons and archetypes are 'different objects according to their nature', and St Theodore the Studite (759-c.826) who states that 'Christ is one thing and his image is another thing by nature'.[35]

The icon thus reflects the archetype and makes the otherwise-unseen visible. This is evident particularly during liturgies, as described by Kallistos bishop of Diokleia and a don of Oxford University:[36]

> As each local congregation prays Sunday by Sunday, surrounded by the figures of Christ, the angels, and the saints, these visible images remind the faithful unceasingly of the invisible presence of the whole company of heaven at the Liturgy. The faithful can feel that the walls of the church open out upon eternity, and they are helped to realize that their Liturgy on earth is one and the same with the great Liturgy of heaven. The multitudinous icons express visibly the sense of 'heaven on earth'.

In the preceding chapter, the co-celebration was described in hymnography for cherubim and seraphim who join in the Liturgy to worship something greater that encompasses us all. Now this co-celebration is described in iconography; it includes saints as well as angels; and its dynamics extend yet further than co-celebration, because there is direct interaction between the angels and saints and the human participants.

Prayers as well as acts of respect are directed by the faithful through the icon to the reality depicted: to Christ, to the saint, or to the angel. Reciprocally, by virtue of its depiction of the sanctified reality, the icon serves as a channel of the reality's sanctified presence, or energy, as expressed clearly and carefully in theological terms during the eighth and ninth centuries especially, when great thinkers were expressing the theology of icons in response to the iconoclasts. Here are some of these statements:

> by means of the icon we venerate the person depicted. For, as St Basil says, 'The honor given to the icon passes to the prototype.' (John of Damascus, Εἰκόν. III.xli)[37]

> When we honor and venerate an icon, we receive sanctification. (6th Act of the 7th Ecumenical Council)[38]

Thus, if one should say there is divinity in an icon, he would not err, as it is also in the figure of the cross, among yet other divine offerings; not by a natural union [not by a union of natures] however, for they are not the deified flesh, yet by a relative participation because they share in grace and honour. (Theodore the Studite, κατὰ Εἰκονομάχων I.xii)[39]

Divine grace is conferred on material icons, by virtue of the persons whom they depict. A robe of purple silk receives no special honor in itself, but if it is worn by a king, the garment shares in the honor that is due to the wearer. So material objects are not venerated in themselves, but if the person depicted is full of grace, the material object shares in this grace to an appropriate extent. (John of Damascus, Εἰκόν. I.xxxvi, II.xxxii [Scholion])[40]

The icon is a point of interaction with the archetype represented. The icon is also a point of intersection between heaven and earth.

We have arrived at a level where now we may see at a glance the similarity between icons and ritual masks by reading two quotations juxtaposed: the first from theology, the *Life of St Stephan the Younger* (+ c.764), written by Stephan deacon of Constantinople in the later eighth century;[41] the second quotation from Alaska anthropology:[42]

The icon is a door.

[Masks are]
eyes into a world or worlds beyond the mundane.

(5) Conclusions

The two quotations in juxtaposition recapitulate the correspondence; and they highlight the *point of comprehension* at the very centre of the ancestral Arctic culture(s): an awareness of spiritual realities in the sacred cosmos, including the awareness of their participation specifically through representations. Whether this awareness was expressed as a concept or remained as a less definite cognitive pattern is inconsequential. In either case, the awareness existed: the dynamics were operative.

This point of comprehension would allow such far northern culture(s) to grasp and to retain the Russian Orthodox Christian faith and practices. Remembering that the ritual masks were usually destroyed or deposited after use, and that their archetypes did not constitute a fixed pantheon, we may well envision the icons' arriving, being engaged by a people who could comprehend them, and then remaining.[43] The realities represented in the icons would be retained for continuing manifest participation.

Did iconographers emerge? Yes, of course, they did. A fine example is Vasilii Vasil'evich Kriukov whom Veniaminov described as follows: 'This young man,

very Aleut in character, alone and without instruction learned to paint icons.'
Some that are attributed to his hand have survived and can be seen in the
church in Unalaska, where they remain part of the liturgical setting today.
(Evidently, he was very gifted as an artist, as described further by Veniaminov:
'By and by he became such a skillful painter of portraits, using water colours,
that he had only to see a person two or three times and he would bring that
person's image alive on paper, covering the whole gamut of facial expressions.')[44]

Within the comparison between icons and ritual masks, differences are evident. It would be a misinterpretation of the evidence if the correspondence
were assumed to imply an equivalence. One difference involves the wearing of
ritual masks: they were often worn, while icons usually are not worn. The dynamic merits attention because of the tripartite fusion that can be engendered
(between the represented, the representation, and the representative or 'representor') when the mask is worn. An oversight would occur here however, should
this obvious disparity be interpreted too quickly as if it indicated a chasm of
non-correspondence. Tripartite fusion does also occur in Orthodox ritual, does
it not? — particularly in the vesting of the priestly celebrants for the Divine
Liturgy. The celebrant becomes iconic himself through his vestments.

The iconic quality of the vested presbyters and deacons is described as follows by St Germanus of Constantinople, whose commentary on the Divine
Liturgy served in the comparison in the preceding chapter:[45]

> The presbyters by imitation of the seraphic powers are covered with stoles as if by
> wings; and with the two wings of their lips, they proclaim the hymn, as they take
> the divine, noetic coal — Christ — bringing it into the altar with the tongs of their
> hands. The deacons, as they go around [in procession], with the wings of their
> linen *oraria*, are types of the angelic powers who have been sent out to minister.

The vested bishop is described next. The bishop's stole, τὸ ὁμοφόριον, is
worn upon the shoulders, hangs front and back to the length of the bishop's
other vestments, and is very wide in comparison with the deacon's stole, τὸ
ὀράριον (plural: *oraria*, mentioned in the preceding quotation). Through
the vivid imagery of Germanus's description, the vested bishop's stole becomes
particularly symbolic of Christ. The vested bishop is referred to as the 'archpriest'
in the following quotation, because he is the main celebrant:[46]

> The archpriest indicates by his stole the stole of Christ: the purple, bloody one
> worn by the immaterial God as porphyry adorned of the undefiled blood of the
> Mother of God and virgin.

The possibility of correspondence in this area becomes even more engaging
when we see the bishop, before entering the altar, standing in the centre of the
nave where he is vested in these garments by men of lower orders. Or, that is

to say, the possibility would become more engaging if evidence were brought forth to show clearly that during ancient Alaskan rituals a primary functionary was dressed in symbolic paraphernalia by assistants, not by his own hands.

An area of correspondence thus exists even to an extent with the dynamic of tripartite fusion. However, again, the correspondence can not be assumed to imply an equivalence. A difference within this area also exists, in the contextualization (the liturgics) and the conceptualization (the theology) that prevents the Orthodox iconic fusion of distinct realities from becoming a confusion. If fusion is allowed as a term to signify a combining of distinct things, then confusion is a disorder that would render these things indistinct from each other. The celebrant's own face remains visible during the Divine Liturgy. His distinct personhood remains immediately manifest, and therefore remains unconfused with any symbol he represents. The 'representor', the representation, and the represented remain *manifestly* distinct realities. The relationship between them remains iconic. The liturgical context furthermore prevents confusion by prescribing a reserved decorum for the religious celebration, so that intellectual processes remain lucid (to be explained in the next chapter).

Just as the liturgical context prevents confusion, so do the theological concepts. The iconic relationship is maintained conceptually as articulated by, for example, Sts John of Damascus, Nicephorus of Constantinople, and Theodore the Studite, all of whom stated (as quoted in this chapter) that the representation is one thing and the represented is distinctly another. The Orthodox context and concepts become even more vital as the symbols are perceived as poetic and experiential, instead of rigidly defined and fixed; so that they become known mainly through participation, instead of by rote: An unfolding participatory experience of symbols can then occur without much risk of confusion.

Important differences notwithstanding, a correspondence within the dynamics of divine participation exists nonetheless. And it may well be argued that, for the sake of the transition, the correspondence comprises the more important factor. Although the dynamics of divine participation occurred in different ritual contexts, and were sometimes channeled toward different archetypes, the very correspondence itself is the key factor. It comprised a point of comprehension that would allow the transition to take place as it did: as an indigenous and corporate movement; because the ability existed in these ancestral far northern culture(s) to comprehend the dynamics of divine participation.

An antithesis

The antithesis is implicit: where this point of comprehension has been diminished or denied, there divine participation would appear incomprehensible.

An example is provided by Lucien Lévy-Bruhl (1857-1939), an epistemologist who attempted a theory of participation from extracts from various ethnographies. Delivering a summary of his views in the Herbert Spencer Lecture at Oxford in 1934, he wrote seven books on the topic beginning in 1910, including *Les Carnets* published posthumously in 1949; and he has been translated into English, then republished in this language throughout the course of this century, most recently by Princeton University Press in 1985. Although he has paled to obsolescence in comparison with culturally-specific studies that have since been achieved, notably the ever timely work by E.E. Evans-Pritchard (1956) and by G. Lienhardt (1961), Lévy-Bruhl warrants some attention because he wrote voluminously on the topic of participation; and he is the only person to have written so much on this topic.

In his opinion, the dynamics of participation bore no relationship whatsoever with the rules of logic and with 'our mentality', as he termed it. 'Ours' would be his own: that which had become prevalent in his own circles. He referred to it also as 'our scientific mentality', a more definite term indicating the type of logic that was involved: the positivism and binary systems governing some then-contemporary fields of science, and exercised within a deistic cosmology if not atheistic.

But are the formal rules of logic actually contrary to the dynamics of divine participation? Such rules require that ontological categories be maintained apart: the attributes proper to one category can not describe another. These rules have been employed in patristic theology to explain the relative participation in iconic relationships.[47] When such rules are applied further than iconic relationships, then a divergence from patristic theology begins. Applied to the very Godhead, they conceptually would subject the divine essence also to these rules that govern created phenomena: the radical transcendence of infinite divinity would then become conceptually limited to the rules which bind finite created things.

Consequences through history from that type of application were the heterodox constructs of Arianism and Nestorianism, mentioned earlier: Arianism subjecting the Trinity to those categorizations, Nestorianism shifting them into the *hypostases* of Christ. From Arius and Nestorius to Barlaam, such constructs would conceptually limit the transcendent divine essence by confining the divine, as if God were Aristotle's Unmoved Mover. None could allow the quality of kinetic immanence as an actual quality of God. Once energetic immanence is described, then the phenomenon would need to be classed as something other than the Unmoved Mover, according to the dictates of those rules. An example closer to Lévy-Bruhl's own time was the application of Aristotelian categories and Porphyry's Tree into definitions of divinity in medieval Latin doctrinal systems.

In any of those constructs however, the potential for the divine to partici- pate within the cosmos was merely limited by the rules of logic (rules that were applied further than to the iconic relationship, to which they are proper, and were thus mis-applied). Divine participation is merely diminished by them. It is not entirely contradicted by them. Why, then, would Lévy-Bruhl reso- lutely insist upon a radical contradiction?

This was due (in my view) not so much to the 'rules of logic' that he asserted would themselves contradict the dynamics of participation, but due more spe- cifically to the deism, if not atheism, of 'our mentality' within which he was exercising those rules. As deism and atheism deny the existence of the divine as an active reality or as an objective reality in the cosmos, any statement that the divine is participating with cosmic phenomena must appear as other than a logical statement, indeed as other than rational, whether it be articulated within ethnography or metaphysics or theology. The deist or atheist may rec- ognize the internal connections that allow a coherence in some cognitive systems involving divine participation, a coherence that Lévy-Bruhl himself admitted. He would have to deny the rationality of any such system nevertheless, regard- less of the coherence: because he presupposes the divine to be ultimately non-existent as an active or objective reality.

Therefore from his first book on the topic to his last notebooks, Lévy-Bruhl described the dynamics of participation as 'prelogical' and 'incomprehensible'. They remained 'non-conceptual' for him, and 'deeply rebellious to intelligi- bility'.[48]

The point of comprehension did not exist for him, neither within his men- tality, nor within the society which had engendered his mentality.

In contrast, the Aleut and Alutiiq societies had developed the possibilities for divine participation, and thus in effect the possibility for a comprehension of patristic panentheism experientially. Whether the corresponding dynamics within their own societies were panentheistic cannot be known. In any case, the very point of comprehension existed at the heart of the ancestral Arctic culture(s), so that they could themselves grasp and retain the new faith and practices.

NOTES

[1] Cf. St Gregory Palamas, περὶ Ἡσυχαζόντων [henceforth: Ἡσυχ.] III.i.21 (1959:597). For the phrase 'Greek Orthodox *ecumene*' that will recur in this chapter, see Intro., sec.3.ii, above. For material in this chapter previously published, see Mousalimas (1997b, 1994, 1990a, 1990b, 1990c, 1988a): the present work super- sedes the previous.

[2] For studies that have begun to articulate the permeability or flexibility of some

categories within specifically Yup'ik cosmology, see esp.: Fienup-Riordan (1990b) and Morrow (1990). These studies were published in winter 1992, issued in periodical volume dated 1990. Also see esp.: Fienup-Riordan (1994).

[3] See, e.g., Gregory Palamas, Ἡσυχ. III.i.29, III.ii.9 (1959:612, 659).

[4] For the development of theism to predominance in European theology, see Williams, esp. Lecture 6 (1927:393-442). For a powerfully argued thesis regarding the development of deism into the scientific worldview, see Sherrard (1987).

[5] Athanasius, 'Ενav. xvii (1971:174); also see ibid. (1973:326).

[6] Ibid.

[7] Dostoyevsky, Possessed (1971:154), cited with reference to the translation quoted.

[8] Dostoyevsky, Karamazov (1982:346), cited with reference to the translation quoted. Cf. the following sources quoted in Ch.6, sec.3.iv, below: Valaam, ed. (1894:140, 182; 1978:86, 109) regarding bears, a mink, and the anchorite Herman of Alaska; also compare Ἱστορία [Historia (anon.)] xxi.15 (1961:127), regarding a hyena and the anchorite Macarius of Egypt.

[9] Dostoyevsky (1982:376).

[10] Athanasius, 'Ενav. xvii (1971:174); also see ibid. (1973:326).

[11] Dostoyevsky (1982:.379).

[12] Dostoyevsky (1971:261).

[13] Pascal (1976:12). Also see the prayer by an Old Believer, Anna Efimova, trans. in Riasanovsky (1985:81-82), citing: A. Pypin, 'Petr Velikii v narodnom predanii', Vestink Evropy [sic] 32, bk.8 (August 1897), pp.640-690, St Petersburg.

[14] Eliade (1988:38); Dostoyevsky, Karamazov (1982:346).

[15] This liturgical service is the Matins of Holy Saturday, sung in parishes on the evening of Good Friday by anticipation and announced in parish calendars for Friday evening. It is sung in monasteries in the middle of the night, properly as the matins of Saturday.

[16] The Praises of Holy and Great Saturday, Ware, trans. (1976:625); cf. Col.1:16-17..

[17] Ibid.., p.631.

[18] Ibid., pp. 626, 636, 640.

[19] Chickalusion (1982). Also see this oral history reported from the village of Kustatan in the journal of Ioann Bortnovskii, entry dated 23 June 1896, in Townsend (1974:18). For another example, see Alexandrovsk, vol.2, p.21: holy water and incense again dispel an evil spirit.

[20] J. Johnson, ed. (1984:12).

[21] See Lawson (1948:119-132). For summaries of Gnostic dualism, see Jonas (1963:250-253) and Rudolph (1983:57-60). For a comprehensive study of views of the Fall prior to and including Irenaeus, see Romanides (1957).

[22] See Parry (1996), Giakales (1994).

[23] Ware (1993:67).

[24] See Mousalimas (1987:284).

[25] John of Damascus, Εἰκόν. I.xxxvi (1975:148).

[26] E.g., Gregory Palamas, Ἡσυχ. III.ii.5-15 (1959:651-671). This vocabulary has been explained among the definitions in this chapter; and was introduced in the pre-

ceding chapter with reference also to: Basil the Great who used the same terms; John Chrysostom who used very similar terms; and Maximus the Confessor who developed much the same theme in terms of λόγοι.

[27] The simile has been assimilated from patristic literature: cf., Athanasius, *'Εναυ.* liv (1971:268); and Basil the Great, *Εἰς τὸν ριε' Ψαλμόν* ii (1857b:105D): but the latter is listed among *dubia* in *Clauis Patrum Graecorum*, vol.2 (Geerard 1974:166).

[28] Mousalimas (1990c).

[29] For the Aleuts, see: Netsvetov (1840:3, 6; 1984b:365-367), Veniaminov (1840b:87; 1984:199);. For the Alutiiqs, see: Black (1977b:86); Birket-Smith (1953:109-110). 'Koniag' and 'Chugach' are mainly anthropoligical terms found in these sources: for these terms, see Ch.5, intro., below. For the Yupiit, see: Morrow (1984:136); Nelson (1899:393-394); Sonne (1988:29-30, 40-45); Zagoskin (1967:226-227); also cf., Hawkes (1913:12). For the Dena'inas and Tlingits, see: Laguna (1972:690), Osgood (1937:178), Townsend (1965:303), Veniaminov (1984:406-407).

[30] Sherrard (1967:58), quoted in Ware (1976:58).

[31] Uspenskii (1960:10-11); trans. in Ware (1976:5). Also see Uspenskii (1982:461-462, 481).

[32] Netsvetov (1840:6; 1984b:367), Black (1982a:35), Edmonds (1966:84), Hawkes (1914:17), Laguna (1956:96, 273), Nelson (1899:359), Sonne (1988:30). Also see Birket-Smith (1953:127).

[33] Kontoglou (1963:99); cited also in Ware (1976:8).

[34] John of Damascus, *Εἰκόν.* III.xvi (1975:125).

[35] Nicephorus, *'Αντίρρησις* I.xxx (1865:280A); Theodore the Studite, *κατὰ Εἰκόνομάχων* I.xi (1860:341B). See 'Nicephorus and the Theory of Religious Images', in Alexander (1958:192) for the operative logic and for the similarity between Nicephorus and Theodore.

[36] Ware (1993a:271-272).

[37] Cited as John of Damascus (1975:143), trans. in Ware (1976:4). Also see *Εἰκόν.* I.xxxv, I.li, II.xxxi, II.xlvii, III.xlviii (1975:147, 154). For the quotation, see Basil the Great, *περὶ τοῦ Ἁγίου Πνεύματος* XVIII (xlv) (1892:92, 1968:406).

[38] 6th Act of the 2nd Council of Nicaea [7th Ecumenical Council, Nicaea, AD 787], in Mansi (1767:269), trans. in Ware (1976:6). Also see Sahas (1986:99).

[39] Cited as Theodore the Studite (1860:344B-C).

[40] Cited as John of Damascus (1975:148), trans. Ware (1976:6).

[41] Cited as Stephan deacon (1860:1113A), trans. in Ware (1976:3)

[42] Fienup-Riordan (1986:51). Also see Fienup-Riordan (1988:267): 'the eyes of the mask ... looked beyond this world into another.'

[43] For photographs of small portable icons including an Even ('Lamut') wooden diptych and a Russian metal triptych, the latter from the Aleutian Islands: see Fitzhugh and Crowell (1988:81), illustrations 87 and 89. So that the icon could be carried, the Russian metal triptych 'had a cord attached for suspension around the neck'; and the Even wooden diptych 'is equipped with a belt hook and leather case'. The Evens, also known in literature as the Lamut, extend from north-central and northeastern Iakutia to the northern coast of the Okhotsk Sea, opposite Kamchatka, including the region around the seaport of Okhotsk: this seaport became the main site for embarkation to

the Aleutian Islands subsequent to the initial contact periods (from the 1770s); embarkation took place from the east coast of Kamchatka during those initial periods, beginning with Bering's voyage from Petropavlovsk in 1741.

For a description of the church near Petropavlovsk in 1779, containing icons that were, according to this source, brought by the Bering expedition, see King (1784:303-304). Significant Aleuts were travelling to and from Kamchatka beginning in the mid-1740s, as explained in Chapter 1, with references, above. These Aleuts included, e.g., Ivan Stepanovich Glotov who visited Kamchatka for the first time in 1762, became the primary *toion* of Umnak and was conducting the services in the village chapel into the 1800s: see Ch.1 at nts 10-11 and 38, above; and Epilogue, sec.2, below.

For icons dated by inscription in the 1770s at Umnak, eastern Aleutians, see Black (1989b:162), also mentioned in Epilogue, sec.2, below. For icons at Kodiak in 1788, see Lopez de Haro (ms.:107), trans. in Moore (1979:69), described in Ch.1, sec.2.iii, above.

[44] Pierce (1990:268-269). Quotations in Pierce are from Veniaminov (1840b; 1984). For the Kriukov family, see Epilogue, nt.10, below.

[45] Germanus, Ἱστορ. ἐκκλη. xvi (1984:66); cf., Isaiah 6:1-6.

[46] Ibid., xxiv, p.74.

[47] See Alexander (1958:192).

[48] Lévy-Bruhl (1975:99). See the original (1949:130): 'la participation implique quelque chose de foncièrement rebelle à l'intelligibilité'. Also see ibid., p.135: 'la participation n'est pas une fonction logique'; p.138: 'pour se rendre compte de la participation, il faut avoir bien soin de se tenir sur le plan affectif, et de ne pas céder à la tentation de se laisser glisser sur le plan cognitif afin de se la rendre *intelligible*.'

CHAPTER 4

Ecstasy

Dynamics of divine participation within nature were operative in southern Alaska in many ways: in masking, as explained in the previous chapter, and in rituals as described in Chapter 2. Yet another way was through shamanizing. Through shamans' ecstatic experiences, the propensity for a participation with spirit(s) was highly evident. It is to a consideration of shamans' practices that our study will proceed.[1]

The shamans' practices comprised only part of wider ritual and spiritual configurations. Periodic ritual festivals were officiated by tradition bearers including song leaders who were not necessarily shamans, and daily domestic rites were observed by elders, who may or may not have been shamans.[2] Yet the shamans' own practices affected virtually the whole of the societies, as a shaman would practice at times regarding his kinship polity and at other times regarding particular members of that society. Therefore while only part of wider ritual and spiritual configurations, the shamans' practices constituted a central phenomenon within these societies nonetheless. They were a 'central societal phenomenon'.[3]

As the transition into Russian Orthodox Christianity involved these societies virtually in their entireties and took place largely through indigenous social and spiritual processes, a certain continuity should be expected from this 'central societal phenomenon' that would be analogous to the transformation of ritual masks into icons. A question rises about the expectation however, inasmuch as this phenomenon was ecstatic. Can a transformation of ecstatic phenomena be expected within a transition such as this?

The question will be addressed through two subsidiary considerations: whether sound patristic criteria exist to distinguish between ecstatic experiences; and if such criteria do exist, whether they were actually applied anywhere in the regions that comprise the focus of this study. Firstly, it will be necessary to define ecstasy as distinct from trance.

(1) Ecstasy, Defined.

Ecstasy must be differentiated from trance. Otherwise, a continuity of ecstatic experiences would involve a persistence of pathology, as trance is itself defined as a pathological state. Theoretical recourse cannot be taken into cultural relativism, because trance has discernable cross-cultural characteristics, including an insensitivity to one's immediate surroundings, an impairment of consciousness about one's experience, and sometimes a debilitation of one's body. A practicable definition is necessary that would allow some scope for ecstasy without trance.

Can a definition be found that will allow the distinction between 'ecstasy' and 'trance'? The following definition from a theologian, P. Christou, provides the distinction and also a scope to encompasses an adequate range of experiences:[4]

> The word 'ecstasy' was changed early from its primary meaning (a transposition from the familiar situation) to the metaphorical, referring to man's psychical level. The term is used particularly to indicate the condition in which the human nous, distanced from the worldly and ceasing from normal reactions to external excitement, experiences another sphere of things, be it a general experience of an other-worldly reality, or a specific comprehension of the divine mystery.

> The external characteristics that typify ecstatics, vary from complete calm to frenzy. In the former instance, the body remains unmoved, while the blood circulation and breathing remain slight; while in the latter instance, observably forceful movements occur. The duration of the ecstasy also varies, depending upon its form, and upon the means through which it occurs.

In this defintion, the constant meaning of 'ecstasy' throughout a range of experiences remains implicit within the etymology of the original word itself: ἐκ-στάσις signifies a *trans-position* and implies a transposition from the commonplace to an experience of other realities. Defined in this sense, the term 'ecstasy' is rather like the phrase 'altered states of consciousness' that has become current in some anthropological literature.[5]

While the definition just quoted derives from a theologian, a differing definition has remained influential in some other circles in the field of academic theology for more than a generation: J. Lemaître defines ecstasy as, and thus limits its content to, divine union.[6]

An adequate scope is allowed through Christou's definition for the *content* of various types of ecstatic experiences. Ecstasy may range in content from 'the comprehension of the divine mystery' to any number of manifestations of the other-worldly; and the latter could either be subjective phenomena such as collective representations and pyschologocial archetypes, or be objective hypostatic phenomena such as actual angels or demons. Thus allowing an adequate scope for the content of various ecstatic experiences, the definition also allows a practicable range for their *forms*, as ecstatic experiences can vary from 'complete calm' to 'frenzy': a range that can encompass the various forms of shamans' experiences described historically from the Aleutian Islands and the Kodiak area, whether they involved composure[7] or extreme animation;[8] unconsciousness (be it momentary or prolonged)[9] or cognizant role-taking.[10]

Trance may be involved in the form of an ecstasy, according to this definition; but trance is not requisite: a 'ceasing from normal reactions to external excitement' could mean an extraordinary quieting or concentrating of one's faculties. This extraodinary quality would be supranormal, 'ceasing from normal reactions' by being heightened above them, not necessarily paranormal or abnormal. This would not necessarily involve an insensivity to one's surroundings or an impairment of consciousness about one's experience, as we shall see. Thus, the possibility exists in this definition for ecstasy without trance.

Has the possibility (for ecstasy without trance) been allowed in studies of shamans' experiences in the far north? A differentiation has been achieved between 'ecstasy' and 'possession': Evidence has been brought forth to demonstrate that a shaman's ecstasy can occur without spirit possession.[11] But has 'ecstasy' been distinguished from 'trance' in this specialized field?

The distinction remains implicit in the monumental study by S.M. Shirikogoroff.[12] While merely implicit, it is very important. Trained in medicine with a speciality in psychiatry, then conducting in-depth field research among the 'Tungus', he recognized the existence of mental stability as well as physical health in the most effective shamans in some locations. Mental stability, he explained, would be required to maintain the ecstatic states effectively without toppling into pathological confusion. Physical health was needed for stamina on that razor's edge. He differentiated these effective shamans from others who manifested psycho-physically pathological conditions. However, while he provides insights for an understanding of various conditions among differing types of shamans, indeed in the very locations where the term 'shaman' originated, he did not involve himself explicitly in the contrast between the terms 'ecstasy' and 'trance'.

We may progress from a counterpoint instead. A categorical equivalence between 'ecstasy' and 'trance', even a synonymity between them, has been posited by Ä. Hultkrantz at Stockholm in his writings about 'shamanism'.[13] Defining 'ecstasy' as 'a state of trance', he has stated that they indicate 'the same thing': 'ecstasy' being used by students of religion and ethnology, 'trance' by psychopathologists and parapsychologists. The definition and statement were published well into his career: Hultkrantz had contributed publications on Native American 'religion' (as he termed the latter generically) since the 1950s; and on far northern Eurasian and American religious phenomena, including 'shamanism', since the 1960s. His definition and statement were neither revised nor contradicted in two full papers that he presented by invitation to the Regional Conference on Circumpolar and Northern Religions, the International Association for the History of Religions, organized by the University of Helsinki Department of the Study of Religions and by the Finnish Society for the Study of Comparative Religions.[14]

A.L. Siikala from Finland presented a full paper in a plenary session in the same conference; she likewise admitted the same equivalence of the terms. Regarding Siberian shamans' practices, she diverged from Hultrantz as she criticized his description of shamans' ecstasies as extreme trance and even hysteria. The Siberian shamans require consciousness to achieve the structured 'role taking' that she studied among them. Her divergence is significant. Yet, while the degree of trance has been mitigated, the equivalence of 'ecstasy' and 'trance' has again been posited nevertheless, as we may read in the following quotation:[15] 'As terms *trance* and *ecstasy* do not differ from one another except that the former is favoured primarily by anthropologists, the latter by students of comparative religion'. This quotation from Siikala could be a paraphrase of the statement by Hultkrantz. Only the attributions to the various academic disciplines differ somewhat in each, due perhaps to an actual overlapping of the uses of these terms in the numerous sources whom these writers have cited in their respective bibliographies.

Where might the equivalence of 'ecstasy' and 'trance' have derived in these Arctic studies more specifically? The equivalence evidently involves an hypothesis that ecstasy is itself a manifestation of a psycho-physically pathological condition. This hypothesis had been propounded in a multi-volume work on the general subject of 'ecstasy' written by E. Arbman, a professor of comparative religions at the University of Stockholm from 1937 to 1958. His work was cited both by Hultkrantz in Sweden and by Siikala in Finland alike when they posited the equivalence themselves.[16]

Earlier than Arbman, 'ecstasy' had been defined categorically as a state of pathological trance by W.R. Inge. Published subsequent to the Bampton Lectures that he delivered in the University of Oxford in 1899 about 'Christian Mysticism', Inge's definition underwent only a slight but significant revision in the Gifford Lectures that he delivered at St Andrew's University in Scotland. In the revision, he extricated the psychological dimension of Plotinus' ecstatic experiences, and thus any like Plotinus's own, from that categorical characteristic. Otherwise, psychological and physical disorder remained definitive of ecstasy.[17]

I am not suggesting that Inge was responsible for the hypothesis. On the contrary, the derivation may be discovered in the wider milieu in which he was lecturing (for an indication, see the translations of the biblical references to 'ecstasy' that are cited in the next section of this chapter, below). Yet he serves as an earlier example of the influence of the hypothesis. He also serves as an example of its currency, as Inge's definition remained current throughout the twentieth century: it has been included in the select bibliography for 'Ecstasy' in the *Encyclopedia of Religion* edited by M.Eliade towards the close of the century.

Once the hypothesis that ecstasy is a manifestation of a psycho-physically pathological condition is challenged, then the equivalence of the terms 'ecstasy' and 'trance' begins to be sundered, as we may notice in the next very influential example. E. Underhill's major book on the subject of 'ecstasy' was published twenty-one times from its first edition in 1911, including twelve revised editions, the last one in 1930 (cited here) reprinted in 1967; and this book has been included in no less than three select bibliographies in the *Encyclopedia of Religion*: those for 'Ecstasy', 'Mysticism' and 'Mystical Union'. Her definition remained even more current than Inge's through the course of the twentieth century. It may have been Underhill's study published in first edition in 1911 that was responsible for Inge's slight but significant revision published in 1918, when he extricated the psychological dimension of Plotinus's experience from the characteristic of pathology. Plotinus had been one of Underhill's primary examples for 'true or sane ecstasy', as she termed it. Other examples provided by her included Teresa of Avila and John of the Cross.

Underhill separated the terms 'ecstasy' and 'trance' when she emphasized the psychological health in instances of 'true or sane ecstasy', as she referred to them.[18] Trance was described as a physical result, to be distinguished from the psychological content as well as from the cause of 'sane' ecstatic experiences. She expected the physical disorder of trance, because she believed that the 'sane' ecstatic would need to strain away from the physical confines of this world, including those of one's own body, in order to sear through them for a direct experience of the divine. Physical disorder would be a manifest result as they 'singed their earth-bound bodies' for 'rapturous union with the divine'. Psychologically healthy they may have been, physically healthy they could not be, however. Yet Underhill's advance is important. She differentiated 'ecstasy' as a psychological phenomenon from 'trance' as a physical condition in these instances.

If the possibility were advanced further, so that physical health was admitted as well as psychological health in certain kinds of ecstasy, then the categorical association ecstasy with trance would need to be sundered. Ecstasy and trance

may coincide, as seen in Underhill's examples. However, they would not necessarily coincide

Where may physical health be admitted along with psychological health in
certain kinds of ecstasy? An answer may be anticipated from the cosmology
introduced in my preceding chapter. The possibility could be admitted within
pantheistic cosmology. An understanding may be obtained through some
short further contrasts. Within atheistic and deistic cosmologies, pathology
(whether psychological pathology alone or psychological and physical pathology combined) would need be definitive of ecstasy when the ecstatic claimed
any contact with divine or spiritual realities, because the divine and the spiritual are denied any objective existence in-and-of-themselves. The ecstatic who
claims to 'see', or to know, the divine or the spiritual must be ill, and the
ecstatic experience must be studied as such, as he insists that the non-existent
exists. Theistic cosmology differs. The objective existence of the divine and
spiritual is admitted, therefore the possibility for the psychological health of
an ecstatic who claims an experience of them is allowed. However the divine is
posited categorically apart from the physical world; and therefore the physically pathological state of trance would be anticipated as a result of even a sane
ecstasy, because the ecstatic would be expected to sear through the physical
confines to reach divine union. A recognizable result of a theistic ecstasy must
be the premature depletion of the ecstatic's physical resources, exhausted by
this straining away from the physical.[19]

In contrast within pantheistic cosmology, a straining away from the physical
would not necessarily be expected for immediate ecstatic participation, because the divine presence is known as immanent. The ecstatic need not
necessarily struggle away from the confines of the physical cosmos, including
the physical nature of one's own self, to reach the divine presence. An ascetic
effort, *ascesis*, for concentration and for self-purification may be required.[20]
This would be a struggle against passions, not necessarily against physical nature. Consequently, the pathological state of trance would not necessarily be
involved in true or sane ecstasy here. While trance might occur in some instances of ecstasy, it would not be a categorical requisite for sane ecstatic
experiences.

The divergence is vital. I believe that the divergence hinges very much on
differing meanings of transcendence (see Ch.3, sec.1). Transcendence is understood here not as positing the divine in a realm away from the cosmos as in
theistic cosmology, but as recognizing the divine as beyond all limitations
while immanent: therefore this transcendence would allow a boundlessness of
divine manifestation and of divine-human participation, even within physical
nature, indeed the physical nature of mortal beings. As a result in a pantheistic

cosmos, some kinds — indeed quite possibly the most intense sane kinds — of ecstatic participation within the divine presence may be expected to nurture the whole human person, even the person's physical nature, because the divine energies are immanent within the physical and vivify the physical. Health may be expected as the all encompassing characteristic in these kinds of ecstasy, physical health as well as psychological health, even physical and mental stamina well into old age. Do we have an example for such a possibility?

Evidence for this possibility — that physical health as well as mental stability may be engendered through ecstasy — is found in *The Life of St Anthony of Egypt*. Extraordinary physical health and longevity are described for him. He lived for about a century and his eyesight remained sharp well into his old age.[21] Whether or not the *vita* was actually written by St Athanasius of Alexandria who knew the Egyptian Anthony in old age and to whom the biography is attributed, the very fact that the *vita* has been valued by so many generations into the present-day should indicate the possibility that physical as well as psychological health in ecstasy has been expected and could occur. Anthony provides a single example. Other examples exist in patristic literature, in whom 'corruptibility and illness diminished' through their immediate ecstatic participation within the divine.[22]

Physical health as well as psychological stability must be permitted as possible characteristics of some kinds of ecstasy if discovery is to be the purpose of research in this field. To accommodate such possible discoveries, the researcher must be equipped with a flexible vocabulary. This flexibility can be obtained when the term 'ecstasy' is separated from the term 'trance'. Explicated above, the distinction will be summarized now. The term 'ecstasy' signifies a transposition from the commonplace to some experience of other realities, be they subjective or objective; and the term 'ecstasy' can encompass a wide range of possible experiences, various types of contents and forms (as in Christou's definition). The term 'trance', on the other hand, signifies the physical abnormality, and sometimes the psycho-physical abnormality, that accompanies some forms of ecstasy but not necessarily all forms.

In some instances, 'ecstasy' and 'trance' may be equivalent (which would accord with Inge's unrevised expectation). In other instances, 'trance' may be merely a consequence of an 'ecstasy' (as in the divine rapture that attracted Underhill's attention); or inversely, 'trance' may be the cause of an ecstatic experience, such as the types of ecstasy induced by frenzied movements or by drugs. But 'ecstasy' need not imply a state of 'trance' at all, neither as a consequence nor as a cause. 'Ecstasy' can be separated from 'trance' clearly and unequivocally.

Once 'ecstasy' is thus distinguished from 'trance', we may see that a continu-

ity of ecstatic phenomena does not necessarily imply a persistence of pathological conditions. On the contrary, a continuity and transformation may
possibly involve states of health of body and soul.

Now, we may proceed to the question: whether a transformation of ecstatic
phenomena may have been involved in the transition to Russian Orthodoxy
in Alaska, analogous to the transformation of ritual masks into icons. The
question will be addressed through two subsidiary considerations (specified in
the introduction to this chapter): firstly, whether sound patristic criteria exist
that would guide such a transformation of ecstatic experiences; and secondly,
whether such criteria were actually applied historically in Alaska.

(2) Patristic Criteria for a Discernment between Ecstatic Experiences

Do patristics provide criteria that would guide and support a transformation
of ecstatic phenomena: in other words, criteria that would allow a discernment between types of ecstatic experiences?

Discernment is evident among early patristic writers when ecstasy represented in scripture was recognized as a means of true prophetic revelation.
Referring to the biblical Book of Zechariah, St Justin the Martyr stated that
the prophet 'had not been in a normal mundane state, but in ecstasy' when
the prophet Zechariah had seen Joshua, the angel, and a demon: οὐκ αὐτοψία,
ἐν καταστάσει ὢν, εοράκει, ἀλλ' ἐν ἐκστάσει.[23]

Justin's disciple St Athenagoras of Athens also recognized ecstasy as a means
of biblical prophecy and revelation. Moses, Isaiah, Jeremiah, and other prophets had 'in ecstasy' spoken of God, because they had been moved by the divine
spirit to speak, just as a flute is inspired by the flautist:[24]

οἱ κατ' ἔκστασιν τῶν ἐν αὐτοῖς λογισμῶν, κινήσαντος αὐτοὺς τοῦ θείου
πνεύματος, ἃ ἐνηργοῦντο ἐξεφώνησαν, συγκρησαμένου (τούτοις) τοῦ
πνεύματος, ὡς εἰ καὶ αὐλητὴς αὐλὸν ἐμπνεύσαι.

Athenagoras and Justin — as well as St Clement of Alexandria (who has
been already mentioned, in Chapter 2) — on the other hand, criticized the
then-contemporary rites and religions, which would induce ecstasies in their
adherents, for instance the rites of the Corybantes and the religion of the
Eleusinian Mysteries. They criticized those sorts of ecstatic practices as being
deceptive and demonic.[25] Similar criticism will be found in subsequent patristic
literature, as we shall see. The criticism indicates a differentiation of the ecstasies induced in some contemporary religions and rites, which were dismissed
as deceptive, from the ecstasy described in the Bible that was considered exemplary of true prophecy.

Because these early patristic writers of the first and second century AD differentiated and emphasized the biblical instances of ecstasy as exemplary of

true prophesy, we should consider the use of the term 'ecstasy' in the Bible before we proceed. The very word ἔκστασις had been written repeatedly in the *Septuagint*, the Old Testament. For instance in Psalm 115:2 (116:11), David exclaims: Ἐγω εἶπω ἐν τῇ ἐκστάσει μου: 'I said in my ecstasy.' Some other instances include: Genesis 2:21-23, Genesis 15:12, Genesis 27:33, and Zechariah 12:4; and there are many more.[26]

The word ἔκστασις was written in the New Testament also. In Acts 10:10, the Apostle Peter experiences 'ecstasy': 'επεπεσεν επ᾽ αυτον εκστασις': 'ecstasy befell him.' 'Ecstasy' occurs for Peter again in Acts 11:5 and for Paul in Acts 22:17. The Acts of the Apostles was originally written in Greek. The *Septuagint* was the Greek translation from the Hebrew and served as the authoritative scripture for early Church. These are the Christian scriptures to which Justin, Athenagoras and Clement (as well as Irenaeus, Epiphanius, Didymus and others, to be cited) were referring.

Because these references to ecstasy are so important, a discrepancy in the English versions of the Bible should be noticed. Instead of the word 'ecstasy', other words have been written into the King James Version (KJV, early seventeenth century) and Revised Standard Version (RSV, mid-twentieth century, from the late nineteenth century Revised Version). David exclaims in 'haste' as written in the KJV, and 'consternation' as written in the RSV, instead of in 'ecstasy' in Psalm 115:2 (116:11 in the KJV and RSV). Divergence occurs similarly in Genesis 15:12, Genesis 27:33, Zechariah 12:4, etc. Significantly in Zechariah 12:4, 'madness' is written into both the KJV and RSV in place of 'ecstasy'.

The divergence occurs also in the translations of the New Testament. Peter and Paul experience 'a trance' in Acts 10:10, Acts 11:5 and Acts 22:17 in the KJV and RSV. As this occurs in New Testament versions that were meant to be direct translations from the original Greek, the same discrepancy in the Old Testament versions can not be attributed to any differences of the Greek *Septuagint* from the Hebrew scriptures (or rather, to any supposed differences from interpretations or variations of the latter). Why wasn't the word 'ecstasy' translated literally? Evidently, an equivalence, even a synonymity, of 'ecstasy' with 'trance' and even with 'madness' was presumed by the translators of the KJV and RSV. But as we have seen in the section above, such equivalence must be refined. Now, to gain insights, we should consider the vocabulary that was used by the patristic writers themselves and the references that would have been authortative for them.

Written in the *Septuagint* and in the Acts of the Apostles and other Christian literature such as that by Justin, Athenagoras and Clement of the first and early second centuries, the word 'ecstasy' for biblical prophecy was set aside by patristic writers during the later second and the third centuries. For example, St Irenaeus of Lyons wrote 'inspiration' and 'prophecy' instead of 'ecstasy' with regard to the biblical instances. (We may notice that his alternative words are affirmative in their connotations.) There was a reason for his reserve about the use of the word 'ecstasy'. In his time, Gnosticism was strident. The Gnostics had involved types of ecstasy in their syncretistic mystagogy, so Irenaeus employed these other words that would mark the difference of biblical prophecy. His concern was with the generalized complex of the Gnostics' syncretism rather than with their forms of ecstasy in particular; therefore evidently, he did not focus on the differing practices of ecstasy itself, but just marked the distinction by using alternative words for the biblical instances. Irenaeus's attitude was explained by J. Lawson during the mid-twentieth century in a comprehensive study of Irenaeus's life and work, as follows:[27]

> S. Irenaeus does not, indeed, disown this theory [expressed by Athenagoras], but he most significantly does not use it. The reason for this is perhaps not far to seek. Irenaeus knows of ecstatic "prophecy" among the Gnostic followers of Marcus, and what he knows fills him with abhorrence. Impressionable women are worked up by incantations and spurious miracles into a state of violent emotion and frenzied speech, and the orgy ends in sexual license. Here is one branch of Gnosticism displaying a well-known aspect of pagan religion.

At the outset of this quotation, Lawson's reference to the theory expressed by Athenagoras in the generation preceding Irenaeus is to Athenagoras's theory about ecstasy that has been indicated here, above. At the end of the quotation, Lawson's allusion to 'a well-known aspect of pagan religion' would be, for example, to that of the Bacchanalia, which was described so vividly by Euripides who also criticized it but implicitly in his drama *The Bacchae* in the fifth century BC.

By the fourth century AD, Gnosticism had met its demise as had the Mystery Religions prior to it. Yet induced ecstasies continued to pose a problem for patristic pastors and writers, now due to the rise of a Christian sect referred to today as the Montanists. A type of ecstasy had been induced to achieve glossolalia and visions by the founder, Montanus, in Asia Minor in the later second century AD, contemporaneous with the Gnostics himself. The movement initiated by him continued in various forms into the fourth century; and in that century, pastoral concerns among the baptized populations necessitated a clarification about ecstasy itself in response. Criteria were written to distinguish the types of ecstatic experiences that typified the Montanists from the kinds of ecstasy that were known to the biblical prophets.

If Montanus had once been a participant in the mysteries of Cybele or of another of the Mystery Religions in his own time, and then continued practicing some of the same techniques of ecstasy after his baptism, then the patristic criticism against the Montanists may be related to the earlier patristic criticisms against the ecstatic rites in the Mystery Religions. It may also be related to Irenaeus's criticism against Gnostic mystagogy, as the Gnostics had been involved in an untoward syncretism with pagan ecstatic elements. Thus the patristic discernment could be traced, in effect, along a line: from Justin, Athenagoras and Clement through Irenaeus and into the fourth century when the criteria for discernment were clearly articulated in two texts.

One of these two texts was the exposition *Against Heresies* by St Epiphanius (c.315 - c.403), bishop of Constantia (Salamis) in Cyprus. The other text was the *Exegesis on the Acts of the Apostles* attributed to Didymus (c.313 - c.398), the director of the Christian catechetical school in Alexandria: the tradition that attributes the latter work to Didymus is the more important factor here.

The agreement between Epiphanius and Didymus regarding this discernment is heightened by a contrast, a fundamental difference between these two men. The head of the catechetical school at Alexandria tended so much towards Platonism that his writings and those attributed to him were censured by the Fifth Ecumenical Council (Constantinople, AD 553). In contrast to Didymus, Epiphanius was opposed to Platonism, particularly in its Origenistic manifestations, and Epiphanius was canonized as an Orthodox saint. Hence, the agreement becomes more significant as they alike drew an initial line of discernment against the type of ecstasy induced by Montanus and his followers.

Epiphanius distinguished between three types of ecstasy: (i) an ecstasy out-of-mind; (ii) an ecstasy through extreme amazement;, and (iii) an ecstasy of sleep. In the first, *the ecstasy out-of-mind*, the person lost cognizance, and sometimes even physical control. The ecstatic was unaware of the meaning of the visions and utterances, and sometimes unaware even of their occurrence. This was the type of ecstasy induced by Montanus, according to Epiphanius.[28]

In the biblical kinds of ecstasy however, the ecstatic's mind was neither upset nor overturned, except perhaps momentarily and then due to astonishment (that was the *ecstasy through extreme amazement*) or due to the natural process of sleep (*the ecstasy of sleep*), as represented for example in Genesis 2:21-23 and 15:12, Psalms 115:2 (116:11), and Acts 10:10-21. Yet in each of these instances also, the biblical ecstatic himself understood, either immediately or soon afterwards, the significance of what had been experienced.[29]

The bishop of Constantia devoted most attention to the ecstasy of sleep, attributed to Adam in Genesis (2:21-23), where the *Septuagint* states: 'God had an ecstasy seize Adam so that Adam slept'.[30] Montanus had evidently claimed that Adam's sleep-ecstasy was the same as his own type of ecstasy during which consciousness was lost. Epiphanius explained however that Adam had experienced natural sleep, which was correctly referred to in scripture as 'ecstasy', because the sleeping person went from one state of activity and sensibility into another state: a state of repose. As the physical senses withdrew without ceasing to exist, the eyes closed, the spirit was quieted, and so Adam became naturally insensible. But when he awoke, Adam was fully aware of what had occurred, why it had occurred, and what it meant. He was able to explain with sobriety and with understanding. Never was Adam out of his mind.[31]

The biblical prophets and apostles went beyond the usual sense perceptions through ecstasies that either diminished the senses (in the ecstasy of sleep) or expanded the senses (in the ecstasy through extreme amazement). Any experience of insensitivity or of confusion among them was momentary, and was superceded by increased rational awareness. Biblical ecstasy was, thus, a going beyond usual consciousness into greater understanding. It was not a going out of consciousness.

Referring to one of the same key texts as Epiphanius, Acts 10:19-21, Didymus, or this exegesis attributed to him, emphasized the same perception. He referred to the Montanists as 'silly' and 'deranged', because they were not 'cognizant of their own thoughts' in their ecstasy; and Didymus contrasted them to the Apostle Peter who was cognizant:[32]

> Nay Peter, in his ecstasy, was strictly cognizant, so as to report what he had seen and heard, and to be sensible of what the things shown were symbolical.

The same was true, according to Didymus (ibid.), of the Hebrew biblical prophets who had ecstatic visions: 'their consciousness kept pace with the things presented to their view.'[33]

Thus Didymus and Epiphanius alike provide the same criteria for an initial line of discernment between types of ecstatic experiences. Beyond this line, where Orthodox patristic and Platonic traditions diverge, the criteria should be expected to differ: patristic discernment should be expected to extend differently from the Platonic.[34] Yet the initial line itself provides the criteria sufficient for the study at hand. On the far side of this initial line, ecstasies were characterized by frenzy and by loss of consciousness to varying degrees. On the near side, the biblical ecstasies were characterized particularly by cognizance as the prophets and apostles understood the content and the significance of their kinds of experiences. Theirs was an increased awareness, neither diminished nor upset except perhaps momentarily and then with good reason: due to a momentary confusion in extreme awe or due to a temporary insensitivity during the natural operation of sleep. Even then, they soon entered into an understanding of the experience, and were able themselves to explain its meaning. Their cognizance, indeed their heightened cognizance, was a factor that distinguished them, as was their composure.

Section (1) conclusion. These criteria would guide the transformation of ancient shamanizing in the Arctic, because the problem was not with all types of ecstasy but with specific types. According to the criteria provided by Epiphanius and Didymus alike, those types of ecstasy involving loss of self-control and consciousness should not be expected to continue into Christianity; or if they did continue, they should be expected to persist in conflict with Orthodoxy, similar to the conflicts of Gnostic mystagogy or of Montantist trance-visions. In contrast, the coherent composed kinds of ecstasy that were known to the biblical prophets and apostles may occur. Whether these kinds did occur in the transition, and whether they were associated with the ancient shamanizing in such a way that they could be seen as a direct transformation, will be considered in Chapters 5 and 6. Currently, the focus of study will remain on the patristic criteria for discernment. Were such criteria actually applied in Alaska?

(3) An Example of Discernment from the Field

Patristic criteria for discernment between types of ecstatic experiences were reflected through an interaction by the priest of the Unalaska parish Ioann (Ivan) Veniaminov. He would have absorbed the patristic tradition through two sources. One would have been the seminary at Irkutsk where he had studied from 1806 until 1818. He remained in the city, ordained to the cathedral, until he departed for Alaska in 1823. The other source would have been a monastery in Irkutsk where his own uncle was a monastic at the same time that young Ivan was at seminary. Whether the youth had learned to locate these criteria in the specific patristic texts that contain them is unimportant for the sake of this example. Relevant is that he had absorbed this living tradition.

Applying these criteria, he discerned ecstatic prophecy of the biblical kind in an Aleut elder of the island of Akun whose baptismal name was Ivan and Slavic surname was Smirennikov. They met in spring 1828, during Veniaminov's first pastoral visit to this island.

We may recall from the history in Chapter 1 that no other priest had ever been assigned to the vicinity before Veniaminov except *hieromonk* Makarii, a member of the religious mission to Kodiak. But Makarii had passed only briefly along Tigalda and Akun islands on his way to Unalaska from Kodiak in summer of 1795, and had then spent only a year at Unalaska island where he allied himself with Aleut leaders against the gross exploitation by the Shelikhov enterprises and departed with six of them in summer of 1796 to journey the distance to Petersburg to protest. Between the missionary Makarii's stay at Unalaska island (summer 1795 to summer 1796) and the parish priest

Veniaminov's arrival at Unalaska (1824), there had only been landfalls made
in transit by *hieromonk* Gideon for a week at Unalaska island on his way to
Kodiak in 1807, and then by a chaplain of a circumnavigational expedition
also at Unalaska island momentarily in 1820 and again in 1821 Otherwise, no
priests had ever been known anywhere in the Aleutian Islands.[35] Makarii's
brief stop at Akun, therefore, would most probably have been the only one by
a priest until Veniaminov's visit in spring 1828, nearly thirty-three years later.

The meeting was reported in writing by both the priest Veniaminov and the
toion of Tigalda and Akun, Pan'kov, who accompanied him; and the report
carries the signature of both these men who attest to the accuracy of the description of the meeting in which they were involved.[36] The description and
the quotations that follow will be taken from this report in translation.[37]

Whether the reader accepts the descriptions as objective (facts about the
actual content of the ecstatic experiences) or interprets them as subjective pro-
jections (perceptions due to the beliefs of these three men: the priest, the *toion*,
and the elder): either way, the example should serve the intended purpose.
Evidently, they spent quite a bit of time together, as Veniaminov and Pan'kov's
report, while itself succinct, contains much insight.

(i) The Interaction

The priest Veniaminov heard of the elder Smirennikov who, people said,
had healed, foreseen future events, and located food sources on various occasions. Indeed he had even predicted the time of Veniaminov's arrival on the
island of Akun and had informed the villagers so that they could gather to
receive the visiting priest. Because Smirennikov had manifested these abilities,
he had become known as a 'shaman, not an ordinary person at least': and
therefore he had been shunned by the *toion* Pan'kov who had 'never entered
into any conversation with the old man'. Veniaminov resolved to meet
Smirennikov 'nevertheless', due to the strength of character of the people who
had described the abilities attributed to him. Veniaminov resolved to discover
'how he knew the future, and what means he employed to learn it'. The *toion*
remained with the priest.

The Aleut elder came to them. He explained to them that he had been baptized by *hieromonk* Makarii, and that 'spirits' then began appearing to him.
They 'continued to appear to him for over thirty years, almost daily'.

> The spirits had the appearance of humans, light of face, dressed in white robes and
> … these robes resembled church vestments and were trimmed with rose bands.

These spirits had told him that they had been 'sent by God to instruct, teach,
and preserve him'. The priest and the *toion* found that the Aleut elder could
relate numerous biblical accounts clearly. Furthermore, 'when I preached,' the

priest reported, 'he was the first to confirm the truth of my words in the tone of a person conversant with Holy Writ.' The priest and the *toion* were astonished that he could have learned so much and could have come to such authority. Smirennikov would not have read these things for himself, he was illiterate. *Hieromonk* Makarii had not had the opportunity or the linguistic facility to teach in such detail. The only person in the region with knowledge enough to have instructed in such detail was the *toion* Pan'kov who had shunned him.

Instructing, these spirits also 'granted his requests, and through Smirennikov they granted the requests of other people, although the latter rather seldom'.

They would appear only to him, not to others. Smirennikov had queried why they did not appear to others, and 'the spirits replied they were so ordered'. The priest asked him to request of 'his protectors, these spirits', that they might make themselves known to Veniaminov himself. In response, the elder departed from his visitors for 'about an hour'. Returning, he relayed the answer:

> What does he want? Does he consider us to be demons? If he insists, he can see and converse with us.

(Veniaminov did not proceed: 'to avoid the pitfall of error, as there was no need for me to meet them,' he wrote.) Veniaminov directed a question to the elder. He asked him about Smirennikov's own internal responses. What did he feel when these spirits appeared to him? Was it sorrow or joy? Smirennikov explained that only if he had misbehaved did he feel 'a twinge of conscience, otherwise he did not feel any fear'.

Having listened to all of this and more, Veniaminov was especially impressed by the man's character:

> Moreover the freedom, fearlessness and even pleasure of his discourse, and above all his clean manner of life, confirmed in me the conviction that the spirits that appear to this old man (if they appear) are not demons.

Veniaminov, therefore, 'did not forbid' the elder from assisting the people who came to him for aid, and furthermore 'instructed' him (— or, rather more probably, respectfully suggested to him, as such a response would be the more appropriate with respect to Smirennikov's age and spiritual stature —) to have these people turn also directly to God themselves:

> Tell those who ask your advice about the future and request your help to address themselves directly to God, as He is common Father to all. ... instruct them to pray diligently and thank the Sole God.

The priest finally addressed the people who were here, telling them *not* to call this man a shaman: 'I told the other Aleuts who were present not to call

him a Shaman.' The distinction was reiterated by Veniaminov when he recorded this meeting also in his journal, entry dated 23 April 1828: 'I conversed
with the elder Ivan Smirennikov who is considered a shaman in these parts. I
found the facts quite to the contrary.'[38]

(ii) An Analysis of the Interaction

Patristic criteria for a discernment of the *form* as well as the *content* of this
Aleut elder's experience are reflected in the report. With regard to the form of
the ecstasy, the Aleut elder of Akun was cognizant. He knew what had occurred. He described his protectors, these spirits, consistently. He relayed their
instructions with detail. His consciousness had 'kept pace with the things
presented'. He 'spoke with an understanding of the depths that had been revealed to him of the knowledge of God'. These quotations that apply to the
elder of Akun come directly from Epiphanius of Constantia and from Didymus
of Alexandria as they differentiated the ecstasy of the Apostle Peter.[39]

Cognizant, the Aleut elder of Akun was also composed while 'seeing other
things besides those seen by people in the everyday course of events', and
while seeing 'not in an everyday manner'. The quotations now come from
Epiphanius again and from Justin, the latter describing the prophet Zacharias
who saw the angel.[40] This is all the more remarkable because the Aleut elder of
Akun experienced ecstasy (when he went to speak to these spirits) during the
meeting with the priest and the *toion*. Veniaminov had just witnessed the man's
descent from such an experience, who returned composed as well as aware.
His composure was evident in the qualities that had so impressed Veniaminov
at that time: 'the freedom, fearlessness and even pleasure of his discourse'. It
was evident furthermore in the stability of his character overall, 'his clean
manner of life'.

It also became evident when Veniaminov differentiated Smirennikov from
typical shamans. Veniaminov was in effect distinguishing this form of ecstasy
from the techniques of typical shamans-of-old on the Aleutian Islands who
would induce trance states that were described by Veniaminov himself in an
ethnography as follows:[41]

> during a shamanistic seance, they [the shamans] leaped, grimaced, beat the drum
> and (entered a state of trance characterized by a loss of conscious control).

Veniaminov was knowledgeable. He equated those techniques with practices by 'shamans everywhere', which would be a reference to his own native
Siberia as well as to southern Alaska. (We may recall that he derived from the
regions where the term 'shaman' had originated: he was from the Irkutsk
gubernia, 'Tungus', or Evenk, and Buriat territory.)[42] This ethnographic view
of his on the eastern Aleutian Islands (quoted) correlates with descriptions of

shamanizing here before his arrival and with descriptions throughout southern and western Alaska: Typically shamans would, although not always, escalate
even into frenzy; and many rite techniques would result in extreme trance
states, even to comatose-like states.[43] None of that occurred with the Aleut
elder Ivan Smirennikov in Veniaminov and Pan'kov's sight; and Veniaminov
differentiated his man decisively.

This contrast by Veniaminov is the same as that expressed explicitly by both
Epiphanius and Didymus: it is the contrast between an ecstasy of the biblical
kind and an 'ecstasy out-of-mind'. The contrast is like the distinction indicated
by Justin and Athenagoras who distinguished the kind of ecstasy experienced
by the biblical prophets and apostles on the one hand, from the frenzied ecstasies induced in some ancient religions and rites on the other hand.

Thus, patristic criteria for a discernment of the *form* of the ecstatic experience are reflected in the report. Furthermore, criteria for a discernment of the
content are also reflected. In this instance, the content is comprised of these
spirits themselves.

These further criteria are indicated subtlety throughout the Gospels and in
the Epistles (see, e.g., 1 Corinthians 12:10). They are made explicit in patristic
literature, for example: repeatedly in the lives of the saints such as the *Life of St
Anthony of Egypt* attributed to St Athanasius of Alexandria in the fourth century
AD; in catechisms such as that by St Cyril of Jerusalem in the fourth century;
and in monastic texts including *The Ladder* by St John Climacus written in the
early seventh century, as well as the *Philocalia* compiled in the eighteenth century from texts written between the fourth and fifteenth centuries.[44]

These criteria involve the discernment of angels from demons. According to
the *vita* of St Anthony for example, the discernment is 'easy when God wills
it', as the appearance of angels comes with tranquility and with joy. If humans
are frightened at first, the angels remove fear with joy: as Gabriel did for
Zacharias, as the angel did at Christ's Nativity for the shepherds, as the angel
did in the sepulchre for the myrrh-bearing women. On the other hand, the
appearance of demons is troubling, if not immediately then inevitably, causing terror and dejection, a 'craving for evil' and 'instability of character'.[45]

The same criteria were reflected when Veniaminov asked Smirennikov about
the spirits who were appearing. He asked about their behaviour. He asked
about their teaching. *And he asked about the elder's response to them.* Perceiving
that Smirennikov was never upset in their presence, although they had been
appearing to him almost daily for more than thirty years, and also perceiving
that these spirits had edified him — qualities that were manifested not only in
the man's answers but also in this own solidly stable character — Veniaminov
recognized that these spirits could 'not be demons'.[46]

An insufficient criterion for this discernment would be merely a manifestation of a spirit in an appearance of an angel. The appearance that Smirennikov described for the spirits would alone not have sufficed. Veniaminov acknowledged this as he wrote:[47]

> Demons may sometimes assume the appearance of Angels of Light, but never for the purpose of instruction, teaching and salvation of human beings, but always for their perdition. As the tree of evil cannot bear the fruit of good, these spirits must be the servants sent to those who seek salvation.

This discernment was vital for Veniaminov due to the importance of the human person's disassociation from the demonic. Veniaminov understood the disassociation as an existential dynamic, and he expressed it at the start of the *Indication of the Way into the Kingdom of Heaven*, a work he authored in the eastern Aleut language during his ministry on the islands, since translated into numerous other languages: there, Veniaminov explained that demons had taken advantage of human suffering to gain control over human beings, but that the devil had been conquered and demonic power had been crushed by Christ for human salvation.[48]

This is a biblical, patristic principle. We saw it also reflected through iconography (Ch.3, sec.2, ii). Aware of this principle, Veniaminov took care to discern the content as well as the form of Smirennikov's ecstatic experience; and he affirmed the experience as God-given.

(4) Conclusions

The question guiding this chapter has been whether a transformation of shamanizing should be expected in the transition, analogous to the transformation of ritual masking. Continuity and transformation would be anticipated because shamans-of-old comprised a central societal phenomenon and because the transition was an indigenous, corporate movement. A central societal phenomenon would most probably continue somehow within a movement that involved a society virtually in its entirety. But this phenomenon was ecstatic, so the question arose about the possibility of the continuity and transformation of ecstatic phenomena.

Vital at the outset was the necessity for us to find a definition of 'ecstasy' that could accommodate the range of forms and contents of ecstatic experiences in the Arctic, and would sunder the categorical association of 'ecstasy' with 'trance' for studies of far northern religions.

The question was then addressed through two subsidiary considerations. Firstly, we considered whether sound criteria existed within patristic theology to support the transformation of ecstatic phenomena. These patristic criteria were identified. Accordingly, a continuity in the forms of ecstatic experiences that involved loss of self-control or prolonged diminution of consciousness should not be expected in the transition; or if they did continue, they should be expected to persist in discord against the patristic principles of Orthodox Christianity.

What could be expected properly in the transition is a kind of ecstasy described for the biblical prophets and apostles, characterized by composure and cognizance, stability and awareness. One could well argue, now in conclusion, that to suppress this kind of ecstasy or even a propensity for it would be to thwart participation in the biblical experience.[49]

Our second consideration was whether patristic criteria for such discernment had actually been applied in the regional focus of this study; and they were found that they had been applied in the example of Ivan Veniaminov's interaction with Ivan Smirennikov. The patristic criteria were evident in the discernment of the form as well as the content of Smirennikov's experiences, when the insightful Russian priest from Siberia met the Aleut elder of Akun.

NOTES

[1] For material in this chapter previously published, see Mousalimas (1995, 1993b, 1993c, 1988b): the current work supersedes the previous. A correction to id. (1998b) should be noted: Veniaminov was not a missionary; he was a parish priest.

[2] See Ch.5, sec.2.vi, below. Also see Veniaminov (1840b:109-110, 258; 1984:211, 290).

[3] For the distinction between shamans' practices either as a central societal phenomenon or as a peripheral societal phenomenon, see Lewis (1971).

[4] Christou (1964:534-535).

[5] E.g., Siikala (1987:31-33), Bourguignon (1973:3, 1974:235).

[6] Lemaître (1953:1863).

[7] For an example from Unalaska Island in the eastern Aleutian Islands, 1791, see Sarychev (1802:141-142, 1807:64-65).

[8] For a generality from Kodiak Island, 1804-1807, see Gideon (1989:59-60). For a generality from the eastern Aleutian Islands, but a secondary source in this respect, see Veniaminov (1840b:123, 1984:219).

[9] For an example at the village of Koshiga in the eastern Aleutian Islands, 1791, see ibid. (1802:147-148, 1807:67-68). For a generality from Kodiak Island, 1804-1807, see Gideon (1989:59-60).

[10] For evidence of a shaman's role-taking on Unalaska Island in the eastern Aleutian Islands, 1791, see Sarychev (1802:141-142, 1807:64-65). For an extended study of shamans' role-taking from Siberian examples, see Siikala (1987).

[11] Siikala (1987, see esp. p.37); Kim and Kim (1993).

[12] Shirikogoroff (1923:247; 1924:369-370; 1935, 274, 350, 363-364, 373, 384).

[13] Hultkrantz (1973:28, 1978:41).

[14] Id. (1990).

[15] Siikala (1987:39).

[16] Arbman (1963:xv); cf. Hultkrantz (1978:41), Siikala (1987:39).

[17] Inge (1912:157); cf. id. (1918:142-146).

[18] Underhill (1930:170, 358-361).

[19] See, e.g., Underhill (1930:58-59, 362).

[20] See Chryssavgis (1989:36-59, 163-194).

[21] Βίος Ἀντωνίου xciii, cited with reference to the edition as Athanasius (1857:973). He lived from AD c.251 until 356, according to Cross and Livingstone (1983:67).

Cf., Rubenson (1990) who argues that an acceptance of the *vita* involves an acceptance of Origenistic presuppositions. Is his categorical association accurate? To what extent has Rubenson (1990) been influenced by the theories established in Sweden regarding ecstasy as pathological, when he insists that the asceticism of Anthony and the desert fathers was categorically Origenistic (dualistic)? If it was Origenistic, then how do we account for the physical health and longevity of the ascetic St Anthony of Egypt, or the extraordinary physical stamina as well as the warm-heartedness and generosity of the ascetic St Herman of Alaska? For the latter, see Ch.6, below.

Notice that I have countered neo-Platonic presuppositions, of which Origenism is a manifestation: see esp.: Ch.3, secs 1 and 3 explicitly; and here, Ch.4, sec.1, implicitly; and again Ch.6, sec.1, implicitly. See esp. nt.34, below.

[22] See, e.g., Chryssavgis (1989:49), from whom the quotation has been taken.

[23] Justin, Διά Τρύφ. cxv.3 (1915:232).

[24] Athenagoras, Πρεσβεία ix.1 (1972:20, 1990:38).

[25] Justin, *1 Ap.* lxiv.1-6 (1914:73-74, 1987:188); Athenagoras, Πρεσβεία xxiv.3-xxvi.5 (1972:58-66 [xxiv.2-xxvi.2]; 1990:79-88). Also see Clement of Alexandria, Προτρεπτικός ii, iii (1919:26-101, 1972:10-35).

[26] See Hatch and Redpath (1897:441, 1906:203); but compare this list from the *Septuagint* with the equivalent verses in the KJV and RSV.

[27] Lawson (1948:29). For references to Gnosticism, see Ch.3, nt.21, above.

[28] Epiphanius, Παν. xlviii.4 (1980:225-226); also see ibid., xlviii.5-7, pp.224-229.

[29] Ibid., xlviii.6-48.7, pp.227-229.

[30] Ibid., xlviii.4, p.226.

[31] Ibid., xlviii.5, pp.227-228.

[32] Didymus, *in Act.* x:10 (1863:1677A-B). Also in Cramer, ed. (1844:176); trans. in Marriott, ed. (1851:315, nt.), also in Schaff, ed. (1899:143, ftnt. 1): but ἔκστασις is rendered as 'trance'; I have inserted the proper translation of the original word.

[33] Ibid. Cf., Origen, *de Principiis* III.iii.4 (1936:227), by whom Didymus was probably influenced:

From this we learn to discern clearly when the soul is moral by the presence of a spirit of the better kind, namely, when it suffers no mental disturbance or abberation whatsoever as a result of the immediate inspiration and does not lose the free judgement of the will. Such for example were the prophets and apostles who attended upon the divine oracles without any mental disturbance.

[34] For differences between patristic and Platonic traditions, see especially Louth

(1981:194-201, 1989:20-24). For the difference in ecstatic experiences, see, e.g., St Gregory Palamas, Ἡσυχ. I.ii.14 (1959:349): Palamas likewise emphasizes cognizance, now against Barlaam who evidently (from the passage cited) considered rapturous trance, that is the insensibility even to one's own self, to be the crowning experience in man's union with God. Palamas's criticism of Barlaam can be interpreted as a patristic criticism against a Platonic type of ecstasy; and the divergence may be related to the difference between panentheistic ecstasy and theistic ecstasy mentioned earlier in this chapter (see sec.1, above).

[35] For the chronology of clergy previous to Veniaminov, see Ch.1, sec.1.i, above.

[36] For the *toion* Ivan Pan'kov, see Ch.1, sec.1.iv, above; and Ch.5, sec.3.i, below.

[37] Letter, Revd Priest Ioann Veniaminov to Archbishop Michael of Irkutsk, 5 November 1829, cited as Veniaminov (1977) with reference to the translation of this report; trans. reprinted in Oleksa, ed. (1987:132-135).

[38] Veniaminov (1993:78, journal entry 23 April 1828).

[39] Cited in sec.2, above.

[40] Epiphanius, Παν. xlviii.5 (1980:227-228); Justin, Διά Τρύφ. cxv.3 (1915:.232).

[41] Veniaminov (1840b:123; 1984:219). The parenthetical phrase in the quotation has been inserted by the translator for Veniaminov's 'изступленіе'.

[42] Shirokogoroff (1935:268); Eliade (1964:4, 1987:202); Tugolukov (1978:426): cited in Intro., sec.1.iii, nt.56, above.

[43] For the Unalaska region, see Sarychev (1802:147-148, 1807:67-68); for Kodiak, see Gideon (1989:59-60); but cf. Sarychev (1802:141-142, 1807:64-65): cited in note 7, above.

[44] Cyril of Jerusalem, Κατήχησις XVI.xiii-xvi (1860:220-226; 1894:118-119); Climacus in Chryssavgis (1989:111-112, 171-172). In the *Philocalia*, see e.g.: Diadochus of Photice, Λόγος ἀσκητικὸς xxxvi-xl (1782:241-243; 1979:263-265); also see Diadochus, ibid. (1955:104-108).

For the *Philocalia* see Ware (1984). The writings in the *Philocalia* were compiled by Sts Nicodemus of the Holy Mountain and Macarius of Corinth in five volumes, published in Greek in 1782. A sizeable selection was translated into Slavonic in Moldavia by the monastic Paisii Velichkovskii who had spent seventeen years on the Holy Mountain himself (1746-1763). In 1791, the translation was taken to the Metropolitan of St Petersburg, Gavriil, who had the texts submitted to two select committees, one comprised of monastics, the other consisting of theology professors. The translation was published in Moscow in 1793. The second edition was published in 1822.

Now let us place these data into the context of our history. The Slavonic translation was published in Moscow in 1793, the same year the monastic missionaries were dispatched to Kodiak. The missionaries were selected, and their mission was organized, in large part by this same Gavriil the Metropolitan of St Petersburg, as well as by Nazarii the *hegumen* of Valaam. It is probable that *hegumen* Nazarii would have been found on the editorial committee comprised of monastics, due to his stature; if not him, then someone else of Valaam, due to the standing of this monastery. The year after the second edition was published, Veniaminov was assigned to the Unalaska parish.

The Slavonic edition was translated into Russian partially in 1857, then completed between 1877 and 1889 (see Ware, ibid., cols 1344-1345).

[45] Athanasius, Βίος Ἀντωνίου (1857:xxxv, cols 893-896, and xxxvi, cols 896-897; also see xxv-xxvii, cols 881-884). Anthony has already been described in this chapter from this *vita* as an example of the possibilities of health inherit in some forms of ecstatic experiences. These further criteria from the same *vita*, now regarding the contents of the experiences, have not been introduced into this study until now.

[46] Veniaminov (1977:102).

[47] Ibid.

[48] Veniaminov, *Indication of the Way*: see the translation by Garrett from the Russian version into English, in Oleksa, ed. (1987:83-84).

[49] See, e.g., James (1988:219, 267, 329).

CHAPTER 5

Transformation, I

We have seen that sound criteria exist for a discernment between types of ectastic experiences, so that we may expect a transformation of ecstatic shamanizing in the Arctic analogous to the transformation of ritual masks into icons. Did this actually take place? Do we have any clear examples from the history of the Aleut and Alutiiq peoples? To address the question, we shall look at the characteristics of shamans-of-old.

Two perspectives will be described. A contrast between them should allow the process of the transformation to be perceived as discontinuity becomes evident through an *ethnographic perspective* but continuity becomes visible in specific instances through a *social perspective*.[1]

A review of the region

It may be useful to describe the region afresh, because the geography and demography will be specific in the descriptions that follow.

The region comprising the primary focus will be referred here to as *southern Alaska*. Like a single brush-stroke, this expanse extends west to east across the length of the Aleutian Island chain, over the Alaska Peninsula, through the Kodiak archipelago, along the Gulf of Alaska, to nearly the Copper River. The peoples of this region are from west to east:

(a) the Aleuts, distinguished in this study very generally as western, central, and eastern Aleuts: the western and central encompassing the Near and Andreanov Islands, and the eastern encompassing the Fox Islands, the Shumagin Islands, and the southwestern tip of the Alaska Peninsula;

(b) the Alutiiqs of the Alaska Peninsula and the Kodiak area, also referred to as Koniags and as Pacific Eskimos in anthropological literature; and

(c) the Alutiiqs of the Chugach Bay (Prince William Sound) area, also referred to as Chugach.

Terms 'Koniag' and 'Chugach' will be used to allow sharper distinctions between the Alutiiq of regions (b) and (c).

Immediately neighbouring people are the Dena'ina Athapaskan and the Yup'ik Eskimo due north, as well as the Eyak and the Tlingit directly east. Descriptions of these neighbouring people will be corroborative. Whenever a characteristic diverges from the general pattern within the region at large, the divergence will be specified.

Encompassing all these peoples and regions like a wider band, this greater territory will be referred to as the *region at large*. It extends from the Bering Strait in the west to the Alexander Archipelago in the east, with the eastern boundary being formed naturally by the great peaks of three mountain ranges: the Chugach Mountains, the St Elias Mountains, and the Coast Mountains.

(1) Intrinsic Meanings

What might the word 'shaman' have meant in context? What might the spirit(s) have been with which the shamans-of-old were associated in southern Alaska? If differences existed, could these have been significant for the transition? Meanings of the words 'shaman' and 'spirit' will be provided from the Alaskan vocabularies that they represent.

If the following definitions appear too specialized for a reader, the reader may proceed to this section's conclusions and then directly into the comparison of the perspectives.

(i) 'Shaman'

The Alaskan words together yield a meaning in regional context: *the shaman was someone possessed of spirit(s) who could therefore accomplish the extraordinary*. The words translated as 'shaman' in the Aleut and Eskimo languages in the region at large are:

> *qugagîx̂*, meaning someone possessed of *quĝax̂*, in central Aleut;
>
> *qugagìq*, someone possessed of *quĝaq*, in eastern Aleut;
>
> *kalla'alek*, someone possessed of *kalla'aq* in Alutiiq (Koniag and Chugach); and
>
> *tungalik*, someone possessed of *tungaq* (Yup'ik).

Variations of the terms *kalla'alek* occur in dialects of Yup'ik; and the term *tungalik* has orthographical as well as dialectical variations. It derives from the Inupiaq (Inuit) farther north. All of these words are cognates.[2]

For each cognate alike, I have used the phrase 'possessed of', because this phrase allows both possibilities: that the shaman was possessed by the spirit(s); and that the shaman possessed, or controlled, them.

An alternative exists in the Koniag and Yup'ik languages: *an'alkuq*, or *angalkuq*.[3] While translated by a source as 'someone of many tricks', it can be understood instead as someone who does the extraordinary.

(ii) 'Spirit'

In the cognates from these Aleut and Eskimo languages, the term 'spirit' is intrinsic: *quǵaq, quǵaх̂, kallaʹaq*, or *tungaq*. Therefore, we should carefully consider this set of term also, as the regional meaning of 'shaman' is linked to it. The consideration is more complicated, because we shall need to ask whether the definitions for this set of terms in the Alaskan languages today can be imputed into the proto-historic languages, at the time of the transition.

How are these terms defined today? *Quǵaq (quǵaх̂), kallaʹaq* and *tungaq* indicate 'evil spirits' according to dictionaries and linguistic studies of the modern languages.[4] The same meaning has been found by or applied by ethnographers, anthropologists and other observers with regional specificity.[5]

This meaning can be reflected furthermore through a contrast with a different set of words designating 'spirit' in the region at large. The other set of words signifies the 'persons of animals' and 'persons of the universe', or of universal phenomena; in other words: the spirits associated with great cosmic forces such as the sun, wind, and moon, and with major species such as the seals. The cognates in this other set in the Eskimo languages are: *yua* in the Yup'ik language; *inua* in Inupiaq and Inuit, found also sometimes in Yup'ik; and *sua* in Sugpiaq, the ancient Alutiiq (Koniag) language.

Significantly, a linguistic relationship exists between these words (*yua, sua,* and *inua)* and respectively the words Yupiit, Sugpiat, and Inupiat or Inuit that signify real human persons. The Aleut word '*tayaruu*' probably conveys similar meaning, and the relationship of '*tayaruu*' with *taiyaǵuq* and *tayaǵuх̂* may correspond; so this word may be included within the set. So (more certainly) should the Tlingit word *kwáani*, as it signifies the spirit(s), or 'persons', embodied in natural phenomena, for example, *teet kwáani*, the 'persons of the waves'. The word *kwáani* has been differentiated from the Tlingit word *yéik*, which indicates the 'disembodied' spirits revealed to the shaman.[6]

Can the difference between these two sets of words — *yua*, etc., on the one hand; and *tungaq, kallaʹaq, quǵaq*, etc., as defined in the modern languages on the other hand — be found in proto-historic contexts? The difference is reflected in some masks that survive from pre- and proto-historic times. (While describing these masks, I shall use the Yup'ik Eskimo word *yua* for its set of words, for expedient brevity and also for congruence with the description of Yup'ik rituals in Chapter 2 where the *yua* were introduced; although the cognate *inua* is more usually found in generalized literature about the Arctic.)

The *yua* masks were symmetric throughout the region at large. Often they were composite. On some composites, an anthropomorphic or zoomorphic *yua* was carved as a smaller part of a mask representing the sun or moon or animal. In other composites, the mask face opened on hinges to reveal its *yua* inside. The *yua* representations could be sublimely beautiful. They were often anthropomorphic, as should be expected due to the linguistic relationship between the words *yua* and Yupiit that signify real human persons. On Kodiak Island, anthropomorphic and zoomorphic traits might have merged for representations of *yua* there.[7] In contrast, in general the masks that represented the *qug̀aq* (in Aleut), *kalla'aq* (in Alutiiq), *tungaq* (in Yup'ik) could be grotesque, with asymmetric faces or elongated heads, even sometimes with blood splattered mouths.[8]

But can this contrast be imputed incisively into the proto-historic languages? A possibility exists that it can not. The definition of *qug̀aq* and *kalla'aq* as 'evil spirit(s)' in the Aleut and Alutiiq languages (squarely within our primary focus of study), as glossed along with *tungaq* in the Yup'ik language by so many modern and relatively modern sources, may derive from Christianity. This does not mean that the Russian Orthodox classed all manifestations of *qug̀aq* (in Aleut) and *kalla'aq* (in Alutiiq) categorically as malevolent; but instead that those terms came to indicate that sort exclusively through history. The possibility is indicated by the use of the term *qug̀aq* and its cognates to translate 'demon' in the Gospels in the Aleut language;[9] while cognates of ἄγγελος entered, through the word ангел, into the Aleut language as *an'gilaq* and into Alutiiq as *aankilaq* to signify God's messengers, the angels.

A precedent exists for this possibility. In the ancient Greek language, the words ἄγγελος (angel) and δαίμων (daemon) did not carry the very definite contrasting meanings that they can convey today. An ἄγγελος was a messenger, anyone who announces something. A δαίμων could be any one of a variety of types of lesser spirits (lesser than the gods). It could indicate intermediaries of any type between the immortal and the mortal. It could also signify various subjective, affective states. It could even signify genius. It was even applied to the spirit inspiring Socrates. The use of the term was supple or fluid. Still today, the English term 'demon' can encompass many meanings (the word 'spirit' is itself ambiguous in modern English, is it not?).[10]

The definite contrasting meanings that these words carry in modern Greek can be found in the *Septuagint*, the Greek translations of the Hebrew scriptures, translated during the third to first centuries BC. The term δαίμονες (demons) is used therein to indicate malevolent spirits only. In vivid contrast, ἄγγελος (angels) is written for the benevolent spirits, God's messengers. This incisive lexical distinction was incorporated into early Christian writings, becoming securely definitive in patristic literature by the second century AD;[11] and the clear lexical distinction has become standard in the vocabulary today. Within this dichotomy, the word 'angels' on the one hand and the term 'demons' on the other hand, can still encompass each a range of states and realities:

affective conditions as well as objective beings.[12] Yet the dichotomy is clear: the range remains benevolent (angelic) on the one hand, but malevolent (demonic) on the other hand.

The incisive dichotomy was transposed into European languages, including Russian, through the translations of Christian scripture. And the dichotomy is found in the Aleut translation of Gospel and in the Aleut and Alutiiq languages today: *an'gilaq* and *aankilaq* for benevolent spirits, God's messengers; in contrast to *quǧaq* and *kalla'aq*, malevolent spirits, demons.

Could the meanings of *quǧaq* and *kalla'aq* have been supple and ambiguous in the ancient Aleut and Alutiiq languages? An ambiguity is evident in the Tlingit language in southeastern Alaska with regard to the term *yéik*, the disembodied' spirits revealed to the shaman. The ambiguity has been underscored, as the definition has been given, by N.M. Dauenhauer and R. Dauenhauer as follows: 'It is our understanding that most of these *yéik* are not intrinsically evil, though some may be; certainly all are powerful and ambiguous at best, and not generically benevolent.'[13]

Section conclusion. If the term *quǧaq* in the ancient Aleut language and the term *kalla'aq* in the ancient Alutiiq language were supple and morally ambiguous, then we should expect that the shamans-of-old whose designations *qugaǧiq* and *kalla'alek* derived from those terms would likewise be morally ambiguous as a group: neither considered benevolent (good) nor considered malevolent (evil) categorically. And we shall see that this was probably the case.

Among the differences that will become evident is a benevolence and stability in some significant individuals perceived through the social perspective, against a moral ambiguity if not malevolence typifying others through the ethnographic perspective. The difference will be related to the nature of the spirits operative among them, indeed to a discernment between ecstatic experiences.

It is not between shamans as a group and any other category of spiritual functionaries that the contrast will be developed next in this study, but between the characteristics typifying shamans-of-old in southern Alaska through two perspectives.

(2) An Ethnographic Perspective on Shamans-of-old in Southern Alaska

Through the ethnographic perspective, shamans can be seen within the very visible and audible characteristics that have attracted the attention of ethnographers and that do recur in ethnographies.[14] These characteristics include: (i) an election by spirits which was normally disorienting and frightening; (ii) training in some but not all cases; (iii) distinctive rites with spirit manifestations; (iv) particular paraphernalia; and (v) ontological and cosmological boundary crossings; and (vi) tasks accomplished through spirit mediation.

(i) The Election

Shamans were chosen by spirits. This occurred invariably throughout the region-at-large. Evidently, a person's heredity and volition determined a propensity for the vocation but did not necessarily secure the vocation itself. Someone was a shaman because the spirit(s) had deemed it.

Sometimes spirits overpowered the shamans-to-be without the latter soliciting the encounter. In these cases, the shamans-to-be did not seek the vocation: if they could not rid themselves of the spirits, they had to learn to deal with them and thus became shamans. A certain Dena'ina managed to evade the vocation by fighting off the spirits as they assaulted him in dreams.

People sought the initial encounters and the vocation in other cases. Even so, the spirits took the final initiative by manifesting themselves to only some of these people. Even among the Tlingits, whose shamans came from the same matrilineal groups and normally sought the spirits, the spirits chose the shamans from those eligible.

The initial experiences that inaugurated the election were frightening and disorienting. What ever the cause might have been that precipitated a conviction of election, the experiences involved fright and confusion. Here is a summary description from the eastern Aleutian Islands:[15]

> While travelling at sea, for instance, suddenly in front of them there would be an inaccessible island or a horrible cliff or fearsome monsters emerging from the sea. If they were travelling on foot, different spectres would show themselves to them, or suddenly it would seem that they were standing on the brink of a precipice ready to be hurled down from it and so on.

In the Chugach region, a shaman named Kalushi realized his election when a 'large fish' capsized his kayak, so that he was lost at sea. Found later safe atop a precipice too steep for him to have climbed, and asked how he had transported himself up there, he said that 'a mask' had carried him up.[16]

Kalushi's experience involved typical emotions and symbols: the shaman-to-be was traumatized, cast into the depths, disoriented, caught by a mask (a spirit), and transported to a precipice. Similar frightening and disorienting initial experiences were reported throughout the region-at-large by other sources.

Those chosen by the spirits were normally men, but they could be women. And on Kodiak Island, they could be transvestites whose propensity to cross ontological and cosmological boundaries as shamans would be reflected in their crossing of social and gender boundaries.[17]

(ii) Training

In general, the encounters with the spirits constituted the training as well as the initiation. Through these encounters, the shamans-to-be learned their spirits' names and their spirits' songs. They learned to interact with the spirits, to control them and to be controlled by them. In this way, they learned to mediate with the powers that influenced or claimed to influence life and death, success and misfortune, food and famine, health and illness.

Shamans-to-be might receive training from experienced shamans. There was regional variation. On the mainland among the Yupiit, and southward among the Chugach, some shamans received training, while others learned on their own. On Montague Island where 'half the population were conjurers', a number had been trained by a renowned shaman whose name was Apuluq. On Kodiak Island, children might have been trained to the role. Eastward among the Yakutat Tlingit, the shamans received some unspecified training. On Nunivak Island, shamans claimed they had received no training, but this claim did not convince the ethnographer who wondered how they could then have learned. Evidently, training of an apprentice or a helper occurred in some cases but not necessarily in all instances.

(iii) Shamans' rites with spirit manifestations

Shamans had their own rites. To steady drum beats they sang songs that they had learned during encounters with the spirits. They sang to make the spirits manifest. Manifestations could occur through sights and sounds apart from the shamans; alternatively, the spirits would appear through the shamans, who would represent them by masks or costumes or by mimicry. Mimicry could often involve cawing like birds, leaping like fish, or growling, crawling, even mock-biting like land animals.

By differing means, shamans sought to influence the spirits which were present. These means varied from gentle persuasion to outright fights. For example, an eastern Aleutian Island shaman coaxed a spirit to cease afflicting a patient, while a Kodiak Island shaman battled and banished a moon-spirit. Another eastern Aleutian Island shaman threatened a spirit by daring to expose it as impotent if it refused to change the weather. In response the spirit knocked the shaman senseless, but finally complied.[18]

Shamans throughout the region-at-large lost consciousness during rites. In the case just cited, this was caused by the shaman being hit by a spirit. In other cases, the shaman induced unconsciousness through rapid body movements, such as running in circles.

Drugs evidently were not normally used: drug use is not reported in the sources. A lone reference to drug use from the central Aleutian Islands was an error, which occurred when 'петрушка' was mistakenly allowed into the English translation as 'opium'.[19] It is a common word for parsley in the Russian language. *Petroushka* is a kind of angelica widely employed in Alaska today as a herbal medicine, and used for body massage in the steam bath on Kodiak Island.

(iv) Paraphernalia

With regard to the shamans' own semblance during their rites, two traditions existed in the region-at-large. One, less ornate, occurred among the Chugach, eastern Aleuts, and Yupiit. The other was ornate and existed among Dena'ina, Eyak and Tlingit. Both traditions converged among the Koniag on Kodiak Island.

According to the less ornate tradition, the shamans either performed in normal *kamleikas* (gut-skin parkas) or performed naked. Elaboration consisted only of the skin-pieces hung from the waist and lined with bird beaks which were worn by some Chugach shamans. In contrast, according to the ornate tradition, the shamans wore combinations of ritual garments and talismans, including headgear, necklaces, animal furs, claws, feathers, and noise-making attachments. The shamans also used rattles and wands. Masks and costumes were changed by Tlingit and Eyak shamans as different spirits became manifest. In both traditions, shamans wore masks during some rites only, probably the most important ones in which the most powerful spirits appeared or in which spirits received special attention.

Shamans constructed masks for their own rites and for some public ritual festivals. This ocurred throughout the region-at-large, including the Aleutian Islands.[20] The masks manifested the types of spirits which the shamans saw. But the shamans' masks were only varieties of masks, mask-making being well developed and varied throughout the region. Other varieties included funerary masks and story-telling or dance masks.

A type of item that evidently was specific to the shamans was the shamans' dolls. The northernmost Yup'ik shamans kept theirs secretly, hiding them in isolated places and consulting them as oracles. Central and western Aleutian Island shamans surreptitiously made human-sized dolls to carry out deeds. These large dolls were self-animating, which after doing the shamans' deeds could act of their own volition, even bringing destruction to whole lineages. They were therefore dangerous and local norms prohibited them, but 'there was always someone among the shamans willing to make one'.[21]

Small dolls in human form and in animal forms were made by Koniag, Chugach, Dena'ina, Eyak and Tlingit shamans. These dolls were used to extract the sources of illness from patients during healing rites. During a shaman's performance, a doll might act according to its shape: a bird-form flying, a halibut-form leaping, a human-form walking. Shamans claimed they could send their spirits into such dolls at will. Apuluq (the powerful Chugach shaman from Montague Island), for example, made one for his grieving, childless wife, and when he put his power into it, it was said to have walked.[22] Such dolls could be made to do deeds: they could help in the hunt; they could rescue people at sea; some could speak. Similar to the large dolls on the western and central Aleutian Islands, some could even act on their own.

(v) Boundary Crossings

Sometimes during their rites, and at other times too, shamans crossed or claimed to cross ontological boundaries to become something other than themselves. They turned into animals or into spirits, as was clearly reported everywhere in the sources that have been cited. This happened during rites through representations involving mimicry or involving the wearing of masks and costumes. It also occurred in powerful shamans in myths whenever they willed it.

Shamans also crossed or claimed to cross cosmological and geographical boundaries by traveling up through the sky to the moon, even through star holes to upper worlds, down through the sea to the depths, far across the earth, and into the land of the dead. Whether in the body or out of the body, it is unclear.[23] The ethnographies simply describe the shamans as disappearing, then reappearing. Folklore simply said the shamans flew, sometimes like birds. In one instance, it was said that he left trails of sparks in the sky.

So much prestige was attached to these crossings that some shamans practised them through dramatic acts. One shaman, for example, had his assistant kinsmen tie him up tightly, throw him in the sea, and leave him to drown. Four days later to the sound of his assistants' drumming, he walked into the village alive and well. Another shaman had his assistants bind him to a pyre. They then set it aflame and burned it to the ground. The next day he reappeared, coming down into the *qasgiq* (*kashim*) through the smokehole in the roof (for the *qasgiq*, and the symbolism of the smokehole, see Ch.2, sec.4.ii, above).

Crossing boundaries, a shaman could become erratic or dangerous. A description among the Chugach may serve as an example:[24]

> [The shaman Tutyiq's] spirit flew away carrying its master. Nobody ever saw the spirit, but they saw Tutyiq in their dreams when he told them he was going to make them sick. People wanted to kill him, but even Apuluq was afraid to do so.

Apuluq was the powerful Chugach shaman from Montague Island (mentioned in subsecs ii, iv): even he was wary of this Tutyiq. A benign shaman lost control of his power, 'too strong for him to control'. A comparatively helpful shaman might be treated with caution: Angauqanga was 'a good man who assisted and cured many people'. His only devious work was the 'stealing' of animals' *yuas*, so that his own sons alone could catch the animals during hunts. Yet, he was kept in his own dwelling away from the home because 'his daughter was afraid to let him live in the house'.[25]

(vi) Tasks

Despite variations, and despite any ambiguity, the main social task associated with shamans throughout the region-at-large centred on their abilities to temper the spirits of illness and thus to heal. Throughout the region-at-large, a shaman would heal by identifying the spirit responsible for the malady, then either driving it away or persuading it to cease acting malevolently. In the southeast where witchcraft and sorcery were believed to be prevalent causes of illness, the Tlingit and Eyak shamans identified the witch or sorcerer.

On the central Aleutian Islands some shamans would also employ herbal medicines.[26] Where herbal remedies were less well known or used, a shaman might massage or use hand pressure.[27]

Next to healing, the tasks most frequently associated with shamans throughout the region-at-large were foreseeing future events and facilitating the hunt. They accomplished the latter by attracting game or by locating food sources. Other tasks reported for particular areas include: changing the weather, identifying transgressors of norms, rescuing people at sea, learning the location or the fate of missing people, and making amulets.

In their capacity as shamans, they did not preside over the ritual festivals. Public ritual festivals were developed throughout the region-at-large. Shamans might perform during them; for example, shamans had specific roles at definite times during *Nakaciuq*, the Yup'ik hunting-related ritual festival that honoured sea mammal *yua* and that escorted the *yua*s ceremoniously on return to the sea (as described in Chapter 2): During the first day of *Nakaciuq*, the shamans would sing and represent the life-death cycle. During a later day, they would 'see' the *yua* to learn if these spirits had been pleased. Also for *Kevig*, the Yup'ik shamans directed the making of specific masks and the singing of songs associated with these masks. However while participating, the shamans did not preside over these festivals.

There were some exceptions. Yup'ik shamans were masters of ceremonies during *Kelek*, another ritual festivity that occurred regularly in many places to honour the shamans' spirits as well as the *yua*. *Kelek* was distinct from *Nakaciuq* and *Kevig*. Across the Bering Sea, central Aleutian Island shamans conducted 'ceremonial feasts', but whether all or only a particular type of 'ceremonial feasts' the source does not say.[28] If they did so at all of them, then this was a unique trait towards the terminus of the island chain; but if they did so only at a particular type, then this and the Yup'ik *Kelek* would be correlative.[29]

These exceptions aside, we may say that shamans throughout the region-at-large usually did not act as masters of ceremonies in public ritual festivals unless they did so as leading men who happened also to be shamans.

Nor did they officiate at life-crisis rites, although Yup'ik shamans on Nunivak

Island and Tlingit shamans performed annual village or lineage purification and preservation rites. Again the generality does not imply that the shamans were never involved: it signfies that their involvement would occur for reasons other than their being shamans.

The shamans' main social tasks throughout the region-at-large clearly were: (a) healing, (b) forseeing future events, and (c) facilitating the hunt, or locating food sources.

(3) The Social Perspective: Two Examples of Transformation

We shall see that two men did not manifest that set of characteristics. Yet these men were referred to as 'shamans' nevertheless. These men were: (i) the elder of Akun, Ivan Smirennikov, among the Aleut people; and (ii) an Alutiiq healer named Kangatyuq, among the Alutiiq people. They reflected the meaning intristic in the regional words for 'shaman' and were fulfilling the shamans' main social tasks.

(i) The elder of Akun: 'an Aleut prophet'

The patristic criteria for the discernment of the form as well as the content of Smirennikov's ecstatic experience comprised the focus in the preceding chapter. The present chapter will focus on the social context where Smirennikov's ecstatic experiences took place. The discernment is a quality proper to the one who exercised it, that is Ivan Veniaminov. The social context is a quality of the one who lived it, that is Ivan Smirennikov. The qualities have been kept distinct, developed each in its own chapter. The sources about Smirennikov and their credibility have been explained in the preceding chapter.[30] Ivan Smirennikov lived on the island of Akun, where the priest Ivan Veniaminov and the *toion* of Tigalda and Akun, Ivan Pan'kov, met him during spring 1828. More detail about these three is necessary to develop the example. We may recall from Chapter 1 that Aleut men from the islands of Tigalda and Akun had created a militant alliance to counter the escalating influx of commercial enterprises into the eastern Aleutians during the 1780s and 1790s, and that the same islands had provided the leadership for the Aleut-led wars during the mid-1760s. A *toion* of this region, Sergei Dmitrievich Pan'kov, had presided at a council at Unalaska in 1791.

In the next generation after the toion Sergei Dmitrievich Pan'kov, now within changed social conditions, we find the current *toion* Ivan Pan'kov who held the same surname as well as the same title of leadership, indicating an affinity between himself and Sergei Dmitrievich. The current *toion* was already knowledgeable in Russian Orthodoxy, providing instruction in this faith and its practices himself in his polity before the parish priest Veniaminov had arrived. (we noticed the processes by which this leadership could emerge on the Aleutian Islands, Ch.1, sec.1.ii-iv). This *toion* of Tigalda and Akun received the parish priest and family on their arrival into the Unalaska district and assisted, even monetarily, with their settlement here in 1824. Elder in age to the priest, he assumed a fatherly concern for him and for his ministry, accompanying him on pastoral visits as on this visit to Akun in 1828. They became intimate. Their cooperation was so close, and the *toion's* knowledge of Christianity was so developed, that Pan'kov and Veniaminov would together coordinate the translation of the Gospel according to Matthew into the Aleut language on the eastern Aleutian islands, and this *toion* would be properly designated on the publication's frontispiece as co-translator with the priest. After Veniaminov's transfer in 1838, Pan'kov continued to provide religious leadership, having chapels constructed for his own people on Tigalda and Akun in 1842 and 1843.[31]

Just as the *toion* of Tigalda and Akun, Ivan Pan'kov, was a generation older than Ivan Veniaminov, so was the Aleut elder of Akun, Ivan Smirennikov. The Aleut elder was approximately sixty years old at this time, the priest was thirty-one years old.[32] Apart from age, the three Ivans would not have been so very different from each other, as Veniaminov derived from a village in Siberia, the Irkutsk *gubernia*, and may have been Eurasian by his own lineage, as Russian settlers had long intermarried with north Asian peoples.[33] This interaction took place between far northerners: all three of these Ivans were men of the Arctic.

The elder of Akun was known to have healed, foreseen the future, and located food supplies on behalf of others in this region on numerous occasions. And he was known in this region as a shaman: 'regarded by the local inhabitants and by many others as well, as a shaman, not an ordinary person at least.' Even the *toion* considered him to be a shaman; therefore Pan'kov, having 'firm faith in the One God' and 'afraid to fall into error', had assiduously avoided the man: he had 'never entered into any conversation with the old man' and had 'protested and tried to restrain others' when they would call on him for help', according to Pan'kov's own account that he co-authored and co-signed.[34] It is likely that Smirennikov also considered himself to be a shaman, because once he had asked his 'protectors', the spirits, to leave him so that he should not be:[35]

> Moreoever as people regard him as a shaman, and he does not want to be a shaman, he asked the spirits to leave him alone; the spirits replied that they ... can not leave him.

He asked them to leave him not because he was frightened by them (he was never frightened by them), but because he did not wish to be a shaman himself.

Smirennikov's interactions with these spirits were different from the typical interactions between shamans and spirits as observed through the ethnographic perspective. His encounters with his spirits were not terrifying or disorienting. Through more than three decades of their appearance to him, these spirits had never caused him anxiety, except a pang of conscience when he had done something amiss: otherwise he never experienced any foreboding in their presence.

Nor did he employ the rites and paraphernalia that were typical of other shamans. This difference can be deduced from three factors. Firstly, these spirits appeared only to Smirennikov. He himself, evidently, found this odd as he had asked them about it: 'To his question, why they do not appear to others, the spirits replied that were so ordered.' The typical shamans' rites and paraphenalia represented the shamans' spirits' manifestations. Furthermore, these spirits had not appeared in order to be propitiated or to be appeased by him. The very nature of their manifestation, even to himself alone, would not necessitate typical rites of summoning and propitiation.

Thirdly, their appearance and the elder's own vocation were endorsed by the priest Veniaminov who was knowledgable about the practices of shamans-of-old on the Aleutian Islands and in Siberia and who refused to have the appellation 'shaman' applied to this man: 'I told the other Aleuts who were present not to call him a Shaman,' Veniaminov emphasized; and he emphasized the same again: 'I conversed with the elder Ivan Smirennikov who is considered a shaman in these parts. I found the facts quite to the contrary.'[36] The insightful younger man from Siberia was, in effect, distinguishing this man's form from the practices and experiences that typified shamans-of-old (see Ch.4, sec.3.ii). We may say that the *toion* came to the same conclusion, because Pan'kov affixed his signature alongside Veniaminov's signature on the report that contained this distinction.

A year later, in July 1829, Veniaminov would require that an actual shaman should promise to cease practicing when that one sought baptism from him in the Nushagak region, western Alaskan mainland, outside the parish.[37] Why? The Siberian was aware that shamans' practices might induce involvement with the demonic. He did not dwell upon the theme with regard to shamans-of-old, nor did he create a generality about them; but he was aware of this type of involvement that did occur among some and he mentioned it in his ethnography as follows:[38]

Many shamans frankly termed their profession a service of the devil and told young people that anyone who could not expect to brave the terrors should not aspire to be a shaman.

As baptism involves a formal renunciation of the diabolical, and as the disassociation from the demonic was vital in Veniaminov's sight for the sake of human salvation (see Ch.4, sec.3.ii), therefore he would require that a shaman should cease from involvment in typical shamans' rites when one sought to be baptized. With regard to the Aleut elder of Akun however, Veniaminov encouraged *him* to continue practising among the Aleuts of Veniaminov's own parish, no less. The distinction is clear. Smirennikov differed in practice from typical shamans-of-old.

Nonetheless this man on Akun island was being referred to as a shaman, regarded as such 'by the local inhabitants and by many others as well'. Indeed, he reflected the intrinsic meaning in the regional terms for 'shaman': He was possessed of spirit(s), and thus was enabled to accomplish the extraordinary. In his case, the phrase 'possessed of spirits' could be understood as their remaining with him.

We may well hypothesize that if the words for 'spirit' had not yet become definite in general usage in the Aleut language, and the meaning of *quĝaq* was still supple in popular usage, then the popular application of the term *qugaĝiq* to him might not have been incongruous, because the term would have described him through the meaning that is implicit in its etymology: he was (in fact) possessed of spirits and he was (indeed) accomplishing the extraordinary. The contradiction in terms would exist for Veniaminov and Pan'kov who were intent on precision in such matters, and perhaps even for Smirennikov himself; however, there might have been little if any contradiction in the popular use of the regional term for him. The hypothesis is possible because the translation of the Gospel according to Matthew had not yet commenced: Veniaminov and Pan'kov would begin the translation a year-and-a-half later, in September 1829. Once *quĝaq* would be fixed as the term for the malevolent, the demonic, then the contridiction would become acute in general and the elder of Akun would cease being referred to as a 'shaman' in common parlance, because this highly gifted and nearly unique man belonged categorically with the angelic. The distinction is incisive. It is this distinction that was given to him by the two other Ivans (a Siberian and a fellow Aleut, both leaders of stature). It was expressed three generations later.

In 1927, the Native Alaskan priest A.P. Kashevarov referred to this elder of Akun, Ivan Smirennikov, as 'an Aleut prophet.'[39]

Kashevarov's reference is accurate. It is not a fanciful analogy. Smirennikov's ecstatic experience was akin to those of the biblical prophets and apostles: his experience was of the biblical prophetic kind, according to patristic criteria that have been applied to him as we have seen (Ch.4, sec.3).

'An Aleut prophet', as he became known, was being referred to as a 'shaman' in his own region in his own times. Thus through him, the transformation does become visible: as the shamans' main and most vital social tasks continued through this man among the baptized Akun Aleuts.

(ii) The Alutiiq Healer

The next example took place virtually concurrently, now among the Alutiiq people in the Kodiak area. The published information about Kangatyuq was collected and written by the ethnographer K. Birket-Smith who conducted fieldwork in the Chugach Bay Area (the Prince William Sound region) from 27 April to 22 July 1933 as part of the First Danish-American Alaska Expedition.[40] Birket-Smith spent six weeks with Makarii Fedorovich Chumovitskii who became the ethnographer's 'primary informant' and whose daughter Matrona acted as *ad hoc* interpreter between them.[41] Makarii Fedorovich was a tradition-bearer with deep roots in the region, a leading man of stature within the community. He said he had known Kangatyuq, which is likely in fact.[42]

The ethnographer collected a number of 'shaman stories' and other descriptions from this same source. Birket-Smith was aware of the distinctions between shamans and other types of healers and knew various regional terms for them.[43] We can not know for certain whether he could have applied his knowledge of these various terms when he collected this account however, because of a disadvantage in the ethnographic fieldwork. Birket-Smith did not speak Alutiiq or Russian, the languages that Makarii Fedorovich spoke. They communicated through Matrona, for whom English was a third language.

There is a further problem involving the ethnographer's own classifications. The Russian-Alutiiq who relayed these descriptions was classed by Birket-Smith as a 'Chugach Eskimo', and some descriptions that contained Orthodox Christian elements were taken by the ethnographer to be 'aboriginal religious ideas'.[44] Therefore when Birket-Smith's publication refers to the healer Kangatyuq as a 'shaman', the term 'shaman' can not itself be taken as the indicative feature. It might have been another projection from the ethnographer's own subjective classifications, as follows: the Russian-Alutiiq tradition-bearer becomes a 'Chugach Eskimo'; the religious descriptions that he conveys become 'aboriginal religious ideas'; and the Alutiiq healer in the account becomes a 'shaman'. The placing of Kangatyuq in the context with shamans-of-old can not depend merely on the designation of him as a 'shaman' in this written account. More indicative and more important is the broader structure of the account, which (we may expect) would more securely reflect the original account and oral tradition.

The structure of this account places Kangatyuq among other men known to have been shamans in the Chugach region. It compares him with them and emphasizes his differences from them. The account about him is the lengthiest and most detailed among the descriptions that the ethnographer published from this same source. Its relative length and detail might indicate the importance of its content for Makarii Fedorovich himself. It is related as a story, which can be read in the publication, while I shall represent the details to analyse the differences that Makarii Fedorovich emphasized in this account

A persistent feeling, or intuition, had prompted Kangatyuq to discover his ability to heal. He tested this intuition during the sea otter hunt by reviving a grounded bird: he 'breathed' on it; the bird strengthened and flew. Yet even this discovery did not inaugurate the vocation. Kangatyuq was encouraged to begin healing later, by a man.

During another hunting expedition, this time into the Kodiak area, Kangatyuq and a cousin went into the forest to visit 'a very holy man, Монах Германъ'.[45] The Cyrillic is written in the published source. It is Russian for 'the monastic Herman'. (We may recall that this monastic was the member of the spiritual mission from Valaam who had arrived at Kodiak in 1794 and who had moved from *Pavlovskaia gavan* to the islet of *Elovoi* by 1818, where he resumed the anchoritic life that he had known in the forests of Karelia. The last surviving of the initial missionaries, he reposed in the forest on this islet in 1836.)

This 'very holy man, Монах Германъ' saw Kangatyuq, recognized his abilities (he recognized him as 'a shaman', in the published account, p.131) and directed him to the 'priest's house' to heal the 'priest's daughter' who was deathly ill. As Kangatyuq had been to church the day before, he knew the priest and so went to the house where he gave the priest a message written by the monastic missionary. Having read the message, the priest took Kangatyuq to the ailing daughter. Thus did this Alutiiq healer's vocation commence.[46]

He healed her as he was enabled by an unnamed spirit to whom he prayed. The prayer was a general supplication, described in the account as follows (ibid.):

> I wish you would help me, whoever you are. You let this girl come back to her parents like that rotten bird ... that I made alive, then I'll believe myself what I am.

He proceeded by 'breathing' on her:

> The first time she did not move, but the second time he blew through his hands, and she opened her eyes as if she was waking up. Now Kangatyuq talked and talked, but they were not able to understand what he said. After he had blown for the third time the girl motioned to him to set her up.

These acts comprised his healing technique at the commencement of his vocation, and the same technique remained throughout his vocation: 'He always used to blow but never did anything else, not even sing' (p.132). He only healed. He never harmed. So remarkable was this quality that it was emphasized in the account:

He never hurt anyone, but he always cured people. He could do so even faster than Apuluq. He always used to blow but never did anything else, not even sing. 'That fellow's got good medicine breath,' people said. He did not know who his spirit was. His son Kalushi did not cure people like [as did] his father.

We saw Apuluq and Kalushi through the ethnographic perspective earlier in this chapter, from stories about themselves: Apuluq was the powerful shaman from Montague Island who was possessed of Adliuq, the fearsome Copper River spirit; and Kalushi had his vocation inaugurated through the capsizing at sea and the subsequent transportation 'by a mask' to the top of a cliff face.[47]

Now let us highlight Kangatyuq's differences from typical shamans such as those in the Chugach region. His vocation as a healer had not been inaugurated through the disorienting initial experiences that typified shamans such as Kalushi. Nor did it involve the subsequent terrifying encounters with spirits. Unlike Apuluq, Kangatyuq did not even know who his spirit was. Therefore, it would have remained unnamed: and this would explain the fact that Kangatyuq did 'not even sing' to heal. Singing for shamans-of-old could be a pronouncing and repeating of a spirit's name to make a spirit manifest. He 'always' healed by breath alone: in other words, the rites and paraphernalia that typified shamans-of-old were not used by him. Finally, his character was remarkably stable: 'he only healed.'[48]

He was securely associated within Russian Orthodoxy by the tradition-bearer who relayed the oral history: Kangatyuq had been to church before he himself went into the forest to seek the monastic missionary Herman; this 'very holy man' recognized the nascent healer's qualities and encouraged the vocation; the vocation commenced in a priest's house, indeed with the clergyman's own daughter.

Yet while differing from typical shamans-of-old in southern Alaska and while effecting his ability of heal differently from theirs (as emphasized in the account), Kangatyuq fulfilled this main vital task that was attributed to shamans-of-old and he did so even better than they. Thus, Kangatyuq the Alutiiq healer becomes another example of the transformation.

(4) Conclusions

Two perspectives on shamans-of-old in southern Alaska have been assumed. The ethnographic perspective brings out a set of visible and audible characteristics that have attracted the attention of ethnographers. The social perspective highlights the main vital social tasks of the shamans-of-old in southern Alaska, especially healing. Within the social perspective, men could be seen who were accomplishing the main social task(s) without the set of other characteristics that typified shamans-of-old. One example arises from among the Aleuts, another from among the Alutiiqs, both virtually concurrently: the first on the Aleutian Islands in 1828, the second in the Kodiak area before 1836.

The two perspectives allow an aspect of the transformation to be perceived: as continuity becomes visible through the social perspective regarding the shamans' major social tasks; but discontinuity becomes evident through the ethnographic perspective regarding some other characteristics of shamans-of-old. As the discontinuity in the set of characteristics included the distinctive rites that induced ecstatic trance in shamans-of-old, a relationship should be recognized between the comparison created in this chapter and the comparison in the preceding chapter, there from patristic literature regarding ecstatic experiences. This relationship is recapitulated in the example who spans these chapters: the Aleut elder Ivan Smirennikov. In the preceding chapter, he comprised an example of prophetic ecstasy of a biblical kind, in contrast to other types of ecstatic experiences. In the present chapter, he has comprised an example of the transformation in contrast to shamans-of-old.

So that these two men could be established as examples of a transformation *from* the ancient shamans' practices, these men had to be associated with shamans-of-old in the region. The Aleut elder and prophet Ivan Smirennikov was associated with regional shamans-of-old by the very term 'shaman' that was being applied to him by Akun Aleuts and by others in general parlance during his own times. His differences notwithstanding, he reflected the broadest meaning of the regional terms for 'shaman' while he was fulfilling the main vital tasks associated with the shamans-of-old in southern Alaska. The Alutiiq healer named Kangatyuq was associated with regional shamans by the overall structure of the Chugach-area account that described him fulfilling their main social task. Healing through the capacity of a spirit, he also was conformed to the broadest meaning of the regional terms for 'shaman' although the account about him emphasized his diffences from them.

Equally, these two men had to be associated with Christianity, so that they may be seen moreover as examples of the transformation *into* Russian Orthodoxy. Both men were associated in this way very clearly; and the association in both instances happened to involve, no less than, men who are venerated as saints in the Russian Church: St Herman for the Alutiiq healer and St Innokentii (Veniaminov) for the Aleut elder and prophet.

Together the Aleut elder and the Alutiiq healer signify a vital aspect of transformation among their respective peoples: a transformation of the characteristics of shamans-of-old into the qualities of healers and even of a prophet of the biblical kind.

This aspect should be expected within a transition that occurred through virtually the whole of the Aleut and Alutiiq societies in their entireties and that involved indigenous spiritual and social processes. Other aspects, glimpsed so-far in this study, include the transformation of ritual masks into icons, and the transformation of ancient ritual festivals into liturgies and into liturgical festivals. But would this specific aspect of a multifaceted transformation be recognized by authorities other than those like the insightful Veniaminov and Herman? Or might some seek to purge the 'natives' from all 'shamans', even all 'shaman stories' and 'aboriginal religious ideas'? The question will be reserved as the study proceeds further into this facet of transformation.

NOTES

[1] The comparative method of study that engendered the two perspectives has been described in my Introduction (Method: Social Anthropology); and the criteria for the credibility of the relevant sources were explained there as well. It should be added now that among the sources that will be cited here, a number are Native Alaskans: Fr Iakov Netsvetov (1840, 1984b), Nora Marks Dauenhauer (Dauenhauer and Dauenhauer 1990:108-127; 1988), and Elsie Mather (1985; for Mather summarized, see Morrow 1984).

For material in this chapter previously published, see Mousalimas (1995, 1993c, 1990d, 1989a): the present work supersedes the previous. A divergence should be noted from id. (1989a): the 'cultural perspective' has been designated the 'ethnographic perspective' to reflect better the types of characteristics that are involved, the highly visible and audible characteristics that would attract the attention of an ethnographer. Futhermore with regard to ibid., see nt.14, below. With regard to id. (1990d), see nt 43, below.

[2] For these terms, see: Bergsland (1986:127, 1980:118), Birket-Smith (1953:124), Jacobson (1984:183, 321, 380), Fienup-Riordan (1983:234), Fortesque (ms.), Geoghegan (1944:117), Hawkes (1914:17), Lantis (1946:197), Leer (ms.), Nelson (1899:428), Ray (1967:11). Orthographic as well as dialectical variations occur. In the Yup'ik language according to Jacobson (1984:380, 742), there are four terms for 'shaman': *kallalek, qelalek, tuunralek, angalkuq* (each of these four terms has a cognate in other Eskimo or Aleut languages); see nt.5, below.

[3] Fitzhugh and Kaplan (1982:188), Jacobson (1984:68), Lantis (1946:197), Morrow (1984:136), Fienup-Riordan (1983:234). The translation, quoted, is from Ray (1967:11).

[4] Bergsland (1986:127, *quGa-*), Fortesque (ms.:*tunraq*), Geoghegan (1944: *quǧaq*), Leer (ms.:*kala'aq*). Also see Veniaminov (1840b:86, 144; 1984:199, 229). For the distribution of the cognates through Alaska and the North American Arctic, and a distribution of synonyms in the Koryak and Chukchi languages in northeast Asia, see Marsh (1954:27-28).

[5] See e.g. Nelson (1899:394), Sonne (1988:93-94). Among the four Yup'ik terms for 'shaman' *(kallalek, qelalek, tuunralek, angalkuq)*, only the term *'tuunralek'* is associated with an evil spirit in that language: see Jacobson (1984:380). This indicates that

distinctions are made linguistically between types of practitioners, not by prefixing an adjective to render a 'good *tuunralek*', which would be a contradiction in terms in the modern language, rather like positing a 'good demoniac'; but by applying different terms to differing types of practitioners. These distinctions collapse in translation into the single term 'shaman'. The term *angalkuq* seems to me to be significant, but I do not have enough knowledge of the language to comment on this.

[6] For the Eskimo language cognates, see Leer (ms.), Jacobsen (1984) and Fortesque (ms.): in these dictionaries, compare *sua*, *yua* and *inua* with *kalla'aq* in Alutiiq, *tuunraq* in Yup'ik and *tunraq* Inupiaq/Inuit. For a general distinction with reference to the wider distribution of the cognates, see Marsh (1954). For the distinction of *yua*, or *inua*, from *tunraq* in ethnography and anthropology, see: Nelson (1899:394) and more recently Sonne (1988:94-95); but the latter has indicated that the distinction was not as definite on Nunivak Island as on the mainland. For the Aleut probable synonym, see Marsh (1954:24), from whom the spellings have been quoted here. For the Tlingit, see Dauenhauer and Dauenhauer (1990:125).

[7] See Lot-Falck (1957) for the Koniag mixture of anthropomorphism and zoomorphism with reference to the masks collected by Pinart; but Lot-Falck might have been overly interpretative in this regard. Further research is being conducted by Dominique Desson, Department of Anthropology, University of Alaska, Fairbanks.

[8] For Aleut masks, see the illustrations in Black (1982a): compare and contrast those in figure 47. For Koniag and Yup'ik masks, see the illustrations in Fitzhugh and Crowell (1988): contrast illustration 368 of an *inua* with 441 of a *tunraq* for the Koniag; and contrast illustration 348 of an *inua* with 351, 353, and 436 of *tunraq* for the Yup'ik. For the Yup'ik, also see Sonne (1988), illustrations 19-20, 25, 29-30, 36-37, 43 and 65 of *inua*: contrast with illustration 55 of a *tunraq* and compare with illustrations 15 and 82 of *irci*, another Yup'ik term for 'spirit' that occurs on Nunivak Island according to Sonne (1988:78-85). For *irci*, also see nt.9, below.

[9] See Mark 1:32, 34, in Atkan (central) Aleut, cited by Bergsland (1980:118). See Matthew 8:31 in Fox Island (eastern) Aleut in Veniaminov, [Pan'kov, et al.] (trans), (1840). The terms *iiraq* and *ii'aq* are the translations for the 'devil' in the Gospel according to Matthew in the Alutiiq language, according to Leer (ms.; and personal communication, March 1988). Close cognates, *iinraq* and *iinruq*, are found in the Yup'ik language from the same verbal root, *iir-*, 'to hide' (Jacobson 1984:160).

[10] For the suppleness of the ancient Greek term δαίμων, see: Dodds (1965:37-38), who says that the term was 'vague'; and Rexine (1985:361), who explains that 'the word had a fluidity', the ancient 'Greeks did not stop to categorize whenever they made use of the word'. For the ambiguity of the English term 'demon', see *The Concise Oxford Dictionary of Current English*, where 'demon' is assigned two senses, or meanings: supernatural being, inferior deity, spirit, ghost, indwelling spirit, genius; [and then separated by a semi-colon and subsequent semi-colons] evil spirit as in demoniac; heathen deity; devil; malignant supernatural being; cruel, malignant, destructive, or fierce person.

[11] Athenagoras, *Πρεσβεία* xxiv.3-xxvi.5 (1972:58-66; [xxiv.2-xxvi.2] 1990:79-88). For an indication of the earlier use of this terminology by St Justin the Martyr, see Wartelle (1987:56-68).

[12] See Chryssavgis (1990:169-176).

[13] Dauenhauer and Dauenhauer (1990:125).

[14] I shall provide references in this section for only: (a) some emphases on the Aleutian, Kodiak area and Chugach area materials, (b) for quotations, and (c) additional information. Also see Ch.4, nts 7-10, 43, above.

Otherwise for the generalities, see: Birket-Smith (1953); Birket-Smith and Laguna (1938:); Black (1977b:); Black (1981b); Chickalusion (1982); Desson (1988); Dauenhauer and Dauenhauer (1992); Dauenhauer and Dauenhauer (1990); Dauenhauer and Dauenhauer (1988); Edmonds (1966); Fienup-Riordan (1994); Fienup-Riordan (1990b); Fienup-Riordan (1988); Fienup-Riordan (1983); Gideon (1909); Iokhel'son (1933); Kamenskii (1985); Krause, A. (1956); Laguna (1972); Lantis (1966); Lantis (1946); Lantis (1938); Lot-Falck (1957); Marsh (1967); Mather (1985); Morrow (1984); Nelson (1899); Netsvetov (1840; 1984b); Osgood (1937); Pinart (ms.); Pinart (1873a); Pinart (1873b); Pinart in Lantis (1938); Ray (1981); Ray, ed. (1968); Sarychev (1802:141-142; 1807:64-65); Swanton (1908:464); Van Stone (1964); Veniaminov (1840a; 1984); Veniaminov (1840b; 1984).

In earlier publications, I allowed a seventh category into this perspective: 'Moral Ambiguity' because of the emphasis on moral stability in the two sources that will provide the contrast through the social perspective. While an emphasis is useful for contrast, I felt that a whole category was not quite fair and now I am convinced that it is not: therefore, this characteristic has been subsumed to 'Boundary Crossings'.

[15] Veniaminov (1840b:125; 1984:220).

[16] Chumovitskii in Birket-Smith (1953:130). For Chumovitskii, see sec.3.ii, below.

[17] Black (1977b:99).

[18] For eastern Aleutians, see Sarychev (1802:141-142, 147-148; 1807:64-65, 67-68). For Kodiak, see Pinart in Lantis (1938:146). Could Pinart's view be a misinterpretation? If it is at all possible that the moon was a patron for males and was invoked by whalers on Kodiak (Black, personal communication), then the moon-spirit as inimical to a powerful male shaman might be incongruous. The question may be answered by the research into Pinart's notes conducted by Desson, yet to be published.

[19] Netsvetov (1840:5); cf. ibid. (1984b:367).

[20] For Aleutians, see: Netsvetov (1840:6; 1984b:367); Veniaminov (1840b:144; 1984:229).

[21] Quotation from the central and western Aleutians, Netsvetov (1840:4; 1984b:366); also see Veniaminov (ed.), nt. in ibid.

[22] Chumovitskii in Birket-Smith (1953:128).

[23] Only two ethnographers specify soul-flight: Birket-Smith (1953:127); Laguna (1972:704).

[24] Chumovitskii cited in Birket-Smith (1953:128).

[25] Chumovitskii cited in ibid., p.129.

[26] Netsvetov (1840:5-6; 1984b:367).

[27] See Lantis (1946:202).

[28] Netsvetov (1840:6; 1984:367).

[29] Nelson (1899:494) described a ritual during which shamans presided: *yu-gi-yhik'*

or *i-t-ka-tah'*, referred to as the 'Doll Festival' because a shaman's doll was a central feature. According to Nelson, this ritual had limited distribution, occurring only at the northernmost rim of the Yup'ik territory along the lower Yukon River and in the neighbouring Ingalik Athapaskan territory upriver. Nelson's information about this 'Doll Festival' is not corroborated by any other source regarding the Yupiit. Morrow (1984), summarizing the list of Yup'ik ceremonies compiled by Mather (1985), does not mention it. However, neither does any information from the region at large contradict Nelson.

[30] Quotations and data for Smirennikov derive from Veniaminov (1977:100-102). See Ch.4, sec.3.

[31] See Ch.1., sec.iv, 'The merging of faith and polity', nts 31-37.

[32] For Smirennikov's age, see: Veniaminov (1977:100); Black (1977a:96). For Veniaminov's age, see Pierce (1990:521).

[33] Photographs of him that I have seen in the museum archives in Iakutsk show Eurasian features. The normalcy of such intermarriages as late as the second decade of the twentieth century impressed M. Czaplicka on the 'Yenesei Expedition', from the summer of 1914 until the summer of 1915. The phenomenon was described with aplomb by this Pole at Oxford (Czaplicka n.d.:242-243): 'in no other colony in the world have ... the *lower* and *higher* races so happily adjusted themselves.' While research is yet needed into Veniaminov's own ancestry, an emphasis can be placed on this overall social context, or general historical background, securely now. Furthermore, a cultural synthesis, or multilateral assimilation, was occurring in these regions and continued as late as the 1890s at least (see, e.g., Ch.1, nt.9, above).

[34] Veniaminov (1977:102).

[35] Ibid., p.101.

[36] Ibid.; id. (1993:78, journal entry dated 23 April 1828).

[37] Id. (1993:108, journal entry dated 2-3 July 1829). The *Novo Aleksandrovskii* redoubt, founded at the mouth of the Nushagak River in 1819, was manned by a few traders in 1829. Veniaminov visited this redoubt only one other time during his decade of ministry within the Unalaska parish. A resident priest was assigned to the region later, in 1842.

[38] Id. (1840b:125; 1984:219-220). The same insights, unsolicited by me, were emphasized to me in Iakutsk in July 1991 by a Iakut old man who claimed to have been an assistant of some local shamans.

[39] Kashevarov (1987:346), cited with reference to the reprint. This priest, A.P. Kashevarov, descended from the same extended family as the priest P. Kashevarov who has been cited in Ch.1, above, and will be cited in Ch.6, below.

[40] In Birket-Smith (1953:130-132).

[41] See ibid., pp.1-2. For a photograph of the ethnographer with Makarii Fedorovich and Matrona, J. Johnson, ed. (1984:iv). The surname, spelled 'Chimovitski' by Birket-Smith, will be spelled Chumovitskii here because the surname is spelled this way as it recurs in Russian-American history and as it occurs in the Kodiak area and the Chugach Bay area today. As the interrelationships may prove to be important for the history of the region, the transliteration of the surname should reflect the relationships here.

Makarii Fedorovich was a descendant of Paramon Chumovitskii according to J. Johnson (Chugach Alaska Corporation, personal communication, August 1991). When J. Johnson mentioned this to me, I did not have the insight that shall express in the following paragraphs of this note. I should have asked whether Makarii Fedorovich was a direct descendant. If he had been raised by or had learned from Paramon, then this relationship is all the more significant, as the following description may indicate.

For Paramon, see Gideon (1989:ix, 98, 110, 116, 119). Gifted intellectually, bilingual and literate Paramon Chumovitskii was selected by *hieromonk* Gideon as one of four senior students of the 'Russian-American school' at Kodiak 'who distinguish themselves both by their exemplary successes in learning and by showing sufficient success in training other pupils at the examination held on the 21st of that month [April 1807]' (p.116). The other three were Ivan Kadiakskii, Kristofor Prianishnikov, and Aleksei Kotl'nikov. Hieromonk Gideon wished to take Paramon, as well as Prokopii Lavrov and Aleksei Kotl'nikov, with him on his return voyage to mainland Russia later that same year, so that the young men could visit Okhotsk (p.98); but Alexander Baranov, the chief manager of the company, would not make the provisions for this. At Gideon's departure, Gideon assigned Ivan Kadiakskii to be the head teacher and Kristofor Prianishnikov to be the associate teacher of the school that he had established, and Aleksei Kotl'nikov was designated by him to be their assistant (p.119). Gideon entrusted Paramon Chumovitskii with the task of finishing the compilation of the Kodiak Alutiiq dictionary and compiling a grammar of this language (ibid.).

Furthermore, Gideon (p.110) specified to the company's chief manager that Paramon should be 'left under special supervision' by the monastic Herman whom Gideon, at his departure, had designated as the head of the spiritual mission; in other words, Baranov was not to interfere by putting Paraman to work for the company. And Gideon told the monastic Herman that this young man should serve as translator. This indicates Paramon's development: that Paramon Chumovitskii should serve as the interpreter for the head of the spiritual mission. When we consider the qualities about this monastic Herman (see Ch.6), then Paramon's formation and character should become clearer yet. This association should gain in significance as the monastic Herman appears vividly in our current chapter.

Paramon Chumovitskii as the spiritual mission's interpreter should be differentiated from an interpreter who preceded him, Osip Prianishnikov whose surname is shared by Paramon's fellow student Kristofor Prianishnikov. Osip had married in the Kodiak area. In 1795, he was commended by Archimandrite Ioasaph in writing to G.I. Shelikhov: 'I recommend for your approval Osip Prianishnikov, a man who knows the native language and wants to become an ecclesiastic' (Ioasaph to Shelikhov, 18 May 1795, in Tikhmenev, ed. 1863:107; 1979:84). But Baranov 'hates' him, the *archimandrite* wrote (ibid.). Baranov ridiculed and demeaned Osip Prianishnikov in writing repeatedly during 1799, because he had taken sides actively with the missionaries and the Kodiak people against Baranov's regime (see Baranov's reports in Tikhmenev, ed., e.g.: 1863:150, 162, 1979:115, 124). In March 1805, *hieromonk* Gideon refused to relinquish two youths. one with the surname Prianishnikov (his Christian name was not specified), 'who are being illegally demanded' by the company to be put to work (Gideon 1989:85). Was this Kristofor? Was Kristofor Osip's son? Whatever the relationship may have been between the Prianishnikovs, we may see through this chronology that Kristofor and his three fellow senior honour students, including Paramon, emerged as teachers and a linguist in 1807, despite the turmoil (to the credit of *hieromonk* Gideon's fortitude and tactfulness). We should see moreover that Paramon came to be with the monastic Herman in this context and that lineage then extends to Makarii Fedorovich.

[42] The span in time between the collection in 1933 and the events in the account would be about one hundred years, as the latest possible date for experience described for Kangatyuq would have been before 1836, the year of the repose of the monastic Herman, a key figure in the account. Makarii Fedorovich Chumovitskii was elderly in 1933. If he had known Kangatyuq in the latter's old age, and if Kangatyuq had been a young man at the time of the events, before 1836, then the lives of these two men could easily have encompassed this span in time. Furthermore, Chumovitskii was relaying an oral tradition.

[43] See, e.g., Birket-Smith (1953:116). During my initial research, these factors were elusive: compare Mousalimas (1990d), where the process of collection by Birket-Smith was not distinquished from that by Veniaminov.

[44] Birket-Smith (1953:.2, 130-131).

[45] Ibid., p.130. We are fortunate that the ethnographer took such care with the transcription in this instance.

[46] The parish priest at that time might have been either Frumentii Mordovskii, assigned to Kodiak to relieve the elderly missionary *hieromonk* Athanasii in 1824, or Aleksei Sokolov who replaced Mordovskii in 1833, as both these married clergymen had daughters: see Pierce (1990:362-363, 476-477). In 'Athanasii' in my text, the 'th' is transliterated from the old Russian consonant 'θ'. In the late 18th century Russian primary sources, 'θ' is found, not 'φ', in this name in other names including place names such as Thebaid; e.g., see Valaam (1894:43) and Murav'ev (1855).

[47] NB: Chumovitskii is the source for these descriptions also, as cited above.

[48] The latter difference can be brought forward vividly by contrast with other stories in the Chugach region, that also derived from Chumovitskii (in Birket-Smith 1953), some of which we saw through the ethnographic perspective (end of sec.2.v, above). They include: (a) the mentor of other shamans in this region, Apuluq who was possessed of the spirit Adliuq; (b) the shaman Tityiq who had been carried away by his spirit and would appear in people's dreams to afflict them; (c) the shaman Chitna Joe who 'cured alot of people' but 'had power too strong for him to control'; and (d) the shaman Old Man Duke who was feared by the Tlingits and Eyaks as well as the Chugach people and who, in a fit of jealously, cursed his own wife so that she died and he then grieved piteously at that deed.

Regarding some of the names that appear in these descriptions, we should be aware that people throughout the region at large have multiple names, each name reflecting an aspect of a person's identity. Different sorts of names occur in various sources: ancestral Alaskan names; Russian Orthodox baptismal names; Slavic, Scandinavian, and English surnames; everyday American names, like Johnny; and nicknames, Chitna Joe or Old Man Duke.

CHAPTER 6

Transformation, II

The same kinds of qualities that can be perceived through the social perspective were also attributed to the anchorite from Valaam whom Kangatyuq met in the forest on the islet of *Elovoi*, today's Spruce Island: that 'very holy man, Монах Германъ'.[1] Associated with spirit(s), he was accomplishing the extraordinary, healing, foreseeing future events, and pacifying the forces of nature. The reader may attribute these qualities either directly to him or to the sources who wrote about him (in the latter instance, these qualities would be attributed to these sources' own beliefs regarding him). The effect upon the argument is one and the same; for in either case, these qualities were associated with the anchorite from Valaam in the forest of *Elovoi*.

A tradition will be traced in this chapter from him, through the Monastery of Valaam, to the desert fathers, and then into the Gospels and the Acts of the Apostles: a deep line of tradition embodied by him, and through him touching a continuing line of indigenous tradition in the Kodiak area where he lived when, for example, he inaugurated the vocation of the Alutiiq healer.

Why should an entire chapter focus solely upon this person when no one else will have been described to such length in this study? Firstly, he remained in the region much longer than any of the other missionaries. Of the seven monastic missionaries and three church servitors who arrived at Kodiak in 1794, five had died by the turn of the century.[2] In 1805, four were mentioned in a report from Kodiak.[3] By 1819, only three remained,[4] and by 1825, only this one of the original ten.[5] He reposed in the forest of *Elovoi* in 1836, after forty-two years in the Kodiak area.[6]

Also, he is considered holy and is venerated in Alaska and at Valaam, known as 'St Herman of Alaska' in the one location and 'St Herman of Valaam' in the other location, as we shall see.

(1) Summary Biography[7]

Embarking upon the monastic life as a young man of about sixteen years old, he went to a *metochion* near the Gulf of Finland, a 'holding' of the monastic establishment *Sviato-Troitskaia Sergievskaia Lavra*, where he remained for five or six years. He then entered the monastery of Valaam, situated on an islet in vast Lake Ladoga in Karelia.

There he sought solitude in a *scete*, consisting of a few monastics, as few as two or three under the guidance of a spiritual father, deeper in the forest than the monastery house itself. Eventually he embarked upon the anchoritic (er- emitic) life for even greater solitude by permission from Nazarii, the *hegumen* of Valaam, who had observed his spiritual development and his ability for these rigours and challenges.

In 1793, Nazarii attached him to the mission for Kodiak. This was a gift from the *hegumen* indeed, as Nazarii was developing his own monastery, yet he sent a man of such calibre to Kodiak. The *hegumen* remained in contact with him through letters, as did the subsequent *hegumeni* of Valaam for forty- two years hence.[8]

The monastic Herman arrived in September 1794. He had practical respon- sibilities, of course. In 1798, he was assigned to oversee the remaining missionaries' domestic concerns when their leader, *archimandrite* Ioasaph, departed.[9] This would hardly have been an easy duty, although these men's far northern backgrounds would have equipped them for the hardships. The company's on-site management at that time was not favourably disposed to- wards these monastic missionaries, as we may recall (Ch.1, sec.2.i.c): no provisions had been made for them, they were not given an adequate supply of food to sustain themselves, their lodgings were demeaning. Later, under administrations that would be better disposed, food stores could be scarce.[10] The missionaries would fish and would garden for food, and in times of dire need they foraged the beaches to sustain themselves.[11]

From 1807, he served as the head of the surviving mission when Gideon, the cathedral *hieromonk* from Petersburg who had arrived in 1804 to examine the mission's conditions, departed. The monastic missionary, in this capacity, cared particularly for the poor and the infirm.[12]

By 1819, he had resumed the anchoritic life, at a site that he named 'New Valaam' in the forest on the islet of *Elovoi*: he would have been about sixty-two years old in this year.[13] The name is itself a manifestation of his continuous links with the monastery of Valaam. In 1830, it became the official designa- tion for this area where he was still living.[14]

'New Valaam' was located on the eastern side of *Elovoi*, a distance of a few 'versts', equivalent to a few miles, over the sea from Kodiak Island's harbour town, *Pavlovskaia gavan*.[15] The location would provide finer quietude, dis- tancing him from the bustle of the harbour. We may assume that it would also serve to distance him from the designs and demands of the colonizers. We should recall that he had involved himself in protests against the gross exploitation by the Russian-American Company's administration, especially in the years 1802, 1805, and 1818; and remember his heartfelt plea in December of the later year on behalf of the oppressed (Ch.1, nt.69). That later year, 1818, immediately preceded his move to Elovoi in 1819.

He resumed a way of life at 'New Valaam' in the forest of *Elovoi* that he had known at Valaam in the forest of Karelia. He 'was living a strictly ascetic life': 'the monk of Valaam ... lived as a hermit' ['св. Старца, монаха Валаамсаго Монастыря... подвизавшагося'. 'О. Германъ ... велъ строгую аскетическую жизнь'].[16]

How would a 'monk of Valaam' have followed a 'strictly ascetic life'? Virtually a single formidable rule exists for all monastics through hourly, daily, weekly, monthly and yearly observances. Varied orders in monasticism do not exist in the Greek Orthodox *ecumene* today, just as they did not in the nineteenth century (and earlier). Variations occur in the ways the monastics organize their living situations, whether in a coenobitic monastery (where all attend the liturgical services and collect in the refectory together), or an idiorhythmic community (comprised of households of monastics who will attend and collect within their households), or *scetes* (already explained), or hermitages (a single monastic even deeper in the wilderness as an anchorite, an eremite, a hermit). And variations occur in the extent to which the entire rigorous rule is observed, not everyone can or ought to follow it entirely. It tends to be observed more fully by hermits and scete dwellers in the depths of the wilderness who have the ability to fast so intensely and to pray continuously for concentration and towards self-purification, ultimately (it is hoped) for union with the divine.

His conformity to this monastic tradition can be inferred further (than the statements quoted just above) from a description of his clothing: he wore ряса and клобукъ,[17] these are the traditional cassock and cowl (τὸ ῥάσο and τὸ κουκούλιον). His conformity is evident moreover in the instructions that he himself provided before his death for the preparation of his body for burial:[18] they accord with monastic tradition, the cowl becoming the shroud. Can we be surer yet? Yes. Into his elderly years, he was 'conducting the Holy Services according to monastic laws'.[19] And the monastics of Valaam themselves recognized him as one who had 'followed the true path of introspection in isolation',[20] in other words their proper traditional way.

What might he have looked like, this anchorite in the far northern forest conforming himself to this tradition of asceticism? A drawing was provided by someone who knew him well.[21] A very impressive feature in the sketch are the eyes: they reflect deep empathy, compassionate soulfulness, as well as steadfastness. He was described in written sources as open-hearted, gentle and generous. They also describe him as being of good physical health and strong, with extraordinary physical stamina waning only towards the end of his mortal existence.[22]

People came to see him from the Kodiak area, the Alaska Peninsula, the Chugach Bay area, and the eastern Aleutian Islands.[23] Alaskans 'of both sexes with their children often came to visit him. ... On Sundays and feastdays many people came to him to pray'.[24] Some people settled here to be near him.[25] He taught at times.[26] Orphans took refuge here.[27] A few people had already been living on the small island when he had arrived. And he himself would paddle the distance to *Pavlovskaia gavan* to visit at times, to counsel and to console.[28]

Thus while his hermitage remained apart deeper on the islet affording him solitude, his move into the finer quietude of the forest was 'above all not a *move away* from the people ... he still continued to see and counsel visitors who came to him' (cf. Chryssavgis 1989:7).

These words written with regard to St John Climacus of the seventh century apply equally to this saintly anchorite from Valaam of the nineteenth. He had a precedent among the earlier fathers in the desert.

Like the extraordinary among them, he is venerated in Alaska and at Valaam as a saint today.[29] His qualities of holiness have been recognized from generation to generation from his own lifetime. For example, 'Монах Германъ' was described as a 'very holy man' in the Chugach Bay area, the Prince William Sound region, by the Russian-Alutiiq tradition bearer M.F. Chumovitskii in 1933 (as cited already). Earlier, in 1894, the Valaam commentary described him as an 'enlightened and exalted personality' who had 'reached a high level of spiritual experience'; and this commentary referred to him as a 'Holy Elder': 'Сватой Старецъ': the memory of him had already become sacred at Valaam by that time:[30]

> To us the memory of this man is sacred, and everything to do with him is dear to us [Длія насъ священна память этого человька, и дорого все что до него относится].

Earlier yet, in 1866, a generation after his repose, the perception was reported by a vicar bishop at *Novo Arkangel'sk*, the vicar of the Kamchatka diocese, who wrote: 'In general all the local inhabitants have a sincere respect for Father Herman as a holy hermit, completely convinced of his godliness.'[31]

This conviction is expressed in sources contemporary and nearly contemporary with him that will be cited in this chapter. The references here to him as 'holy' and 'sacred' are based directly on these sources: the words reflect statements in these sources at the very time of the transition itself.

(2) Sources for the Descriptions of this Missionary's Attributes

Sources contemporary or nearly contemporary with him describe him being associated with spirits, healing, foreseeing, and pacifying the forces of nature. These sources are:

(a) S.I. Ianovskii, a Russian naval officer;

(b) K. Larionov, Russian-Alutiiq church warden at Kodiak;

(c) Ignatii Alig'iaga, an 'Aleut' long-time resident at 'New Valaam';

(d) Gerasim, the elder's 'disciple' at 'New Valaam'; and

(e) G.M. Lazarev, a 'pilgrim' from Valaam.

These descriptions are mutually corroborative regarding the kinds of qualities attributed to him. Found in the materials collected about him by *hegumen* Damascene of Valaam in the 1860s and published by Valaam Monastery in 1894, these descriptions are supported to lesser degrees by:

(f) other sources, useful for clarification, including: Innokentii, archbishop of Kamchatka, a primary source; P.F. Kashevarov, priest of Kodiak, a secondary source; and modern residents of Kodiak, specifically here M.H. Naumoff, conveying oral traditions. Attention is due to Sophia Vlasova as well.

(i) The Sources Themselves

(a) *Sem'en Ivanovich Ianovskii, 'Letters to Damascene'.* A naval officer acting as the chief manager of the Russian-American Company from mid-1818 until mid-1820, Ianovskii came to know the monastic missionary. They first met during November 1819, when Ianovskii was thirty years old and the monastic elder would have been about sixty-two years of age.[32] They became close: 'he loved me as a son', Ianovskii wrote in retrospect.[33] By Ianovskii's own account, Herman converted him from deism (which is Ivanovskii's own term).[34] He eventually became a monastic himself, at Kaluga, southwest of Moscow, in 1864, subsequent to his wife's death.[35] He wrote his recollections about the elder monastic Herman for *hegumen* Damascene between 1865 and 1867. These recollections particularly highlight Herman's interactions with imperial naval officers who had been in Russian-America.

(b) *Konstantin Larionov, 'Information about Father Herman'.* Larionov recalled his parents, an Alaskan mother and a Russian father, being visited by 'Father Herman' at their home while Konstantin was still a young child.[36] Later during his boyhood, he himself would visit 'the elder' at the hermitage in the forest of *Elovoi*. For instance in 1835 (this was a year before the elder's repose), when Konstanin was 'hardly more than twelve years old', he went with a younger boy named Stepan and an Alutiiq named Peter, also 'known as Shtuluk'.[37] Reaching the hermitage, they recited aloud a prayer the elder had taught them. From within, the elder from Valaam answered, 'Amen'; and they entered to find him sitting on the ground, cutting potatoes. Then as Konstantin remembered:

> He told me to take down a book from the shelves and made me find the articles
> which had to do with his discourse. As I was not reading fluently at that time, he
> told me or showed me the pages and explained the Church script to me.

The youngster huddled over the book, intent on reading letter-by-letter across
the Slavonic script, while 'apa' sat at a distance on the ground cutting the
potatoes and listening and telling 'stories'. It seemed to the twelve year old
that the elder recalled 'the contents of the books by heart'. Perhaps he had
memorized the contents; or perhaps he was guiding the boys through a passage that he knew well, had chosen especially for them and was augmenting.
In either case, this was the way he taught them: in his cell, or one-man yurt, in
the forest as an old man to his grandsons or grand-nephews.

As an adult Larionov became the староста, warden, of the Kodiak church.
In this position, he wrote his recollections about the missionary monastic and
he compiled memories from Alutiiq and Russian-Alutiiq people older than
himself in the Kodiak area, many of whom he cited. These recollections span
the period from 1825 to the late-1830s, and include accounts of the elder's
repose.

Larionov's 'Information about Fr Herman' was conveyed to the auxiliary
bishop at *Novo Arkhangel'sk*, who dated the manuscript 21 May 1867. In that
year, 1867, Larionov would have been approximately forty-four years old.
The manuscript was forwarded by this bishop to Damascene with confirma-
tion of the authorship and with attestation of the author's character, 'worthy
of trust'.[38]

(c) *Ignatii Alig'iaga, in Larionov's 'Information about Fr Herman'.* One of the
key people from whom Larionov collected memories in the generation older
than himself was Ignatii Alig'iaga who had lived alongside the anchorite for
many years. He was with him at his repose, and Alig'iaga remained at 'New
Valaam' after the elder's repose. They were so close that the monastic elder
entrusted him with instructions and confidences; and so close that Alig'iaga
could say in retrospect, '*Apa* led a hard life which no one else could imitate.'[39]
Alig'iaga's descriptions are vivid.

Alig'iaga is referred to as an 'Алеут' ('Aleut') by Larionov. Whether a 'Kodiak
Aleut' (Alutiiq) is unspecified yet probable. We should be reminded that the
word Алеут designated a civil status in Russian-America and that ethnic distinctions between Алеут groups were rendered by predicating the term with
regional specifications, for example: 'Atka Aleut', 'Fox [Island] Aleut', 'Kodiak
Aleut', etc. (see Intro., sec.3.i). Now, let us ask: Wouldn't a native Kodiak
writer such as Larionov have been prone to use a prefix such as 'Fox Island
Aleut' if Alig'iaga were other than a Kodiak native?

(d) *Gerasim, in the 'Narrative of the Pilgrim Lazarev'.* Gerasim was an orphan who had taken refuge on *Elovo*i. He was raised under the elder's guidance, learned the skill of literacy and also learned a proficiency in rubrics. As he matured, he was sent by the elder to conduct services in the villages, and he received the elder's church books as an inheritance from him. Gerasim remained devoted to him until the end. At the elder's repose, Gerasim kept the vigil by reading the Acts of the Apostles. In the last moments, he held the elder's head. The elder rested his head on Gerasim's chest and then reposed.[40]

In those last days, he was advised by the monastic missionary to wed and to remain on *Elovoi*, where the pilgrim Lazarev met him around the year 1864. Gerasim is identified in Lazarev's introductory paragraph, and he is cited throughout Lazarev's narrative. No description of Gerasim's civil status or ethnicity is specified by Lazarev, which is remarkable as evidently it appeared irrelevant to the 'pilgrim'.

Thus with Gerasim as with Ignatii Alig'iaga, we have another eyewitness account from many years; and it too was compiled and relayed by another trustworthy source, as we shall see next.

(e) *Grigorii Mikhailov Lazarev, 'Narrative of a Pilgrim from Valaam Monastery ... concerning the life of the monk Herman'.* (For brevity, I shall refer to this work as the 'Narrative of the Pilgrim Lazarev'.) A 'townsman from Tsarskoe Selo' in central Russia, Lazarev had evidently made the journey as a pilgrimage from Valaam across the breadth of Russia to the hermitage on *Elovoi*. Reaching 'New Valaam', he collected accounts about the saintly monastic as relayed to him by numerous people here. As the introductory paragraph of his narrative was dated in October 1864, we may safely assume that was the year of the collection. The collection was included by *hegumen* Damascene in Valaam's centennial publication of sources. Indeed this pilgrim from Valaam provides the very first source in the collection.

Lazarev's own personal data is minimal, as his narrative was not a travel journal. The information about the intent of his journey as a pilgrimage and about his civil status was noted. Otherwise he remains virtually anonymous. The *genre* of his writing, including his near anonymity, is very significant, and the significance will be brought out soon.

(f) *Other sources, useful for clarification.* These include: (i) Innokentii, archbishop of Kamchatka, a primary source;[41] (ii) Peter, bishop in Novo Arkhangel'sk, vicar bishop of the Kamchatka diocese, a secondary source;[42] (iii) the priest P.F. Kashevarov of the Kodiak parish, a secondary source;[43] and (iv) Michael Harold Naumoff, conveying Kodiak oral tradition.

M.H. Naumoff related virtually one of the same oral traditions that Larionov had, and Naumoff provided a significant detail. It will be quoted later, in context with Larionov's statement. Naumoff derived from the village of Afognak, and was living in the town of Kodiak. He was seventy-eight years old at the time of my conversation with him, and he was trilingual. The conversation was in English. He was fluent.

Sophia Vlasova. Sophia Vlasova appears in these sources and is of such stature that she merits attention.[44] She was one of the first people to settle near the elder on the islet of *Elovoi*. In 1820, when she was 'no more than twenty' years old, she heard him preach the Gospel and she insisted on learning from him. He himself described her resolve as follows:[45]

> To the Glory of the holy mystery of God He has recently, through his unfathomable workings, shown me something which in all my twenty-five years here on Kodiak I had never seen before. Just after last Easter , a young woman of no more than twenty who spoke good Russian and who was previously unknown to me and whom I had never seen, came to me and heard about how the Son of God was made flesh, and about eternal life, and she was so filled with love for Jesus Christ that she would not leave me, but she pleaded with me with great conviction, against my inclination and my love of solitude and in spite of all the obstacles and difficulties I brought up, to take her on, and she has been living with me now for more than a month and is not bored. I have observed this with great amazement...

This conviction of hers indicates a resolve that is so firm as the way is rigorous. Its 'obstacles and difficulties' were explained to her by him, and the elder from Valaam observed with 'great amazement' that she was not discouraged and she persevered.

Other women who saw her wished to do the same, wrote the elder in 1820, just a month after her decision; and the number 'twelve' was reported in 1864 in retrospect by the pilgrim Lazarev. Evidently, they coalesced to form a woman's community at 'New Valaam', living an appropriate span away from the hermitage. He would join them for prayers, particularly on Sundays. (At other times, they would probably have observed corporate and private prayer on their own while he dwelt and maintained the monastic rule deeper in the forest.)[46]

Sophia Vlasova became these women's 'supervisor'. This is an indication of her spiritual development and stature. Another indication is reflected in the elder's advice for her to continue in this way of life after his repose. He advised the other women, and also advised Gerasim, that they should find spouses for themselves and wed after his death — and we may well imagine the result if these women each became a progenitress of an Alaskan family: mothers teaching this faith and its practices to their children, then grandmothers imparting the traditions to generations of their own kin. Yet he told Sophia Vlasova to continue in this way of life on her own.[47]

(ii) Vocabularly in these Sources

Some terms might require clarification before the quotations are read: 'elder' (старец), 'disciple' (ученик, ученица), 'father' (отец), and *'apaa'* (апа).

The word старец, elder, indicates spiritual stature as well as age. The spiritual dimensions become paramount as this word was combined with 'holy' for 'Сватой Старець': the 'Holy Elder'. The word 'Старець' and the combination 'Сватой Старець' are used by Ianovskii and also by the Valaam commentary as well as by Larionov. 'Старець' is directly synonymous with γέρων, found in patristic literature for the desert fathers.

The words ученик in the masculine gender and ученица in the feminine gender, found in most of the sources, can be translated as 'disciple' or 'student'. The direct synonyms μαθητής, μαθήτρια, can be translated in either way, too. The proper translation should be indicated by the textual context.[48] These are the words for Christ's disciples, and for John the Baptist's disciples, etc., in the Bible. Reflecting the relationship of a person who learns a way of life from someone of deeper spiritual qualities, the use of these words continues through patristic literature into monastic settings to the present day, for women as well as men. The continuity can be perceived here in the frequent occurrences of 'ученик' and 'ученица' in conjuncton with 'старец' in the 'Narrative of the Pilgrim Lazarev'. The *genre* of this narrative is equivalent in tone and in content to a type of patristic literature, known as 'the sayings of the desert fathers'. As the *genre* is the same, the translation should be the same: 'disciple'. The equivalence of *genre* will be highlighted.

'Fr Herman' ('отец Германъ'): this usage by almost all of the sources should not be misleading. He was not a priest, not even a deacon. He remained an unordained monastic. The term can be used to refer to unordained monastics when a formal mode of reference or address is needed for them also. As a formal term of respect, it is synonymous with πατήρ; and as a formal term of address, it may lack the higher spiritual meaning of γέρων (старец) and the deeper interpersonal meaning of *'abba'*, while it can assimilate these meaning as it does here for him.

'Apaa' is an Alutiiq word used by Alig'iaga and Larionov, who explained: 'апа, a term used by all of us inhabitants of Kodiak and which means, in translation, uncle or father.'[49] It is still applied to St Herman in the Kodiak area where it is spelled *'apaa'* today and can mean 'grandfather';[50] for example, Naumoff referred to him as *'apaa* Herman' during our conversation. In sound and meaning, this word resembles *abba*, used in patristic literature for the desert fathers.[51] The resemblance will become significant.

(3) Descriptions of the Attributes

The same general kinds of qualities that were visible through the social perspective in the preceding chapter of this study are attributed to the elder from Valaam in the forest of *Elovoi*: associated with spirit(s), he healed, foresaw future events, and pacified the forces of nature. Only a very few examples will be quoted. More examples for each and every one of these qualities can be found in the sources.

(i) Associated with spirit(s)

Once I asked him: 'Father Herman, how can you live on this island, alone in the forest? Do you not get lonely?'

He replied, 'No, I am not alone. God is there, just as He is everywhere, and the Holy Angels are there also. How can I be lonely? With whom is it better and more pleasant to speak — people or angels? Angels, of course.'[52]

The elder conversing with angels in the forest of *Elovoi* is also seen dispelling demons:

The Elder had busied himself in his cell with handiwork when his disciple Gerasim suddenly entered without offering the customary prayer. As he came into the cell he asked for the Elder's blessing; the latter did not answer and the disciple repeated his request several times and still the Elder said nothing. The disciple stood around for several hours and finally decided to leave the cell. When he came the following day he offered the normal prayer and the Elder answered, 'Amen.'

The disciple asked to be blessed; the Elder did so and then sat down again to his task. Then Gerasim asked him, 'Father, why did you not bless me yesterday nor answer when I asked?'

To this the elder replied, 'When I first arrived on this island the devils came to my cell many times, sometimes in human form, for things they wanted; sometimes they came disguised as animals and caused me much distress and that is why I would not admit anyone unless they offered a prayer.'[53]

(ii) Healing
Associated with angelic spirits, the elder healed:

The disciple noticed that at the Feast of the Epiphany the Elder went to the bank of the river which ran near his abode and sat there until midnight, after which he collected some water in a dish and then returned home. One day the disciple Gerasim asked the Elder why he fetched water at night and not during the day. To this the Elder answered: that night the water was made holy by the Angel of God. The disciple asked him how he knew the water had been made holy. The Elder answered that when the Angel of God comes down from the heavens and buries a cross of our Lord in the waters, then the waters tremble. The disciple noticed that whenever one of the women disciples was ill, or one of his visitors, the Elder would take this water and make them drink it or wash the affected part with it, and this cured them.[54]

The traditional icon for this feast-day depicts angels on the banks of the Jordan attending the Epiphany (see Ch.3, sec.2, final part). Rubrics for this day recommend that the festal service should take place at naturally running water if possible; and indeed it will take place at the sea or at a river, or sometimes at a lake for expedience, even in northern climates although the month is January. The water is blessed at a point in the liturgical celebration by a clergyman who, vested and chanting, will plunge a cross into and out of the water — through a hole in the ice if need be. But this monastic was unordained: he was not a priest, not even a deacon.

He could not bless the water himself, because this ritual is normally reserved for the ordained. Who, then, would bless it? The angel did. The water thus sanctified, became a healing agent as the elder would afterwards collect it and distribute it to the infirm. The angel blessing the water for him, enabled him to heal.

(iii) Foreseeing[55]

According to Ignatii [Alig'iaga] who lives on *Elovoi* to this day, Father Herman once told him that all the people living on Spruce Island would die and that he, Ignatii, would be left alone, and would grow old and poor, and that the people would remember Father Herman and thirty years after his death Ignatii would still be alive. He is amazed at this saying: 'How could a man like us know something like this so long in advance; he must have been a very special man, because he could read our thoughts, which we involuntarily revealed to him, and he would use these thoughts to teach us things.'[56]

Quotations from other sources follow:

The Elder's forecasts very quickly came true.[57]

Once his disciple Sophia (it was a Sunday) wished to travel to a nearby island to gather seaweed. The Elder said to her and her companions: 'Do not travel today, go tomorrow.' But they said amongst themselves, 'There hasn't been any fine weather for a whole week and only God knows whether it will be fine tomorrow or not'; so they set off without the Elder's blessing. As they set off, the *baidarka* suddenly ran onto a rock and capsized, because it was only made of leather, and one person was drowned in the sea. When they arrived home, the Elder called them to him and said: '... When I went out to the seashore that morning, I saw a ghastly figure sitting on the rock and splashing the water with his arms.'[58]

He once said to me: 'You are going to Russia, to Petersburg. Do not take with you there your wife, who was born here and who has not seen the wide world, its captivating luxuries, its temptations and its sins. Better to leave her with your mother in the Ukraine, while you yourself go about your business in Petersburg!' I gave him my word, but I did not keep it. She did not want to be without me on any account. I took her with me and within a year I had lost her. She died in Petersburg.[59]

Thirty years after the elder's repose, a source stated: 'Many people have told me that he had from God the gift of second sight — telling the future.'[60]

(iv) Pacifying the forces of nature

The Apa would ... feed the birds that were constantly around his cell, and what was even more remarkable, the mink which lived under his cell. It is strange that it is normally impossible to approach this little animal when it has pups, yet Father Herman would feed them by hand. Was what we saw not miraculous, Ignatii would ask? After Herman's death the birds and animals left.[61]

He would feed fish to the birds and to the mink., an essential staple that the elder would gather for himself, especially during the springtime:

Then the Elder would adopt the following procedure, as related by Ignatii: *Apa* would order the fish to be caught and stunned and then gutted and cut into two strips.[62]

Whom had he ordered so that the fish would be caught? '*Apaa* Herman had dug a trench from the river, and he would call the fish to come up it, so he could catch them.'[63]

Others have told me how ... they had seen bears near his dwelling, [and] how he would feed them and then they would wander off again.[64]

When Father Herman settled on *Elovoi*, there was during the early years a flood or flood-tide (doubtless caused by an earthquake); and the people there, the inhabitants, were frightened and came to tell the Elder. He left his cell and went to his disciples' house, where he celebrated the service every Sunday because there was no chapel or church. He took the icon of the Mother of God from its place and carried it out into the meadow where the tide had earlier been and, placing the icon on the ground, he began to pray to God. When he had finished his prayers, he told those who were present that they should not be afraid, saying: 'The sea will not come farther or higher than where the holy image stands.' And this is in fact what happened. And this was confirmed by those who heard it.

When it was necessary to carry the icon back, after the people had been instructed, Father Herman is reputed to have said to Sophia Vlasova ... that if the waters began to rise again she should place the icon on the beach, and he promised that the sea would not go beyond that point where it stood. This icon of the Mother of God is still to be found to this day on *Elovoi* in the place called New Valaam.[65]

In fact, it happened that in 1842, as we were sailing to Kodiak, we had been at sea for a long time and we were in very difficult circumstances. Only half a case of water remained for fifty-two passengers; and before we could make the harbour of

Kodiak, we encountered a contrary wind that blew for three days and nights. During this time, our ship was going backwards and forwards (or, in seafaring terms, it was tacking) from the southern tip of Kodiak to *Elovoi*, where Father Herman had lived and died. On the third day, towards evening, when our ship again approached *Elovoi* (maybe for the twentieth or thirtieth time), I looked at the island and said to myself: 'If, Father Herman, you have found the Lord's favour — then let the wind change.' And in fact hardly a quarter of an hour had passed when the wind suddenly became favourable, and that same evening we entered the harbour and stood at anchor![66]

Section conclusion. In these descriptions, the elder from Valaam, *apaa* in the forest of *Elovoi*, is associated with spirit(s) as he healed, foresaw future events, and pacified the forces of nature (the latter included food gathering). These attributes are of the same general kinds as those seen through the social perspective in the preceding chapter.

In light of these descriptions, we may gain a clarification about him as he appeared in the 'Chugach' account about Kangatyug (Ch.5, sec.3.ii). It may be recalled that this folk history was collected in 1933 by an ethnographer from a tradition bearer and that a linguistic distance existed between the collector and the source. Kangatyug's initial meeting in the forest with the 'very holy man, Монах Германъ' was transcribed by the ethnographer as follows (Birket-Smith 1953:130-131):

They caught sight of a bright ray of light shining on a small log cabin. They walked in and saw an old man praying on his knees. The old man asked them: 'How did you come here? Are you dead or alive?' Only dead persons came there, and the old man was able to see dead people.

But on the contrary, living human beings visited, as Kangatyuq did in this instance and as so many others did. The adverb 'only' must therefore be omitted from the last sentence in the passage. Now, let us replace the term 'dead people' by the more comprehensive word 'spirits'. The sentence becomes like the other descriptions: *Spirits came there, and the elder was able to see spirits.*

The question assigned to him begins to become clearer too, once these corrections are made. He asked Kangatyug, 'Are you dead or alive?' (Those words probably were not his own, however they are adequately indicative.) In effect, the elder of Valaam was discerning human beings and angels on the one hand from, on the other hand, demons: because the latter could assume various guises to distract and mislead people who had embarked on the spiritual ascent to heaven, the descent into the heart.

This kind of discernment was described by sources contemporary or nearly contemporary with him: an example can be found in the second quotation among those just presented, above. A similar kind of discernment was being exercised by Veniaminov for the same reasons and virtually concurrently (Ch.4, sec.3.ii): Veniaminov's encounter took place on the island of Akun in 1828, while *apaa* Herman was following the anchoritic life on the islet of *Elovoi*.

These processes of discernment are described likewise for the desert fathers as well (an example will be found in the second quotation to be presented, below).

(4) A Line of Tradition

These qualities attributed to him can be identified within a line of tradition that extends from *apaa* in the forest through the monastery of Valaam to the *abba*s in the desert, that is to say the desert fathers. Four links secure this line from him to them through Valaam (in addition to the fact that they all adhered to the same religion and followed very similar ways of life for the same purposes).

He was respected at Valaam. He embodied a tradition that was recognized there as he lived this acknowledged tradition in the forest of *Elovoi*.[67] This serves as the first link in the line.

Next, the region in which Valaam was located had become known as the 'Russian Thebaid' by affinity with the Egyptian Thebaid. Monastic, including anchoritic, activities had flourished in numbers and with vitality in the desert especially between the fourth and sixth centuries AD. These activities developed with magnitude also in the *taiga* and on the tundra, now particularly from the fourteenth century, through networks of many monasteries with their *scetes*, hermitages and other 'holdings' (*metochia*). This 'Russian Thebaid' extended from Karelia in the west and Komi-land in the east, to the White and Pechora Sea coasts in the north.[68]

The third link is the *genre* of one of our main sources. The 'Narrative of the Pilgrim Lazarev' is remarkably similar both in tone and in content to a type of patristic literature regarding the desert fathers. An example is Ἡ κατ' Αἴγυπτον τῶν μοναχῶν Ἱστορία [*Historia Monachorum in Aegypto*]. It is a 'history of the monastics in Egypt' whose anonymous author had made a pilgrimage to elders' hermitages in the desert in the fourth century and had recorded their 'wonders', miracles (θαύματα), and their sayings as recalled by their disciples.[69] Likewise, Lazarev made the pilgrimage to the hermitage in the far northern forest and wrote about this elder's wonders and sayings as recalled by his disciples.

Finally, the line is secured by the 'wonders' (θαύματα) themselves, as described alike about this *apaa* in the forest and the *abba*s in the desert. Four 'categories of wonders' have been analysed from Ἡ κατ' Αἴγυπτον τῶν μοναχῶν Ἱστορία: (i) 'dreams and visions', (ii) 'healing', (iii) 'clairvoyance', and (iv) 'nature miracles'.[70] These 'categories' are basically the same as the kinds of qualities attributed to *apaa* Herman. The wording slightly differs, while the content is similar throughout: (i) the 'dreams and visions' involve associations with spirits; (ii) the 'healing' does not differ even in name; (iii) the 'clairvoyance' includes many instances of foresight and prophetic foresight; and (vi) the 'nature miracles' are instances of nature being pacified — with a desert lion or a hyena appearing instead of a bear or a mink, as we shall see.

The descriptions are voluminous, beyond this collection in the Ἱστορία [*Historia*].[71] I have selected just one or two examples for each category to trace the line as succinctly as possible from *aapa* to the *abbas*:

(i) Associated with spirit(s)

Abba Anouf said to them, ... 'an angel has fed me the heavenly food everyday ... an angel has been with me always, showing me the dynamics of the cosmos; the light of my understanding was not extinguished. Every request of mine to God, I received straightaway.' (*Historia* xi.5-6, p.91)

[John of Lycopolis], like a father counseling his children, ... explaining to them many ... things about the exercise [of asceticism], edified them greatly. ... 'Firstly, exercise [yourselves in] humility ... so that you not be led astray by demons raising up images before you. But if anyone should come to you, whether a brother, or a friend, or a sister, or a wife, or a father, or a teacher, or a mother, or a child, or a servant, stretch out your hands in prayer at once; and should it be a phantasm it will flee from you.' (*Historia* i.56, i.59-60, pp.31, 32-33)

(ii) Healing

Blessed John did not accomplish cures himself; instead he healed more often by giving oil to the ill. ... He sent [a certain woman, for example] some oil; and as she said, having anointed her eyes herself three times, she regained her sight after the third day, and gave thanks manifestly to God. (*Historia* i.12, pp.12-13)

(iii) Foreseeing

(Abba Anouf, 'the great confessor' said to his spiritual sons, themselves already advanced in such matters): 'Blessed be God, who has made your conditions and conduct known to me'. Telling of the deeds or achievements of each of them, he then described even his own [to them ... and said,] 'God has hidden nothing that he has not made known to me. Light has never left my eyes.' (*Historia* xi.5-6, p.91)

(iv) Pacifying the forces of nature

Another time, they say, Macarius was praying in the cave in which he dwelled in the desert. There happened to be a cave of a hyena nearby. Once while he was at prayer, it suddenly imposed, and began licking his feet; then taking him gently by the edge [of his cassock] it drew him towards her own cave. He followed her saying, 'What does this beast want?' It led him as far as her own cave, went in, and brought out to him her own cubs, born blind. Having prayed for them, he gave them back to the hyena with their sight healed. And as a gift, in thanksgiving, she brought to him a large skin of a great ram, and laid it at his feet. Smiling at her, as she was sensible and sensitive, he took the gift, and spread it beneath himself. This skin is preserved by someone yet today. (*Historia* xxi.15, p.127)

This line can be traced yet further, into the Acts of the Apostles and the very Gospels. From many examples that abound in these scriptures also, I shall again present just a brief few to indicate the depth of this tradition:

(i) Associated with spirit(s)

And the angel answering said unto him [Zacharias, father of John the Baptist] I am Gabriel, that stands in the presence of God; and am sent to shew thee these glad tidings. (Luke 1:19)

Then was Jesus led up of the Spirit into the wilderness to be tempted of the devil. (Matthew 4:1)

And he [Christ] was there in the wilderness forty days, tempted of Satan; and was with the wild beasts; and the angels came and ministered unto him. (Mark 1:13)

(ii) Healing

For an angel went down at a certain season into the pool [of Bethesda], and troubled the water: whosoever then first after the troubling of the water stepped in was made whole of whatsoever disease he had. (John 4:4)

When he [Christ] had thus spoken, he spat on the ground and made clay of the spittle, and he anointed the eyes of the blind man with the clay, and said unto him, 'Go, wash in the pool of Siloam' (which is by interpretation, Sent). He went his way therefore, and washed, and came seeing. (John 9:6-7)

(iii) Foreseeing

And it shall come to pass in the last days, saith God, I will pour out of my Spirit upon all flesh: and your sons and your daughters shall prophesy, and your young men shall see visions, and your old men shall dream dreams. (Acts 2:17; cf.Joel 2:28-32)

(iv) Pacifying the forces of nature

And he [Christ] said unto them [His disciples], 'Cast the net on the right side of the ship, and ye shall find.' They cast therefore, and now they were not able to draw it for the multitude of the fishes. (John 21:6)

(5) Conclusions

A line of tradition becomes evident that extended from *apaa* in the forest to the *abbas* of the desert: in other words, from this holy elder through the monastery of Valaam to the desert fathers. He lived within this tradition securely.

This patristic tradition can be likened to a vertical line. If we liken the indigenous tradition in the Kodiak area to a horizontal line, then we may see the vertical meeting the horizontal in the forest of *Elovoi*. He appears at the very point where these lines crossed.

Apaa in the forest of *Elovoi* was associated with spirit(s) as he healed, foresaw future events, and pacified the forces of nature. These qualities have been traced firmly into patristic and biblical experience from the descriptions about him in sources contemporary with him. These are the same kinds of qualities that became visible likewise through the *social perspective* on shamans-of-old in southern Alaska. Thus even within himself, that broad horizontal line of far northern tradition (that he also manifested) met the deep vertical line of patristic tradition (that he embodied).

This 'very holy man' was sought in the forest by Kangatyuq. It was not necessarily their first or only meeting, but it was the one in the Alutiiq account and marked a key event. From this meeting, Kangatyuq became a healer. When the vocation of the Alutiiq healer was inaugurated through his meeting with this 'very holy man', a continuing line of indigenous tradition in the Kodiak area was touched by a continuous line of patristic tradition: The horizontal line of indigenous tradition can be said to have been transformed by the vertical at this point of intersection when the two men met. And the Alutiiq healer became a primary example of transformation.

The lines also intersected in the Aleutian Islands when Ivan Smirennikov met *hieromonk* Makarii and received baptism. According to the account, angels then began appearing to him on Akun Island almost daily for nearly thirty-three years hence, into his old age; and they enabled him to fulfill the vital tasks: healing, foreseeing and locating food. The elder man of Akun became known as an 'Aleut prophet'.

Apaa in the forest of *Elovoi* joins with the Aleut prophet and the Alutiiq healer as their qualities correspond with earlier phenomena, now transformed.

'Correspondence' signifies similarity, not equivalence. Differences are evident for him, just as they are evident for the Aleut prophet and the Alutiiq healer, in contrast to some characteristics of shamans-of-old in southern Alaska that we observed through the *ethnographic perspective* instead — just as differences were manifest also in the transformation of ritual masks into icons. *Apaa* in the forest of *Elovoi* was never referred to as a 'shaman' by any source, not even in the Chugach-region account in which he figured so vividly. Even in the 'shaman story', he was referred to as 'a very holy man, Монах Германъ'. To assert that he had been thought of as a 'shaman', because he was in effect fulfilling the main vital tasks associated with shamans-of-old in southern Alaska, would be to mistreat the evidence and misrepresent the idea that have been put forward here. We can not know how the Alaskans contemporary with him interpreted him beyond the sources that have been cited. Through these sources, we may recognize his differences.

He was assisted by angels and spoke to them: he discerned and spurned demons. Healing is the quality known about him: harming is not a characteristic attached to him. As he pacified the forces of physical nature, so furthermore he tempered the forces of social nature as he helped the poor and the needy, consoled the distressed, and was an advocate for the oppressed.

We may mark these differences by words for St Herman of Alaska, just as for the Aleut prophet and the Alutiiq healer. This is important. Yet so is the correspondence.

A certain correspondence is evident in him also; and we may (again now, as for icons earlier) state that the correspondence comprises the more important factor for the sake of this transition. The correspondence needs to be seen if his place in the transition is to be perceived, a place belonging to this missionary monastic who remained here the longest in a transition that was itself an indigenous movement: One who remained here the longest indeed at a very point of intersection (and comprehension) where a deep line of continuous patristic tradition met and touched a broad line of continuing indigenous tradition in the Arctic.

Notes

[1] The quotation is from Chumovitskii in Birket-Smith (1953:130): see Ch.5, sec.3.ii, above.'Herman' is a softening of Германъ, deriving from Γερμανός. Some dialects of Russian normally soften the pronunciation of 'g' to 'h': for instance, Гавриил is pronounced as 'Havriil' while yet spelled with an initial г. Perhaps this softening was assimilated in Alaska. In any case, it occurs for this name in English pronunciation here today.

[2] The ten who arrived in 1794 were (i) Archimandrite Ioasaph, (ii) *hieromonk* Iuvenalii, (iii) *hieromonk* Makarii, (iv) *hieromonk* Athanasii (for the transliteration, see Ch.5, nt.46, above), (v) *hierodeacon* Stefan, (vi) *hierodeacon* Nektarii, (vii) monastic Herman, (viii) church servitor Dmitrii Avdeev, (ix) church servitor Nikita Sem'enov, and (x) church servitor Kosma Alekseev. The latter was tonsured at Kodiak by the head of the mission, Archimandrite Ioasaph and, receiving the same name, became the monastic Ioasaph.

This number with their names and ranks derive from research by L.T. Black into Petersburg archives, May-June 1993 (personal communications: Iakutsk, June 1993;

Fairbanks, March 1994), to be published with further details in her forthcoming book, provisionally titled *Russians in Alaska, 1741-1867.*

Before Black's research, some confusion existed about the church servitor Kosma Alekseev in written histories. Brief references to him as a monastic at Kodiak (e.g., Veniaminov 1840b:155; 1984:234) caused the presumption in, for example, Tikhmenev (1978:36) that the original ten had been comprised of eight monastics and two servitors.

Avdeev drowned in the Kodiak area in 1796 (Black, as cited; cf. Veniaminov 1840b:155, nt., 1984:235, nt.). *Hieromonk* Iuvenalii was sent as a missionary from Kodiak Island to the mainland where he disappeared (see Ch.1, nts 61 and 126, above; Ch.6, nt.29, below). In 1799, Archimandrite Ioasaph, *hierodeacon* Stefan and *hieromonk* Makarii drowned in the wreck of the *Phoenix.* Archimandrite Ioasaph had travelled from Kodiak to Irkutsk to be elevated to the episcopacy. *Hierodeacon* Stefan had accompanied him. They were returning to Kodiak on the *Phoenix. Hieromonk* Makarii was returning with them, as he had been ordered subsequent to his protest in Petersburg (see Ch.1, sec.1.iv, above). Another church servitor had been attached to the mission at the elevation in Irkutsk: Dmitrii Popov, a cantor ('chorister') who was Veniaminov's own first cousin (Veniaminov 1840b:158 nt., 1984:236 nt.), also lost in the shipwreck.

[3] *Hieromonk* Gideon, Secret Report to Metropolitan Amvrosii, 2 June 1805, in Gideon (1989:80). No one else is listed by this qualified primary source, other than these four who were: *hieromonk* Athanasii, *hierodeacon* Nektarii, monastic Herman, and monastic Ioasaph. Monastic Ioasaph should not confused with the head of the mission, Archimandrite Ioasaph.

[4] Monastic Herman to *hegumen* Ionafan of Valaam, 13 Dec. 1819, in Valaam, ed. (1894:192-193; 1978:114-115). *Hierodeacon* Nektarii had returned to Irkutsk in 1806, and he became an *hieromonk* in the Kirenskii Monastery, according to Veniaminov (1840b:154 nt.; 1984:234 nt.) and Pierce (1990:379).

[5] The monastic Ioasaph had died in the Kodiak area in 1823, and *hieromonk* Athanasii had been relieved and transported from Kodiak in 1825, according to Veniaminov (1984:234) and Pierce (1990:3, 201).

[6] The date is based on Kodiak documents from that year, according to Pierce (1990:164; and personal communication, November 1989) and also according to Black (personal communication, March 1988). Also see 'German (Herman)', in Index [Pierce, ed.] in Veniaminov (1984:502). The date of his repose was given as 1837 by Veniaminov twice (1840b:5 nt., 1840a:22; see: 1984:235 nt., 1978:44); and then by Peter, vicar bishop at *Novo Arkangel'sk*, in a marginal note that Peter affixed to another man's account in May 1867 (in Valaam, ed. 1894:181; 1978:108). The error was repeated in OCA (1970:12, 66, 81), at that church group's canonization of Herman as a saint. Why weren't qualified historians and archivists brought in to assist?

[7] Biographical data derives mainly from the centennial collection of primary and secondary sources published by Valaam, ed. (1894, 1978), comprising Appendix 1 in Valaam (1894a, 1978). Among these sources, the letters by Ianovskii are especially valuable for their biographical content. Some of these letters in translation in Valaam, ed. (1978) are reprinted in Oleksa, ed. (1987). Efforts were inaugurated by 1994 by

R.H. Pierce, History Department, University of Alaska at Fairbanks, for a revised edition of the 1978 translation.

More primary source material containing biographical information about Herman can be found in the Shur collection in the materials from Russian archives on microfilm in the Rasmuson Library, University of Alaska at Fairbanks, as yet unpublished. Further information pertaining to him in the Kodiak area could be gleaned from Russian-American Company documents, segments of which have been published in translation in the Limestone Press Alaska History Series (Pierce, ed. and trans. 1976, 1984). A document that Herman signed, which also has yet to be published, exists in the Golder collection (HRS/RR/LCM 564:1-5, cited in Ch.1, nt.96, above).

A biography was written by Valaam (1894b), as another contribution (in addition to Valaam 1894a) for the centennial of the arrival of the religious mission to Kodiak: it is an inspirational *vita*, in which primary source material is merged with secondary source material indiscriminately and without references into a single readable narrative. In contrast, Valaam ed. (1894) distinguishes between sources and identifies them.

[8] For the term '*hegumen*' and its transliteration, see Ch.1, nt.4, above. *Hegumen* Nazarii remained in contact with him (Herman to *hegumen* Nazarii, 19 May 1795, HRS/RR/LCM 643:53-58). Nazarii's successor, *hegumen* Ionafan, corresponded with the monastic Herman (Herman to Ionafan, 13 Dec. 1819, in Valaam, ed., 1894:190-194, 1978:113-115; and for Ionafan to Herman, see ibid. 1894:189, 1978:113). Ionafan's successor, *hegumen* Damascene, compiled the monastic Herman's letters and collected material about him from credible sources in the 1860s. Valaam's concern that he should be known, and known correctly, is reflected in their publication of the primary and secondary source material collected about him (Valaam, ed., 1894), and the commentary they wrote (1894a), and even the *vita* they composed about him (1894b).

[9] Archimandrite Ioasaph to Monastic Herman, 8 June 1798, in Valaam, ed. (1894:187; 1978:111).

[10] Administrators for whom respectful or helpful attitudes are described include: L.A. Gagemeister (L. von Hagemeister), on-site chief manager for a brief few months at the beginning of 1818 (see Ch.1, nt.121, above); S.I. Ianovskii in this capacity from mid-1818 to mid-1820 (see Ch.6, sec.2.i.a, here below); and probably F.P. Vrangel (Wrangel) in this capacity from late-1830 to early-1835 (see nt.14, below). Both Gagemeister and Ianovskii were deeply influenced by Herman. A primary source, Larionov in Valaam, ed. (1894:175-176, 180; 1978:104-105, 107), describes a respectful and helpful attitude for V.I. Kashevarov, local manager at Kodiak mid-1830 into 1838; but the accounts collected by a secondary source, Lazarev in ibid. (1894:124; 1978:76-77), differ.

Ianovskii to Damascene, 22 Nov. 1865, in Valaam, ed. (1894:140; 1978:86). Ianovskii is a credible primary source for the information about the food shortage, as he was the company's chief manager at the time of the events he recounted. 'It should be noted here,' he wrote, 'that the employees of the American Company [*sic*] issue from the stores grain and other supplies for the up-keep of the monks, but sometimes there is no grain.' Further research could probably substantiate that the latter was more often the case: that they were rarely supplied. For the Shelikhov company's pretences about support that was not forthcoming, see Ch.1, nt.90, above.

[11] For the monastics foraging the beaches at Kodiak, see Archimandrite Ioasaph to Shelikhov, 18 May 1795, RAC/Iudin/LCM, also see this document in Tikhmenev (1861:103; 1979:80). For Herman gathering fish at *Elovoi*, see Ianovskii, as cited in this note. For Herman supplementing his gathering of food with his gardening, see esp. Larionov and Peter in Valaam, ed. (1894:183, 158; 1978:109-110, 95-96).

[12] For the designation, see Gideon (1989:116). For the charity, see the references in Pierce (1978:178); also see Ianovskii to Damascene, 22 Nov. 1865, in Valaam, ed. (1894:136-137; 1978:83-84).

[13] Herman to Ionafan, 13 Dec. 1819; Herman to Ianovksii, 20 June 1820; Herman to Ianovskii, 10 August 1821; and Ianovskii to Damascene, 22 Nov. 1865: in Valaam, ed. (1894:193, 149, 168, 133; 1978:115, 92, 100, 81), respectively. Also see Ianovksii to Damascene, 22 Nov. 1865, in Valaam, ed. (1894:133; 1978:82).

His age of sixty-two years in 1819 is calculated as follows: he was forty-eight years old in June 1805, according to Gideon to Amvrosii, 2 June 1805, in Gideon (1989:80). For his age of sixteen years when he originally embarked on the monastic life, see: Ianovksii to Damascene, 22 Nov. 1865, in Valaam, ed. (1894:131; 1978:80).

[14] Communication, Chief Manager F.P. Wrangel [Vrangel], 18 June 1831, Communication of the Governors no. 354, cited by Pierce (1978:178).

[15] Herman to Ionafan, 13 Dec. 1819, in Valaam, ed. (1894:193; 1978:115). Also see, Ianovskii to Damascene, 22 Nov. 1865, in ibid. (1894:133; 1978:81). A verst is a 'Russian measure of length, 3,500 feet', according to *The Concise Oxford Dictionary*, 5th ed.; or '0.66288 mile (1.06 kilometre)', according to the *Encyclopedia Britannica*, 15th ed.

[16] Ianovskii to Damascene, 22 Nov. 1865 and 12 Dec. 1866, in Valaam, ed. (1894:133, 161; 1978:81, 97). Relayed by Ianovskii in writing to Damascene at these dates in 1866, the eyewitness accounts derive from 1819-1820.

[17] Ianovskii to Damascene, 22 Nov. 1866, in Valaam, ed. (1894:142; 1978:87).

[18] Larionov in Valaam, ed. (1894:180; 1978:107). More completely, we see that he wore a deerskin shirt, canvas breeches under an old threadbare habit, patched and darned in many places, as well as wearing the cowl and some shoes of a sort (*bashmaki*), according to Ianovskii to Damascene, 22 Nov. 1865, in Valaam, ed., 1894:142; 1978:87).

[19] Peter to Damascene, 12 May 1866, in Valaam, ed. (1894:158; 1978:96) from retrospective accounts that the vicar bishop Peter had heard in Alaska, corroborated by the primary sources in nts 17 and 18, above. Peter served at *Novo Arkhangel'sk* from 1860 until 1867: see nt.38, below.

[20] Valaam (1894a:51; 1978:31-32).

[21] Ianovskii, plate 1 in Valaam (1894a; 1978). I am referring to Ianovksii's drawing (which is unlike a sort of icon that has recently been drawn about him, depicting a skinny creature glaring at us through piercing eyes and admonishing us with a boney hand). Ianovksii describes the eyes as 'twinkling', with (what we might call) a joyfulness despite sorrows: 'His face was pale and lined, his eyes grey-blue and twinkling' (Ianovksii to Damascene, 22 Nov. 1865, in Valaam, ed., 1894:143, 1978:88). Ianovskii describes him furthermore in a letter attached to the drawing (Ianovskii to Dama-

scene, 12 Dec. 1866, in Valaam, ed., 1894:161, 1978:97):

> My memory came alive with recollections. I remembered all the feaures of his face, shining with the Holy Spirit: the pleasant smile on his lips, his humble gaze, his quiet and gentle manner, his warmly welcoming words – his height, his manner of walking, the attractive nature of his gaze: his blue-grey eyes – the Lord brought all this before my eyes again as a result of your holy prayers. It was as though I could see the Holy Elder myself and was only a guide and an indicator as the portrait was being drawn.

[22] See Ch.4, sec.1, above. For warmth of heart, see especially Ianovskii to Damascene, 22 Nov. 1865, 3 Sept. 1866, and 12 Dec. 1866, in Valaam, ed. (1894:143, 153, 161; 1978: 88, 93, 97). For physical health, see Lazarev, Ianovksii, and Larionov in ibid. (1894:122, 142, 183; 1978:76, 87, 110). For his eyesight weakened by the year 1835, and perhaps earlier: see Larionov in ibid. (1894:177; 1978:105); Lazarev in ibid. (1894:126; 1978:78).

This quality really is extraordinary. For example let us see that from November 1819 and into the following year at least (probably longer, but the source spans these two years) while he was *sixty-two and sixty-three years old* (!): he would paddle a kayak himself the distance of miles from his hermitage to the Kodiak harbour town, and back, over the open water. This can be an arduous crossing, as anyone who has done it today knows: today in a motorized boat on a relatively calm sea, all but the most seaworthy find themselves sick from the swells of the waves, including men in the height of their youthfulness. These are far northern sea waters. Consider the roughness off the coast of *Elovoi* that imperiled the ship carrying Veniaminov to Kodiak in 1842, adverse winds causing the vessel to tack backwards and forwards between the islet and Kodiak harbour for three days and nights and causing Veniaminov to offer up fervent prayers for the ship's safety (see sec. 2.i.f., below). The *sixty-two year old and then sixty-three year old* hermit would paddle across these waters. And he would walk overland in all types of weather, as also reported by Ianovskii during those years (in Valaam, ed., 1894:135-136; 1978:83):

> Neither rain, nor blizzard, nor storm could prevent the enthusiastic elder from visiting me and then making the half-verst journey home alone at mid-night! He would come to see me every day dressed in an ancient habit without a topcoat ... Then at midnight or later, the elder would return home alone, leaning on his staff, whatever the cold and however stormy the weather.

Older yet, in his later sixties and perhaps into his seventies, he alone would regularly carry a loaded box from the seashore to his hermitage, which is quite a distance (I have walked it myself; although I can not say exactly how long the distance is: it takes quite a while). The box contained seaweed that he would collect to fertilize the vegetable garden. 'This caused people to wonder how the Elder could carry such a weight for such a great distance' (Larionov, as cited already in this note: the accounts that Larionov collected extend retrospectively from 1836 to 1825, therefore I have said that the elder woud have been in his later sixties). His 'blanket' was a board on which he slept, about which no one knew except Ignatii Alig'iaga and another old man Isai who were very close to him (Larionov ibid.: 1894:180; 1978:108): he needed, or wished to have, nothing more in this far northern climate.

Under his cassock, he wore a heavy cross on a heavy chain, the weight of which would have served to temper the reserves of his physical energy, the weight from which he did not divest himself until his most elderly times. For the cross, cf. Larionov ibid. (1894:180; 1978:107) with ibid. (1894:182-183; 1978:109). Larionov admits that he did not understand Alig'iaga about this. By comparing Larionov's two but confused statements, we can glean the factors. These items were entrusted by the elder in his dying days to Alig'iaga with instructions about how Alig'iaga and Isai were to use them, not for ascetic labours, different from the elder's own type of use. These instructions are clear enough as relayed from Alig'iaga through Larionov and can be read in the source. Entrusted to Alig'iaga, the items were then placed behind an icon in the hermitage chapel (probably for the designated use), and were discovered by others when the cross fell from the resting place; the items were then kept in the chapel at 'New Valaam' as holy objects, and they remain treasured in the church in Kodiak today. The 'holy elder' from Valaam wore these under his clothes, out of sight (so that not even Alig'iaga knew about them until the final days of the repose), and his strength was extraordinary and his demeanour was pleasant.

[23] For the Kodiak area see, e.g., various sources in Valaam, ed. (1894:124, 153, 176-177, 182, 185; 1978:76, 93, 105, 109, 111). For the Alaska Peninsula see ibid. (1894:148; 1978:91). For the Chugach Bay area see Birket-Smith (1953:130-131). Also see Lazarev in ibid. (1894:122; 1978:76). For Russian visitors to New Valaam, see, e.g.: Ianovskii to Damascene, 3 Sept. 1866, in Valaam, ed. (1894:153, 1978:93); Lazarev, in ibid. (1894:124, 1978:76).

[24] Ianovskii to Damascene, 22 Nov. 1865, in Valaam, ed. (1894:134; 1978:82). Ianovskii describes the service for Sundays and feastdays at 'New Valaam' as follows: The elder recited 'the Hours, the Acts [sic] and the Gospel, and sang and preached'. If we understand 'Acts' as, or as including, the Epistles, then this is clearly the order of Divine Liturgy conducted by laity: an abbreviated service beginning with the Third and Sixth Hours, and continuing into the Liturgy of the Word that includes the Epistle and Gospel readings plus the designated regular and seasonal hymns, while omitting the parts reserved for the clergy. This would have been the service he conducted, because he was not a priest.

[25] Herman to Ionafan, 13 Dec. 1819, in Valaam, ed. (1894:193; 1978:115); Herman to Ianovskii, 20 June 1820, in ibid. (1894:147-148; 1978: 90-91); Lazarev in ibid. (1894:122-123; 1978:76); Larionov in ibid. (1894:176; 1978:105).

[26] Herman taught the skill of literacy to people who came to him at 'New Valaam', including Gerasim, Sophia Vlasova and the women who coalesced around Vlasova (see Lazarev in Valaam, ed.1894:123, 1978:76): these people will be introduced in section 2 of this chapter. A school is not mentioned in Ianovksii's recollections of 'New Valaam', a primary source from 1819-1820; however, Ianovksii does describe an epidemic during a period at that time (see nt.27, below). The epidemic caused many deaths, leaving many orphans, widows and widowers; so, a school might have come about afterwards to be known to Larionov, a primary source whose accounts begin in

the later-1820s and continue in the 1830s, and to be reported by secondary sources in retrospect in 1866.

The responsibility for the schooling of pupils is attributed to 'the guidance of a worthy woman of character,' by the vicar bishop, a secondary source, in retrospect in 1866 (Peter to Damascene, 12 May 1866, in Valaam, e.d, 1894:158, 1978:95). Herman is said to have taught 'God's law in both sections of the school,' according to the Kodiak parish priest, another secondary source, in retrospect in 1866 (P.F. Kashevarov in Valaam, ed., 1894:185, 1978:110).

It is noteworthy that the teaching of literacy had been in place since the initial contact periods: Russian literacy had been adopted by Aleuts by the 1790s, and Russian language and religion were being studied at the initial settlement on Kodiak Island in 1788 (as indicated in Chapter 1, above). Plans for formal education had been projected by Archimandrite Ioasaph from 1794. A school had been organized at Kodiak by *hieromonk* Gideon in 1805 (see Gideon 1989, index 'school'). He planned to establish lessons in the French language as well as in the Alutiiq and Russian languages, and lessons in the arts as well as in the practical sciences (L.T. Black, personal communication). Also see Ch.5, nt.41, above.

These activities are different from the role of schoolteacher as career trainer that was expected for the missionaries by some colonial administrators and company shareholders during the first two decades of the religious mission. A school with missionaries as the teachers to assimilate the natives was imagined by, for example, I. A. Pil and N. P. Rezanov; see: Order, Governor-General at Irkutsk I.A. Pil to G.I. Shelikhov, 12 May 1794, in Andreev, ed. (1948:323-335), summary rendition in Appendix 7 in Shelikhov (1981:132-134); Letter, Rezanov to Hieromonk Gideon, 21 Dec. 1804, in Valaam (1894a:253; 1978:152); Letter, Rezanov to the Directors of the Russian-American Company Directors, 6 Nov. 1805, in Tikhmenev, ed. (1863:215), see trans. in Gideon (1989:90) and in Tikhmenev, ed. (1979:168).

A general problem exists when the mission school was imagined by a colonial administrator such as Pil and a shareholder such as Rezanov to render the colonized useful to the colonists. The problem becomes specific if Herman is hastily described as a missionary schoolteacher without differentiation. In contrast to that sort of colonial design, Herman's involvement with his disciples, including his teaching them literacy and other skills, rises in admirable contrast; and Gideon's vision about education on Kodiak soars upwards alongside. This contrast between Gideon's and Herman's complementary approaches to education on the one hand, and Pil and Rezanov's purpose on the other hand, could be developed thematically, even though Gideon's actitivies took place in mesh with Rezanov's plans.

[27] See sources in nt.25, above. For an epidemic that swept through the Kodiak area leaving many orphans, see Ianovskii in Valaam, ed. (1894:136-137; 1978:83-84).

[28] Larionov in Valaam, ed. (1894:175-177; 1978:104-106); Ianovskii to Damascene, 22 Nov. 1865, in Valaam, ed. (1894:135-136; 1978:83).

[29] My statements about the qualities attributed to Herman including holiness will be made by reference directly to sources contemporary and nearly contemporary with him and will reflect the perceptions of these sources themselves. The references here to him as holy and saintly are not due to any act of canonization about him. A formal

act occurred for him in Alaska in 1970, but by a new church group ('OCA', formed in that year) whose standing is not entirely acknowledged among all the Orthodox patriarchates and autocephalous Churches. That group has since canonized other 'American saints'. Particularly problematic are two 'martyrs' canonized in 1980 from no more than a very few written sources, secondary, tertiary and quaternary: none of them primary; and without sufficient evidence of veneration for those (so-called) saints previous to the canonizations. In one case, the location and circumstances of the death of the person have been described since as differing from those in the Act of Canonization (Oleksa 1990; compare OCA 1980). Pronouncements from such a group, therefore, can not be included as credible and authoritative (also see nt.6, above).

[30] Valaam (1894a:49-50, 53; 1978:31, 33).

[31] Peter to Damascene of Valaam, 12 May 1866, in Valaam, ed. (1894:159; 1978:96).

[32] Ianovskii to Damascene, 22 Nov. 1865, in Valaam, ed. (1894:134-135; 1978:82). Ianovskii's predecessor for a brief few months at the beginning of 1818 was L.A. Gagemeister (L. von Hagemeister) who also had a special regard for Herman: see nt.10, above. A naval administration had replaced the private mercantile company administration in Russian-America in January 1818, after the Napoleonic Wars.

[33] Ianovskii to Damascene, 22 Nov. 1865, in Valaam, ed. (1894:143; 1978:88).

[34] Ibid. (1894:135; 1978:82).

[35] Valaam (1894a:57-58; 1978:36); also see Pierce (1990:199).

[36] Larionov in Valaam, ed. (1894:177; 1978:106).

[37] Ibid. (1894:176-177; 1978:105).

[38] Bishop Peter's attestation and signature in Larionov, in Valaam, ed. (1894:184; 1978:110). The manuscript was sent from Iakutsk with the cover-letter: Peter, bishop of Iakutsk, to Damascene, 9 Sept. 1867, in Valaam, ed. (1894:171, 1978:102). The designation 'bishop of Iakutsk' should not cause confusion. Peter had arrived in Russian-America in 1860 (see Pierce 1990:398), and remained here as the auxiliary bishop of the Kamchatka diocese until summer 1867. In May of that last year, he wrote his own, very brief biography of Herman as requested from Damascene (cited here in nts 11, 19, 26 and 31, above). Peter dated this letter on 12 May 1867 and evidently dispatched it straightaway from *Novo Arkhangel'sk*, as it was received at Valaam in October. Therefore, he is designated in that letter as bishop of *Novo Arkhangel'sk*. A few days later, he affixed his signature, the attestation and the date 21 May 1867 onto Larionov's manuscript, which he had received; and he also wrote the marginal remark on a page of this manuscript as cited in nt 6, above. But he did not, perhaps could not, send Larionov's manuscript from *Novo Arkhangel'sk*. Very soon afterwards, Russian-America was sold: Alaska became a possession of the USA. He vacated the see. By September 1867, Peter had already become bishop of Iakutsk. He then dispatched the manuscript to Damascene, and attached his own cover letter for the transmittal, signed by him now as 'bishop of Iakutsk'.

[39] See Larionov in Valaam, ed. (1894:180; 1978:107-108). For some of the instructions and confidences to Alig'iaga, see the last paragraphs in nt 22, above: e.g., it was to Alig'iaga that the elder entrusted his cross.

[40] See Lazarev in Valaam, ed. (1894:123, 127; 1978:76, 78-79).

[41] This is Veniaminov: archbishop Innokentii is the same person as the priest Ioann

(Ivan) Veniaminov who has figured so importantly throughout this study. Having served as the parish priest of the Unalaska parish and then the *Novo Arkhangel'sk* parish, he travelled to Petersburg where, in 1840, he was tonsured a monastic and was elevated to the episcopacy with the name Innokentii. See Intro., sec.2: Summary Chronology, years 1840-c.1852, above.

He was mentioned in the narrative by Lazarev who had recorded an account about him in relation to the 'holy elder'; so, in December 1866, *hegumen* Damascene requested verification or correction from the archbishop himself. Receiving the request in his far eastern archdiocese, Innokentii replied in spring of 1867 and explained that: At a perilous time in a difficult sea crossing to Kodiak in 1842, he had sought aid through a brief prayer to 'Fr Herman' (by then deceased); the contrary weather conditions quickly subsided; and the passage was completed safely. He thus verified this much of the account. He corrected it at another point however. Lazarev presumed that Innokentii had a vision of Herman. But Innokentii stated: 'I did not see any visions.' (Innokentii, archbishop of Kamchatka, to Damascene, 1 March 1867, in Valaam, ed. 1894:128, 169-170; 1978:79, 101.)

[42] See nt.38, above.

[43] Born in *Novo Arkhangel'sk* of 'Creole' parents, P.F. Kashevarov had been schooled in the seminary there and was ministering in the cathedral before his assignment to the Kodiak parish in 1848. The widely extended Kashevarov family were predominant in both the Kodiak and the Sitka areas: in a later generation, the priest A.P. Kashevarov appears, whose insight was so important at the end of Ch.5, sec.3.i, of this study.

P.F. Kashevarov sent a 'Note about Fr Herman', dated in September 1866, from Kodiak to the vicar bishop in *Novo Arkhangel'sk*, Peter (probably by request from him), who forwarded it to *hegumen* Damascene. That year, the priest P.F. Kashevarov would have been thirty-seven years old. In this 'Note', a few events described by Ianovskii and Larionov alike are also conveyed by him, now from people older than himself in the Kodiak area. A few other factors are clarified through him also. Cf. Ianovskii, Lazarev, and Kashevarov respectively in Valaam, ed., 1894:142, 174-175, 185-186; 1978:87-88, 104, 111): Ivanovskii's coincidence with both Larionov and Kashevarov is perhaps the most indicative factor, as Larionov was the church warden and Kashevarov was the priest of the same parish at this time.

[44] Sophia Vlasova comprises one side of an equation that brings forth a balanced result. Her resolve, about which we shall read, is an attribute found in many of the lives of monastic saints when they embark on the ascetic way. It reflects their freedom as they choose, nay as they insist on, this way of life. St Herman stands on the other side of this equation. During his previous twenty-five years in the Kodiak area, he had not brought anyone into the way of life that he was himself following: in other words, he had not imposed this on this anyone. When Sophia Vlasova approached him, he attempted to discourage her.

His own stature needs to be recognized clearly in this context when a Kodiak person sought to learn this way of life from him; therefore I shall emphasize his stature by delineating three points that may serve as a guideline. (i) He derived from a related people, or folk, himself and thus would have had certain affinities; in any case, he clearly had deep empathy, understanding. His background was related, he understood. (ii) He was already over sixty years of age and had about forty-six years of monastic formation and experience by the time Vlasova sought him to learn this tradition from him. His experience was substantial. (iii) During those many years of monastic formation and experience, he had been supervised by the *hegumeni* of Valaam, an institution of high repute, of solid standing. This institution remained in contact with him while he was in Russian-America. When he named his hermitage 'New Valaam', the affiliation was real, not feigned. He was a monastic of a monastery of high repute: he was securely attached to an institution of solid standing. These three points may serve as a guideline, should any men or women who lack these qualities come to Spruce Island (*Elovoi*), having wrapped themselves in Orthodox garb, boasting of a monastic tonsure, and claiming to be carrying the tradition lived by St Herman, even perhaps using his name. Also consider the description in nt.21, above.

[45] Herman to Ianovskii, 20 June 1820, in Valaam, ed. (1894:147-148; 1978:91).

[46] Ibid. Also read in ibid.: 'There are also many young men who would like to come but there is no room for them.' For the number twelve, see Lazarev in Valaam, ed. (1894:123; 1978:76). For the distance from the hermitage, see: P.F. Kashevarov in Valaam, ed. (1894:185; 1978:110), who is a secondary source but the pattern he describes is typical. For the Sunday gatherings, see Larionov in Valaam, ed. (1894:172; 1978:102). For the translation of ученица, which should be 'disciple' not 'pupil' in this context, see nt.48, below.

[47] Larionov in Valaam, ed. (1894:172; 1978:103); Lazarev in ibid. (1894:126-127; 1978:78).

[48] For instance, when Gerasim is referred to in his youth, the translation might be 'pupil'; and when the children supervised by Sophia Vlasova at 'New Valaam' are mentioned, then the translation should be 'pupils'. But another word, воспитанники, is also used for 'school pupils' whom Vlasova supervised or whom 'Fr Herman' taught: see Larionov in Valaam, ed. (1894:172, 183; 1978:109); also see Rezanov in Tikhmenev, ed. (1863:216). Cf., воспитанники as 'school pupil' and ученик as 'pupil, apprentice, and disciple', in *The Oxford Russian-English Dictionary*, 2nd edition (M. Wheeler, ed.); also see 'disciple' as ученик in *The Oxford English-Russian Dictionary* (P.S. Falla, ed.).

But when Vlasova herself and the women who had coalesced around her in a community near the 'Holy Elder' are described, then the translation proper for them must be 'disciples'. When Gerasim is described from the 1830s, and Alig'iaga is described, the proper translation must be the elder's 'disciples'. The proper translation renders their relationship with the старец. It reflects the dynamics of these inter-relationships as well as these people's own stature. To render Gerasim who had been raised by the 'holy elder' and on whose breast the elder lay his head at final repose; to render Alig'iaga who had lived so closely alongside the elder, who was himself mature in age, and to whom the elder had entrusted confidences; to render Sophia Vlasova around whom (no less than) a women's community had coalesced: as 'pupils' is to demean their stature.

An interesting and significant factor is the earliest ages of these and other key people when they sought the elder in the forest of *Elovoi*: Gerasim was a boy, Larionov was twelve, Vlasova was about twenty, Ianovksii was thirty. The monastic missionary would have been in his sixties when they first met him. As for Alig'iaga, no age is specified for him while an age older than these others is indicated.

[49] Larionov in Valaam, ed.,(1894:177; 1978:105).

[50] J. Leer, Alaska Native Language Center, University of Alaska at Fairbanks (personal communication, March 1988), who specified *apaa* as the correct spelling in Roman script and provided the translation as 'grandfather'. *Apa* is the word for grandfather in the Yup'ik language also, according to S.A. Jacobson (1984:75).

[51] See, e.g.: *Apophthegmata Patrum* (1908-1913, 1975a, 1975b); *Historia,* anon., (1961); Palladius of Helenopolis (1904, 1974), *Vita Pachomii* (1932, 1980).

[52] Ianovskii in Valaam, ed. ((1894:140; 1978:86).

[53] Lazarev in ibid. (1894:125; 1978:77).

[54] Ibid. (1894:123-124; 1978:76).

[55] 'Foresight' has been written as the heading for this section, because foresight can be distinguished from prophecy without positing them as mutually exclusive categories. Foresight is the gift of foreknowledge. Prophecy involves words spoken about God within the divine presence. These terms can be combined when the dynamics coincide: prophetic foreknowledge. A further distinction can be rendered through the term 'clairvoyance', a dynamic seen in the second part of the initial quotation in this section. For clarification and finer terminology, see Ware (1974:101-109) whose insights can be applied here. 'Three gifts in particular distinguish the spiritual father,' Ware explains:

> The first is insight and discernment (*diakrisis*), the ability to perceive intuitively the secrets of another's heart, to understand the hidden depths of which the other is unaware. ... This power is spiritual rather than psychic; it is not simply a kind of extra-sensory perception or a sanctified clairvoyance but the fruit of grace, presupposing concentrated prayer and an unremitting ascetic struggle. ... The second gift is the ability to love others and to make others' sufferings his own. ... The third gift is the power to transform the human environment, both the material and the non-material.

Healing is identified by Ware as 'one aspect' of this 'power to transform the human environment'. Other aspects are reflected in the verb 'to transform', rendered also as 'to transfigure': The spiritual father perceives the divine transfiguring the mundane, and also through himself this transfiguration is made manifest. Ware draws examples from the fourth century through time into the mid-twentieth century. While the gender reference is masculine, these qualities are found equally in women of the same formation and stature throughout the centuries.

[56] Larionov in Valaam, ed. (1894:178-179; 1978:106-107). *Elovoi* is found in the original: Spruce Island is the modern designation.

[57] Lazarev in ibid. (1894:124; 1978:77).

[58] Ibid. (1894:126; 1978:78).

[59] Ianovskii in ibid. (1894:141; 1978:87).

[60] Peter, vicar bishop, in ibid., ed. (1894:158-159; 1978:96).

[61] Larionov, in ibid. (1894:182; 1978:109).

[62] Ibid.. (1894:182; 1978:109).

[63] M.H. Naumoff, personal communication, Kodiak, March 1988. Naumoff also said of *apaa*, 'He's helped me many times.'

[64] Ianovskii in Valaam, ed. (1894:140; 1978:86). Ianovksii was surprised not only because bears would come to visit, but also because the 'holy elder' was sharing his scant food with the bears during a season of dearth, despite his own scarcity (see ibid.).

[65] Larionov in ibid. (1894:172-173; 1978:102-103).

[66] Innokentii, archbishop of Kamchatka, in ibid. (1894:169-170; 1978:101).

[67] Also see, e.g.: Βίος Ἀντονίου xxxv, xl, cited as Athanasius (1857:889-891); also see ibid. vi, viii, xiii, xxv-xvi, cols 849-852, 853-856, 861-864, 881-884. See others in: *Historia*, anon. (1961), *Apophthegmata Patrum* (1908-13, 1975a, 1975b), Palladius of Helenopolis (1902, 1974), *Vita Pachomii* (1932, 1980). Also see: Sts Cyril of Jerusalem, John of the Ladder, and Diadochus of Photice, as cited in Ch.4, sec.3.ii of my text, above.

[68] For the analogy, see A.N. Murav'ev (1855). For the Egyptian desert including the Thebaid, see esp. Chitty (1964). A.N. Murav'ev was an ecclesiastical historian who was himself contemporary with the later phase of Russian-America. The vividness of his analogy was retrospective, as the reforms by Emperor Peter I had destroyed many of the activities, yet the 'Russian Thebaid' remained. Two examples should illustrate its magnitude: the network belonging to Valaam Monastery and the network belonging to *Sviato-Troitskaia Sergievskaia Lavra*. We may recall that Herman embarked on the monastic life in a *metochion* of this *Lavra* in the mid- eighteenth century, about the year 1763, and then entered Valaam five or six years later. (The year of his embarcation is calculated from his age of forty-eight in 1805 and his age of sixteen at this early juncture, as cited above).

As many as six subsidiary monasteries plus many *scetes* and hermitages extending from Lake Ladoga to the White Sea coast were attached to Valaam by the sixteenth century (Valaam 1983:87). The monastic system of *Sviato-Troitskaia Sergievskaia Lavra* had developed to similar magnitude northwards from Moscow already in the fourteenth century, and yet more *scetes* and hermitages developed within just this one network during the early fifteenth century. These were only a couple of the networks among many others in the 'Russian Thebaid'.

The origins of Valaam may be of interest. The monastery derived from an anchorite who had settled near the shores of Lake Ladoga and was joined by a native man from the region who became his disciple, during the reign of Olga of Kiev, early to middle tenth century, according to Murav'ev (1842:18). The mid-tenth century is the earliest possible date for this anchoritic settlement, according to Valaam Monastery (1983:26-27). Written historical records begin in the mid-twelfth century, by which time both of these men were already being venerated as saints, their relics were enshrined, and icons had been made of them; and by this time, the monastery house had been established on the islet in Lake Ladoga.

[69] *Historia*, anon. (1961). For the historicity of the pilgrimage, see Ward (1980:4): 'Despite the doubts of some modern scholars, I am confident that the *Historia*

Monachorum describes a real journey.' For the authorship (anon.), see Ward (1980:6-7) accepting research by Butler (1904) that the Ἱστορία Μοναχῶν [*Historia*] is independent from the πρὸς Λαῦσον Ἱστορία into which it had been incorporated. Also, Festugière (to be cited below) has presented it as an anonymous work independent from Palladius's own. For the relationship of the Greek text to the Latin rendition authored by Rufinus, and for the dating of both, see Ward (1980:7-9). For numerous pilgrimages in the deserts from the fourth to the sixth centuries, see Chitty (1966:206), also see the entry 'Pilgrimages' in Subject Index, ibid.

[70] Ward (1980:40).

[71] Also see, e.g.: *Apophthegmata Patrum* (1908-1913, 1975a, 1975b); Palladius of Helenopolis (1902, 1974); *Vita Pachomii* (1932, 1980). For clarification, see Ware, cited in nt 55, above.

CONCLUSIONS

'Christianization of the Religion of their Ancestors'
Mircea Eliade, *Myth and Reality*

(1) A Two-fold Question

A twofold question has been involved throughout these chapters: how did the transition occur; and what were its implications for these ancestral cultures?

(i) How Did the Transition Occur?

The communication of the Russian Orthodox faith and its practices took place along lines of personal attachments, engendered by certain affinities, from like to like: that is to say, from northeast Asians and far northern Eurasians to Aleuts and Alutiiqs within the far northerners' own culture(s); and it took place throughout the whole bodies of peoples' societies, or kinship based polities. Even in the Kodiak area where the historical circumstances at the initial contacts differed from those on the Aleutian Islands, the main characteristics were fundamentally the same: indigenous and corporate, predicated on affinities and close interpersonal relationships.

Native leadership emerged within this movement from the start, including for instance the *toion* Ivan Glotov, the *toion* Ivan Pan'kov, as well as the leader of the Valaam elder's women disciples Sophia Vlasova, and many more. Key people of extraordinary spiritual gifts emerged, such as the Aleut prophet of Akun Ivan Smirennikov. Significant interactions, a synergy, occurred between them and the remarkably few clergy and formal missionaries who were here in place in this vast region and who were talented men of deep spiritual gifts themselves: such as, the parish priest Ioann (Ivan) Veniaminov, the parish priest and missionary Iakov Netsvetov, and the missionary monastic Herman. (Not all were of such caliber however, and the divergence of others has been indicated: Archimandrite Ioasaph at Kodiak was ambiguous in this respect, *hieromonk* Filaret at Ikogmiut was mentally unstable and dangerous, the vicar bishop Peter at *Novo Arkhangel'sk* (Sitka) was heavy-handed; *et cetera*.)

The gifted clergy and formal missionaries reflected an affirmative outlook in their interactions, an outlook that is available to us from a long unbroken line of patristic tradition stemming from the first and second centuries AD. This affirmative outlook recognizes the dissemination of the divine presence and therefore would recognize and allow areas of correspondence between the ancestral cultures and the new faith and practices. This outlook is not naïve or overly sentimental. It was reflected through sturdy men of stable characters with steadfast dedication who insightfully marked differences, and these men were an integral part of the far northern experience themselves. Their kind of attitude would allow a creative appropriate synthesis, one that did take place indeed.

A vital area of correspondence existed about the dynamics of divine participation. The divine participates in the cosmos, reciprocally the cosmos participates in and is vivified by the divine presence. This participation is made manifest not only through the reflections of the divine in nature but also through ritual symbols and acts. These are essential dynamics in the new faith and its practices. These were essential dynamics in the ancestral Arctic culture(s): the dynamics of divine participation within nature were operative in southern Alaska in many ways, in masking, in various rituals, and in shamanizing

These dynamics of divine participation comprised a vital *point of comprehension* where the ancestral far northern culture(s) could engage and retain the new faith and practices — to comprehend not merely in a theoretical manner, but in a profoundly existential way. At this point of comprehension, we could see the ritual masks become icons, the ritual festivities become liturgies and liturgical festivals, and the shamanizing become an ecstasy of the biblical prophetic kind. Each of these was an aspect of a multifaceted transformation that involved yet more dimensions, as we should expect within a movement that was indigenous and corporate, occurring through virtually the whole of the Aleut and Alutiiq societies in their entireties.

Perhaps it needs to be emphasized in these Conclusions, just as it was mentioned in the Introduction, that an indigenous movement is not necessarily insular: People entered into close interpersonal relationships with others; and key people travelled extensive distances to centres to absorb traditions and to bring these traditions home. An indigenous movement in the Arctic does not imply a coarseness either: Cultures that could engage and retain something as sublime and formal as the Divine Liturgy of St John Chrysostom must have a sensitivity for decorum and must be endowed aesthetically, albeit in their own ways. It is with these qualities, including formality, in mind that we may say: Their antiquity is *retained transformed* — drawn up in their own way from their own roots unsevered.

(ii) Implications for these ancestral cultures

Antiquity retained transformed: This implies a 'Christianization of the religion of their ancestors'. The quotation is from Mircea Eliade with reference to his own ancestry.[1] Referring to a whole body of traditions (designs, lore, food, song, dance) belonging to Romanian culture, and those belonging to neighbouring Slavic cultures, he expressed the continuity that he perceived: they 'incorporated into their new faith the cosmic religion that they had preserved from prehistoric times.'[2] These words apply to the Aleut and the Alutiiq peoples of Alaska also. The same may be said for other Arctic peoples as well.

This process — the Christianization of the ancestral religion — is differentiated by Eliade from the antithesis, which would be the paganization of Christianity, as he emphasized:[3]

> For the peasants of Eastern Europe this in no sense implied a 'paganization' of Christianity, but, on the contrary, a 'Christianization' of the religion of their ancestors. When the time comes for the history of this 'popular theology' to be written on the evidence that can be traced in seasonal festivals and religious folklores, it will be realized that 'cosmic Christianity' is not a new form of paganism or a pagan-Christian syncretism. Rather it is an original religious creation, in which eschatology and soteriology are given cosmic dimensions.

Aspects of this 'cosmic Christianity' were forthcoming in this study through examples from popular literature and folk traditions as well as iconography, liturgical traditions and patristic literature (Ch.3, sec.2). They express the transcendence of the divine ('yet beyond all'), the immanence of the divine ('vivifying all, and existing in everything'), and this immanence made specific in the Incarnation in Jesus Christ. It is the immanence that has comprised the most significant dynamic here. It was expressed by Dostoyevsky through his character Zossima in conversation with a peasant: 'Christ has been with the birds of air, the beasts of the field, the leaves, and the blades of grass, even before us.' Zossima describes even the minute creatures partaking 'in the mystery of God'. And Zossima exclaims: 'Love all men, love everything, seek that rapture and ecstasy.' These cosmic dimensions are expressed by the Greek shepherd in Arcadia who dances in celebration of the Resurrection. They are expressed by the Russian peasant in the north who atones to the earth. They are expressed by the Orthodox Yup'ik hunter in Alaska who greets the seasonal coming and going of the flocks of birds by singing to them, and who atones to restore harmony with the animals on whom his subsistence depends by honouring them and the spirit that sent them.

The difference of these dynamics from naïve pantheism was highlighted with reference to a major tale among the Orthodox Dena'ina and a folktale among the Orthodox Alutiiq (Ch.3, sec.2). The Alaskan folklore provides examples of the 'popular theology' that Eliade has mentioned in the quotation, above. This 'popular theology' became evident also in the Chugach-area folk history about the meeting of the Alutiiq healer Kangatyug with 'a very holy man, Монах Германъ,' an account that was shown to contain vital elements from the patristic tradition (Ch.5, sec.3.ii; and again Ch.6, sec.3, sec. conclusion).[4]

(2) A Question of Categories

It is significant that the Chugach-area tradition and the tradition-bearer himself were both misrepresented by the ethnographer who collected the account. The Russian-Alutiiq tradition bearer of stature was categorized as a 'Chugach Eskimo', this account was placed among the 'shaman stories'. The categorization indicates the existence of a distant perspective. Evidently very well meaning, the ethnographer Birket-Smith was simply too far removed, so that his perspective encompassed elements of patristics and 'shamanism' indiscriminately.

A problem with the distant perspective is that it identifies Christianity as 'the white man's religion', or euphemistically more recently in Arctic studies 'the European religion'; and therefore tends to cast indigenous phenomena wholesale into categories other than Christian. Folk-healing, folklore, folk dancing, folk epics, are all cast away into another category simply because they are not Western. In other words, things Western are presumed to be things Christian; therefore non-Western phenomena are classed as something other, even in regions where Christian identity has been observed as central to the indigenous peoples' self-identity for generations as on the Aleutian Islands and the Kodiak area or regions where Christianization took place many centuries ago as in Iakutia.

Two more examples of the same type of categorization as this ethnographer's were brought forward in my Introduction (sec.1). The cause was simpler in those examples: in both instances, the commentators' task was to describe the 'native religion', so the commentators affected pre-Christian patterns even though Russian Orthodoxy had been manifestly recognized as central to these peoples' self-identity. The affectation is tantamount to declaring the Olympian pantheon as the religion proper to the Greeks, disregarding the thorough ingrafting of mainstream Christianity into the very heart of the Greek culture and *vice versa*. A retrospective description of that sort can be valuable and enriching: the problem would occur if the description were presented as contemporary and categorical.

The result in the Arctic is a confusion, sometimes understandably as when Birket-Smith confused some subtle yet essential distinctions, but other times to an extent that is absurd when the categorization becomes absolute. 'Shamanism', itself an artificial term, is being propounded by some today as a religion proper to the Arctic peoples, replete with its own clergy ('shamans') and even its own 'temples'. Reminiscent of the Gnostic movements in European history in the first centuries AD, this is unprecedented in Arctic history. Therefore I would refer to it as 'neo-shamanism', to mark it as an innovation. It is occurring in northeast Asia, far more so than in Alaska; and it is being led by some foreign academics in league with a few former Marxists. I mention the derivations in order to underscore an important factor: that the proponents are too distant to be aware of the deeper dimensions of mainstream Christianity. These deeper dimensions were known to Eliade, whose own background provided the affinities for a closer perspective; and he was at the forefront of the study of shamanism.

The artificiality of neo-shamanism aside, the stance otherwise merits some serious attention. In some instances, the distancing of indigenous Arctic phenomena categorically away from Christianity is meant to reinforce the vitality or the revitalization of indigenous Arctic cultures against unnecessary intrusions. If a commentator or an activist does believe that Christianity and Westernization are categorically linked, then the commentator or activist may attempt to buffer the intrusion by creating a distance for things native from all things Christian. The attempt is not meant as buffer with regard to Westernization only. It occurs in the Arctic with regard to Russification also; and in our study we have seen examples of some Russian churchmen who would laud the wholesale assimilation of other ethnic groups (Ch.1, sec2.i.d). The reaction against this, be it against Westernization or wholesale Russification, can not be dismissed too easily. Personally, I have sympathy for it. But it remains merely the inverse of the actions projected by the oppressors. For their own interests, the latter would interpret and use Christianity to reform conquered peoples. Inversely, reactive commentators and activists tend to disdain and dispel Christianity so that native peoples are not made to conform to those designs. While there is something to commend in the stance, the perspective remains an equally distant one, never-the-more.

A closer perspective is required: one that would see the difference between the depth and the breadth of mainstream Christianity on the one hand, and the intrusion of Westernization in particular on the other hand. Discovery, or re-discovery and re-orientation, is available to us all. Re-discovery could involve deeper self-recognition.

To appreciate this necessity yet further, let us assume the distant perspective and project it without modification from the far northern forests into the desert. How would it observe the activities of the *abba*s, the desert fathers of old, as they healed, conversed with angels, shunned demons — as something other than 'Christianity', as 'shamanism', perhaps? And if so, then let us project it earlier into Galilee, and ask how might it observe the same acts, there in context at that time?

From a closer perspective, we would recognize certain affinities when a Chugach-area tradition-bearer of stature distinguished an Orthodox Alutiiq healer from other sorts of ecstatics and reflected a distinction that has recurred in the patristic tradition for centuries; and more over when the tradition-bearer described phenomena about 'a very holy man' that also recur in the patristic tradition. The recognition should be easy as the tradition-bearer, Makarii Fedorovich Chumovitskii, was an Alutiiq (or Russian-Alutiiq) mature man of stature: a leader of his people's church.

From a most insightful perspective, a man from Siberia was able to discern the spiritual gifts of the biblical prophetic kind in an Aleut elder, indeed in someone through whom a thorough Christianization of the Aleutian ancestral ways had taken place, and within virtually unchanged Aleut material culture — the Aleut Ivan Smirennikov, the Siberian Ivan Veniaminov.

From a close perspective we should see that ancestral modes of dance and music, feasting and foods, mourning and healing, lore and language, have continued transformed and are lived with vitality. The mainstream Christianity of this wide *ecumene* has provided substance for spiritual, including cultural, verve and resilience, and has always embraced a rich tapestry of kinds of cultures.[5] This religion has been lived concurrently in the dwelling-camps of fishermen, in the yurts of subsistence hunters, in the huts (*kalivya*) and tents of nomadic herders, in the honeycombed villages of cultivators, in the neighbourhoods of city-dwellers, in the houses of merchants, on the estates of aristocracy: and, yes, within palaces indeed.

For the Aleut and Alutiiq peoples, a close perspective should allow us to say: This faith and its practices are the peoples' own. This faith and its practices have always been rooted in these peoples' own ways of life and own communities. This religion is theirs. And through this religion, their antiquity is retained transformed — drawn up from their own roots unsevered. These Alaskans today have an unbroken communion with their deepest ancestral past through their Russian Orthodoxy, chosen and maintained as an inheritance for them by their ancestors — *that is, as long as their churches remain their own.*

Here is a viable way of life with roots deep in antiquity and with fruit in the modern world. Or alternatively expressed, here is deepest antiquity existing unsevered transformed.

NOTES

[1] Eliade (1988:38).

[2] Id. (1959:164).

[3] Id. (1988:38). Regarding 'cosmic Christianity', Eliade (ibid.) recognizes the involvement of all of the natural world — 'All Nature sighs, awaiting the Resurrection' — as being a central motif in 'the religious folklore of Eastern Christianity' (quoted and cited in Ch.3, sec.2.iv, at nt.14, above).

[4] Chumovitskii in Birket-Smith (1953:2, 130-131). Perhaps the affinity is closer yet between this account, along with the other accounts, regarding *apaa* in the forest and the patristic accounts regarding the *abba*s in the desert, because the earlier likewise derive from folk histories, or oral traditions. So does the supreme expression of the Christian faith, the Gospels themselves, conveyed originally by word of mouth until transcribed, or placed in writing, which is the reason we have the four accounts.

[5] For the word '*ecumene*', see Intro., sec.3ii, above. The plurality that I am indicating is not a flight of fancy or a literary flourish on my part. This plurality in unity is real. It reflects the central belief about the Holy Trinity: the Godhead is indivisibly one while known in three hypostases. Just as the Godhead is one, so one formal set of doctrines, and formal set of cycles of worship, exist. The unity is manifest. The diversity is not unbound. Just as the Godhead is known in three hypostases, so these peoples (ἔθνη: народи) live this faith in their own way: with their own languages, even alphabets, lore and other customs. And just as the hypostases in Trinity co-inhere, so the peoples co-participate. They co-participate through the unity of ritual. They co-participate furthermore through mutual interaction. Their integrity is not isolated, or insular. A contrast may be found here with religions that insist absolutely on the oneness and therefore demand nearly total cultural uniformity.

If a qualification were to be set on the indicative description in my text, then it should be that the rich plurality has diminished since the mid-twentieth century. The diminution had begun earlier in the twentieth century: because of the militant imposition of Bolshevism across Russia; and because of the brutal expulsion that was suffered by the Greek and Orthodox Turkic populations wholesale from their ancestral homelands in Asia Minor, following the genocide that was suffered relatedly there by the Armenians (see, e.g., Dobkin 1988). Asia Minor had been one of the heart-lands of Christianity from biblical times until the political events of the twentieth century. Most of the Ecumenical Councils took place in cities on the Aegean seacoast of Asia Minor. These upsets in the earlier twentieth century preceded the widespread upsets of the Second World War and its aftermath, when many other traditional cultures were chronically damaged. But that was not long ago; and the richer plurality has only diminished, it has not disappeared.

An example might be useful. This is a single example that I hope will suffice. The Orthodox Vlach people of Greece, who are related linguistically to the Romanians, lived their traditional existence as nomadic or semi-nomadic herders throughout the centuries. (See, e.g., Ward and Thompson 1914, from ethnographic observations during

1909-1910; esp. Ch.6: Birth, Baptism, Betrothal, Marriage, Burial Customs; and Ch.7: Festivals and Folklore). Only after the Second World War did they become sedentary as a group. Yet even as sedentary, the Vlachs retain many of their customs and their language: a main centre is the town of Metsovo in Thessaly today. Nor did their nomadic way of life marginalize them as a people: on the contrary, wealthy Vlach merchants were also known in earlier times, and Vlach statesmen have assumed influential roles in Greek, hence European, statesmanship. Other examples would derive from Karelia, diminishing mainly because of the migrations into Finland as a result of WW2. Examples derive from Iakutia, the Altai and throughout northeast Asia, diminishing because of the forced collectivization, urbanization and industrialization in the USSR during the Cold War, the aftermath of WW2.

An example derives also from the Aleutians. The abrupt expulsion of the Aleut population from their villages by the USA military (which was mentioned in my Introduction, sec.1) caused not only the unprecedented displacement of every village in the archipelago but also caused the deaths of many elderly people who were tradition-bearers: they just could not survive the trauma. It remains my hope that my many years of labour to produce this study may serve to say some of things they, in their own way, might have said to their descendants.

The Nikolski Tree

(1) Let the Children Speak

Firstly something about Pascha on the Aleutian Islands as published in *Taniisi* ('*To Shed Light*', '*Shine On*'), volume 3, by the Aleutian Region School District:[1]

Another tradition of the Orthodox Church is a special bread called Artos. Artos is blessed with prayer and Holy Water. It is carried around the church during the Easter Week procession and remains in the middle of the church during the entire week. Upon it is placed a small icon of the Resurrection of Jesus. There is a tradition which states that when the Apostles sat down to break bread for their meal, they would leave one place empty where Jesus Christ sat and would place a piece of bread in the empty space to remind them that He was always present among them.

Easter Kulich is a sweet bread with some dried fruits and sometimes nuts. It is an Orthodox traditional bread which is eaten during Easter season. It is brought to church during Easter midnight service and blessed. Kulichax is the Aleut term. There are many recipes from place to place. Here is the recipe that Lavera Dushkin uses: ...

Tom Merculief and William Dushkin

Grades 8 and 6, Aleutian Region School District

Furthermore from the same two young men on the Aleutian Islands:

The word Easter is the name of the pagan 'goddess of spring'. In Europe this name was applied to the Christian festival celebrating the Resurrection of Christ.

In Eastern Christendom, the Greek word 'Paskha' has been used. It means 'the passover', from the Hebrew Pesekh. Paskha is the new Passover of Death, hence the name and significance of the Hebrew Paskha was devoutly accepted and used by the Early Christians and the Orthodox Church.

... [and for the date of this feastday:] The Orthodox still observe the rule laid down by the First Ecumenical Council in Nicaea, in the year 325 A.D.

Tom Merculief and William Dushkin

Grades 8 and 6, Aleutian Region School District

227

Something from the village of Akutan on the Aleutian island of the same name:

The Friday before Easter is called Good Friday. On that day we wear dark clothing to church. On Easter morning we wear light clothing.

Easter means having fun, because for seven weeks before Easter there is Lent. During the seven weeks, Jesus was helping people and preaching. He also told his disciples to help people, too. The first week of Lent is the strictest week, along with the fourth and the last week. The other weeks are not as strict as they were before. Long ago, all the days in Lent were carried on with great respect for the church rules. ...

At Eastertime the thing I like best is when everyone makes Kulitch and everyone passes them out to different people. I like that best because Kulitch is very good to eat. People usually put frosting on top ...

Mike Shelikoff
Grade 11, Aleutian Region School District

Something from Alexandrovsk, English Bay, on the Kenai Peninsula:

Easter is a very special holiday in English Bay. The night before Easter we go to church from 11:00 at night till 3:00 or 4:00 in the morning. The church is decorated with flowers. Around two in the afternoon before Easter, the black cloth is taken off the icon stands and the members of the church put lighter colored cloth like light green, pink or light blue on the stands.

We sing Lenten songs. Then at midnight we walk around the church three times with lighted candles and sing Easter songs. Then we go back into the church and we start singing again. The priest blesses the Easter bread (recipe follows the article) and the eggs with holy water before we take them out of church. ... The big Easter dinner is at the end of a busy Easter day. Easter is a very special day for everybody.

Roberta Kvasnikoff
Alexandrovsk, no.3
English Bay Elementary / High School
Kenai Peninsula Borough School District

Again from the Kenai Peninsula:

Easter Lent, called the Great Lent, usually starts in the early part of March. It is the time of preparation for the Feast of the Resurrection. It lasts about six weeks. During this time, we (Russian Orthodox) don't eat meat starting from Meatfare Sunday, one week before Great Lent. We don't eat dairy products from Cheesefare Sunday: that is one day before Great Lent. We don't dance or listen to music much. This is the time when people get closer to everybody. We do this by helping the people who need help. We carry packages, help clean their houses and do what good neighbors do.

During Lent, 'the royal gates' to the altar area in the church remain closed to signify man's separation from the kingdom of God through sin. The church vesting is a somber color usually black. ...

Good Friday is the anniversary of Christ's death. People go to church dressed in black. Before the people go to church they don't eat anything. At church men bring the picture of Jesus from the altar room. The priest walks under the picture in the middle of the church. It is surrounded by a black cloth and flowers.

A procession of the people on Holy Saturday bears witness to the total victory of Christ over the powers of darkness and death. And this time the people with lighted candles follow the priest around the church, he has the winding sheet over his head and a Holy Gospel in his hands.

Becky Kvasnikoff
Alexandrovsk, no.3
English Bay Elementary / High School
Kenai Peninsula Borough School District

Something from Naknek in the Bristol Bay area too:

Black is not used in the church often. It is only used on Good Friday when Christ was crucified on the cross. Just for a few hours black would be used, then immediately it is changed to white. ... The other church colors are usually gold, red, green, white, and blue. These are kind of basic church colors that are used for different seasons, like Christmas, Easter, to remember Saints. On Saint Herman's Day, the gold signifies preciousness. ...

Owen Johnson, interviewing Alexei Askoak
Uutuqtwa, vol.11, no.1
Bristol Bay High School

About the Aleut language:

The development of written Aleut (Al-ë-yüt) language was started by a Russian priest named Ivan Veniaminov. When he came to the Aleutian Chain in 1825, he started the first written Aleut alphabet in cyrillics. He had the help of Tigalda Chief Ivan Pan'kov and Stepan Kriukov of Nikolski; Iakov Netzvetov of Atka and Amlia Chief Nikolay Dediukhin helped adapt it to the Atkan dialect. This cyrillic alphabet was used strictly for religious translations of the Bible. ...

Simeon Snigeroff
Grade 8, Aleutian Region School District

Next from Atka in the centre of the Aleutian archipelago:

There are many things that are important to the people of Atka. One of the most important things is the Russian Orthodox Church.

There have been four Russian Orthodox Churches built in Atka. Before the first regular church in Old Harbor, they used a prayer chapel made of sod which was built by Vasil'yev, a Russian, in the year 1811. Then a snowslide broke it up, so they moved the village further down the mountain. The church at the new location was named St. Nicholas, and it was started in 1828 and finished in 1829.

Since the church was not finished when Father Iakov Netsvetov arrived in 1828, they used a prayer tent.

A second church was built in the 1870s because the villagers moved to a new site on Nazen Bay. This second church was located where John. L. Nevzoroff's house is presently located. For reasons, unknown, the second church was vacated and a third church built on the site of the present church. This church was burned down during World War II. The fourth and present church was built between 1945-46. Some of the important saints, holidays and other things remain important to the people of Atka. A few of the most important saints are: St. Nicholas of Myra-Lycia (the Atka Church is named after him); St. Herman is important to Atkans because he was the first Alaskan priest to become a saint; St Innocent was important because he later became a Bishop after serving in Alaska. He was canonized a saint for the work he did in the Russian Orthodox Church. ....

The Russian Orthodox Church has been the center of Atkan life since the Russians came in the late 1700s. Since almost 100 percent of the people of Atka are Russian Orthodox, the church will continue to be the center of Atkan life for many years to come.

Mary Snigaroff
Grade 7, Aleutian Region School District

Now from Nikolski on the island of Umnak in the Aleutians:

From the beginning of the 1900s, the Village of Nikolski was called Umnak. The problem was, the whole island was called Umnak, so in order to distinguish the village, the island, and the post office, they had to choose another name. ... Since St. Nicholas was the patron saint of the church, a name was taken from Nicholas. To get the name, they replaced the 'ch' with 'k', the 'a' was taken out, and 'ki' was added to the end. The final result was Nikolski.

Myron Merculieff and Susan Dushkin
Grades 5 and 8, Aleutian Region School District

Let us concentrate on Nikolski.

(2) An Old Man's Tale

Spending two months at Nikolski collecting material for a master's thesis, a USA field researcher noticed the stump of a 'pole' in front of the village church. It was enclosed in a 'monument house'. This 'pole', he said, was seen by the Aleuts to be 'very powerful'; for instance, they told him of a boy who had hit the 'monument house' with darts while playing and the boy's arm swelled. The pole had once been so very high, they told him, that a raven perched on top looked as small as a sparrow from below; but now, just a stump of the pole remained, and when it was gone, they said, the Aleuts would be gone too.[2]

Years later, an anthropologist published the same description of the 'pole' and its 'monument house', replete with the legend of the raven once on the top. He reiterated the belief: 'Anyone who touches the house in a mood of challenge or disbelief will suffer fearfully.' He repeated the legend: 'Legend has it that Nikolski will survive and its Aleuts, as long as the pole stump remains.'[3]

What could this 'pole' be? Why is it so important to the Umnak Aleuts, so that it remains even as a 'stump', cordoned into a monument, and their future is tied to it by legend? Where did it come from? The anthropologist assumed that it had its origin before Russian contact, because he had been told that 'the Russians' had tried to destroy it'.

Let us heed an oral tradition from the village, collected by the Unalaska City School in 1975 from Sergei Sovoroff, an elderly Umnak Aleut, translated and published the following year.[4] Seventy-four years of age, he admits that no one in the village could properly remember its origins, yet he will bring forth whatever he knows. He heard the story as a child, and will relay it now.

He speaks of *ikax*, 'the tree' or 'the wood', that stands in front of the present village church:

> I don't know the year when it was first noticed; to my knowledge I think it was the year 1765 or before. No one told me the exact date so I don't know who put it there or how it got there. My father's mother was the one who told the story about the *ikax*. ... My father's great-grandfather told the story to the grandchildren and it was passed on to me.

The '*ikax*', he explains, was originally built at the old village site. It was so tall that the top could not be seen in the fog. 'The structure itself was like a wood shed, and the long pole it had was something the people talked about and held in awe.' Originally, it was something new to behold: 'The first time they saw it nobody knew what it was.'

It was reduced in size 'when the Russians occupied Alaska':

> A Russian boat came to Nikolski. [...] When they came to the village they had no place to stay so they tore the *ikax* down to make themselves a shelter. The villagers told them not to destroy the *ikax* but they didn't listen to them and instead built themselves a place to live in. After they were finished they went out to pick driftwood for burning in the same way that the Aleuts did. While getting driftwood and picking it along the way they would stop to rest. Wherever they sat down to rest they died. And one went for a walk behind the village in a place with a small river. Its a kind of swamp place. He bent down to drink some water but he fell in and drowned. The place where he died is called *inglakun* (whiskers) because the Russians who died there had lots of whiskers. So up to today we still call it "Whisker River" in Aleut.
> [...] The only thing I know is that all those Russian men who used the wood for themselves died mysteriously.

In 1900, after a fire, the chapel was relocated to 'the other side of the river', he explains. The *ikax* was placed in the ground at this site; and the 'house was built over the *ikax*' (to enclose and protect it). His own father dug the foundations for the relocated *ikax* and its house, using an *ixulax*, a whale bone spade; and his father recorded the event in writing, but the account, written in pencil, has since faded and has become illegible, Sovoroff relates.

When he himself was a boy, he threw darts at it for target practice. The next day, his arm swelled painfully. His father sent for village elders; the 'two old men and women' examined the boy; and his father then confronted him, 'I bet you were spearing the *ikax*.' That was when, Sergei Sovoroff says, he realized that 'they were telling the truth about the *ikax*': it had 'power'.

In 1930, the 'house over the *ikax*' was repaired with his own assistance, he explains. He mentions no other reconstruction.

Sergei Sovoroff's tradition is as succinct and unembellished. Obviously, the 'house over the *ikax*' that he built or assisted in building in 1930 is the same as the 'monument house' containing the stump of a 'pole' in front of the Nikolski chapel that the scholar observed in 1952, and the anthropologist described in 1980.

But let us ask ourselves: Might Sovoroff be reserved about projecting his knowledge, as someone is apt to be reserved in a society where self-projection is considered rude and self-effacement polite? Might he be exercising care to relate a tradition without the risk of a slightest embellishment or speculation? Or is he being playfully cryptic? — or perhaps just tactful.

With these questions in mind, let us extend extra attention to the oral tradition, considering it as a reserved message from an elderly Aleut of stature, not as a primitive tale from a native. While he candidly admits the limits of his knowledge, and is sparse with his words, he may be providing all the information necessary for us to discover what this 'stump of a pole' really is. Let's look.

When was this 'tree', or 'wood', first noticed? 'I think it was the year 1765 or before,' he says. The time corresponds with the date of the first, or the first known, baptism in the Unalaska region: This was the baptism of the youth who became the primary *toion* of Umnak, Ivan Stepanovich Glotov, his journey to Kamchatka with his godfather, and his return to Umnak. I shall reproduce and rearrange parts of my text about him from Chapter 1 (sec.1.iii, iv and sec.3), so that this can re-read easily here now (the references can be found in that chapter):

> Shushak, a leading man of Umnak Island, entered into alliance with Stepan Gavrilovich Glotov, a hunter who had come from northeastern Asia and who remained in the Umnak region from 1759 to 1762. Shashuk entrusted a nephew to him [a dynamic predicated on the general Aleutian Island custom of kin exchange], and the ally baptized the youth. This was the first baptism, or among the

first, in the Unalaska region. Names were given and shared: the godson received the baptismal name Ivan (Ioann) and he assumed his godfather's names as his own patronymic and surname; thus the youth Mushkal (Mushkalyax) became the Aleut Ivan Stepanovich Glotov.

A tall cross was erected by Stepan Gavrilovich at that time at this site, where the first baptism in the Unalaska region took place: This fact comes from Veniaminov conveying a tradition communicated to him in the 1830s and 1830s by elderly people in the Unalaska region.[5] So, Sergei Sovoroff says: 'Originally, it was something new to behold: 'The first time they saw it nobody knew what it was.' Yes, of course, it would have been something new: the first.

What did the *ikax* look like? 'The structure itself was like a wood shed, and the long pole it had was something the people talked about and held in awe,' Sergei Sovoroff tells us. His simile is clear. A wood shed has a roof of the same shape as the typical covering over a Russian cross that is placed outdoors. Just above the vertical axis, or center pole, of the cross, two pieces of wood form a pointed cap. Each piece extends outward from the apex, each in an opposite direction, each to an upper extremity of the longest horizontal bar of the Russian cross, thus forming the pointed structure that covers the full height and width of the three-barred cross: like the roof of a wood hut. Its outline does appear like a 'wood hut' supported upon a long centre pole.[6]

But its size was cut. What happened? Sergei Sovoroff explains (as quoted above): when the Russians 'occupied' Alaska, a boat came to the village: 'they had no place to stay so they tore the *ikax* down to make themselves a shelter. The villagers told them not to destroy the *ikax* but they didn't listen to them [...] The only thing I know is that all those Russian men who used the wood for themselves died mysteriously.' The same information is given by Veniaminov, from eyewitnesses, as follows:[7]

> In the course of time, other Russians used this cross in the construction of their *kazarma* for sleeping benches or beds and, one must state, this was done without any need. Old men, who were eyewitnesses, assert that as soon as the builders moved into their new lodgings a strange disease broke out among them. More than one half of those living in the barracks died while the Aleuts living close by remained untouched. And this was because they used the cross for the sleeping benches. Now because of this, the Aleuts there do not dare to take a chip of wood lying near the oratory.

Could Sovoroff have read Veniaminov's account and simply repeated it in a loose rendition? He states that he has 'read many Aleut books which were written by Father Veniaminov and many others,' but has never 'come across anything mentioning the *ikax* (the tree)'. Veniaminov's *Notes on the Islands of the Unalaska District* (1840) was written and published in Russian, and the reference it contains to Glotov is merely a paragraph in this two volume work.

Sergei Sovoroff does not leave us with the date only, '1765 or before'. He provides a lineage for this tradition too. Let us follow the lineage to see where it leads. He tells us that he heard the story from his grandmother when he was a 'child'. Because a child needs to be old enough to remember, therefore I shall ask to be permitted to estimate the child's age as ten to twelve-years-old, give-or-take a few years. He would have been ten to twelve-years-old in 1911 to 1913 (calculated from his birth-date in 1901, and from his age of seventy-four years in 1975 when his account was transcribed). His grandmother would have heard it from her grandfather, as Sergei Sovoroff has told us: 'My father's great-grandfather told the story to the grandchildren and it was passed on to me.' In other words, it descends from four generations prior to Sovoroff him-self, as follows: self, (i) own father, (ii) own grandmother, (iii) own great-grandparent, (vi) father's great-grandfather. Now if we allow a modest average of twenty-five years for each of these four generations, the lineage descends to a century before Sergei Sovoroff received the tradition. And if we subtract these one-hundred years from the date of his childhood, where do we arrive? — at the years 1811 to 1813 approximately. This would be the time of the generations who would, later, in the 1820s and 1830s, communicate the tradition to Veniaminov also.

What was happening at Umnak during the years 1811 to 1813, or slightly before or after? To see, we shall return to the history of Ivan Stepanovich Glotov (Ch.1, sec.ii, iii, iv). He succeeded his uncle Shushak and became the primary *toion* of Umnak. In 1792, he was awarded a gold medal by leaders of the imperial Russian Billings/Sarychev expedition. In 1796, this primary *toion* led twenty-two other men, each of whom was a leader of this region, in a protest directed to the imperial capital Petersburg against the escalation of ruthless commercial enterprises on these islands — in other words, against the ruthless types who had 'invaded Alaska', as Sovoroff has said; and who had cut the *ikax*. In 1807, he travelled to Unalaska to receive a blessing and anointing from *hieromonk* Gideon, who was here while travelling from Kodiak to Kamchatka.

Bilingual and literate, this *toion* was conducting the Orthodox services in the village chapel for the Umnak Aleuts. Here is the observation, of 23 October 1807, by *hieromonk* Gideon:[8]

> On the Island of Umnak, through the efforts of the literate toion Ivan Glotov, a chapel has been built which is dedicated to the Church Teacher Nikolai [St Nicho-las]. He himself conducts there morning and evening prayer services and the Hours on Sundays and Feastdays.

The chapel had been built at the site where the baptism had taken place and where the cross had been erected, according to Veniaminov.[9]

So, at the time of Sovoroff's father's great-grandfather, this man Ivan Stepanovich Glotov — whose baptism was commemorated by a cross at the site — was the *toion* and church reader of Umnak.

Two of the icons in the Chapel of St Nicholas at Umnak date by inscription from the 1770s. In 1826 or somewhat after that year, the chapel was re-built by Stepan Ivanovich Kriukov who had become the *toion* by then; and his descendants have retained the offices of chief (*toion*) and church reader.[10]

The village chapel was relocated to a site nearby at the turn of twentieth century, 'after a fire', Sergei Sovoroff tells us; and the *ikax* was taken to the new site. His own father dug the foundations for the relocated *ikax,* he explains; and 'a house' was built over it. In 1930, Sergei Sovoroff himself repaired or assisted in repairing the 'house over the *ikax*'. Thus we should see that he, following his father and remembering his grandmother (and thus their grandparents), took care to honour this relic. And he kept the story about it, with reserve, while most everyone else had forgotten the story of its origin.

But why would he refer to it as *ikax*, 'the tree', 'the wood'? The translation renders *ikax* unambiguously as 'tree' in the opening sentence, which reads verbatim: 'This *ikax* (tree) we are talking about is a few yards in front of the church.' We also find the word 'wood' as well as the word 'tree' used, each at various times, in the translation for *ikax*. The Aleut word *ikax* does translate as 'tree' and also as 'wood', according to the linguist R.H. Geoghegan from Veniaminov's research.[11]

There is an Aleut word for 'the cross': it is *kamagaq* in the Fox Island dialect according to Geoghehan.[12] If this *ikax*, this tree, really is the cross, wouldn't the Aleut speaker have said: '*kamagaq*', 'the cross'? Let's see. The word '*kamagaq*' is glossed as 'ecclesiastical'; so we may assume that it would be a formal term. As for the words 'tree' and 'wood', another Aleut word is given in the dictionary for both alike: *yagaq*. This term *yagaq* is glossed as the translation into Aleut for the Russian words 'tree and 'wood'.[13] *Yagaq* is glossed furthermore with derivative forms for various types of wood and trees. Unlike *yagaq*, the word *ikax* is glossed only from the Aleut and is not given any derivative forms. Thus, we find more than one word for 'tree', 'wood', in this language. Sergei Sovoroff used this one (and the Aleut translators maintained it in their publication).

This word *ikax* is the one found in Aleut translation of the Gospel according to Matthew, chapter 26, verse 4, corresponding properly to the original Greek word ξυλον, also found in the Act of the Apostles (5:30, 11-39-40, 13:29) to refer to the Cross of Christ. Equivalents are found in the Slavonic translation and English versions (KJV, RSV) of these biblical verses; for instance, in the

King James Version we can read:

> The God of our fathers raised up Jesus, whom ye slew and hanged on a tree. (Acts 5:30)
> ... whom they slew and hanged on a tree: Him God raised up the third day, and shewed him openly. (Acts 11-39-40)
> And when they had fulfilled all that was written of him, they took him down from the tree, and laid him in a sepulchre. (Acts 13:29)

This word 'tree' from these biblical verses is incorporated into hymns of the Crucifixion intoned during the Matins of Great Friday of Holy Week, such as this line from a major hymn known as the fifteenth *antiphon*:[14]

> Today is hung on the tree, He who suspended the land in the midst of the waters.

This line is repeated three times, slowly, before the hymn continues. The same word as well as the word 'cross' (σταυρον in the original Greek, as found in other verses of the Bible) are incorporated into hymns of the *Apokathelosis* during Vespers of Great Friday; for example, this *sticheron*, *apostichon*, and *apolytikion*:

> All creation was changed by fear [awe] when it saw thee O Christ hanging upon the cross; the sun was darkened, and the foundations of the earth were shaken. All things suffered with the Creator of all. O Lord, who for us didst willingly endure, glory to thee.
> O Thou who puttest on light like a robe: When Joseph, with Nicodemus, brought thee down from the tree and beheld thee dead, naked, and unburied, he mourned outwardly and grievously, crying to thee with signs and saying: Woe is me, sweet Jesus: When but a short while ago the sun beheld thee suspended on the cross, it covered itself in darkness, the earth quaked with fear ...
> The noble Joseph took down from the tree thy spotless body, and when he had enwrapped it in clean linen with aromas, he laid it for burial in a new sepulchre.

The first and last examples that have been brought forward here are more widely known, because the line in the *antiphon* (the first example) is repeated three times at a climatic point during the Matins of Great Friday of Holy Week; and the *apolytikion* (the last example), sung during the Vespers of Great Friday, is repeated as the *troparion* during Matins of Holy Saturday. Furthermore, references to the Cross as 'the Tree' and references to 'the Wood of the Cross' occur at other times through the liturgical year, for example in the hymns of the fast-day commemorating the Holy Cross, the fourteenth day of the month of September.

With this insight in mind, let us listen again to the Aleut elder's opening words: 'This *ikax* (tree) we are talking about is a few yards in front of the church.'

Once we re-read the quotations from him in this light, the 'stump of the pole' in its 'monument house' becomes quite clear. This Tree, this Wood of the Cross, commemorates the first baptism (or the first known). The remnant is enclosed and protected. Its significance shines forth.

Sergei Sovoroff, the tradition-bearer, concludes with these words about himself and his wife (she derives from Kodiak, I believe):

> Even though I am gone, they could mention my name concerning the old stories. Moreover, if someone would mention my name in their prayers I will thank you all very much. My wife's name is Agnes. She was Agnes Stepetin before I married her. This year we will celebrate our 51st anniversary on June 9th. I tried to find more about the *ikax* but so far that is all I know.

NOTES

[1] Many other examples can be found in the same and other issues of these school publications, and furthermore in student publications from more school districts. It just happens that I have at hand these issues of *Taniisi* from the Aleutian Region School District, *Alexandrovsk* from the Kenai Peninsula Borough School District, and *Uutuqtwa* from Bristol Bay High School, from which I have drawn the quotations. They serve the purpose entirely, and their dates complement the parameters that I set in my Introduction (sec.1) without extending too far forward. Also see, e.g., Layattienakoff (1987a, 1987b).

[2] Berreman (1953:149-150).

[3] Laughlin (1980:138-139). Also see photo, ibid. In the photograph, G. Marsh is seen resting his arm on the 'monument house' while enjoying a pipe, nonchalant. I have heard that he eventually became an Orthodox priest of a parish in Arizona: 'Anyone who touches the house ...,' perhaps? If he did become a priest, then the effect is rather ironic: as we saw him once causually stripping this religion as a designation from the Aleuts (Intro., sec.1, above), then would find him later enveloped in it himself.

[4] Sovoroff (1976), translated from Aleut by I. Gromoff and N. Galktionoff, City School, Unalaska. All data and quotations derive from this source unless otherwise indicated.

[5] Veniaminov (1984:233).

[6] For then-contemporary drawings of such crosses on Unalaska about 1805, and on Kodiak Island in 1790, see the illustrations in Makarova (1975). For those on Kodiak Island, also see the illustrations in Shelikhov (1981).

[7] Veniaminov (1984:233).

[8] Gideon (1989:122).

[9] Veniaminov (1984:233).

[10] Pierce (1990:269). For the dates of the inscription on the icons, see Black (1989b:162).

Who built the chapel of St Nicholas at Umnak? Gideon (cited, nt 8, above) said in 1807 that it had been built by the *toion* Ivan Stepanovich Glotov who was conducting the services diligently and who was already over sixty years old in that year. However, the construction has also been attributed to Ivan Vasil'evich Kriukov, the father of the *toion* Stepan Ivanovich Kriukov who succeeded to this position after *toion* Ivan Stepanovich Glotov (see Pierce 1990:268-269).

A remarkable man, Ivan Vasil'evich came to Russian-America as a *promyshlennik* from Siberia, married and settled in the Aleutians Islands. He was responsible for attracting Veniaminov to become the first parish priest of the Unalaska parish, as Veniaminov himself stated. Ivan Vasil'evich Kriukov visited Irkutsk from the Unalaska District and described the piety of the Aleuts so vividly that Veniaminov was inspired to request the assignment. Furthermore according to Veniaminov, Ivan Vasil'evich had forty years on the islands when he met him in Irkutsk. This Russian-Siberian Ivan Vasil'evich Kriukov who intermarried and settled would have been at oldest about the same age as, or probably younger than, the Aleut *toion* Ivan Stepanovich Glotov, certainly not older than him. Either this Russian-Siberian Ivan Vasil'evich Kriukov or the Aleut Ivan Stepan Glotov built the first chapel at the site of the cross at the old village *Recheshnoe* on Umnak Island.

We must be careful to distinguish the father Ivan Vasil'evich Kriukov from his son Stepan Ivanovich Kriukov ('Steven Krukoff'), who succeeded Ivan Stepanovich Glotov as *toion* (chief) of Umnak and whose descendants continued to hold the office of *toion*, chief, and church reader. The son, Stepan Ivanovich Kriukov ('Steven Krukoff'), rebuilt the chapel in or near the year 1826. His brother was Vasilii Vasil'evich Kriukov, the iconographer (see Ch.3, at nt.44, above).

[11] Geoghegan (1944) spells this word differently: *ygax*. I have reproduced the translators' spelling, rather than Geoghegan's entry, for conformity with my source. The variation appears minor. The initial vowel and consonant *ik-* are only slightly more gutteral that the initial dipthong and consonant *yg-*. Geoghegan's *g* is almost as far back in the throat as a k, like the g in garden (see 1944:8). So much said for the gutteral consonant, the discrepancy in the initial vowel might perhaps be explained as follows: *ikax* is Sovoroff's spoken word transliterated into the Roman alphabet, while *ygax* is Geoghegan's rendering of the written Cyrillic, from Veniaminov's dictionary and other early texts. Geoghegan's *ya* represents the last letter of the Cyrillic alphabet (pronounced ya or ia), which might perhaps have been the way this word was pronounced in the early nineteenth century, a century and a half before Sovoroff's pronunciation in 1975. Whatever the cause for the discrepancy, the two spellings in Roman script represent the same word in the Aleut language.

[12] Geoghegan (1944:136).

[13] Ibid., pp.166; 168.

[14] Cf. Ch.3, sec.2.v, above. The translations of the hymns quoted here derive from Papadeas (1977).

BIBLIOGRAPHY

Abbreviations

AA	*Arctic Anthropology.*
ANLC	Alaska Native Language Center, University of Alaska, Fairbanks.
APUA	*Anthropological Papers of the University of Alaska.*
CC	*Crossroads of Continents: Cultures of Alaska and Siberia*, ed. W.W. Fitzhugh and A. Crowell, Smithsonian Institution, Washington, DC.
CCSL	Corpus Christianorum, Series Latina, Turnholt.
CSEL	Corpus Scriptorum Ecclesiasticorum Latinorum, Vienna (and Prague).
ÉIS	*Études/Inuit/Studies*, University of Laval, Quebec.
GCS	Die Griechischen Christlichen Schriftsteller, Berlin.
GOTR	*Greek Orthodox Theological Review.*
HNAI	*Handbook of North American Indians*, general ed. W.C. Sturtevant, vol.5: *Arctic*, ed. D. Damas, Smithsonian Institution, Washington, DC.
IAHR	International Association for the History of Religion, Regional Conference on Circumpolar and Northern Religion, University of Helsinki, Department of the Study of Religion, 1990.
JAF	*Journal of American Folklore.*
JASO	*Journal of the Anthropological Society of Oxford.*
LPAH	The Limestone Press Alaska History Series, general ed. R.A. Pierce, Kingston, Ont. (and Fairbanks).
NPNF	A Select Library of Nicene and Post-Nicene Fathers of the Christian Church, general ed. P. Schaff (and H. Wace), Oxford and NYC.
OECT	Oxford Early Christian Texts, Oxford.
PG	Patrologiae Cursus Completus, Series Grecae, general ed. J.P. Migne, Paris.
PTS	Patristische Text und Studien, Berlin and NYC.
RLHT	The Rasmuson Library Historical Translation Series, general ed. M.W. Falk, University of Alaksa, Fairbanks.
SC	Sources Chrétiennes, Paris.

Works Cited

Afonsky, G., 1990, Orthodoxy in Alaska, *Russia in North America: the Proceedings of the 2nd International Conference on Russian-America*, ed. R.H. Pierce, pp.289-297, LPAH.

——, 1977, *A History of the Orthodox Church in Alaska (1794-1917)*, Kodiak.

Alekseev, A.I., 1987, *The Odyssey of a Russian Scientist: I. G. Voznesenskii in Alaska, California and Siberia, 1839-1849*, trans. W. Follette, LPAH.

Alexander, P.J., 1958, *Patriarch Nicephorus of Constantinople: Ecclesiastical Policy and Image Worship in the Byzantine Empire*, Oxford.

Alexandrovsk, 1982, no.3, Kenai Peninsula Borough School District, English Bay School, Homer, AK.

——, 1980-1981, no.2, Kenai Peninsula Borough School District, English Bay School, Homer, AK.

Al'kor, Ia.P. [Ia. P. Koshkin] and Drezen, A.K. (eds), 1935, Колониальная Политика царизма на Камчатке в XVIII веке, Institute of the Peoples of Siberia, Leningrad.

Andreev, A.I. (ed.), 1948, Русские Открытия в Тихом Океане и Северной Америке в XVIII веке, Moscow.

Apophthegmata Patrum, 1975a, *The Wisdom of the Desert Fathers: Apophthegmata Patrum (the Anonymous Series)*, trans. B. Ward, Oxford.

——, 1975b, *The Sayings of the Desert Fathers, the Alphabetical Collection*, trans. B. Ward, London.

——, 1908-1913, Apophthegmata Patrum: the Anonymous Series, ed. F. Nau, in Histoires des Solitaires Égyptiens, *Revue de l'Orient Chrétien*, 2nd series, vol.3 (xiii), no.1, pp.47-57; vol.4 (xiv), no.4, pp.357-379; vol.7 (xvii), no.2, pp.204-211; vol.8 (xviii), no.2, pp.137-146, Paris and Leipzig.

Arbman, E., 1963-1970, *Ecstasy or Religious Trance, in the Experience of Ecstatics from the Psychological Point of View*, 3 volumes, trans. D. Burton, ed. Ä. Hultkrantz, Uppsala.

Arutiunov, S.A., 1988, Koryak and Itel'men: Dwellers of the Smokey Coast, *CC*, pp.31-35.

Arzhanukhin, V.V., 1997a, Greek Patristics in Russia of the 17th -18th Centuries, Pembroke College, Oxford Symposium, 14-15 April 1997: Bishop Innokentii Veniaminov and the Patristic Background for 19th Century Missionary Work, International Bicentennial of the Birth of Innokentii Veniaminov. In *GOTR*, vol. 4, nos 1-4 (1999), pp. 565-574.

——, 1977b, Russian Theological Schools in Alaska, Centre for the Study of Christianity in the Non-Western World, University of Edinburgh, 16-17 April 1997, Christian Identities in the Arctic, International Bicentennial of the Birth of Innokentii Veniaminov.

Athanasius of Alexandria, 1973, Λόγος περὶ τῆς Ἐνανθρωπήσεως τοῦ Λόγου καὶ τῆς διὰ σώματος πρὸς ἡμᾶς ἐπιφανείας αὐτοῦ, *Athanase d'Alexandrie, sur l'Incarnation du Verbe*, ed. and trans. C. Kannengiesser, SC, vol.199.

——, 1971, Λόγος περὶ τῆς Ἐνανθρωπήσεως τοῦ Λόγου καὶ τῆς διὰ σώματος πρὸς ἡμᾶς ἐπιφανείας αὐτοῦ, *Contra Gentes and de Incarnatione*, pp.134-277, ed. and trans. R. Thomson, OECT.

——, 1857, Βίος καὶ πολιτεία τοῦ Ὁσίου Πατρὸς ἡμῶν Ἀντωνίου, PG, vol. 26: Ἀθανασίου ἀρχ. Ἀλεχανδρίας τὰ εὑρισκομένα πάντα, vol.2, cols 835-976.

Athenagoras of Athens, 1990, Ἀθηναγόρου Ἀθηναίου φιλοσόφου χριστιανοῦ Πρεσβεία περὶ Χριστιανῶν, *Athenagoras: Legatio pro Christianis*, ed. M. Marcovich, PTS, 31.

——, 1972, Ἀθηναγόρου Ἀθηναίου φιλοσόφου χριστιανοῦ Πρεσβεία περὶ Χριστιανῶν, *Athenagoras: Legatio and de Resurrectione*, pp.2-87, ed. and trans. W. Schoedel, OECT.

Augustine of Hippo, 1969, Enchiridion ad Laurentium de fide et spe et caritate, ed. E. Evans, CCSL, vol.46: *Sancti Aureli Augustini Opera (pars xii, 2)*, pp.49-114.

——, 1956, Letter to Valentine [c. Easter 426 or 427], trans. W. Parsons, *The Fathers of the Church, a new translation*, vol.32: *St Augustine, Letters*, pp.57-62, NYC.

——, 1953, *Enchiridion or Manual to Laurentius*, trans. E. Evans, London.

——, 1930, Epistula [ccxiv] ad Valentinum: Letter to Valentinus (AD 426 or 427), ed. A. Goldbacher [reprinted from Augustine (1911)], trans. J. Baxter, *St Augustine, Select Letters*, pp.405-415, Loeb Classical Library, London and NYC.

——, 1913, De peccatorum meritis et remissione, et de Baptismo Paruulorum, eds C. Urba and J. Zycha, CSEL, vol.60: *Sancti Aureli Augustini Opera (sect. viii, pars 1)*, pp.1-151.

——, 1911, Epistula ccxiv [214] ad Valentinum, ed. A. Goldbacher, CSEL, vol.57: *Sancti Aureli Augustini Operum sectio II: S. Augustini Epistulae (clxxxv-cclxx)*, pp.380-387; reprinted id., 1930.

——, 1902, De peccato originali, eds C. Urba and J. Zycha, CSEL, vol.42: *Sancti Aureli Augustini Opera (sect. viii, pars 2)*, pp.167-206.

——, 1887, On the Merits and Remissions of Sins, and on the Baptism of Infants [de peccatorum meritis ... et ... Baptismo]; On Original Sin [de peccato originali]; and Two Letters written by Augustine to Valentinus and the Monks of Adrumentum [Ep. 214 and 215], trans P. Holmes, R. Wallis and B. Warfield, NPNF, vol.5: *Saint Augustine: Anti-Pelagian Writings*, pp.15-78, 237-255, 347-440.

Aulén, G.E.H., 1931, *Christus Victor: A Historical Study of the Three Main Types of the Idea of the Atonement*, London; reprinted, London, 1950.

Balzer, M.M., 1980, Strategies of Ethnic Survival: Interactions of Russians and Khanty (Ostiak) in the 20th Century, PhD thesis (Bryn Mawr College), University Microfilms, Ann Arbor.

Bancroft, H.H., 1886, *The Works of Hubert Howe Bancroft*, vol.33: *The History of Alaska, 1730-1885*, San Francisco.

Barnes, T.D., 1971, *Tertullian: A Historical and Literary Study*, Oxford.

Barsukov, I., 1883, Иннокетій Митрополтъ Московскій и Коломеичкій, по его сочинуніямъ, письмамъ и разсказамъ современниковъ, Moscow; reprint 1997, Якутский Дом, Moscow.

Bashkina, N.N., et al. (eds), 1980a, Россия и США: Становление Отнощений, *1765-1815*, Moscow.

—— and Trask, D. (eds), [1980b], *The United States and Russia: the beginnings of relations, 1765-1815* [Россия и США:..., Moscow, 1980], Washington, DC.

Basil of Caesarea, 1968, Περὶ τοῦ Ἁγίου Πνεύματος πρὸς Ἀμφιλόχιον ἐπίσκοπον Ἰκονίου, SC, vol.17: *Basile de Césarée sur la Saint-Esprit*, 2nd edn, ed. and trans. B. Pruche.

——, 1966, Ἐπιστολαί, ed. Y. Courtonne, *Saint Basile, Lettres*, vol.3, Paris.

——, 1892, Περὶ τοῦ Ἁγίου Πνεύματος πρὸς Ἀμφιλόχιον ἐπίσκοπον Ἰκονίου, *The Book of Saint Basil the Great, Bishop of Caesarea in Cappadocia, on the Holy Spirit, written to Amphilocius, Bishop of Iconium, against the Pneumatomachi*, ed. C. Johnston, Oxford.

——, 1857a, Ἐπιστολαί [Epistola ccxxxiv], PG, vol.30: *Βασιλείου ἀρχιεπισκόπου Καισαρείας Καππαδοκίας, τὰ εὑρισκόμενα πάντα*, vol.4, cols 367E-872A.

——, 1857b, Εἰς τὸν ριε' Ψαλμόν [in Psalms cxv], PG, vol.30: *Βασιλείου ἀρχιεπισκόπου Καισαρείας Καππαδοκίας, τὰ εὑρισκόμενα πάντα*, vol.2, cols 103B-116A.

Basilov, V.N., 1989, Introduction, *Nomads of Eurasia*, ed. V.N. Basilov, trans. M. Zirin, Natural History Museum of Los Angeles County, Seattle and London.

Beaglehole, J.C. (ed.), 1967, *The Journals of Captain James Cook on his Voyages of the Discovery: the Voyage of the Resolution and Discovery, 1776-1780*, Hakluyt Society, extra series, vol.36, Cambridge.

Bebis, G.S., 1964, Σύμβολαι εἰς τὴν περὶ τοῦ Νεστορίου Ἔρευναν: ἐξ ἐπόψεως ὀρθοδόξου, Athens.

Befu, H., 1970, An Ethnographic Sketch of Old Harbor, Kodiak: an Eskimo Village, *AA*, vol.6, no.2, pp.29-42.

Bergsland, K., 1990, Introduction, *Unangam Ungiikangin kayux Tunusangin: Unangan Uniikangis ama Tunuzangis: Aleut Tales and Narratives*, pp.1-56, comp. V. Iokhel'son [W. Jochelson], eds K. Bergsland and M.L. Dirks, ANLC.

——, 1986, Comparative Eskimo-Aleut Phonology and Lexicon, *Aikakauskirja Journal: Suomalais-Ugrilaisen Seuran/ de la Société Finno-Ougrienne*, vol.80, pp.63-80 (Helsinki).

——, 1980, *Atkan Aleut - English Dictionary*, National Bilingual Materials Development Center, Rural Education, University of Alaska, Anchorage.

Berkh, V.N., 1979, *Wreck of the Neva* [Описаниie Нещастнаго [*sic* (Несчастнаго)] Кораблекрушенiя фрегата Россiйко-Американсой Компанiи Невы, St Petersburg, 1817], trans. A. Shalkop, Alaska Historical Society and Sitka Historical Society, Anchorage.

Berreman, G.D., 1964, Aleut Reference Group Alienation, Mobility, and Acculturation, *AA*, vol.66, no.2, pp.231- 250.

——, 1955, Inquiry into Community Integration in an Aleutian Village, *AA*, vol.57, no.1, pp.49-59.

——, 1953. A Contemporary Study of Nikolski: an Aleutian Village, unpublished MA thesis, University of Oregon.

Bettenson, H. (ed.), 1963, *Documents of the Christian Church*, 2nd edn, London.

Biblia Latina, 1949, *Nouum Testamentum Domini Nostri Iesu Christi Latine*, 4th part, 2nd edn, eds J. Wordsworth and H. White, Oxford.

Birket-Smith, K., 1953, *The Chugach Eskimo*, Ethnografisk Raekke 6, Nationalmuseets Skrifter, Copenhagen.

Birket-Smith, K., and Laguna, F. de, 1938, *The Eyak Indians of the Copper River Delta, Alaska*, Copenhagen.

Black, L.T., n.d. (in print), The Conquest of Kodiak, *APUA*, vol.24.

——, 1997, Veniaminov's Philosophy of Education, Oxford Symposium, 14-15 April 1997: The Greek Patristic Background for Nineteenth Century Missionary Work, International Bicentennial of the Birth of Innokentii Veniaminov.

——, 1994, Religious Syncretism as Cultural Dynamic, *Circumpolar Religion and Ecology: an Anthropology of the North*, pp.213-220, eds T. Irimoto and T. Yamada, Tokyo.

——, 1992, Russian Orthodoxy in Alaska, *Northern Religions and Shamanism*, pp.100-107, eds M. Hoppál and J. Pentikäinen, Ethnologica Uralica 3, Budapest and Helsinki.

——, 1991, *Glory Remembered: Wooden Headgear of Alaska's Sea Hunters*, Alaska State Museum, Juneau.

——, 1989a, Russia's American Adventure, *Natural History*, December, pp.46-57.

——, 1989b, Introduction, Notes and Appendices, *The Round the World Voyage of Hieromonk Gideon, 1803- 1809*, Alaska State Library Historical Monograph, and LPAH.

——, 1984a, *Atka: an Ethnohistory of the Western Aleutians*, LPAH.

——, 1984b, Introduction, Notes and Appendices, in I. Veniaminov, *Notes on the Islands of the Unalashka District*, RLHT and LPAH.

——, 1984c, Introduction, Notes and Appendices, *The Journals of Iakov Netsvetov: The Yukon Years, 1845-1863*, LPAH.

——, 1982a, *Aleut Art: Anangam Aguqaadangin*, Aleutian/Pribilof Islands Association, Anchorage.

——, 1982b, The Curious Case of the Unalaska Icons, *Alaska Journal*, Spring, pp.7-11.

——, 1981a, The Daily Journal of Rev. Father Juvenaly, *Ethnohistory*, vol.28, no.1, pp.33-58.

——, 1981b, The Nature of Evil: of Whales and Sea Otters, *Indians, Animals, and the Fur Trade*, pp.111-151, ed. S. Krech, Athens, GA.

——, 1980a, Early History, *Alaska Geographic*, vol.7, no.3: *The Aleutians*, pp.82-105, ed. L. Morgan.

——, 1980b, Introduction, Notes and Appendices, *The Journals of Iakov Netsvetov: The Atkha Years, 1828-1844*, LPAH.

——, 1978, Epilogue to Ivan Pan'kov -- an Architect of Aleut Literacy, *Orthodox Alaska*, vol.7, no.4, pp.29-33 (Kodiak).

——, 1977a, Ivan Pan'kov -- an Architect of Aleut Literacy, *AA*, vol.14, no.1, pp.94-107.

——, 1977b. The Konyag (the inhabitants of the island of Kodiak) by Ioasaf [Bolotov] (1794-1799) and by Gideon (1804- 1807), *AA*, vol.14, no.2, pp.79-103.

Bolshakoff, S., 1977, *Russian Mystics*, Cistercian Studies Series, vol.26, Kalamazoo, MI, and London.

——, 1943. *The Foreign Missions of the Russian Orthodox* Church, London and NYC.

Bourguignon, E., 1974, Cross-Cultural Perspectives on the Religious Use of Altered States of Consciousness, *Religious Movements in Contemporary America*, pp.228-243, eds I. Zaretsky and M. Leone, Princeton.

Bourguignon, E., 1973, Introduction: A Framework for the Comparative Study of Altered States of Consciousness, *Religion, Altered States of Consciousness, and Social Change*, pp.3-35, ed. E. Bourguignon, Columbus, OH.

Bria, I. (comp.), 1986, *Go Forth in Peace: Orthodox Perspectives on Mission*, World Council of Churches Mission Series, Geneva.

Bright, W. (ed.), 1880, Concilium Arausicanum Secundum, de Gratia et

Libero Arbitrio [AD 529], *Select Anti-Pelagian Treatises of St Augustine, and the Acts of the Second Council of Orange*, pp.384-392, Oxford.

Brown, P., 1967, *Augustine of Hippo: A Biography*, London.

Burtsev, A.A., 1997, The Influence of Church Translations on Subsequent Sakha (Yakut) Literature, Pembroke College, Oxford Symposium, 14-15 April 199T Bishop Innokentii Veniaminov and the Patristic Background for 19th Century Missionary Work, International Bicentennial of the Birth of Innokentii Veniaminov. In *GOTR*, vol. 4, nos 1-4 (1999), pp. 616-622.

Bryant, C., 1870, Reports, *Executive Document no.32*, 41st Congress, US Senate, 2nd Session (20 January), Washington, DC.

Buynitzky, S.N., 1871, St Paul Island, Alaska, *Executive Document* no.122, 41st Congress, US House of Representatives, 3rd Session (11 February), Washington, DC.

Calvin, J., 1962, *Opera Selecta*, vol.3: *Institutionis Christianae religionis 1559 libros I et II continens*, 2nd edn, ed. P. Barth and G. Niesel, Berlin.

——, 1961, *Concerning the Eternal Predestination of God*, trans. J. Reid, London.

——, 1870, De aeterna Dei praedestinatione, *Corpus Reformatum*, vol.36: *Ioannis Calvini: opera quae supersunt omnia*, vol.8, cols 258-366, ed. G. Baum, *et al.*, Brunswick.

——, 1845, *Institutes of the Christian Religion*, vol.1, trans. H. Beveridge, Edinburgh; reprinted, London, 1949.

——, 1552, De aeterna Dei praedestinatione, *Ioannis Caluini opuscula omnia in unum volumen collecta: quibus accessit libellius [de. aet. Dei praedes.]*, pp.879-946, ed. N. des Gallars [N. Gallasius], Geneva.

Cassian of Marseilles, J., 1894, The Conferences, trans. E. Gibson, NPNF, vol.11: ... *John Cassian*, pp.291-545.

——, 1886, Conlationes, ed. M. Petschenig, CSEL, vol.13: *Iohannis Cassianis Opera*.

Chadwick, H., 1986, *Augustine*, Oxford.

——, 1966, *Early Christian Thought and the Classical Tradition: Studies in Justin, Clement and Origen*, Oxford; reprinted Oxford, 1987.

——, 1951, Eucharist and Christology in the Nestorian Controversy, *The Journal of Theological Studies*, vol.2, no.2, pp.145-164.

Chadwick, O., 1968, *John Cassian*, 2nd edn, London, Cambridge University Press.

Chaffin, Y., Krieger, T.H. and Rostad, M., 1983, *Alaska's Konyag Country: Kodiak from Sea Otter Settlement to King Crab Capitol*, Anchorage.

Chickalusion, M., 1982, *Kustatan Bear Story: Qezdeghnen Ggagga*, ANLC.

Chitty, D.J., 1964, *The Desert a City: an Introduction to the Study of Egyptian and Palestinian Monasticism under the Christian Empire*, Oxford.

Christou, P.K., 1973, Ὁ Ἰωάννης Χρησόστομος καὶ οἱ Καππαδόκαι, *Symposium: Studies on St John Chrysostom*, pp.13-22, Ἀνάεκτα Βλατάδων, vol.18, Thessalonica.

——, 1964, Ἔκστασις, Θρησκευτικὴ καὶ Ἠθικὴ Ἐγκυκλοπαιδεία, vol.5, pp.534-539, Athens.

Chryssavgis, J., 1997, The Spiritual Legacy of Innokentii Veniaminov. Reflections on 'The Indication of the Way into the Kingdom of Heaven', Pembroke College, Oxford Symposium, 14-15 April 1997: Bishop Innokentii Veniaminov and the Patristic Background for 19th Century Missionary Work, International Bicentennial of the Birth of Innokentii Veniaminov. In *GOTR*, vol. 4, nos 1-4 (1999), pp.565-596.

——, 1989, *Ascent to Heaven: the Theology of the Human Person according to Saint John of the Ladder*, Brookline, MA.

——, 1983, The Theology of the Human Person in St John Climacus, DPhil thesis, Oxford University.

Clark, D.W., 1987, On a Misty Day You Can See Back to 1805: Ethnohistory and Historical Archaeology on the Southeastern Side of Kodiak Island, Alaska, *APUA*, vol.21, nos 1-2, pp.105-132.

——, 1984, Pacific Eskimo: Historical Ethnography, *HNAI*, pp.185-197.

Clapsis, E., 1989, The Eucharist as Missionary Event in a Suffering World, *Your Will Be Done: Orthodoxy and Mission*, pp.161-171, ed. G. Lemopoulos, Commission on World Mission and Evangelism, Consultation of Eastern Orthodox and Oriental Orthodox Churches (April 1988), Geneva and Katerini, Greece.

Clement of Alexandria, 1985, Στρωμάτες τῶν κατὰ τὴν ἀληθῆ φιλοσοφία γνωστικῶν ὑπομνημάτων, *Clemens Alexandrinus*, vol.2: *Stromata 1-VI*, ed. O. Stahlin, *et al.*, GSC, vol.52.

——, 1972, Προτρεπτικὸς πρὸς Ἕλληνας, *Clemens Alexandrinus*, vol.1: *Protrepticus und Paedagogus*, pp.3-86, 3rd edn, ed. O. Stahlin and U. Treu, GSC, vol.12.

——, 1919, *Exhortation to the Greeks*, ed. and trans. G. Butterworth, Loeb Classical Library, London; reprinted London, 1979.

Clerq, Caroli de (ed). 1963. Concilium Arausicanum, 529 (Secundum), *Corpus Christianorum, Series Latina*, vol.148A: *Concilia Galliae, A. 511 - A. 695*, pp.53-76, Turnholt.

Cook, James, 1784, *Voyage to the Pacific ... 1776 [to] 1780*, vol.2, London.

Cramer, J.A. (ed.), 1844, *Catenae Graecorum Patrum in Novum Testamentum*, vol.3: *Acta Ss. Apostolorum*, Oxford.

Cross, F.L. and Livingstone, E.A., 1983, *Oxford Dictionary of the Christian Church,* 2nd edn, Oxford.

Crowell, A., 1988, Prehistory of Alaska's Pacific Coast, *CC,* pp.130- 141.

Cyril of Alexandria, 1983, Ἐπιστολαὶ πρὸς Νεστόριον, *Cyril of Alexandria: Select Letters,* pp.2-33, ed. and trans. L. Wickham, OECT.

Cyril of Jerusalem, 1894, The Catechetical Lectures, trans. E. Gifford, NPNF, 2nd series, vol.7: *S. Cyril of Jerusalem.*

——, 1860, Κατηχήσεις: Catechesis, *Τοῦ ἐν ἁγίοις Πατρὸς ἡμῶν Κυρίλλου ἀρχ. Ἱεροσολύμων,* vol.2, ed. J. Rupp, Munich.

Czaplicka, M.A., ms. (n.d.), Notes, unpublished, in PS-III-B-1, Asiatic Russia, Tylor Library, Institute of Social and Cultural Anthropology, Oxford University.

——, n.d., *My Siberian Year [1914-1915],* London.

——, 1917, On the Track of the Tungus, *The Scottish Geographical Magazine,* vol.33 (July), pp.289-303.

——, 1914, *Aboriginal Siberia: a Study in Social Anthropology,* Oxford.

Dal, V., 1882, Толковый Словарь Живого Великорусского Языка, vol.3, St Petersburg and Moscow; reprinted Moscow, 1980.

Dall, W.H., 1884, On Masks, Labrets, and Certain Aboriginal Customs, *Third Annual Report of the Bureau of Ethnology, 1881-1882,* pp.73-202, Smithsonian Institution, Washington, DC.

——, 1870, *Alaska and Its Resources,* London.

Daniélou, J., 1973, *A History of Early Christian Doctrine before the Council of Nicaea,* vol.2: *The Gospel Message and Hellenistic Culture,* ed. and trans. J. Baker, London and Philadelphia.

Dauenhauer, N.M., and Dauenhauer, R., 1992, Spiritual Aspects of Tlingit Oratory, [IAHR,] *Northern Religions and Shamanism,* pp.90-99, eds M. Hoppál and J. Pentikäinen, Budapest and Helsinki.

——, 1988, Treatment of Shaman Spirits in Contemporary Tlingit Oratory, *Shamanism: Past and Present,* vol.2, pp.317-330, eds M. Hoppál and O. von Sadovszky, Budapest and Los Angeles.

——, 1990, *Classics of Tlingit Oral Literature,* vol.2: *Haa Tuwunaagu Yis, for Healing Our Spirit: Tlingit Oratory,* Seattle and London.

——, 1987, *Classics of Tlingit Oral Literature,* vol.1: *Haa Shuka, Our Ancestors: Tlingit Oral Narratives,* Seattle and London.

Dauenhauer, R., 1980, Conflicting Visions in Alaskan Education, unpublished paper presented at the Alaska Pacific University, Anchorage, Alaska.

Davis, N.Y., 1984, Contemporary Pacific Eskimo, *HNAI,* pp.198-204.

——, 1971, The Effects of the 1964 Earthquake, Tsunami, and Resettlement on Two Koniag Eskimo Villages, PhD thesis (University of Washington), University Microfilms, Ann Arbor.

———, 1970, The Role of the Russian Orthodox Church in Five Pacific Eskimo Villages as Revealed by the Earthquake, *The Great Alaska Earthquake: Human Ecology*, pp.125- 146, US National Research Council, Division of Earth Sciences, Committee on the Alaska Earthquake, Washington, DC.

Davydov, G.I., 1977, *Two Voyages to Russian-America, 1802-1807* [Двукратное Путешест- вie в Америку, vols 1-2, St Petersburg, 1810-1812], trans. C. Bearne, LPAH.

Deicha, S., 1997, Patristics in Russia, the 19th Century, Pembroke College, Oxford Symposium, 14-15 April 1997: Bishop Innokentii Veniaminov and the Patristic Background for 19th Century Missionary Work, International Bicentennial of the Birth of Innokentii Veniaminov. In *GOTR*, vol. 4, nos 1-4 (1999), pp. 575-584.

Desson, D., 1988, Alphonse Louis Pinart: Ethnographic Notes on Masks, unpublished paper presented at the 15th Annual Meeting of the Alaska Anthropology Association (25-27 March), and the 1st Kodiak Island Culture Heritage Conference (28-30 March).

Diadochus of Photice, 1979, On Spiritual Knowledge and Discrimination: One Hundred Texts, *Philokalia*, vol.1: *The Complete Text compiled by St Nikodemos of the Holy Mountain and St Makarios of Corinth*, pp.263-265, trans G. Palmer, P. Sherrard, and K. Ware, London and Boston.

———, 1955, Διαδόχου ἐπισκόπου Φωτικῆς τῆς Ἠπείρου κεφάλαια γνωστικὰ ρ': de Diadoque Évêque de Photicé en Épire, cent chapitres, *Diadoque de Photicé, Oeuvres Spirituelles*, ed. and trans. É. des Places, SC, 5 bis.

———, 1782, Λόγος ἀσκητικὸς: Διῃρημένος εἰς ρ' κεφάλαια πρακτικὰ γνώδεως καὶ διαρίσεως, *Φιλοκαλία τῶν ἱερῶν Νηπτικῶν*, vol.1, pp.241-243, comps Nicodemus of the Holy Mountain and Macarius of Corinth, Venice; reprinted Athens, 1957.

Didymus of Alexandria, 1863, Fragmenta ex Didymi Expositione in Actus Apostolorum, ed. J. C. Wolf, PG, vol.39: Διδύμου τοῦ Ἀλεξανδρίας τὰ σωζόμενα παντά, cols 1653D-1678C.

Diószegi, V. and Hoppál, M. (eds), 1978, *Shamanism in Siberia*, Bibliotheca Uralica, vol.1, Budapest.

Dirks, M., 1988, Foreword (Atka, AK, September 1987), in E.R. Oliver, *Journal of an Aleutian Year*, Seattle and London.

Dmytryshyn, B., Crownhart-Vaughan, E.A.P. and Vaughan, T. (eds and trans), 1985-89, *To Siberia and Russian America: Three Centuries of Russian Eastward Expansion*, 3 volumes, Oregon Historical Society, Portland.

Dobkin, M.H., 1988, *Smyrna 1922: the Destruction of a City*, Kent, OH, and London.

Dodds, E.R., 1965, *Pagans and Christians in an Age of Anxiety: some Aspects of Religious Experience from Marcus Aurelius to Constantine*, Cambridge; reprinted, NYC, 1970.

Dostoyevsky, F., 1982, *The Brothers Karamazov*, trans. D. Magarshack, London.

——, 1971, *The Devils* [*The Possessed*], trans. D. Magarshack, London.

Dragas, G.D., 1991, St Athanasius on Christ's Sacrifice, *Sacrifice and Redemption: Durham Essays in Theology*, pp.73-100, ed. S. Syke, Cambridge.

——, 1988, Πατερικὲς Προοπτικὲς περὶ τῆς Δημιουργίας, Patriarchate of Jerusalem.

——, 1985, *St Athanasius contra Apollinarem* [*Church and Theology*, vol.6], Athens.

Dumond, D.E., 1977, *The Eskimos and Aleuts*, revised edn, London.

During, I. (ed.), 1961, *Aristotle's Protrepticus: An Attempt at Reconstruction*, Stockholm.

Edmonds, H.M.W., 1966, The Eskimo of St Michael and vicinity as related by H.M.W. Edmonds, ed. D.J. Ray, *APUA*, vol.13, no.2, pp.1-143.

Eliade, M., 1988, Survivals and Camouflages of Myth, *Symoblism, the Sacred, and the Arts*, pp.32-52, ed. D. Apostolos-Cappadona, NYC; reprinted from *Myth and Reality*, pp.161-193, NYC, 1963.

——, 1987, Shamanism: an Overview, *Encyclopeda of Religion*, vol.13, pp.202-208, ed. M. Eliade, NYC.

—— (ed.), 1987, *Encyclopedia of Religion*, NYC.

——, 1982, *Ordeal by Labyrinth: Conversations with Claude-Henri Roquet*, trans. D. Coltman, Chicago.

——, 1964, *Shamanism: Archaic Techniques of Ecstasy*, trans. W. Trask, Princeton.

——, 1959, *The Sacred and the Profane: The Nature of Religion*, trans. W. Trask, San Diego, NYC, London.

Elliot, H.W., 1881, *The History and Present Condition of the Fishery Industries: The Seal Islands*, US Department of the Interior, 10th Census (1880), Washington, DC; reprinted, LPAH, 1976.

Epiphanius of Constantia (Salamis), 1980, Κατὰ αἱρέσεων τό ἐπικληθὲν Πανάριον εἴτουν Κιβώτιον, [Adversus haereses], *Epiphanius*, vol.2: *Panarion haer. 34-64*, ed. K. Holl; revised edn J. Dummer, GCS, 31.

Ertiukova, N.S., 1997, [representing the Iakutsk State Museum], The History of Christianity in the Collections of the Yakutsk State Museum of the History and Culture of the Peoples of the North, Pembroke College, Oxford Symposium, 14-15 April 1997: Bishop Innokentii Veniaminov and the Patristic Background for 19th Century Missionary Work, International Bicentennial of the Birth of Innokentii Veniaminov. In *GOTR*, vol. 4, nos 1-4 (1999), pp.633-638.

Evans-Pritchard, E.E., 1981, *A History of Anthropological Thought*, ed. A. Singer, London.

——, 1965, *Theories of Primitive Religion*, Oxford.

——, 1963, *The Comparative Method in Social Anthropology*, the L.T. Hobhouse Trust Lecture delivered at the University of London, School of Economics and Political Sciences, London.

——, 1956, *Nuer Religion*, Oxford; reprinted Oxford, 1977.

Fassett. H.C., 1890, Sea Otter Hunting: How the Aleuts Conduct the Chase, *San Francisco Chronicle*, 28 December; reprinted in R.F. Heizer, The Aleut Sea Otter Hunt in the Late Nineteenth Century, *APUA*, vol.8, no.2 (May 1960), pp.131-135.

Fedorova, S.G., 1973, *Russian Population in Alaska and California, late 18th century - 1867* [Русское Население..., Moscow, 1971], trans. R.A. Pierce and A.S. Donnelly, LPAH.

——, 1971, Русское Населени, Аляски и Калифорнии, конец XVIII века - 1867 г., Moscow.

Fienup-Riordan, A., 1994, *Boundaries and Passages: Rule and Ritual in Central Yup'ik Oral Tradition*, Oklahoma.

——, 1990a, *Eskimo Essays: Yup'ik Lives and How We See Them*, New Brunswick and London.

——, 1990b, The Bird and the Bladder: the Cosmology of Central Yup'ik Seal Hunting, *ÉIS*, vol.14, nos 1-2, pp.23-38.

——, 1988, Eye of the Dance: Spiritual Life of the Bering Sea Eskimo, *CC*, pp.256-270.

——, 1986, Nick Charles, Sr., in Ann Fienup-Riordan *et al.*, *Artists behind the Work: Life Histories of Nick Charles, Sr., Frances Demientieff, Lena Sours, Jennie Thlunaut*, pp.25-57, University of Alaska Museum, Fairbanks.

——, 1983, *The Nelson Island Eskimo: Social Structure and Ritual Distribution*, Anchorage.

Fischer, B., 1977, *Novae Concordontiae Bibliorum Sacrorum iuxta vulgatum versionem critice editam*, vol.4, Tübingen.

Fisher, R.H., 1943, *The Russian Fur Trade, 1500-1700*, Berkeley and Los Angeles.

Fitzhugh, W.W. and Crowell, A. (eds), 1988, *Crossroads of Continents: Cultures of Alaska and Siberia*, Smithsonian Institution, Washington, DC.

Fitzhugh, W.W. and Kaplan, S.A. (eds), 1982, *Inua: Spirit World of the Bering Sea Eskimo*, US Museum of Natural History, Washington, DC.

Florovsky, G., 1979, *Collected Works of George Florovsky*, vol.5: *Ways of Russian Theology*, part 1, trans. R. Nichols, Belmont, MA.

Fortesque, M., ms., Comparative Eskimo Dictionary, University of Copenhagen.

Frost, O.W. (ed.), 1988, *Journal of a Voyage with Bering, 1841-1742, by Georg Wilheim Steller,* trans. M. Engel and O. W. Frost, Stanford.

Garrett, P., 1979, *St Innocent, Apostle to America,* Crestwood, NY.

Geerard, M., 1974-1987, *Clauis Patrum Graecorum,* 5 volumes, Turnhout.

Geoghegan, R.H. (ed. and trans.), 1944, *The Aleut Langauge: the Elements of Aleut Grammar with a Dictionary in two parts containing Basic Vocabularies of Aleut and English,* ed. F. I. Martin, US Department of the Interior, Washington, DC; reprinted Seattle, 1973.

Germanus of Constantinople, 1984, Ἱστορία ἐκκλησιαστικὴ καὶ μυστικὴ θεωρία, ed. N. Borgia, *Il commentario liturgico di S. Germano patriarca Constantinopolitano e versiona latina di Anastasio Bibliotecario,* Studi Liturgici, vol.1, Grottaferrata, 1912; reprinted in P. Meyendorff, *St Germanus of Constantinople: On the Divine Liturgy,* Crestwood, NY.

Giakalis, Ambrosis, 1994, *Images of the Divine: the Theology of Icons at the Seventh Ecumenical Council,* Leiden.

Gibson, J.R., 1969, *Feeding the Russian Fur Trade: Provisionment of the Okhotsk Seaboard and the Kamchatka Peninsula, 1639-1856,* Madison.

Gideon, 1989, *The Round the World Voyage of Hieromonk Gideon, 1803-1809,* trans. L. T. Black, Alaska State Library Historical Monograph, and LPAH.

Gilbert, G., 1982, *The Journal of Midshipman George Gilbert,* ed. C. Holmes, Honolulu.

Glazik, J., 1954, *Die Russisch-Orthodoxe Heidenmission seit Peter dem Grossen,* Munich.

Golder, F.A., 1968, *Father Herman, Alaska's Saint,* San Francisco.

——, 1925, Preface, in Sergei Fedorovich Platonov, *History of Russia,* pp.v-vii, London.

——, 1917, *Guide to Materials for American History in Russian Archives,* Carnegie Institution Publications, no.239, Washington, DC.

——, 1914, *Russian Expansion on the Pacific: an Account of the ... Expeditions made by the Russians along the Pacific Coast of Asia and North America, 1641-1850,* Cleveland, OH.

——, 1909, Eskimo and Aleut Stories from Alaska, *JAF,* vol.22, no.83, pp.10-24.

——, 1907a, A Kadiak [*sic*] Island Story: the White-Faced Bear, *JAF,* vol.20, no.79, pp.296-299.

——, 1907b, Tlingit Myths, *JAF,* vol.20, no.79, pp.290-296.

——, 1907c, The Songs and Stories of the Aleuts with Translations from Veniaminov, *JAF,* vol.20, no.77, pp.132-142.

——, 1905, Aleutian Stories, *JAF* vol.18, no.70, pp.215-222.

——, 1903a, Tales from Kodiak Island, II, *JAF*, vol.16, no.61, pp.85-103.

——, 1903b, Tales from Kodiak Island, *JAF*, vol.16, no.60, pp.16-31.

Gorokhov, S.N., 1997, Veniaminov's Pastoral Ministry among the Nomadic Ethnic Minorities of Northeast Asia, Pembroke College, Oxford Symposium, 14-15 April 1997: Bishop Innokentii Veniaminov and the Patristic Background for 19th Century Missionary Work, International Bicentennial of the Birth of Innokentii Veniaminov. In *GOTR*, vol. 4, nos 1-4 (1999), pp.643-648.

——, 1992-1993, The Small Peoples [Minorities] of the North: the Challenge Today, Text in temporary exhibit: Before Columbus: into American from Northeastern Asia, Balfour Building, Pitt Rivers Museum, Oxford University.

Graves, K., 1981, Russian New Year in Port Graham, *Tundra Times* (7 January), pp.5, 10.

Gregory Palamas of Thessalonica, 1959, Λόγος ὑπὲρ τῶν ἱερῶν Ἡσυχαζόντων, *Defense des saints hesychastes*, ed. J. Meyendorff, Louvain.

Gulaieva, E.P., 1997 [representing the Sakha Republic National Library), Publishing Activities of the Russian Orthodox Mission in Yakutia (1812-1916), Pembroke College, Oxford Symposium, 14-15 April 1997. Bishop Innokentii Veniaminov and the Patristic Background for 19th Century Missionary Work, International Bicentennial of the Birth of Innokentii Veniaminov. In *GOTR*, vol. 4, nos 1-4 (1999), pp.607-616.

Hahm, Pyong-choon, 1988, Shamanism and the Korean World-View, Family Life-Cycle, Society and Social Life, *Shamanism: the Spirit World of Korea*, pp.60-97, eds C. Yu and R. Guisso, Berkeley.

Hale, C.R., 1877, Innocent of Moscow, the Apostle of Kamchatka and Alaska, *American Church Review*, vol.29, pp.402-419, ed. E. Boggs, NYC and London.

Hammerich, L.L., 1954, The Russian Stratum in Alaskan Eskimo, *Slavic Word*, vol.3 [*Word*, The Linguistic Circle of New York, vol.10, no.4], pp.401-428.

Hatch, E. and H.A. Redpath, 1906, *A Concordance to the Septuagint .... Supplement*, Oxford.

——, 1897, *A Concordance to the Septuagint and other Greek versions of the Old Testament (including Apocryphal Books)*, part 1, Oxford.

Hawkes, E.W., 1914, The Dance Festivals of the Alaskan Eskimo, *University of Pennsylvania Museum Anthropological Publications*, vol.6, no.2, pp.3-45.

——, 1913, *The Inviting-in Feast of the Alaskan Eskimo*, Geological Survey Memoir, no.45, Canada Department of Mines, Ottawa.

Historia [Ἱστορία] (anon.), 1961, Ἡ κατ᾽ Αἴγυπτον τῶν μοναχῶν Ἱστορία [*Historia Monachorum in Aegypto*], ed. A. Festugière, Société des Bollandistes,

Subsidia Hagiographica 34, Brussels.

Holmberg, H.J., 1985, *Holmberg's Ethnographic Sketches*, RLHT.

———, 1856, Ethnographische Skizzen über die Völker des Russischen Amerika, *Acta Societatis Scientiarum Fennicae*, vol.4, pp.410-417, Helsinki.

———, 1855, *Ethnographische Skizzen über die Völker des Russischen Amerika*, Helsinki.

Holy Ruling Synod [of the Russian Church] Documents, mss, in Russian Reproductions, US Library of Congress Manuscript Division, Washington, DC.

Hoppál, M., 1993, Studies on Eurasian Shamanism, *Shamans and Cultures: Selected Papers of the First Conference of the International Society for Shamanistic Research*, pp.258-288, ed. M. Hoppál and K. Howard, Budapest and Los Angeles.

Hosley, E.H., 1966, Factionalism and Acculturation in an Alaskan Athapaskan Community, PhD thesis (University of California at Los Angeles), University Microfilms, Ann Arbor.

———, 1961. The McGrath Ingalik, *APUA*, vol.9, no.2, pp.93-113.

Huggins, E.L., 1981, *Kodiak and Afognak Life, 1868-1870*, LPAH.

Hutchinson, I., 1942, *The Aleutian Islands: America's Back Door*, 2nd edn, London.

Hultkrantz, Ä., 1990, Arctic or Circumpolar Religions, paper presented at IAHR.

———, 1978, Ecological and Phenomenological Aspects of Shamanism, *Shamanism in Siberia*, pp.27-58, ed. V. Diózegi and M. Hoppál, Bibliotheca Uralica, vol.1, Budapest.

———, 1973, A Definition of Shamanism, *Temenos: Studies in Comparative Religion* (Finnish Society for the Study of Comparative Religions, Helsinki), vol.9, pp.25-37.

Huntington, S.P., 1997, *The Clash of Civilizations and the Remaking of World Order*, London, New York.

Iakutsk Church Brotherhood, 1897, Якутское Церковное Братство во имя Христа Спасителя вь 1895/96 г., Iakutsk.

Inge, W.R., 1918, *The Philosophy of Plotinus*, the Gifford Lectures of 1917-1918, 2 volumes, London.

———, 1912. Ecstasy, *Encyclopedia of Religion and Ethics*, vol.5, pp.157-159, ed. J. Hastings, Edinburgh.

———, 1905, *Studies of English Mystics*, the St Margaret's Lectures of 1905, London.

———, 1899, *Christian Mysticism, considered in eight lectures delivered before the University of Oxford*, the Bampton Lectures of 1899, London.

Inouye, R.K., 1990, Starring and Slava: a Legacy of Russian America, *Russia in North America: Proceedings of the 2nd International Conference on Russian America*, pp.358-378, LPAH.

Iokhel'son, V. [W. Jochelson], 1933, *History, Ethnography and Anthropology of the Aleut* (expanded from the reports of the Kamchatka-Aleutian Expedition of the Imperial Russian Geographical Society, 1909-1910), Carnegie Institution Publications, no.432, Washington, DC.

Irimoto, T. and T. Yamada, eds, 1994, *Circumpolar Religion and Ecology: an Anthropology of the North*, Tokyo.

Ivashintsov, N.A., 1980, *Russian Round-the-World Voyages, 1803-1849*, trans. G. R. Barratt, LPAH.

Jacobson, S.A., 1984, *Yup'ik Eskimo Dictionary*, ANLC.

Jaeger, W., 1947, *The Theology of the Early Greek Philosophers*, Oxford.

James, W., 1988a, Introduction, *Vernacular Christianity: Essays in the Social Anthropology of Religion, presented to Godfrey Lienhardt*, ed. W. James and D. Johnson, JASO Occasional Papers, no.7.

——, 1988b, *The Listening Ebony: Moral Knowledge, Religion, and Power among the Udak of Sudan*, Oxford.

John Chrysostom, 1970, Περὶ ἀκαταλήπτου πρὸς Ἀνομοίους λόγοι α'-ε', SC, vol.28: *Jean Chrysostom. Sur l'incompréhensibilité de Dieu*, vol.1: *Homélies I-V*, ed. A. Malingrey.

——, 1862, Ὁμιλία β' εἰς Ἰωάννην, PG, vol.59, Ἰωάννου τοῦ Χρυσοστόμου, τά εὑρισκόμενα πάντα, vol. 7: Ὑπόμνημα εἰς τὸν Ἰωάννην τὸν Ἀπόστολον καὶ Εὐαγγελιστήν, cols 29-38.

——, 1860, Ὁμιλία χβ' εἰς Ματθαῖον, PG, vol.57-58: Ἰωάννου τοῦ Χρυσοστόμου, τά εὑρισκόμενα πάντα, vol.7: Ὑπόμνημα εἰς τὸν Ἅγιον Ματθαῖον τὸν Εὐαγγελιστήν, cols 595-604, ed. F. Fields.

——, 1847, Ὑπόθεσις τῆν πρὸς Κορινθίους Πρώτης Ἐπιστολῆς, ed. F. Fields, *Joannis Chrysostomi, Interpretatio omnium epistolarum Paulinarum*, vol.2, Oxford.

John of Damascus, 1975, Λόγοι ἀπολογιτικοὶ πρὸς τοὺς διαβάλλοντες τὰς ἁγίας εἰκόνας, PTS, 17: *Die Schriften des Johannes von Damaskos*, ed. P. Kotter.

——, 1973, Ἔκδοσις ἀκριβῆς τῆς ὀρθοδόξου πίστεως, PTS, 12: *Die Schriften des Johannes von Damaskos*, ed. P. Kotter.

Johnson, J.F.C. (ed.), 1984, *Chugach Legends: Stories and Photographs of the Chugach Region*, Chugach Alaska Corporation, Anchorage.

Jonas, H., 1963, *The Gnostic Religion: the Message of the Alien God and the Beginnings of Christianity*, 2nd edn, Boston.

Jones, D.M., 1980, *A Century of Servitude: Pribilof Aleuts under U.S. Rule*, Washington, DC.

——, 1976, *Aleuts in Transition: a Comparison of Two Villages*, University of Alaska Institute of Social, Economic, and Government Research, Seattle and London.

——, 1969. A Study of Social and Economic Problems in Unalaska, an Aleut Village, PhD thesis (University of California at Berkeley), University Microfilms, Ann Arbor.

Justin the Martyr, 1987, Ἀπολογία ὑπὲρ Χριστιανῶν πρὸς Ἀντωνίνον· Ἀπολογία ὑπὲρ Χριστιανῶν πρὸς τὴν Ῥωμαίων Σύγκλητον: Apologie en faveur des chrétiens adressée à Antonin; Apologie en faveur des chrétiens adressée au Sénat de Rome, *Saint Justin, Apologies*, pp.98-195, ed. and trans. A. Wartelle, Paris.

——, 1915, Ἀπολογία ὑπὲρ Χριστιανῶν πρὸς Ἀντωνίνον τὸν Εὐσεβῆ· Ἀπολογία ὑπὲρ Χριστιανῶν πρὸς τὴν Ῥωμαίων Σύγκλητον· Διάλογος πρὸς Τρύφωνα Ἰουδαῖον, *Die ältesten Apologeten: Texte mit kurzen Einleitungen*, pp.26-265, ed. E. Goodspeed, Göttingen; reprinted, New York, 1950.

Kamenskii, A., 1985, *Tlingit Indians of Alaska*, trans. S. Kan, RLHT.

Kan, S., 1990, Recording Native Cultures and Christianizing the Natives — Russian Orthodox Missionaries in Southeastern Alaska, *Russia in North America: the Proceedings of the 2nd International Conference on Russian-America*, pp.298-313, LPAH.

——, 1989, *Symbolic Immortality: Tlingit Potlatch of the Nineteenth Century*, Washington, DC.

——, 1987, Memory Eternal: Orthodox Christianity and the Tlingit Mortuary Complex, *AA*, vol.24, no.1, pp.32-55.

——, 1983, Words that Heal the Soul: Analysis of the Tlingit Potlatch Oratory, *AA*, vol.20, no.2, pp.47-59.

KANA [Kodiak Area Native Association], 1987, Oral history project for the Old Harbor Tribal Council, supplemental to 104(a) grant no.E01G14207009 from the Bureau of Indian Affairs (cover letter to BIA's Juneau Area office, dated 29 September).

Kashevarov, A.P., 1987, John Veniaminov, Innocent, Metropolitan of Moscow and Kolomna, *Alaska Magazine*, vol.1 (1927); reprinted in M.J. Oleksa (ed.), *Alaskan Missionary Spirituality*, pp.341-362, NYC.

Kilbuck, J., and Kilbuck, E., 1988, *The Yup'ik Eskimos*, ed. A. Fienup-Riordan, LPAH.

Kim, Tae-gon, 1988, Regional Characteristics of Korean Shamanism, *Shamanism: the Spirit World of Korea*, pp.119-130, eds C. Yu and R. Guisso, Berkeley.

—— and Kim, Kwang-iei, 1993, Deities and Altered States of Consciousness of Korean Shamans, *Shamans and Cultures: Selected Papers of the First Conference of the International Society for Shamanistic Research*, pp.47-51, ed. M. Hoppál and K. Howard, Budapest and Los Angeles.

King, J., 1784, *A Voyage to the Pacific Ocean performed under the direction of Captains Cook ..., 1776 [to] 1780*, vol.3, London.

Kobtzeff, O., 1984, La Colonisation Russe en Amérique du Nord, 18-19 siecles, unpublished PhD thesis, University of Paris 1 (Sorbonne).

Kodiak (anon.), 1985, *The Arctic Willow: A History of an Alaskan Seminary, St. Herman's Theological School*, Kodiak.

Kontoglou, P. [F.], 1963, ʿΗ Βυζαντινὴ Ζωγραφικὴ καὶ ἡ ἀληθινὴ ἀξία τῆς, ʿΗ Πονεμένη Ρωμιοσύνη, pp.96-119, Athens.

Koranda, L.D., 1968, Three Songs for the Bladder Festival, Hooper Bay, *APUA*, vol.14, no.1, pp.27-31.

Korsakovskii, P., and Vasilev, I.Ia., 1988, *Russian Exploration in Southwest Alaska: the Travel Journals of Petr Korsakovskiy (1818) and Ivan Ya. Vasilev (1829)*, trans. D. Kraus, RLHT.

Kotzebue, O., 1821, *A Voyage of Discovery into the South Sea and the Beering's [sic] Straits ... 1815-1818*, 3 volumes, London.

Kovach, M.G., 1957, The Russian Orthodox Church in Russian-America, unpublished PhD thesis, University of Pittsburg.

Krasheninnikov, S.P., 1764, *The History of Kamtschatka and the Kurilski Islands* [Описание... Камчатки..., St Petersburg, 1754], trans. J. Grieve, Glocester [sic]; reprinted, Chicago, 1962; Surrey, 1973.

Krause, A, 1956, *The Tlingit Indians*, trans. E. Gunther, Seattle.

Krause, M.E., 1988, Many Tongues — Ancient Tales, *Crossroads of Continents: Cultures of Siberia and Alaska*, pp.145-150, eds W.W. Fitzhugh and A. Crowell, Smithsonian Institution, Washington, DC.

——, 1980, *Alaska Native Languages: Past, Present, and Future*, ANLC Research Papers 4.

——, 1973, Eskimo-Aleut, *Current Trends in Linguistics*, vol.10: *Linguistics in North America*, pp.796-902, ed. T.A. Sebeok, the Hague and Paris.

Krech, S., 1989, *The Travels and Collections of the fifth Earl of Lonsdale 1888-9*, London.

Lada-Mocarski, V., 1969, *Bibliography of Books on Alaska published before 1868*, New Haven and London.

Laguna, F. de, 1988, Potlatch Ceremonialism on the Northwest Coast, *CC*, pp.271-280.

——, 1972, *Under Mount Saint Elias: The History and Culture of the Yakutat Tlingit*, Smithsonian Institution, Washington, DC.

——, 1956, Chugach Prehistory: the Archaeology of Prince William Sound,

Alaska, *University of Washington Publications in Anthropology*, vol.13.

Langsdorff, G.H., 1814, *Voyages and Travels to Various Parts of the World during the years 1803, 1804, 1805, 1806, and 1807*, part 2: *The Voyage to the Aleutian Islands and the Northwest Coast of America, and return by land over the Northeast parts of Asia, through Siberia*, London.

——, 1812, *Bemerkungen auf einer Reise um die Welt in den Jahren 1803 bis 1807*, vol.2. Frankfurt.

Lantis, M., 1990, The Selection of Symbolic Meaning, *ÉIS*, vol.14, nos 1-2, pp.169-190.

——, 1984, Aleut, *HNAI*, pp.161-184.

——, 1966, *Alaskan Eskimo Ceremonialism*, American Ethnographical Society Monograph 11, Seattle.

——, 1950, The Religion of the Eskimos, in V. Ferm (ed.), *Forgotten Religions*, pp.311-339, New York.

——, 1946, Social Culture of the Nunivak Eskimo, *Transactions of the American Philosophical Society*, new series, vol.35, no.3, pp.153-323.

——, 1938, The Mythology of Kodiak Island, Alaska, *JAF*, vol.51, no.200, pp.123-172.

Lantzeff, G.V., and Pierce, R.A., 1973, *Eastward to Empire: Exploration and Conquest on the Russian Open Frontier to 1750*, Montreal.

Laughlin, W.S., 1980, *Aleuts: Survivors of the Bering Land Bridge*, NYC.

Lavrischeff, T.I., 1928, Two Aleut Tales, *AA*, new series, vol.30, pp.121-124.

Lawson, J., 1948, *The Biblical Theology of Saint Irenaeus*, London.

Layattienakoff [Goforth], A., 1987a, Ounalashka and Akutan, *Theata*, vol.12, pp.39-44 (Department of Cross Cultural Communications, University of Alaska, Fairbanks).

——, 1987b, Spraznekum, *Theata*, vol.12, pp.296-300.

Ledyard, J., 1963, *John Ledyard's Journal of Captain Cook's Last Voyage*, ed. J. Munford, Corvallis, OR.

Leer, J., ms., Alutiiq Dictionary, ANLC.

Lemaître, J. [I. Hausherr], 1953, Mystique Extatique: Contemplation chez les Grecs et autres Orientaux Chétiens, in M. Viller *et al.* (eds), *Dictionnarie de Spiritualité*, vol.2, cols 1862-1872, Paris.

Lessa, W.A. and Vogt, E.Z., 1979, The Purposes of Shamanism: Introduction, *A Reader in Comparative Religion: an Anthropological Approach*, 4th edn, NYC.

Levin, M.G., and Potapov, L.P., 1964, *The Peoples of Siberia*, trans. Scripta Technica, ed. S. Dunn, Chicago.

Lévy-Bruhl, L., 1985, *How Natives Think* [*Les Fonctions dans les Sociétes Inférieures*, Paris, 1918], trans. L. Clare, 3rd edn reprinted, Princeton.

——, 1975, *The Notebooks on Primitive Mentality*, trans. P. Riviere, Oxford.

——, 1949, *Les Carnets de Lévy-Bruhl*, ed. Bibliothèque de Philosophie Contemporaine, Paris.

——, 1918, *Les Fonctions dans les Sociétes Inférieures*, 3rd edn, Paris.

Lewis, I.M., 1971, *Ecstatic Religion: an Anthropological Study of Spirit Possession and Shamanism*, London.

Liapunova, R.G., 1987, Relations with Natives of Russian America, *Russia's American Colony*, ed. S. Starr, Durham, NC.

Liddel, H.G., and Scott, R. (comps), 1940, *A Greek-English Lexicon*, ed. H. Jones, Oxford.

Lienhardt, G., 1964, *Social Anthropology*, London, NYC and Toronto.

——, 1961, *Divinity and Experience: the Religion of the Dinka*, Oxford.

Litke, F. [Lutke, F.], 1987, *A Voyage Around the World, 1826-1829*, vol.1: *To Russian America and Siberia*, trans. R. Marshall and J. Moessner, LPAH.

——, 1835, *Voyage autour du Monde, execute par ordre de sa Majeste l'Empereur Nicolas Ier ... dans les annees 1826 [-] 1829 ...*, vol.1, Paris.

Lopez de Haro, G., ms., Diario de Navigación que con el auxilio Divino, y protección de nuestra Señora del Carmen, espera hacer, el primer Piloto de la Real Armada, y Capitán del Paquebot, de S. M. nombrado San Carlos (alias el Filipino) ..., 29 June - 1 July 1788, Huntington Library, Department of Manuscripts, San Marino, CA.

Lot-Falck, E., 1957, Les masques Eskimo et Aléoutes de la collection Pinart, *Journal de la Société des Américanistes*, new series, vol.46, pp.5-43.

Louth, A, 1997, The Church's Mission: Patristic Presuppositions, Pembroke College, Oxford Symposium, 14-15 April 1997: Bishop Innokentii Veniaminov and the Patristic Background for 19th Century Missionary Work, International Bicentennial of the Birth of Innokentii Veniaminov. In *GOTR*, vol. 4, nos 1-4 (1999), pp.649-656.

——, 1989, *Denys the Areopagite*, Wilton, CT.

——, 1981, *The Origins of the Christian Mystical Tradition from Plato to Denys*, Oxford.

Makarova, R.V., 1975, *Russians on the Pacific, 1743-1799* [Русские на Тихом Океане во второй половине XVIII в, Moscow, 1968], trans R.A. Pierce and A.S. Donnelly, LPAH.

——, 1968, *Русские на Тихом Океане во второй половине XVIII в*, Moscow.

Mansi, J.D. (ed.), 1767, *Sacrorum Conciliorum Nova et Amplissima Collectio*, vol.13: *787 AD - 841 AD*, Florence.

[Marriott, C. (ed.)], 1851, *A Library of Fathers of the Holy Catholic Church, anterior to the division of East and West*, vol.33: *The Homilies of S. John Chrysos-*

tom, archbishop of Constantinople, on the Acts of the Apostles, part 1: *Hom. i-xxviii*, trans J. Walker, J. Sheppard, and H. Browne, Oxford and London.

Marsh, G.H., 1967, A Comparative Survey of Eskimo-Aleut Religion, *The North American Indians: a Sourcebook*, pp.143-159, eds R. Owen, *et. al.*, London and NYC.

——, 1954, A Comparative Survey of Eskimo-Aleut Religion, *APUA*, vol.3, no.1, pp.21-36.

Martin, L., 1986, *Michael Z. Vinokouroff: A Profile and Inventory of his Papers (Ms 81) and Photographs (PCA 243) in the Alaska Historical Library*, Alaska Division of State Libraries, Department of Education, Juneau.

Mather, E.P., 1985, Cauyarnariuq, the Lower Kuskokwim School District, Bethel, AK.

McClanahan, A.J. (ed.), 1986, *Our Stories, Our Lives: a Collection of Twenty-Three Transcribed Interviews with Elders of the Cook Inlet Region*, CIRI [Cook Inlet Region Inc.] Foundation, Anchorage.

McIntyre, H.H., 1870, Alaska, in *Executive Document no.36*, 41st Congress, US House of Representatives, 2nd Session (11 January), Washington, DC.

Merculieff, I., 1997, Eco-Tourism Development on St Paul Island, the Pribilofs, Alaska, *Arctic Ecology and Identity*, pp.133-142, ed. S.A. Mousalimas, Hungarian Academy of Sciences and ISTOR, Budapest and Los Angeles.

——, 1984, Narration, *Amiq: The Aleut People of the Pribilof Islands, a Culture in Transition, 1981-1983*, documentary film directed and produced by S. Swibold and H. Corbett, Flying Tomato Productions, Alberta.

Meyendorff, P., 1984, Introduction, *St Germanus of Constantinople on the Divine Liturgy*, Crestwood, NY.

Miyaoka, O., 1978, Alaska Native Languages in Transition, *Alaska Native Culture and History*, pp.169-203, eds Y. Kotani and W. Workman, Senri Ethnological Studies, vol.4, Osaka.

Moore, K.H., 1979, Spain Claims Alaska, 1775, *The Sea in Alaska's Past, Conference Proceeding*, pp.62-74, Alaska Division of Parks, History and Archaeology Publication Series, no.25, Anchorage.

Morrow, P., 1990, Symbolic Actions, Indirect Expressions: Limits to Interpretation in Yupik Society, *ÉIS*, vol.14, nos 1-2, pp.141-158.

——, 1984, It is a Time for Drumming: A Summary of Recent Research on Yup'ik Ceremonialism, *ÉIS*, vol.8, pp.113-140.

Mousalimas, S.A., in print (a), [Russian trans., '...If Reports Can Be Believed, 1990e], *Язык, Миф Культура Народов Сибири*, Sakha State University, Iakutsk.

——, in print (b), Nature and Space: Patristic Theology and Native Cosmologies towards 'Indigenization' Today, *EFOM Lectures*, Endowment Fund for Orthodox Missions, Lancaster, PA.

——, in print (c), Time and Place: Historical Contexts of Christianity for 'Contextualization' Today, *EFOM Lectures*, Endowment Fund for Orthodox Missions, Lancaster, PA.

____, in print (d), Alaska Native Orthodoxy, *Encyclopedia of Religions and American Cultures*, eds G. Laderman and L. Leon, ABC-Clio, Santa Barbara.

____, in print (e), Shamanism, *Encyclopedia of the Arctic*, ed. M. Nuttal, Fitzroy Dearborn Publishers, London.

____, in print (f), Archbishop Innokentii Veniaminov, *Encyclopedia of the Arctic*, ed. M. Nuttal, Fitzroy Dearborn Publishers, London.

____, in print (g), Sergey Mikhailovich Shirokogoroff, *Encyclopedia of the Arctic*, ed. M. Nuttal, Fitzroy Dearborn Publishers, London.

——, 1997a, Introduction, *Arctic Ecology and Identity*, pp.1-30, ed. S.A. Mousalimas, Hungarian Academy of Sciences and ISTOR, Budapest and Los Angeles.

——, 1997b, Immanence and Transcendence through the Seven Councils [paper presented at the 12th International Conference on Patristic Studies, Oxford], *GOTR*, vol.42, nos 3-4.

——, 1997c, Three Levels (and Modes of Discernment) in the Ministry of St Innokentii (Veniaminov) in Alaska, Sakha Republic International Conference, Iakutsk, 12-14 Sept. 1997: St Innokentii (Veniaminov), Enlightener of the Peoples of Alaska and Siberia, International Bicentennial of the Birth of Innokentii Veniaminov.

____, 1997d, Introduction, Pembroke College, Oxford Symposium, 14-15 April 1997- Bishop Innokentii Veniaminov and the Patristic Background for 19th Century Missionary Work, International Bicentennial of the Birth of Innokentii Veniaminov. In *GOTR*, vol. 4, nos 1-4 (1999), pp. 531-556.

——, 1995, [Russian trans., A Question about the 'Chugach Shaman', Alaska (an Inquiry into Ecstasy and Continuity), 1993c], *Язык, Ммф Культура Народов Сибири*, vol.4, pp.99-112, Sakha State University, Iakutsk.

——, 1994, Непрерывность и Прерывность в Религиозных Культах Аляски, trans. E.Iu. Pogibeleva, *Язык, Ммф Культура Народов Сибири*, vol.3, pp.55-61, Sakha State University, Iakutsk.

——, 1993a, Introduction, *Journals of Ioann Veniaminov in Alaska, 1823-1833*, pp. xiii-xxxix, RLHT.

——, 1993b, 'Ecstasy' in Epiphanius of Constantia (Salamis) and Didymus of Alexandria, *Studia Patristica: Proceedings of the International Conferences on Patristic Studies held in Oxford*, vol.25, pp.434-437, Louvain.

——, 1993c, A Question about the 'Chugach Shaman', Alaska [an Inquiry into Ecstasy and Continuity], *Shamans and Cultures: Selected Papers of the First Conference of the International Society for Shamanistic Research*, pp.147-159, eds M. Hoppál and K. Howard, Budapest and Los Angeles.

——, 1993d, 'Saints' of the 'Orthodox Church in America', *The Hellenic Journal*, vol.19, no.22 (2 December), San Francisco.

——, 1992, The Transition from Shamanism to Russian Orthodoxy in Alaska, DPhil thesis, Oxford University.

——, 1991, The Account from Old Harbor regarding the Baptism of the Kodiak Alutiiq, 1794/95, *GOTR*, vol.36, no.2, pp.155-168.

——, 1990a, The Concept of Participation in Lévy-Bruhl's 'Primitive Mentality', *JASO*, vol.21, no.1, pp.33-46.

——, 1990b, The Divine in Nature: Animism or Panentheism? [paper presented at IAHR], *GOTR*, vol.35, no.4, pp.367-375.

——, 1990c, The Name, an Icon: Naming as Imaging in Southwestern Alaska, unpublished paper presented at the 7th International Inuit Studies Conference, Symposium on Inuit Symbolism and Iconography, University of Alaska, Fairbanks.

——, 1990d, Russian Orthodox Missionaries and Southern Alaska Shamans: Interactions and Analysis, *Russia in North America: Proceedings of the 2nd International Conference on Russian-America*, pp.314-322, LPAH.

——, 1990e, '...If Reports Can Be Believed, Russian Priests Destroyed All the Masks They Could Find', *ÉIS*, vol.14, nos 1-2, pp.191-208.

——, 1990f, The Formation of the Unalaska Parish, *GOTR*, vol.36, no.1, pp.21-35.

——, 1989a, Shamans of Old in Southern Alaska, *Shamanism: Past and Present* [selected papers from the 12th International Congress on Anthropological and Ethnological Sciences, Symposium on Shamanism], vol.2, pp.307-316, ed. M. Hoppál and O. von Sadovszky, Budapest and Los Angeles.

——, 1989b, Contrasting Theological Outlooks on Ancient Kodiak Culture [paper presented at the 1st Kodiak Island Culture Heritage Conference], *GOTR*, vol.34, no.4, pp.365-378.

——, 1988a, Continuity and Discontinuity in Belief Systems in Southern Alaska, unpublished paper presented at the 15th Annual Meeting of the Alaska Anthropological Association.

——, 1988b, Patristics and Missionary Work: an Example from the Russian Orthodox Mission in Alaska [paper presented at the 10th International Conference on Patristic Studies, Oxford], *GOTR*, vol.33, no.3, pp.327-334.

——, 1988c, An Aleut among the Yup'ik [Yupiit]: Alaskan Cosmologies in Contact [paper presented at the Conference on the Cosmologies of Polar Peoples, University of Edinburgh], *Shadow: Journal of the Traditional Cosmology Society*, vol.5, no.2, pp.38-44.

——, 1987, The Consequences of Nestorius' Metaphysics, *GOTR*, vol.32, no.3, pp.279-284.

——, 1980, The Defense of the Council of Chalcedon in the Patriarchate of Jerusalem, 415-518 AD, unpublished MDiv thesis, Holy Cross Greek Orthodox School of Theology, Brookline, MA.

Müller, G. F., 1986, *Bering's Voyages: the Reports from Russia*, trans. C. Urness, RLHT.

[Murav'ev] Mouravieff, A.N., 1855, *Русская Фиваида на Съверъ*, Moscow.

——, 1842, *A History of the Church in Russia*, trans. R. Blackmore, Oxford.

Nelson, E.W., 1899, The Eskimo about the Bering Strait, *18th Annual Report, Bureau of Ethnology*, Smithsonian Institution, Washington, DC.

Netsvetov, Ia., 1984a, *The Journals of Iakov Netsvetov: The Yukon Years, 1845-1863*, trans. L.T. Black, LPAH.

——, 1984b, Notes on the Former Customs and Beliefs of the Atkha Aleuts [Записки... Атхинскихъ Алеутовъ, ed. I. Veniaminov, St Petersburg, 1840], in I. Veniaminov, *Notes on the Islands of the Unalaska District*, pp.365-379, trans. L.T. Black and R.H. Geoghegan, RLHT and LPAH.

——, 1980, *The Journals of Iakov Netsvetov: The Atkha Years, 1828-1844*, trans. L.T. Black, LPAH.

——, 1840, Записки о Прежнихъ [Обычаях и Верах] Атхинскихъ Алеутовъ, ed. I. Veniaminov, in I. Veniaminov, *Записки объ Островахъ Уналашкинскаго Отдьла*, part 3, pp.1-19, St Petersburg.

Niarchos, C.G., 1991, Aristotle's Categories in St John of Damascus' Dialectica, unpublished paper presented at the 11th International Conference on Patristic Studies, Oxford.

Nicephorus of Constantinople, 1865, Ἀντίρρησις καὶ Ἀνατροπὴ τῶν παρὰ τοῦ δυσσεβοῦς Μαμώνα, PG, vol.100: Νικηφόρου Ἀρχιεπισκόπου Κωνσταντινουπόλεως τα εὑρισκόμενα πάντα, cols 205-534.

Nicholson, S. (comp.), 1987, *Shamanism: an Expanded View of Reality*. Wheaton, IL and London.

OCA ['Orthodox Church in America' (*sic*)], 1980, *Act of Canonization [of the Holy Martyrs Hieromonk Juvenaly and Peter the Aleut]*, resolution by Bishop Gregory of Alaska, 17 October 1979, to the Holy Synod of Bishops of the Orthodox Church in America [*sic*], Syosset, NY.

——, 1970, *Booklet for the Canonization of Saint Herman of Alaska*, Syosset, NY.

Oleksa, M.J., 1992, *Orthodox Alaska: a Theology of Mission*, Crestwood, NY.

——, 1990, The Death of Hieromonk Juvenaly, *Russia in North America: Proceedings of the 2nd International Conference on Russian-America*, pp.322-257, LPAH.

—— (ed.), 1987, *Alaskan Missionary Spirituality*, NYC.

Oliver, E.R., 1988, *Journal of an Aleutian Year*, Seattle and London.

Origen, 1936, *Origen on First Principles*, trans. G. Butterworth, London.

Osgood, C., 1937, *The Ethnography of the Tanaina* [Dena'ina], Yale University Publications in Anthropology, vol.16, New Haven.

Oswalt, W., 1963a, *Napaskiak: an Alaskan Eskimo Community*, Tuscon.

——, 1963b, *Mission of Change in Alaska: Eskimos and Moravians on the Kuskokwim*, San Marino, CA.

Padgen, A., 1982, *The Fall of Natural Man: the American Indian and the Origins of Comparative Ethnology*, Cambridge.

Palladius of Helenopolis, 1974, Ἡ πρὸς Λαῦσον Ἱστορία [Παλλαδίου Λαυσιακόν], *Palladio, la Storia Lausiaca*, ed. G. Bartelink, trans. M. Barchiesi, Vite dei Santi 2, Milan and Verona.

——, 1904, Ἡ πρὸς Λαῦσον Ἱστορία [Παλλαδίου Λαυσιακόν], *Texts and Studies: Contributions to Biblical and Patristic Literature*, general ed. J. Robinson, vol.6, no.2: *The Lausiac History of Palladius, II*, ed. C. Butler, Cambridge.

Palmer, G.E.H., Sherrard, P. and Ware, K. (trans), 1979, *Philokalia*, vol.1, London and Boston.

Papadeas, G.L., comp., 1977, *Ai Ierai Akolouqia thj M. Ebdomadoj kai tou Pasca: Greek Orthodox Holy Week and Easter Services*, Dayton Beach, FL.

Parry, K., 1996, *Depicting the Word: Byzantine Iconophile Thought of the Eighth and Nineth Centuries*, Leiden.

Pascal, P., 1976, *The Religion of the Russian People*, trans. R. Williams, London.

Pentikäinen, J.Y., 1989, *Kalevala Mythology*, trans. and ed. R. Poom, Bloomington, IN.

——, 1978, *Oral Repretoire and Worldview: an Anthropological Study of Marina Takalo's Life History*, Folklore Fellows Communication, vol.219.

Percival, H.R. (trans. and ed.), 1900, The Seven Ecumenical Councils of the Undivided Church: their Canons and Dogmatic Decrees, NPNF, 2nd series, vol.14: *The Seven Ecumenical Councils of the Undivided Church*.

Petrivelli, A., 1993, Foreword, *Journals of Ioann Veniaminov in Alaska, 1823-1833*, p.vii. RLHT.

Petroff, I., 1884, *Alaska: Its Population, Industries, and Resources*, US Department of the Interior, 10th Census (1880), vol.8, Washington, DC.

——, 1881, Population and Resources of Alaska, *Executive Document, no.40*, 46th Congress, US House of Representatives, 3rd Session (15 January), vol.18, Washington, DC.

Pharos, P. [F.], 1981, *Τό Πένθος: ὀρθόδοξη, λαογραφικὴ καὶ ψυχολογικὴ θεώρησις*, Σειρά, Athens.

Pheidas, V., 1988, *Ἐκκλησιαστικὴ Ἱστορία τῆς Ρωσσίας (988-1988)*, 3rd edn, Athens.

Pierce, R.A., 1990, *Russian-America: A Biographical Dictionary*, LPAH.

——, 1986, *Builders of Alaska: The Russian Governors, 1818-1867*, LPAH.

—— (trans. and ed.), 1984, *The Russian-American Company: Correspondence of the Governors, Communication Sent: 1818*, LPAH.

——, 1981a, Introduction, *A Voyage to America, 1783-1786, by Grigorii I. Shelikhov*, LPAH.

——, 1981b, Introduction, in E. L. Huggins, *Kodiak and Afognak Life, 1968-1870*, LPAH.

——, 1978, Notes, in Valaam Monastery, *The Russian Orthodox Religious Mission in America*, pp.176-181, LPAH.

—— (ed.), 1976, *Documents on the History of the Russian-American Company*, trans. M. Ramsay, LPAH.

——, 1964, A note on 'Ivan Petroff and the Far Northwest', *Journal of the West*, vol.3, no.4, pp.436-439.

Pinart, A., ms., Field Notes from the Kodiak Island Region, 1871-72, Bancroft Library, University of California, Berkeley.

——, 1874a, Les Aléoutes et leur Origine, *Mèmoires de la Société d'Ethnographie: Revue Orientale et Américaine*, 1st series, vol.12, pp.155-165.

——, 1874b, Voyage de la Cote Nord-Ouest d'Amerique d'Ounalashka a Kodiak (Iles Aléoutienne et Péninsule d'Aliaska), *Bulletin de la Société de Géographie* (Dec. 1873), extract, Paris.

——, 1873a, Les Aléoutes, leurs origines et leurs légendes, *Actes de la Société d'Ethnographie*, 2nd series, vol.7, no.3, pp.87-92.

——, 1873b, Eskimaux et Koloches: Idées Religieuses et Traditions de Kaniagmioutes, *Revue d'Anthropologie*, vol.2, pp.673-680.

Porter, R.P., 1893, *Report on the Population and Resources of Alaska at the Eleventh Census: 1890*, US Department of the Interior, Washington, DC.

Prokopovich, F., 1723, *The Russian Catechism composed [by F. Prokopovich] and published by order of the Czar*, trans. J. Phillips, London.

Prossoff [Prokoff], A., 1988, Alex Prossoff's Story [personal account dictated 16 March 1947], Appendix 2 in E.R. Oliver, *Journal of an Aleutian Year*, pp.241-248, Seattle and London.

Pullar, G.L., 1991, Ethnic Identity, Cultural Pride, and Generations of Baggage: a Personal Experience, unpublished paper presented at 18th Annual Meeting of the Alaska Anthropological Association.

Radchenko, Iu., 1981, Extract from 'Kolumbu Rosskomu ...', trans. M. Ramsay, Appendix 9, in G. I. Shelikhov, *A Voyage to America, 1783-1786*, pp.138-145, LPAH.

——, 1979, Колумбу Росскому..., *Панорама Искусств*, vol.78, pp.341-351.

Ransom, J.E., 1947, Stories, Myths, and Superstitions of Fox Island Aleut

Children, *JAF*, vol.60, no.235, pp.62- 72.

——, 1945a, Writing as a Medium of Acculturation among the Aleut, *Southwestern Journal of Anthropology*, vol.1, no.1, pp.333-344.

——, 1945b, Aleut Religous Beliefs: Veniaminov's Account, *JAF*, vol.58, no.230, pp.346-349.

—— (ed.), 1941, Wreck of the Umnak Native [by A. Ermelov, trans. G. Kochergin], *Alaskan Sportsman*, vol.7, no.2 (February), Ketchikan, AK.

Rathburn, R.R., 1981, The Russian Orthodox Church as a Native Institution among the Koniag Eskimo of Kodiak Island, Alaska, *AA*, vol.18, no.1, pp.12-22.

Ray, D.J., 1981, *Aleut and Eskimo Art: Tradition and Innovation in South Alaska*, Seattle and London.

—— (ed.), 1968, St Michael Eskimo Myths and Tales: Collected by J. Henry Turner and J.M. Edmonds, *APUA*, vol.14, no.1, pp.43-83.

——, 1967, *Eskimo Masks*, Seattle and London.

Rexine, J.E., 1985, Daimon in Classical Greek Literature, *GOTR*, vol.30, no.3, pp.335-362.

Riasanovsky, N.V., 1985, *The Image of Peter the Great in Russian History and Thought*, NYC and Oxford.

——, 1968, Afterword: The Problem of the Peasant, *The Peasant in Nineteenth Century Russia*, ed. W.S. Vucinich, pp.263-284, 306-307, Stanford.

Rydving, H., 1993, *The End of Drum-Time: Religious Change among the Lule Saami, 1670s-1740s*, Uppsala.

Romanides, J.S., 1989, Introduction, Τὸ Προπατορικὸν Ἁμάρτημα, 2nd edn, Athens.

——, 1981, *Franks, Romans, Feudalism and Doctrine: an Interplay between Theology and Society*, the Patriarch Athenagoras Memorial Lectures of 1980, Brookline, MA.

——, 1957, Τὸ Προπατορικὸν Ἁμάρτημα:... ἐν τῇ μέχρι τοῦ Ἁγίου Εἰρηναίου Ἀρχαίᾳ Ἐκκλησίᾳ..., Athens.

Rostad, M., 1988, *Time to Dance: Life of an Alaska Native* [I. Matfay], Anchorage.

Rubenson, S., 1990, *The Letters of St Anthony: Origenist Theology, Monastic Tradition and the Making of a Saint*, Lund.

Rudolph, K., 1983, *Gnosis: the Nature and History of an Ancient Religion*, trans. R. McLachlan, Edinburgh.

Russian American Company Documents, mss, the G. V. Iudin [Yudin] collection, US Library of Congress Manuscript Division, Washington, DC.

Sahas, D.J., 1986, *Icon and Logos: Sources in Eighth Century Iconoclasm: an annotated translation of the Sixth Session of the Seventh Ecumenical Council (Nicea, 787) ...*, Toronto, Buffalo and London.

Salomatov, L., trans., 1959, Gospel according to St Mark, *The Transactions of the American Philosophical Society at Philadelphia*, new series, vol.49, no.3: *Aleut Dialects of Atka and Attu*, pp.87-103.

Sardy, M., 1985-1986, Early Contact between Aleuts and Russians, 1741-1780, *Alaska History*, vol.1, no.2, pp.43-58.

Sarychev [Sarytschew], G., 1807, *Account of a Voyage of Discovery to the Northeast of Siberia, the Frozen Ocean, and the Northeast Sea*, vol.2 [Путешествіе..., St Petersburg, 1802], trans. anon., in *A Collection of Modern and Contemporary Voyages and Travels*, vol.6, London.

——, 1802, *Путешествіе Флота Капитана Сарычева ... съ 1785 по 1793 годъ*, 2 volumes, St Petersburg.

Sauer, M., 1802, *An Account of a Geographical and Astronomical Expedition to the Northern Parts of Russia ... performed ... by Commodore Joseph Billings in the years 1785-1794*, London.

Shade, C. I., 1951, The Girls' Puberty Ceremony of Umnak, Aleutian Islands, *AA*, vol.53, pp.145-148.

——, 1949, Ethnological Notes on the Aleuts, unpublished BA honours thesis, Harvard University.

Shelikhov, G.I., 1981, *Voyage to America, 1783-1786* [Россійскаго Купца Григорья Шелехова Странствованіе въ 1783 году..., St Petersburg, 1791; 2nd edn, 1792; 3rd edn revised, 1793], ed. R. H. Pierce, trans. M. Ramsey, LPAH.

Sherrard, P., 1990, Confronting the Ecological Challenge, *Southeastern Review*, vol.1, no.1, pp.139-148 (Southeastern College, Athens).

——, 1987, *The Eclipse of Man and Nature: an Enquiry into the Origins and Consequences of Modern Science*, West Stockbridge, MA.

——, 1967, The Art of the Icon, *Sacrament and Image: Essays in the Christian Understanding of Man*, ed. A. Allchin, London.

Sherwood, M.B., 1964, A Note on the Petroff Note, *Journal of the West*, vol.3, no.4, p.440.

——, 1963, Ivan Petroff and the Far Northwest, *Journal of the West*, vol.2, no.3, pp.305-315.

Shirokogoroff, S.M., 1935, *Psychomental Complex of the Tungus*, London.

——, 1924, What is Shamanism?, *The China Journal of Science and Arts*, vol.2, nos. 3-4, pp.275-279, 368-371.

——, 1923, General Theory of Shamanism among the Tungus, *Journal of the North China Branch of the Royal Asiatic Society*, vol.54, pp.246-249.

Shishigin, E.S., Yakutia, *A Dictionary of Eastern Christianity*, ed. K. Parry, Oxford, Blackwell, 1999, pp. 253-255.

——, 1997a, Prelate Innokentii (Veniaminov) and Yakutia, Pembroke College, Oxford Symposium, 14-15 April 1997: Bishop Innokentii Veniaminov and the Patristic Background for 19th Century Missionary Work, International Bicentennial of the Birth of Innokentii Veniaminov. In *GOTR*, vol. 4, nos 1-4 (1999), pp.597-606.

——, 1997b, Prelate Innokentii Veniaminov in Iakutia, Centre for the Study of Christianity in the Non-Western World, University of Edinburgh, 16-17 April 1997, Christian Identities in the Arctic, International Bicentennial of the Birth of Innokentii Veniaminov.

——, 1997c, Metropolitan Innokentii (Veniaminov) and his Place in the History of the Peoples of Alaska, Siberia and the Far East, Sakha Republic International Conference, Iakutsk, 12-14 Sept. 1997: St Innokentii (Veniaminov), Enlightener of the Peoples of Alaska and Siberia, International Bicentennial of the Birth of Innokentii Veniaminov.

——, 1991, *Распространение Христианства в Якутии*, Якутский Государственный Объединенный Музей Истории и Культуры Народов Севера, Iakutsk.

Siikala, A.L., 1987, *The Rite Technique of the Siberian Shaman*, Folklore Fellows Communications, vol.93.

Sitnikov, L.A., 1990, Григорий И. Шеликов, Irkutsk.

Smirnoff, E., 1903, *A Short Account of the Historical Development and Present Position of Russian Orthodox Missions*, London.

Smith, B.S., 1980, *Russian Orthodoxy in Alaska: a History, Inventory, and Analysis of the Church Archives in Alaska with an Annotated Bibliography*, Alaska Historical Commission, Anchorage.

Sonne, B., 1988, *Agayut: Nunivak Eskimo Masks and Drawings from the 5th Thule Expedition, 1921-24, collected by Knud Rasmussen*, Report of the 5th Thule Expedition, vol.10, part 4, Copenhagen.

Sovoroff, S., 1976, History from Nikolski and Umnak, including the Story of the Nikolski Tree, trans [from Aleut] I. Gromoff and N. Galaktionoff, City School, Unalaska.

Spaulding, P.T., 1955, An Ethnohistorical Study of Akutan: an Aleut Community, unpublished MA thesis, University of Oregon.

Stamey, R., 1979, The Restoration of the St. Nicholas Russian Orthodox Church, Juneau, Alaska, *Orthodox Alaska*, vol.8, nos 3-4, pp.73- 78.

Stamoolis, J., 1986, *Eastern Orthodox Missionary Theology Today*, Minneapolis.

Starr, J.L., 1961, The Cultural and Educational Development of Aborigines and Settlers in Russian-America, 1784-1867, PhD thesis (New York University), University Microfilms, Ann Arbor.

Stephan deacon of Constantinople, 1860, Εἰς τὸν βίον καὶ μαρτύριον τοῦ παμμάκαρος καὶ ὁσίου μάρτυρος Στεφάνου τοῦ Νέου... PG, vol.100, cols 1069-1186.

Swanton, J.R., 1908, Social Conditions, Beliefs and Linguistic Relationships of the Tlingit Indians, *26th Annual Report, 1904-1905, of the Bureau of American Ethnology*, pp.391-485, Smithsonian Institution, Washington, DC.

Sweetland, M.M., ms. [1945], Faith of Our Fathers, Living Still: In Spite of Dungeon, Fire and Sword, Barabara Sweetland Smith, Anchorage.

Taft, R., 1980-1981, The Liturgy of the Great Church: an Initial Synthesis of Structure and Interpretation on the Eve of Iconoclasm, *Dumbarton Oak Papers*, vol.34-35, pp.45-78.

Taniisi, 1982, vol.3, Aleutian Region School District.

Taylor, K.L., 1966, A Demographic Study of Karluk, Kodiak Island, Alaska, *AA*, vol.3, no.2, pp.211-240.

Tertullian, 1960, *Q. Septimii Florentis Tertulliani de Resurrectione Carnis Liber: Tertullian's Treatise on the Resurrection*, ed. and trans. E. Evans, London.

——, 1950, On the Soul [de Anima], trans. E. Quain, *The Fathers of the Church*, vol.10: *Tertullian Apologetical Works*, pp.179-309, Washington, DC.

——, 1947, *Quinti Septi Florentis Tertulliani de Anima*, ed. J. Waszink, Amsterdam.

——, 1870, A treatise on the Resurrection in the Flesh [de res. car.]; A treatise on the Soul [de anima], trans. P. Holmes, *The Ante-Nicene Christian Fathers*, general eds A. Roberts and J. Donaldson, vol.15: *Writings of Tertullian*, vol 2, pp.215-332 and 410-541, Edinburgh.

Theodore the Studite, 1981, *On the Holy Icons*, trans. C. Roth, Crestwood, NY.

——, 1860, Ἀντιρρητικοὶ κατὰ εἰκονομάχων, PG, vol. 99: Θεοδώρου τοῦ Στυδίτου τὰ εὐρισκόμενα πάντα, cols 327-351.

Theophilus of Antioch, 1970, *Ad Autolycum*, ed. and trans. R. Grant, OECT.

——, 1948, Θεοφίλου πρὸς Αὐτολύκον, SC [no number]: *Théophile d' Antioche: Trois Livres à Autolycus*, ed. G. Bardy.

Thunberg, L., 1985, *Man and the Cosmos: the Vision of St Maximus the Confessor*, Crestwood, NY.

——, 1965, *Microcosm and Mediator: the Theological Anthropology of Maximus the Confessor*, Copenhagen.

Tikhmenev, P.A. (ed.), 1979, *A History of the Russian-American Company*, vol.2: *Documents* [Историческое Обозрѣніе Образованія...; part 3: Приложеніе, St Petersburg, 1863], trans. D. Krenov, LPAH.

——, 1978, *A History of the Russian-American Company* [*Историческое Обозрѣніе Образованія Россійско-Американской Компаніи и дѣйствій ея до настоящаго времени*, parts 1-2, St Petersburg, 1861-1863], trans and eds R.A. Pierce and A.S. Donnelly, Seattle and London.

—— (ed.), 1863, *Историческое Обозрѣніе Образованія Россійско-Американской Компаніи и дѣйствій ея до настоящаго времени*, St Petersburg.

Torres, F., 1985, Rois Chasseurs, un Essai de Définition de la Structure Sociale Aléoute, *Inter-Nord*, vol.17, pp.115-129.

Townsend, J.B., 1979, Indian or Eskimo? Interaction and Identity in South Alaska, *AA*, vol.16, no.2, pp.160-182.

——, 1975, Mercantilism and Societal Change: an Ethnohistorical Examination of Some Essential Variables, *Ethnohistory*, vol.22, no.1, pp.21-32.

——, 1974, Journals of Nineteenth Century Russian Priests to the Tanaina [Dena'ina]: Cook Inlet, Alaska, *AA*, vol.11, no.1, pp.1-30.

——, 1965, Ethnohistory and culture change of the Iliamna Tanaina [Dena'ina], unpublished PhD thesis, University of California, Los Angeles.

Toynbee, A.J., 1946, Preface, in [D. C. Somervell], *A Study of History by Arnold Toynbee*, Royal Institute of International Affairs, London, NYC, Toronto.

——, 1935, *A Study of History*, vol.1: *Introduction*, 2nd edn, Oxford.

Tugolukov, V.A., 1978, Some Aspects of the Beliefs of the Tungus (Evenki and Evens), trans. S. Simon, in *Shamanism in Siberia*, pp.419-428, eds V. Diózegi and M. Hoppál, Budapest.

Turner, C.G., 1976, The Aleuts of Akun Island, *Alaska Journal*, vol.6, no.1, pp.25-31.

Turner, E., 1989, From Shamans to Healers: The Survival of an Inupiaq Eskimo Skill, *Athropologica*, vol.21, no.1, pp.3-24.

Unangam Ungiikangin, 1990, *Unangam Ungiikangin kayux Tunusangin: Unangam Uniikangis ama Tunuzangis: Aleut Tales and Narratives*, comp. V. Iokhel'son [W. Jochelson], ed. K. Bergsland and M.L. Dirks, ANLC.

Underhill, E., 1930, *Mysticism: a Study in the Nature and Development of Man's Spiritual Consiousness*, 12th edn, London; reprinted London, 1967.

Uspenskii [Ouspensky], L., 1982, *La Théologie de l'icône dans l'Eglise orthodoxe*, Paris.

——, 1960, *Essai sur la Théologie de l'icône dans l'Eglise orthodoxe*, Paris.

Uutuqtwa, 1987, vol.2, no.1, Bristol Bay High School, Naknek, AK.

Valaam Monastery, 1983, *Valamo and Its Message*, Helsinki and London.

——, 1978, *The Russian Orthodox Religious Mission in America, 1794-1837* [*Очеркъ изъ Исторіи...*, St Petersburg, 1894], trans. C. Bearne, LPAH.

—— (ed.), 1978, Documents [Приложенія], Appendix 1, *The Russian Orthodox Religious Mission in America, 1794-1837*, trans. C. Bearne, LPAH.

——, 1894a, *Очеркъ изъ Исторіи Американской Православной Духовной Миссіи (Кадьякской Миссіи 1794-1837 гг.)*, St Petersburg.

——, 1894b, *Жизнр Валаамскаго Монаха Германа, Американскаго Миссіонера*, St Petersburg.

—— (ed.), 1894, Приложенія, Appendix 1, *Очеркъ изъ Исторіи Американской Православной Духовной Миссіи (Кадьякской Миссіи 1794-1837 гг.)*, pp.121-194, St Petersburg.

Valaam Monastery Documents, mss, in Russian Reproductions, US Library of Congress Manuscript Division, Washington, DC.

Vancouver, G., 1984, *A Voyage of Discovery to the North Pacific Ocean and Round the World, 1791-1794*, vol.4, ed. W. Lamb, Hakluyt Society, London.

——, 1798, *A Voyage of Discovery to the North Pacific Ocean and Round the World, 1791-1794*, vol.3, London.

Van Stone, J.W., 1979, Athabascan-Eskimo Relations in West-Central Alaska: an Ethnohistorical Perspective, *AA*, vol.16, no.2, pp.152-159.

—— (ed.), 1977, *A.F. Kashevarov's Coastal Explorations in Northwest Alaska, 1838*, trans. D. Kraus, Fieldiana Anthropology, vol.69, Chicago.

—— (ed.), 1973, *V.S. Khromchenko's Coastal Explorations in Southwestern, Alaska, 1822*, trans. D. Kraus, Fieldiana Anthropology, vol.64, Chicago.

——, 1967, *Eskimos of the Nushagak River: an Ethnographic History*, University of Washington Publications in Anthropology, vol.15.

——, 1964, Some Aspects of Religous Change among Native Inhabitants in West Alaska and the Northwest Territories, *AA*, vol.2, no.2, pp.21-24.

——, 1960, Three Eskimo Communities, *APUA*, vol.9, no.1, pp.17-56.

Veniaminov, I., 1993, *Journals of Ioann Veniaminov in Alaska, 1823-1833*, trans. J. Kisslinger, RLHT.

——, 1984, *Notes on the Islands of the Unalashka District* [Записки..., St Petersburg, 1840], trans L.T. Black and R.H. Geoghegan, RLHT and LPAH.

——, 1977, Letter to the Archbishop of Irkutsk (June 1828) [ms., filed 5 November 1829, Tobol'sk; transcript, Russian Church, Miscellaneous Papers, Alaska Historical Library Archives, Juneau], trans. L.T. Black, *AA*, vol.14, no.1. pp.100-102.

——, 1975, The Russian Orthodox Church in Alaska: Innokentii Veniaminov's Supplementary Account (1858), trans. R. Croskey, *Pacific Northwest Quarterly*, vol.65, no.1, pp.26-29.

——, 1972, The Condition of the Orthodox Church in Russian America: Innokentii Veniaminov's History of the Russian Church in Alaska [Состояніе Православной Церкви..., *Иннокентій... его Творенія*, vol.2, ed. I. Barsukov, Moscow, 1887, pp.1-42], trans and eds R. Nichols and R. Croskey, *Pacific Northwest Quarterly*, vol.63, no.2, pp.41-54.

——, 1944, The Elements of Aleut Grammar [and] A Grammatical Essay on the Aleut Language [in *Опытъ Грамматики Алеутско-Лисьевскаго Языка*, St Petersburg, 1846], trans. R.H. Geoghegan, *The Aleut Language*, pp.13-83, ed. F. Martin, US Department of the Interior, Washington, DC; reprinted Seattle, 1973.

——, 1840a, Состояніе Православной Церкви въ Россійской Америкь, *Journal of the Ministry of Public Education*, vol.26, no.5 (1840), pp.15-58, extract, St Petersburg.

———, 1840b, *Записки объ Островахъ Уналашкинскаго Отдѣла*, part 2, St Petersburg.

Veniaminov, I. [Pan'kov, I., *et al.*] (trans), 1840, *Евангеліе наптсанное Апостоломъ МатФьемъ съ Русскаго языка на Алеутско-Лисьевской*, Moscow.

Veniaminov, I., and Netsvetov, Ia. (trans), 1840, Начатки Христіанскаго Ученія, St Petersburg

Vernadsky, G., 1959, *The Origins of Russia*, Oxford.

Vita Pachomii (anon.), 1980, The First Greek Life, *Pachomian Koinonia*, vol.1: *The Life of Saint Pachomius*, pp.297-407, trans. A. Veilleux, Cistercian Studies Series, vol.45, Kalamazoo.

———, 1932, Βίος τοῦ Ἁγίου Παχουμίου [vita prima], *Sancti Pachomii Vitae Graecae*, pp.1-96, ed. F. Halkin *et al.*, Société des Bollandistes, Subsidia Hagiographica, vol.19, Brussels.

Voulgarakes, E.A., 1971, Ἡ Ἱεραποστολὴ κατὰ τὰ Ἑλληνικὰ Κείμενα ἀπὸ τοῦ *1821 μέχρι τοῦ 1917*, Athens.

Wace, A.J.B and M.S. Thompson., 1914, *Nomads of the Balkans: an Account of Life and Customs among the Vlachs of Northern Pindus*, London.

Ward, B., 1980, Introduction, *The Lives of the Desert Fathers: the Historia Monachorum in Aegypto* [Ἡ κατ' Αἴγυπτον τῶν Μοναχῶν Ἱστορία], London and Oxford.

Ware, K. [T.], 1997, 'The Light that Enlightens Everyone': The Knowledge of God among Non-Christians according to the Greek Fathers and St Innocent, Pembroke College, Oxford Symposium, 14-15 April 1997: Bishop Innokentii Veniaminov and the Patristic Background for 19th Century Missionary Work, International Bicentennial of the Birth of Innokentii Veniaminov. In GOTR, vol. 4, nos 1-4 (1999), pp.557-564.

———, 1993a, *The Orthodox Church*, new edn, London.

———, 1993b, Forword, *Journals of Ioann Veniaminov in Alaska, 1823-1833*, p.ix, RLHT.

———, 1984, Philocalie, *Dictionnaire de Spiritualité*, vol.12, part 1, cols 1335-1352, eds M. Viller *et al.*, Paris.

———, 1976, The Theology of the Icon: a Short Anthology, *Eastern Christian Review*, vol.8, no.1, pp.3-10.

———, 1974, The Spiritual Father in Orthodox Christianity, *Cross Currents* (Summer/Fall).

Ware, K., and M. Mary (trans), 1978, *The Lenten Triodon*, London.

——— (trans), 1969, *The Festal Menaion*, London.

Wartelle, A., 1987, Introduction, *Saint Justin, Apologies: Introduction, Texte, Critique, Traduction, Commentaire et Index*, pp.15-94, Paris.

Williams, N.P., 1950, The Origins of the Sacraments, *Essays Catholic and*

Critical by Members of the Anglican Communion, pp.367- 423, ed. E. G. Selwyn, 3rd edn, London.

——, 1927, *The Ideas of the Fall and of Original Sin: A Historical and Critical Survey*, the Bampton Lectures at Oxford University, London.

Worl, R., 1988, Alaska Natives Today, CC, pp.319-325.

Wrangell, F. P., 1980, *Russian America: Statistical and Ethnographic Information*, trans. M. Sadouski, LPAH.

——, 1839, *Statistische und Ethnographische Nachrichten über die Russischen Bestizungen an der Nordwestkuste von Americka*, St Petersburg.

Yakimov. O.D., 1997a, Saint Innocent and the Modern World, Sakha Republic International Conference, Iakutsk, 12-14 Sept. 1997a: St Innokentii (Veniaminov), Enlightener of the Peoples of Alaska and Siberia, International Bicentennial of the Birth of Innokentii Veniaminov.

——, 1997b, The Unalaska Period of Ioann Veniaminov's Life and Activity: The Formation of a Church Leader and State Leader and of an Enlightener, Pembroke College, Oxford Symposium, 14-15 April 1997: Bishop Innokentii Veniaminov and the Patristic Background for 19th Century Missionary Work, International Bicentennial of the Birth of Innokentii Veniaminov. In GOTR, vol. 4, nos 1-4 (1999), pp. 623-632.

Yannoulatos, A., 1989, Orthodox Mission: Past, Present, Future, *Your Will Be Done: Orthodoxy and Mission*, pp.63-92, ed. G. Lemopoulos, Commisssion on World Mission and Evangelism, Consultation of Eastern Orthodox and Oriental Orthodox Churches (April 1988), Geneva and Katerini, Greece.

——, 1983, *Κύριος τῆς Λαμπότητος: ὁ Θεος παρὰ τὸ ῎Ορος Κέννα Φυλῶν*, 3rd edn, Athens.

Zaehner, R.C., 1957, *Mysticism — Sacred and Profane*, Oxford.

Zagoskin, L., 1967, *Lieutenant Zagoskin's Travels in Russian-America*, ed. H. Michael, Arctic Institute of North America, Toronto.

Made in the USA
Coppell, TX
06 December 2020